RELIGION IN CONSUMER SOCIETY

Ashgate AHRC/ESRC Religion and Society Series

Series Editors:

Linda Woodhead, University of Lancaster, UK
Rebecca Catto, University of Lancaster, UK

This book series emanates from the largest research programme on religion in Europe today – the AHRC/ESRC Religion and Society Programme which has invested in over seventy-five research projects. Thirty-two separate disciplines are represented looking at religion across the world, many with a contemporary and some with an historical focus. This international, multi-disciplinary and interdisciplinary book series will include monographs, paperback textbooks and edited research collections drawn from this leading research programme.

Other titles in the series:

Contesting Secularism
Comparative Perspectives
Edited by Anders Berg-Sørensen

Religion in the Neoliberal Age
Political Economy and Modes of Governance
Edited by Tuomas Martikainen and François Gauthier

Social Identities Between the Sacred and the Secular
Edited by Abby Day, Giselle Vincett and Christopher R. Cotter

Discourses on Religious Diversity
Explorations in an Urban Ecology
Martin D. Stringer

Understanding Muslim Chaplaincy
Sophie Gilliat-Ray, Stephen Pattison and Mansur Ali

Ageing, Ritual and Social Change
Comparing the Secular and Religious in Eastern and Western Europe
Edited by Peter Coleman, Daniela Koleva and Joanna Bornat

Religion in Consumer Society
Brands, Consumers and Markets

Edited by

FRANÇOIS GAUTHIER
University of Fribourg, Switzerland

TUOMAS MARTIKAINEN
University of Helsinki, Finland

Routledge
Taylor & Francis Group
LONDON AND NEW YORK

First published 2013 by Ashgate Publishing

Published 2016 by Routledge
2 Park Square, Milton Park, Abingdon, Oxfordshire OX14 4RN
711 Third Avenue, New York, NY 10017, USA

First issued in paperback 2016

Routledge is an imprint of the Taylor & Francis Group, an informa business

British Library Cataloguing in Publication Data
Religion in consumer society : brands, consumers and markets. --
(Ashgate AHRC/ESRC religion and society series)
1. Religion and sociology. 2. Globalization--Religious aspects. 3. Consumption (Economics)--Religious aspects.
4. Religion and state--History--21st century.
I. Series II. Gauthier, Francois. III. Martikainen, Tuomas.
306.6-dc23

The Library of Congress has cataloged the printed edition as follows:
Religion in consumer society : brands, consumers, and markets / edited by François Gauthier and Tuomas Martikainen.
pages cm. -- (Ashgate AHRC/ESRC religion and society series)
Includes bibliographical references and index.
ISBN 978-1-4094-4986-7 (hardcover)
1. Religion--History--21st century. 2. Consumption (Economics)--Religious aspects. 3. Neoliberalism. 4. Religion and state. 5. Religion and sociology. I. Gauthier, Frangois. II. Martikainen, Tuomas.

BL98.R385 2013
306.3--dc23

2012044684

ISBN 13: 978-1-138-24772-7 (pbk)
ISBN 13: 978-1-4094-4986-7 (hbk)

Contents

PART II: COMMODITISED SPIRITUALITIES

List of Figures and Tables

Figures

Table

Notes on Contributors

Lars Ahlin is an Associate Professor of Sociology of Religion at the Aarhus University, Denmark, where he is working in the section for the Study of Religion in the Department for Culture and Society, Faculty of Arts. His areas of interest include contemporary religious expressions and their relations to the economic and political changes in late modern societies. His publications include *New age: konsumtionsvara eller värden att kämpa för* [New Age: Consumer Good or Values Worth Fighting For] (University of Lund, 2001), *Pilgrim, turist eller flykting? En studie av individuell religiös rörlighet i senmoderniteten* [Pilgrim, Tourist or Refugee: A Study of Individual Religious Mobility in Late Modernity] (Symposion, 2005), *Krop, sind – eller ånd? Alternative behandlere og spiritualitet* [Body, Mind – or Soul? Alternative Therapists and Spirituality] (Forlaget Univers, 2007) and several articles in books and journals.

Marion Bowman is Senior Lecturer in Religious Studies at the Open University, UK. She was the William James Visiting Professor at the University of Bayreuth, Germany in 2009, and has been a visiting lecturer at the Universities of Pecs (Hungary), Bergen (Norway) and Åbo Åkademi (Finland). A past president of both the British Association for the Study of Religions and the Folklore Society, and an executive board member of the Working Group on the Ethnology of Religion, SIEF (Societe Internationale d'Ethnologie et de Folklore), she works at the interstices of religious studies and folklore/ethnology. Her research interests include vernacular religion, pilgrimage, material culture, the spiritual economy and a long-term study of Glastonbury, England, on which she has published extensively. Her latest book is *Vernacular Religion in Everyday Life: Expressions of Belief*, co-edited with Ülo Valk (Equinox, 2012).

Andrew Dawson is a Senior Lecturer in the Department of Politics, Philosophy and Religion at Lancaster University, UK. He has studied at universities in the UK and USA and has degrees in social science, religious studies and theology. Andrew's academic interests revolve around the interface of religion and modern society which he engages through the sociology of religion. He has recently completed a book on the global expansion of the Brazilian new religion of Santo Daime titled *Santo Daime: A New World Religion* (Bloomsbury, 2013). Andrew's major publications include *New Era – New Religions: Religious Transformation in Contemporary Brazil* (Ashgate, 2007), *Sociology of Religion* (SCM Press, 2011) and, as editor, *Summoning the Spirits: Possession and Invocation in Contemporary Religion* (I.B. Tauris, 2011).

Stephen Ellingson is Associate Professor of Sociology at Hamilton College, USA. He earned a doctoral degree in sociology from the University of Chicago. He is the author of *The Megachurch and the Mainline: Remaking Religious Tradition in the Twenty-First Century* (University of Chicago Press, 2007), co-author of *The Sexual Organization of the City* (University of Chicago Press, 2004), co-editor of *Religion and Sexuality in Cross-Cultural Perspective* (Routledge, 2002) and co-author of *Organizational Ethics in Health Care: Principles, Cases and Practical Solutions* (Jossey-Bass, 2001). He has also been published in the *American Journal of Sociology*, *Journal for the Scientific Study of Religion*, *Review of Religious Research* and *Journal of Contemporary Ethnography*. His additional articles on megachurches can be found in *Sociology Compass* and *The New Blackwell Companion to the Sociology of Religion* (2010). His current research examines the emergence and influence of religious environmentalism.

François Gauthier is Professor in the Sociology of Religion at Fribourg University (Switzerland), formerly at the Département de sciences des religions of the Université du Québec à Montréal (UQAM). He is also Researcher at the Chaire de recherche du Canada en Mondialisation, citoyenneté et démocratie (UQAM) and at the Groupe Société, Religions, Laïcités (GSRL EPHE-CNRS, Paris). His areas of interest include the impact of consumerism and neoliberalism on contemporary societies, as well as issues linked to religion and politics, religion and public space, and the application of the Maussian theory of gift in religion and culture. His publications include edited volumes on 'Religion in Consumer Society' (*Social Compass*, 58/3, 2011), Sacred and Economic Growth (*Entropia*, 11), 'Youth and Religion' (*Jeunes et religion au Québec*, Presses de l'Université Laval, 2008) and 'Techno Culture and Religion' (*Religiologiques*, 24), as well as numerous articles in books and journals.

Anne-Christine Hornborg is Professor in the History of Religions at the Centre for Theology and Religious Studies, Lund University, Sweden. Hornborg has produced several publications concerning indigenous worldviews, the phenomenology of landscape, the new spirituality, ecology and religion and ritual studies. In recent years, she has examined new, ritualised practices in contemporary Sweden, including nonspiritual therapies and coaching. In her latest book, *Coaching och lekmannaterapi: en modern väckelse?* [Coaching and Laymen Therapy: A Modern Spiritual Movement?] (Dialogos, 2012), she analyses the phenomena of coaching and layman therapy as products of neoliberal cosmology and the market.

Tuomas Martikainen is Professor in Ethnic Relations in the Swedish School of Social Science at the University of Helsinki, Finland. He is also a member of the executive general management team of the Post-Secular Culture and a Changing Religious Landscape (PCCR) centre of excellence in research at Åbo Akademi University. His areas of interest include contemporary religious and ethnic diversity, the governance of religion, religion in the consumer society and the incorporation of immigrant Muslims in Europe. His publications include *Religion, Migration, Settlement: Reflections on Post-1990 Immigration to Finland* (Brill, 2013), *Immigrant Religions in Local Society: Historical and Contemporary Perspectives in the City of Turku* (Åbo Akademi University Press, 2004), several edited volumes and numerous articles in books and journals.

John S. McKenzie is an Associate Lecturer with the University of Aberdeen and the Open University in Scotland. He has conducted research into the transplantation of Tibetan Buddhism to the West and his current research interests include the sociology of religion and tradition, Western Buddhism, globalisation, qualitative research and social theory. Publications include '"You Don't Know How Lucky You Are To Be Here!": Reflections on Covert Practices in an Overt Participant Observation Study' (*Sociological Research Online*, 14/2–3), 'Keeping It Real!: Constructing and Maintaining Traditional Authenticity in a Tibetan Buddhist Organisation in Scotland' (*Sociological Research Online*, 16/3) and 'Tartan Buddhists: A Typology for Understanding Participation in a Tibetan Buddhist Organization in Scotland' (*Fieldwork in Religion*, 7/1). He has also presented papers at the British Sociological Association annual conference on a number of occasions.

Francesca E.S. Montemaggi is a PhD candidate at Cardiff University, Wales. Her research develops Georg Simmel's sociology of religion to account for the construction of individual religious identity and authenticity within a Christian evangelical church. Her research focuses on belief, spirituality, and the social action of faith-based organisations. She has published on spiritual capital in the peer-reviewed journals *Implicit Religion* and the *International Journal for Interdisciplinary Social Sciences*. Francesca holds an LLB from the University of Kent at Canterbury, an MSc in Nationalism Studies from the University of Edinburgh and an MSc in Social Sciences Research Methods from Cardiff University. Francesca has also worked in politics and public affairs in the UK and Europe.

Mira Niculescu is a doctoral candidate at the Ecole de Hautes Etudes en Sciences Sociales (EHESS) in Paris and member of the Centre d'Etudes Interdisciplinaires du Fait Religieux (CEIFR), France. She is currently a Visiting Scholar at the Institute for Israel and Jewish Studies at Columbia University New York, and a Research affiliate at the Initiative for the Material and Visual Culture of Religion (MAVCOR) at Yale University, New Haven, and a former Visiting Research Fellow at the Hebrew University of Jerusalem (HUJ). Her doctoral research examines the contemporary "spiritual turn" in American Judaism in the light of the "Jewish-Buddhist" phenomenon. Her areas of interest include Western Buddhism, contemporary Judaism, Jewish Renewal, neo-Kabbalah, neo-traditionalism, religious individualism, dual belongings, syncretism and hybridity, religion and identity, religion and spirituality, religious globalisation and transnational flows, religion and consumer society, popular culture and popular religion. Her publications include book chapters such as 'Women with Shaved Heads: Western Buddhist Nuns and Haredi Jewish Wives' (in *Religion and the Body*, Åbo Akademi University Press, 2011), '"I the Jew, I the Buddhist": Multi-Belonging as inner dialogue.' (*CrossCurrents*, September 2012) and other articles.

Stefania Palmisano is Lecturer in the Sociology of Organisation at the University of Turin, Italy, where she teaches the sociology of religious organisations. She is Visiting Research Fellow, Department of Politics, Philosophy and Religion at Lancaster University, UK. She also has been Visiting Research Fellow at the Department of Sociology in Boston University, USA. At the moment she is doing research on new monasticism and its relationship with monastic tradition. She is also editing a book in Italian on the study of relations between religion and economics. Recent publications include 'Ambiguous Legitimation: Grassroots Roman Catholic Communities in Italy and Ecclesiastical Hierarchies' (*Temenos*, 47/1), 'Moving Forward in Catholicism: New Monastic Organizations, Innovation, Recognition, Legitimation' (*Journal for the Study of New Religions*, 1/2) and 'Spirituality and Catholicism: The Italian Experience' (*Journal of Contemporary Religion*, 25/2).

Per Pettersson is Professor of Sociology of Religion at the Service Research Centre (CTF) at Karlstad University, Sweden. He is also Guest Professor at the Uppsala Religion and Society Research Centre (CRS) at Uppsala University and Director of the CRS ten-year-long research programme *The Impact of Religion: Challenges for Society Law and Democracy, 2008–2018*. He is mainly involved in international comparative research. Recent publications include 'A European Perspective on the Churches' Role as Social Agents in South Africa' (with M. Middlemiss Lé Mon, *Journal of Theology for Southern Africa*, 2012), 'State and Religion in Sweden: Ambiguity between Disestablishment and Religious Control' (*Nordic Journal of Religion and Society*, 24/2), 'Majority Churches as Agents of European Welfare: A Sociological Approach' (in *Welfare and Religion in 21st Century Europe*, Ashgate, 2011), 'Confirmation Work in Sweden' (in *Confirmation Work in Europe: Empirical Results, Experiences and Challenges. A Comparative Study in Seven Countries*, Gütersloher Verlagshaus, 2010) and 'Nordic Majority Churches as Agents in the Welfare State: Critical Voices and/or Complementary Providers?' (with A.B. Pessi and O.H. Angell, *Temenos*, 45/2).

Simon Speck is Senior Lecturer in Sociology at the University of Derby. His research interests are in classical and contemporary social theory with a particular focus on the social, cultural and political dimensions of modernity. He has written on the place of religion in sociological theories of late, liquid and reflexive modernity and is currently researching the ubiquity of humour and comic phenomena in the age of reflexive modernity.

Linda Woodhead MBE DD is Professor of the Sociology of Religion at Lancaster University. She was Director of the £12m UK Religion and Society research programme from 2007 to 2013. Her research involves theoretical and empirical explorations of religion, with a particular focus on religious change in contemporary Western societies. Her publications include *Everyday Lived Islam in Europe* (ed., 2013), *Religion and Change in Modern Britain* (ed., 2012), *A Sociology of Religious Emotion* (2010, with Ole Riis) and *The Spiritual Revolution* (2005, with Paul Heelas).

Preface

This volume on religion in consumer society is part of our joint effort to further the sociological study of contemporary religion. We have set our agenda in our first coedited volume, *Religion in the Neoliberal Age: Political Economy and Modes of Governance* (Ashgate, 2013), and we deepen and explore it further in this one. In brief, our key thesis is that the twin forces of neoliberalism and consumerism are penetrating and transforming the 'religious' worldwide, though in locally-embedded forms. After having explored issues relating to institutional and political aspects in book one, this volume shifts the gaze towards consumerism, understood as a dominant and globalizing cultural and social ethos. It should be well understood that these two volumes can be taken together as interpreting a single, complex and multi-faceted phenomenon.

We both, as children of the consumer society in Canada and Finland, shared the same concern and dissatisfaction about the normative critique of consumerism in much of the sociology of religion: the proposal that consumption in religion is necessarily and by definition bad, or less worthy than other forms of religion. Our guts said there is something wrong with a general devaluation of consumerism. It goes without saying that consumption, like any other human practice, comes with many faces, that capitalism can be an exploitative force, and that conspicuous consumption is not exactly good for sustainable development. However, we now live in consumer societies where consumerism is a culturally dominant ethos. In this context, people live the life they have under the conditions which are available to them, and lead meaningful lives just as they have in other societies. They have practices, experiences and beliefs that cannot be discredited on the grounds that they do not correspond to post-Reformation institutional, nationally bound versions of Christianity. While we believe that there certainly are legitimate grounds for critiquing consumerism, just as there are for critiquing capitalism, we feel it should not lead us to devalue all of those cultural phenomena that are born and have grown out of consumer cultures. On the contrary, it was becoming more and more apparent to us, that in order to understand and analyse a growing number of religio-cultural phenomena, it seemed almost impossible not to acknowledge the massive impact of consumerism upon them. The message of this book is not that consumerism is good or bad, but rather that it is here and now, and allowing us to see the world of religions through those lenses clarifies many discussions on contemporary religious change. Hence we believe that consumerism and consumption need to be understood rather than seized from a priori normative analytics if we are to advance in our grasping of contemporary phenomena.

It is useful to recall that religion was at the very core of sociology's founding fathers' endeavours, especially Durkheim and Weber. After decades of specialization within social sciences and the marginalisation of the interest for religion, we believe it is time that religion finds its way back as a core issue of investigation and analysis well beyond the disciplinary frontiers of the sociology of religion. We also believe that the differentiation of social/institutional spheres hypothesis is just that: a working hypothesis, and that it has been exaggerated in its capacity. Today, it fails to provide a meaningful and heuristic basis from which to renew our perspectives. Instead, the contemporary boundary blurring that has been diagnosed in almost every social field argues in favour of more general, synthetic, ambitious and global approaches set to understand contemporary realities with respect to transversal forces, and with a specific attention to culture and social practices, not only institutions.

The sociology of religion has been from its outset framed within the secularisation paradigm. While numerous critiques have been directed at the very heart of these theories and the idea that religion is either declining or making a return, there is still much work to be done in defining an alternative paradigm. Attempts at substituting theories of 'religious change' have failed up to now to provide anything more than partial outlooks that generally end up supporting the same claims of religious deregulation, fragmentation, individualisation, even incoherence. We believe that the future of social sciences with respect to religion lies in the definition of a global, comprehensive analytic able to seize the diversity of contemporary religious phenomena with respect to wider and globalizing social changes. By focusing on the structuring effects of neoliberal ideologies, management, marketization and consumerism, and by showing the dialectical rapports between these and religion, a new coherence appears which delineates the contours of a new mode of regulation of religion within the context of a new globalised, hyper-mediatized political and cultural economy. This volume is a contribution to such a task with the idea that it can only be realised through the collective and complementary efforts of scholars from different countries around the world working on a wide variety of objects and who agree to side-step dominant and specialized conceptualizations. As such the chapters in this volume are in no way applications of a single and totalizing theoretical frame, but rather insightful openings onto renovated perspectives for research and analysis by an interesting mixture of established, new and upcoming academics.

The origins of this collection date back to the ISSR conference in Aix-en-Province in July 2011, where many of the contributors met for the first time. We would like to thank our contributors for the hard work they have done. A special thank you is directed to Professor Peter Nynäs and the Post-Secular Culture and Changing Religious Landscape in Finland (PCCR) Centre of Excellence in Research at Åbo Akademi University that made the linguistic proofing of the volume possible, conducted with great professionalism by Sarah Bannock. Tuomas Martikainen has also conducted his contribution to the volume within the PCCR Project. MA Linda Annunen from Åbo Akademi University receives thanks for helping us in drafting the bibliography. Diletta Guidi, research assistant at the University of Fribourg, has collaborated on the index. A special thank you and 'Rock on!' is directed to Professor Linda Woodhead, who has been an extremely valued companion in this adventure and who is a powerful inspiration through her outstanding work. We even owe her the suggestion for this forum of publication, the Ashgate AHRC/ESRC Religion and Society Series. We finally thank the wonderful staff at Ashgate who, in the midst of tough economic times for publishers, have been thoroughly professional and a pleasure to work with.

François Gauthier, Fribourg University, Switzerland
Tuomas Martikainen, University of Helsinki, Finland

Introduction: Consumerism as the Ethos of Consumer Society

François Gauthier, Linda Woodhead and Tuomas Martikainen

> An open, competitive religious economy makes possible an expanded spiritual marketplace which, like any marketplace, must be understood in terms both of 'demand' and 'supply'.[1]
>
> – Wade Clark Roof

> Brands are the equivalent of religious objects. … Branding is similar to religion as it aims to create the experience of an affective community. … Brand management is the economic use of a religious element.[2]
>
> – Adam Arvidsson

This volume, like the companion which preceded it,[3] seeks to change the bias of the existing scholarship on religion by giving primary attention to religion's relation not with the political but with the economic domain. The main exception to this bias – the work on relations between religion and economics by Max Weber and those who take their inspiration from him – focused on work and production. Our earlier book focused on a different aspect of (modern) economic life by looking at how the ideology and practice of market liberalism, expressed in neoliberal forms and ideas, has impacted on the nature and practice of religion in late modern societies. This second book ventures into another under-explored territory by giving attention to the interplays between religion and consumerism.

We live in consumer societies. The signs are obvious, in the West and far beyond. What would globalisation be without the expansion of consumerism, the spreading of instantaneous communication, and participation in the new

---

1 Wade Clark Roof, *Spiritual Marketplace: Baby Boomers and the Remaking of American Religion* (Princeton, NJ, 1999), 78.

2 Adam Arvidsson, 'Entretien avec Adam Arvidsson. "Les marques sont des reliques modernes"', *Les Grands Dossiers des Sciences Humaines*, 22 (2011): 56.

3 Tuomas Martikainen and François Gauthier (eds), *Religion in the Neoliberal Age: Modes of Governance and Political Economy* (Farnham, 2013). See also François Gauthier, Tuomas Martikainen and Linda Woodhead (eds), 'Religion in Consumer Society', special issue, *Social Compass*, 58/3 (2011).

global culture of mobility, fluidity, success, and affluence? Is consumerism not 'the cement of the global society'?[4] In recent decades, the rise of shopping as a leisure pursuit (six hours per week in the US),[5] the pervasiveness of advertising in everyday life, the omnipresence of brands, the liberalisation of credit and the growing access to consumption, the commoditisation of more and more areas of life, the rise of lifestyles as loci for identity, the political identification of freedom with personal choice, the emergence of the consumer as an identity – all of these attest to the inextricable interpenetration of consumption and everyday life.

Consumption as an ethos and consumerism as a cultural backdrop are certainly among the salient features of our societies. Yet far from being the backdrop and starting point of social, political, and cultural analyses, consumption remains relatively understated and under-theorised in the social sciences – especially in relation to religion. Consumption has occupied an increasingly determining place in social practice in modernity. Still, 'consumption has a profound but often problematic and unrecognized place in the social sciences over the modern period'.[6] 'Why, in the floodtide of Enlightenment enthusiasms for freedom … was consumption never articulated as a social goal … [w]hy is it … that consumption, which is the linchpin of our modern social system, has never been the linchpin of our theories explaining modernity?'[7] The starting point of this volume is the observation that consumption and consumerism are driving forces of globalisation, hand in hand with the hyper-mediatisation of culture. Together, they have profound consequences on religious practices, beliefs, expressions, and institutions worldwide, and as such deserve more scholarly attention.

Consumption, consumerism, and hyper-mediatisation participate in a wider phenomenon which is characterised by the ever-increasing pull of economics on all aspects of social and cultural life, along with the rapid rise of the 'new' political economy of neoliberalism, and the spreading of management and governance ideologies and practices. As we explored in the previous volume, neoliberalism believes in the efficiency and rationality of markets, and seeks to place as many social functions as possible on a market footing, thus introducing the element of profit into every 'service'. Neoliberal theorists such as Hayek also justify this marketisation in terms of the greatest possible expansion of human freedom. Whilst such marketisation is different in ethos, perhaps fatally so, from a consumer ethos (Daniel Bell), they share this belief in the value of freedom, and the centrality of choice. And the two are linked by an inner logic, whereby the successful pursuit of endless and increasing profit (an essential element of growth) can only be sustained

---

4 Peter Stearns, 'L'expansion globale du désir', *Les Grands Dossiers des Sciences Humaines*, 22 (2011): 17.

5 Celia Lury, *Consumer Culture* (New Brunswick, NJ, 2011), 4.

6 Don Slater, 'The Sociology of Consumption and Lifestyle', in Craig Calhoun, Chris Rojek and Bryan Turner (eds), *The SAGE Handbook of Sociology* (London, 2005), 174.

7 Joyce Appleby, quoted in Don Slater, *Consumer Culture and Modernity* (Cambridge, 1997), 58.

by provoking continuous consumer demand for new products. Both processes also result in a 'commodification' whereby all aspects of life, even the ecosphere, are viewed as available to be bought and sold at a price (Sandel).

A consumer culture is a culture of consumption, meaning that 'the dominant values' of this society are not only 'organized through consumption practices but are also in some sense derived from them',[8] be it wellbeing, hedonism, happiness, personal satisfaction, choice, sovereignty, individuality, reflexivity or autonomy. A growing premium is also put on self-presentation and the promotion of the self, which itself becomes a commodity vying for attention in the marketplace of life. Consumer culture is the culture of a market society, in the sense that increasingly the various areas of social life are mediated by market relations in the form of the consumption of commodities.[9] It is a culture in which marketisation, commoditisation, advertisement, and branding are fundamental processes. Consumer culture is a capitalist culture in a globalising, highly mediatised world. It is 'constituted as a culture both *for* consumers and *of* consumers: both a set of commodities for people to consume, and a set of representations of people as consumers'.[10] Perhaps most profoundly, consumer culture is the means of expression and actualisation of the modern project of the individualised self, as it 'provides a very particular set of material circumstances in which individuals come to acquire a reflexive relation to identity'.[11]

Consumerism – of course – has its adversaries. As consumption is based on monetary economy, those at the fringes of consumer proficiency are filled with wants, lusts and desires that they are unable to fulfil. News reports of the London riots of August 2011 were, to the reporters' astonishment, less concerned with describing a protest against injustice, urban poverty and racism than about the carrying home of flat screen televisions, expensive sneakers, and fashion items – the rioters were like crows behaving as a kind of consumerist cargo cult. The 'political' aspect of the protest was the issue of being fully participating members of the consumer society, a 'crisis in social expectation',[12] today's alienation *par excellence*. Even nativist, fundamentalist and xenophobic movements are emerging as critical voices of consumer lifestyles and mourn a soon-to-be-forgotten, communitarian past. Still, even there, the threat of consumerism does not lie in the comforts of modern life, but rather in the inherent relativism which is embedded in consumerism. Another aspect of anti-consumerism is found in the anti-globalisation movement and in other contemporary social movements which critique the penetration of the market into all spheres of life and the uneven

---

8 Slater, *Consumer Culture and Modernity*, 24–5.

9 Ibid., 25.

10 Roberta Sassatelli, *Consumer Culture: History, Theory and Politics* (London, 2007), 195.

11 Lury, *Consumer Culture*, 29.

12 See for example Olivier Roy, *Globalized Islam: The Search for a New Ummah* (New York, 2004), 172.

spreading of the fruits of capitalism. The slogan of the Occupy Movement – 'We are the 99%' – catches the tone well. However, these protests are directed not only against the super-rich, the new global elite, but even more against the comfortable middle-class way of life which is supporting the status quo. Consumption should be rendered fairer and available to more people, even if at the same time there is a nod to sustainable development.

While the omnipresence of consumption in everyday life is in little doubt, the nature of consumption, its processes, dynamics, and incidences, remain contentious, as does its relation to religion. The rise of consumption as a dominant social ethos and ideology in the second half of the twentieth century has coincided with a radical transformation of the religious field, particularly in the West, but increasingly in all parts of the world. Traditional forms of religion have declined dramatically; national churches find themselves being challenged by forms of transnational or global recasting favoured by progress in communication technologies, new religions are springing up in the wake of waves of immigration, and new religious trends such as holistic spiritualities and charismatic movements have emerged as novel, yet durable popular phenomena. While debates in the sociology of religion have revolved around the issue of the 'decline of religion' for decades, the idea that religion has reconfigured and recomposed into new forms has finally gained the acceptance of a majority. Still, the study of religion continues to be largely deployed within the paradigm of secularisation. This paradigm is increasingly showing its limitations with respect to some of the most obvious changes since the 1980s, including the move towards more experiential rather than creed-based forms of religion, in other words, a move from a regime of *orthodoxy* towards a regime of *orthopraxy*;[13] the reconfiguration of religion with respect to identities and life ethics; the immanentisation of salvation and the interweaving of health and therapeutics with religion; the erosion of the nation state as comprehensive framework for understanding religion and the rise of transnational reconfigurations of religious (real and/or virtual) communities; the radical critique of institutional authority within contemporary culture, challenging the social sciences' methodological focus on institutional dynamics in favour of more 'liquid' (Zygmunt Bauman) and transient realities; the blurring and reshaping of institutional spheres; the impact of the internet and electronic media in religious governance, community, communication, and their emergence as primary resources for information on religion; the multidimensional and variegated transformation

[13] On the shift from orthodoxy to orthopraxy, see François Gauthier, 'Primat de l'authenticité et besoin de reconnaissance. La société de consommation et la nouvelle régulation du religieux', *Studies in Religion/Sciences religieuses*, 41/1 (2012): 93–111; François Gauthier and Jean-Philippe Perreault, 'Jeunes et religion dans la société de consommation: État des lieux et prospective', in François Gauthier and Jean-Philippe Perreault (eds), *Jeunes et religion au Québec* (Québec, 2008), 9–28.

of traditional religious institutions with respect to these changes, and so on.[14] These processes are perhaps best seen among new religious formations, such as megachurches and new spiritualities, but they are also present among traditional religions and fundamentalist groups. Religious authenticity and experience is, however, increasingly being legitimated *via* new means.

A core element of secularisation theory is an acceptance of the differentiation of institutional spheres as an essential element of modernisation.[15] Combined with the specialisation of the social sciences, this has resulted in a tendency to isolate the study of social spheres from one another. While this perspective has proved fecund and adequate on a number of issues over a certain period of time, more recent developments are increasingly highlighting its biases and shortcomings. There is a need for more transversal and global perspectives that include religion in a de-differentiating focus. The hypothesis of this volume is that much is to be gained by recognising the impact of economics on the whole of society. This volume and its sister volume suggest that religion today is not as diffuse, disorganised, fragmented, and deregulated, in the sense of free-floating and purely cultural, as most contemporary work on religion explicitly or implicitly claims it to be. The first volume, *Religion in the Neoliberal Age: Modes of Governance and Political Economy*, is concerned with the more institutional dimensions entailed by such an approach, as it examines the changing landscape of relations between religions and states with respect to the pressures exerted by market-oriented, neoliberal modes of governance and management, as well as some changes occurring within religious organisations. The present volume focuses on the interplays between religion and consumerism, management, marketisation, and branding, from a perspective concerned with the vast and complex varieties of religion as they are lived, be it with respect to transformations within institutional religions or less easily charted charismatic trends, quest culture, contemporary spiritualities, life coaching, and so on.

Of course the subject of religion in relation to economics is by no means new. In the introduction to the first volume, we engage in a critical discussion of classical interpretations and suggest a fourfold typology of contemporary work. This discussion builds on this work. Since the hypothesis guiding this endeavour stresses the complementarities of both institutional and cultural perspectives, we hope very much that the reader considers these volumes as they were meant to be, that is to say, as a whole. In what follows, we continue to define the terms that constitute the socio-economic backdrop by discussing the nature and dynamics of the market, consumption, and branding.

---

14 For an analysis of these shifts as manifest in the UK context, see Linda Woodhead, ‘Introduction’, in Linda Woodhead and Rebecca Catto (eds), *Religion and Change in Modern Britain* (London, 2012).

15 On secularisation, see especially David Martin, *On Secularization: Towards a Revised General Theory* (Farnham, 2005); José Casanova, *Public Religions in the Modern World* (Chicago, IL, 1994).

Economic Theory and Rational Choice

A logical place to start is to consider what classical economic theory has to say about consumption. Economic theory – liberal economics – understands consumption as the counterpart of production in the mechanism of price, which 'typically has the function of calibrating the market by coordinating supply and demand through the circulation of information'.[16] Consumption is the act of purchase within an isolated time-space medium called a market. Consumers appear in the market essentially as buyers. In a market, then, sellers oppose buyers, and price represents the resolution of this 'conflict' of interests (sellers want to sell at the highest price, and buyers to purchase at the lowest) between calculating, rational, maximising agents. All events occurring within a market are understood as deriving from the pursuit of individual interests. From the perspective of economic liberalism, there is no society, only interactions between self-interested individuals. From this perspective, the market emerges as an impersonal, neutral, and self-instituted social regulator of conflicting desires, coordinating the allocation of resources across different spheres of production and consumption. Hence for classical liberalism up to neoliberalism, the market is defined as a non-political, non-metaphysical, non-hierarchical, and non-coercive, dynamic, open mechanism for social regulation. As such, the market is not seen as a social authority, or even a 'social institution': '[r]ather, social coordination through the market is achieved when all individuals, with their disparate desires, rationally orient themselves to the common denominator of *price*'.[17] This conception of the market, which goes back to the founding works of Adam Smith in the eighteenth century, was conceived well before anything like a 'market' existed in reality, in the sense of being free from traditional determinations, social bonds, and political dependency. In other words, the 'market' was born as a utopian ideology, an economic answer to modernity's problem *par excellence*: social regulation outside of a theologico-moral frame. As Don Slater writes: '[p]rice is not, for liberal economic thought, a reflection of the "value" of goods: this is regarded as a metaphysical concept. Price is simply a compromise between the agendas of wants followed by each private individual.'[18] Thus the market is a supposedly autonomous, rational, and formal mechanism freed from particularisms, values, and metaphysics.

Within mainstream economic theory, the consumer is the demand side, and demand is an aggregate of individual purchase decisions based on individual cost-benefit analysis. Economic theory does not ask in depth and detail why consumers buy goods, but only answers how: through rational action and the calculation of utility. Demand is therefore treated as a given, something which is unquestioned and unquestionable:

---

16 Celia Lury, *Brands: The Logos of the Global Economy* (New York and London, 2004), 4.

17 Slater, *Consumer Culture and Modernity*, 41.

18 Ibid., 42.

> Desire is a private matter and individuals enter the market already knowing what they want and how much they should pay for it. ... Price is therefore considered an efficient mechanism for allocating social resources in terms of the only standard liberalism recognizes: the preferences of individuals. These preferences discipline the behaviour of firms automatically: they need not desire to satisfy individual's needs but must march in close step with the marginal utility calculations of those individuals in order to stay in business.[19]

Although the individual is at the centre of liberal thought, it is something the theory can say little about. As consumers, individuals are abstracted from their particular needs and contexts and emotions, save for one quality which is said to govern all actions: utility, 'defined simply as the capacity of an object to satisfy a desire. The nature of the desire is irrelevant: utility simply represents the abstract, empty desire-satisfying attribute of a good.'[20] Utility, as the principle underlying the mechanism of price, is that by which qualitative features – values, preferences, beliefs, morality, and so on – are translated into quantitative measure. It is that which allows one to 'compare apples and oranges'.[21] Defined by Jeremy Bentham at the end of the eighteenth century as 'that property in any object whereby it tends to produce benefit, advantage, pleasure, good, or happiness, or reduce pain',[22] utility is a purely formal concept: content (substance) is left to the individual. Hence economic theory has little, if anything, to say about particular needs and desires. The complexity of these needs and desires and their social and particularistic contexts are boiled down to a single motive for action. Defined as the 'total sum of satisfaction', utility replaces society and culture with 'reason', understood as formal and abstract calculation.[23]

For the normally-constituted sociologist or anthropologist, the hazardous nature of such a reductionism and formal abstractionism is obvious. It is perhaps good to recall that Émile Durkheim's entire sociological project was constructed in opposition to utilitarianism and economic liberalism, which had come to seduce many of the positivist thinkers of his time.[24] Constructed on ideological grounds rather than empirical findings, economists have had a problem in supporting the neoclassical model in the twentieth century, finding they have to try to integrate a wider variety of social variables. While hallmark figures such as Gary Becker made declared attempts in this direction, and even though Raymond Boudon worked to limit the scope of the self-interested model, issues 'of power,

19 Ibid., 41–2.

20 Ibid., 44.

21 Ibid., 44.

22 Ibid., 44.

23 Ibid., 44–5.

24 Christian Laval, *L'ambition sociologique* (Paris, 2002); Philippe Steiner, *L'école durkheimienne et l'économie: sociologie, religion et connaissance* (Genève, 2005).

institutions, emotions and values'[25] continue to be eschewed by economic theory. Even though the economic model of human action has been shown to be highly problematic when confronted with social reality, 'economic science' continues to promote monolithically the neoclassical model in its faculties across the world.[26] Mainstream economics are, incidentally, not a numerous array of theories invested in the study of a social 'field', that of the various means of exchange and ways in which 'human societies provision themselves',[27] but rather a 'discipline' constituted around a single theory. The result is the reduction of all human actions to rational, self-interested behaviour, a model that is then extended to all societies over time and space.[28]

This approach to economic theory has entered into the study of religion by way of a 'rational choice' approach. It is noteworthy that the economic approach to the study of religion emerged as a critique of the 'old' paradigm of secularisation, self-declaring itself a 'new paradigm' fit for making sense of religion today. Without engaging in an in-depth discussion of rational choice theory (RCT), we must highlight how it diverges from our volumes' proposal on both methodological and theoretical grounds. For partisans of the economic approach to religion, religion can be understood in terms of the logic of the marketplace; 'supply' and 'demand'.[29] Religious organisations are accordingly defined as 'competing' in 'religious markets', in other words, seeking to maximise 'market shares', by the provision of 'religious products' 'in exchange for resources – most notably, time, money, and commitment'. Such a conception is radically individualistic, with religion defined as the answer to a fundamental human (individual) need for 'meaning and belonging'.[30] In so doing, the anthropology that underlies capitalism, that of humans characterised by insatiable needs, *homo oeconomicus*, is universalised and naturalised, made to be that from which religion itself is to become understandable. This approach therefore short-circuits social, cultural and historical determinations in the study of religion, with specific contexts translated as being more or less 'open' religious markets.

Most importantly with regards to our problematic, RCT takes a very narrow, theoretical approach to the economic aspects of religious phenomena, and does not discuss the real-world dynamics of marketisation, management, neoliberalism, commoditisation, consumption, and related changes affecting religion in contemporary societies. Instead it states that religion behaves – timelessly – as in the formal model of economic theory. It is not interested in the complex rapports between religion and economics as it sets out to think religion in all societies and

25 Sassatelli, *Consumer Culture*, 72.

26 Alain Caillé, *Dé-penser l'économique. Contre le fatalisme* (Paris, 2005).

27 Karl Polanyi, *The Great Transformation: The Political and Economic Origins of Our Time* (Boston, MA, 2001).

28 Slater, *Consumer Culture and Modernity*, 52.

29 Roof, *Spiritual Marketplace*, 78.

30 Ibid., 79–80.

in all epochs in economic terms – that of the neoclassical model. As such, the rational choice approach to religion itself constitutes a vibrant example of what needs to be explained: the propensity today of perceiving social realities through economic categories.

Marketing and Branding, Emotions and Identity

Notwithstanding the claims of economists, every marketing specialist knows that companies today are not simply selling goods or services. From chewing gum to automobiles and insurance, companies are instead knowingly providing identity markers, ideals, experiences, and authenticity.

For the marketing guru Douglas Atkin, brand construction amounts to creating religious cults. In his bestselling book *The Culting of Brands*,[31] Atkin lists Apple and Harley Davidson as examples of companies that have been successful at this, with ensuing economic success. 'Brands are symbols', he writes, and today's economy is not a formal economy in which products are made to compete in rational terms – it is a 'spiritual' and 'symbolic economy' in which what is sold is 'community', meaning, and shared experiences. Rather than reducing religious phenomena to economic terminology, Atkin exemplifies the very opposite trend which animates marketing today: thinking of economics in religious terms. Far from casting consumers as rational actors seeking to maximise utility, let alone applying this rationale to religious 'consumers', looking at the evolution of marketing is instructive as to how consumerism actually works. Is it religion today that behaves like neoclassical economics, or is it consumerism that functions according to religious anthropology?

There is ample evidence that consumption is coextensive with the process of modernisation, and that a consumer society emerged in a developed and widespread form in the late nineteenth century, sparked by the mass production of consumer goods. Consumer society continued to thrive in this wake, as the 1920s were 'probably the first decade to proclaim a generalized ideology of affluence'.[32] A powerful association was then made between consumption *and* the desirable utopia of modernisation. Marketing was already not only about selling durable, efficient goods, but about selling pathways to modernity: 'the world was to be modernized partly through consumption'.[33] The incentive was for people to modernise *themselves*, their homes, their means of transport, and so on. Interrupted by the Great Crash of 1929 (due to excessive deregulation of financial markets…) and the Second World War, the rise of the consumer society became irreversible from the late 1950s on. Matching Taylorist management and Fordist productivism

---

31 Douglas Atkin, *The Culting of Brands: When Customers Become True Believers* (New York, 2004).

32 Slater, *Consumer Culture and Modernity*, 12.

33 Ibid., 12.

that relied on discipline and rational control, marketing until then was first of all about the 'rational' marketing of a product in terms of its utility, and then about making consumers adopt pre-programmed forms of behaviour, in accordance with the idea that the motive for consuming goods was status achievement and the participation in the ideals of modernity.[34]

With the late 1950s came the 'realisation' that the 'symbolic dimensions' of the product, distilled in the 'brand image', counted for a great deal:

> The brand image … represents a 'public image, a character or personality that may be more important for the over-all status (and sales) of the brand than many technical facts about the product'. The brand results from the product's existence as a complex 'public object', 'it is made up of the meanings that advertising, merchandising, promotion, publicity, and even sheer length of existence have created'. … Without such symbolic distinctions, 'how else can they decide whether to smoke Camels or Lucky Strikes; to use Nescafe or Borden's instant coffee; to drive a Ford or a Chevrolet or a Plymouth?'[35]

Pioneers in marketing were keen on noting that individual self-expression was the motor of consumption, transforming everyday, insignificant consumer decisions into vehicles for the expression of a newfound desire for individuality that accompanied the postwar boom. The new standard in marketing was henceforth self-realisation. It was no longer how long the washer would last, but 'what it would do for your soul':

> Above all, marketing had to abandon the idea that consumers made rational decisions in relation to a socially given hierarchy of needs or values. Rather, in this new area of self-expression, human desire was best regarded as plastic and open. Indeed people lived in a world of goods to which they were emotionally attached and to which they owed large parts of their own personality. … It was to these unrecognized, irrational, emotional bonds that progressive market researchers now had to turn.[36]

In a consumer society, subjectivity is to be produced rather than given by traditional social structures, and goods are a prime means for this creation. Hence the turn towards marketing techniques which were increasingly oriented towards brand

---

[34] This is the essence of Pierre Bourdieu's famed theory of distinction, which for that matter falls short of understanding contemporary phenomena.

[35] Adam Arvidsson, *Brands: Meaning and Value in Media Culture* (London and New York, 2006), 55. Quotes from Burleigh B. Gardner and Sidney J. Levy, 'The Product and the Brand', *Harvard Business Review*, March–April (1955): 33–9.

[36] Arvidsson, *Brands*, 58.

image management and lifestyle advertising which associated products to certain immaterial qualities such as attitudes, values, feelings, and meanings.[37]

The 1980s drove consumerism to new heights, both because economic growth now depended on consumption more than production and because the consumer now represented the 'very model of the modern subject and citizen'[38] for the rising neoliberal ideology. The policies of Margaret Thatcher and Ronald Reagan in favour of privatisation and deregulation of media, public space, and public institutions facilitated the omnipresence of brands in schools, museums, and public spaces in general, normalising this aspect of consumerism within everyday life. At the same time, neoliberalism 'radically promoted consumer sovereignty as the link between freedom and dynamism. The model of consumer choice came to be seen as the most adequate model for all forms of modern citizenship and social action, the market as the only means of social coordination that secured both freedom and progress.'[39] Increasingly, commoditisation became the normal means of social existence, and individual freedom became equated with the 'freedom to choose'. Consumerism and neoliberalism are thus linked: '[n]ot only are modern subjects able to think of themselves primarily as consumers (as opposed to workers or citizens), and to understand consumption as a primary site for their identities, but the language and values of consumption as market choices seem to predominate in other social spheres.'[40]

The Social and Individual Dimensions of Consumption

Despite the emphasis so far placed on the ways in which late modern consumerism reinforces individual identity construction, the social dimensions of consumerism deserve more consideration. In their 1979 book *The World of Goods*, British anthropologist Mary Douglas and economist Baron Isherwood opened an avenue that has since been trodden by cultural studies.[41] For the authors, consumption is a social fact as well as an economic one, and its essential function has to do with 'meaning, value, and communication'. In their understanding, consumer goods are not acquired in order to satisfy (individual) needs, as they are markers of social relations and socially constructed meanings. Goods are the visible part of culture, and it is through their exchange that social life is made to exist. This perspective acts out a radical critique of economic theory by insisting that the autonomy of the economic sphere is a myth and does not resist analysis. For example, shopping is a highly social practice, as it involves going to commercial avenues or

---

37 Ibid., 61.

38 Slater, *Consumer Culture and Modernity*, 10.

39 Ibid., 37.

40 Slater, 'The Sociology of Consumption', 176.

41 Mary Douglas and Baron Isherwood, *The World of Goods* (New York and London, 1996).

shopping malls – socially designated places at given times. Shopping also usually involves other social activities and social relations. Even a quick observation of the practice of shopping suggests that consumption is best understood in terms of market*place* rather than through the supply and demand curves of individual rational calculations making up the enclosed system of the 'market'.[42] In the wake of the heterodox economist and historian Karl Polanyi's work, economic sociology has used the notion of 'embeddedness' to show that exchange is less impersonal than it may seem. However much they claim to shut themselves off from other social spheres, markets are constituted within social networks and are not purely economic, but complex social events and institutions.[43] The social constitution of markets and economic exchange in general is important, as it supports the argument that consumption is a web of practices that involve not only the satisfaction of needs but also social functions, and that these practices carry and express values. Markets and morals are not mutually exclusive, contrary to classical liberal thought.[44]

Cultural studies have been at the forefront in highlighting the ways in which consumerism has been renewed by a 'self-realisation turn' in marketing in recent decades. The rise of brands is a significant factor in this evolution. Marketers have taken advantage of their understanding that consumption is not about rational decisions in an isolated economic sphere and have knowingly contributed in establishing the brand as a 'total social fact'.[45] Brands are social facts that totalise and create what we have called consumer society. A total social fact resonates throughout the social, that is to say, within and across the social's differentiated spheres (politics, religion, law, aesthetics, education, and so on), as do brands. As cultural theorists have argued, the shift towards branding, which came into full effect in the 1980s (at the same time as the neoliberal surge), constitutes a new mechanism for the co-construction of supply and demand in a way which pulls us ever further from the rationalist and autonomist paradigm of neoclassical theory. Branding vividly illustrates how today's markets are profoundly social and cultural forms.

No longer aimed at 'imposing a particular structure of needs and tastes on consumers, which was characteristic of Fordist marketing, 'new marketing's' aim is, in the words of British marketer John Grant, to seek to fill 'the great gaps of meaning that exist in people's lives' and to propose brands as 'ideas that people can live by'.[46] Rather than working by discipline, brands espouse new liberal governance principles by working with the freedom of consumers: they say 'not

42 Slater, *Consumer Culture and Modernity*, 54.

43 Ibid., 54; Sassatelli, *Consumer Culture*, 160, 195.

44 Caillé, *Dé-penser l'économique*.

45 Lury, *Brands*, 15. See Marcel Mauss, 'Essai sur le don', in *Sociologie et anthropologie* (Paris, 1973), 149–279.

46 John Grant, *The New Marketing Manifesto* (London, 1999), 15, quoted in Lury, *Brands*, 38.

"You Must!" but "You May!"'.[47] It is no longer a product that is sold but a right to a relationship with a brand and with others who 'worship' the same brand.[48] Branded goods are experiential and social commodities.[49] What is sold is not an object but an *experience* that must appear *authentic* if it is to be meaningful. As Adam Arvidsson writes,

> [i]t is not about imposing ways of using goods, or behaving or thinking as a consumer. Rather, it is about proposing goods as tools, or building blocks whereby consumers can create their own meanings. What people pay for, the idea goes, is not so much the brand itself as what they can produce with it: what they can *become* with it. To quote one successful American pop-management book: 'The power of any brand is simply how your associations with it make you feel'.[50]

Consumer capitalism does not isolate exchange from social relations; on the contrary. Brand marketing functions by making the most of our hyper-mediatised, globalised culture by tying brands to social relations. In a consumer culture as in the archaic cultures studied by classical anthropology, goods are symbols in the deepest sense as they represent, enact, give substance, actualise, and help reproduce social relations.[51] Branding reverses the rapport supposed by economic theory between the brand and the product: it is the product that refers to the brand and not the contrary. The brand provides a context, an ambience, a promise, a predetermined yet open-ended frame of action in which products are used. Brands are avenues of possibility. Incidentally, for the consumer, brands are means of production of meaning, identity, and subjectivity, and they are active in mediating belonging and community. Consumption and identity are thus intricately knit together today as every choice, however routine, has potentially profound existential consequences. This is why the 'market for identities is the biggest market of all'.[52] As the means of production and an expression of identity, brands are also producers of what Adam Arvidsson calls a 'common social world'.[53] As indicators of lifestyles (a certain pattern of values, aesthetics, ethics, ideals, and so on), brands are recognisable symbols around which social relations and communities coalesce. An important aspect of this type of identity production is that it must be expressed in order to be warranted and recognised by others, which the brand allows for.

---

47 Arvidsson, *Brands*, 8.

48 Lury, *Brands*, 3.

49 Arvidsson, *Brands*, 35.

50 Ibid., 68; quote from Daryl Travis, *Emotional Branding: How Successful Brands Gain the Irrational Edge* (Roseville, CA, 2000), 10.

51 Douglas and Isherwood, *The World of Goods*.

52 Don Slater, *Consumer Culture*, 85.

53 Arvidsson, *Brands*, 14.

The twentieth century has seen the identity regime embodied by the universalistic, nation-state-grounded model of the citizen break up into a myriad of competing and complementary lifestyle-based identities. Hence 'identity' is at the heart of recent transformations affecting religion and wider culture. Figures such as Giddens, Bauman, and Beck have highlighted the ways in which the 'post-traditional self' is constructed by choices and negotiations between multiple and contrasting identities. Consumerism is central to this immanent eschatology which revolves obsessively around the self and the means for its recognition. Consumer society is a 'society of identities'.[54]

The Canadian philosopher Charles Taylor is one of the few to have considered the importance of consumerism in this development. According to Taylor, the postwar transformation of Western societies into fully-fledged consumer societies amounts to a 'cultural revolution' which has deepened the 'subjective turn' of modernity. The spread of the ethos of consumption across our societies has been the vehicle through which the modern project of the self is actualised and the modern 'culture of authenticity and expressivity' radicalised. Consumerism has been accompanied by the massification of the nineteenth-century Romantics' 'expressive individualism' which consisted in the new belief that every person has his own unique individuality, and that life consists in discovering and realising this authentic and unique self, rather than conforming to normative models imposed from 'without' by society, especially political and religious authorities.[55] The importance of consumption cannot be explained by the overwhelming spread of alienation, brought about by the irresistible *telos* of simulacra, reification, or disenchantment which are supposedly inherent to merchandise, as 'critical theory' and the rationalisation thesis would argue. Rather, consumption rapidly developed as an all-encompassing cultural ethos because consumer objects were the new ways through which the modern culture of individualism could find an expression.

If the cultural revolution of consumerism is a step further into individualism, approaching the issue from the standpoint of a radicalisation of the authenticity and expressivity tropes highlights its social moorings and cultural dynamics. It does not isolate the individual and her choices from social determinations and cultural processes and values, while showing how the exercise of choice is constitutive of subjectivity today – how 'free choice' is a *social* imperative. The resulting individualism is consequently not narcissism, as the expression of one's identity supposes the constant (real or virtual) presence of others to ensure recognition. The web of signs and meanings that makes up our consumer and media culture is the background that gives meaning to our actions. As Taylor illustrates with the example of fashion, consumerism is a general social structure in which the collective is not oriented towards a common action and a shared destiny but rather takes the form of an arena for mutual exposition. Consumer culture is therefore

54 Jacques Beauchemin, *La société des identités* (Montreal, 2004).

55 Charles Taylor, *Varieties of Religion Today: William James Revisited* (London and New York, 2002), 79–80.

paradoxically one which is as intensely individualistic as it is one in which social relations and collective experiences, be it in intimate circles or massive gatherings, are of paramount importance.

Consumerism and Religion Today

From our perspective, consumerism appears to be far from superficial: it is bound to the very founding and directing principles of modern culture. The primacy of authenticity that it carries has profoundly affected even the most institutionalised and traditional of religions, by questioning the authority mechanisms that concretely ensured their competence regarding Truth.[56] Experience – of one's own, tested in exchange with trusted others including charismatic figures – has superseded tradition (in Weber's sense) as the measure and means of Truth. This process tends to value emotion over reason, hence the increasing appeal to the emotions across the religious spectrum, from holistic spiritualities to charismatic trends, Pentecostalism, and certain types of fundamentalisms. The rise of emotional religiosities is consequently not the lightened expression of some postmodern trend. It is 'one of the results of a long process by which Moderns have learned to think of themselves as beings endowed with interiority and to think of their presence in the world no longer with respect to an order inscribed in the nature of things or willed by God, but as a quest for happiness and wellbeing'.[57] As Charles Taylor has shown, the roots of this phenomenon go back well before the twentieth century to Descartes and even Saint Augustine; but consumer culture gives them a new inflection, force, and reach.

Thus religion shifts from obedience and a compliance to pre-existing schemes to personal commitment, even within the 'world religions'. Religion and faith become operational with respect to the widespread eschatology of self-realisation. The individual becomes pivotal in this regime. One could expect in this situation that individualisation would lead to a solipsistic and ultimately inordinate, fragmented, deregulated, and highly heterogeneous reality. This has indeed been the report made by a majority of scholars. Yet this conclusion is founded on a very shallow acknowledgement of social reality – just because older forms of regulative mechanism seem obsolete it does not mean that there is no regulation.

As Danièle Hervieu-Léger has remarked in a forceful article, the movement towards individualisation is accompanied by a certain homogenisation of religion.[58] If we remove our gaze from the face value of practices and contents of belief to view things from a wider and deeper perspective, we see that beliefs and

[56] Danièle Hervieu-Léger, 'Quelques paradoxes de la modernité religieuse. Crise de l'universel, planétarisation culturelle et renforcements communautaires', *Futuribles*, 260 (2001): 101.

[57] Ibid., 105.

[58] Ibid.

practices are isolated from the webs of meaning in which they were previously inscribed, and reintegrated in the new globalised networks of consumer culture in which expressive individualism and associated sociality thrives. If the contents of belief appear to be diverse and heterogeneous, the *modes* of religious belief and practice have perhaps never been so homogeneous. There is no longer a deep cultural difference between a Christian and a Jew, let alone a Protestant and a Catholic, but rather something like a difference in lifestyles and life ethics – and networks of association. The turnaround is complete since the times analysed by Max Weber: it is no longer the different Christian cultures that shape capitalism – it is consumer culture that shapes Christianity (and religion in general).

An indication of this homogenisation is the popular universalistic idea that all religions are particularistic paths that highlight different aspects of a single truth.[59] The same goes for the idea according to which 'we all seek the same thing in the end', and so on. The effect of this is to pare down what used to be insurmountable differences only a few decades back (think of the abysmal divide between Protestants and Catholics) and validate a common core that embraces the entire religious spectrum (with some variations and derogations, of course). It is because of this homogenisation of the modes of belief and practice that contemporaries can as easily circulate between different religious groups and collate elements that are *a priori* contradictory and impervious. Another example that supports the hypothesis of a newly regulated religious landscape is the theme of 'healing' and 'wellbeing' – major themes in consumer culture – which reaches across the spectrum of religiosities, from Pentecostals to holistic spiritualities and self-help psychology.[60]

To explain this phenomenon, Danièle Hervieu-Léger suggests a parallel with the emergence of consumer and neoliberal societies. As the markets have been deregulated, she explains, so have 'symbolic goods' been freed from the hands of traditional, institutional monopolies, creating a standardising effect. While the recourse to economic categories in the sociology of religion is often highly problematic, she writes that in this case their use is called for in a way that is not simply analogical. Unfortunately, the argument goes no further, and the rapport between the present state of religion and economics is only suggested. Likewise, an increasing number of scholars are writing on the branding, marketisation, and commoditisation of religious phenomena. Yet what does this mean? Is religion reducible to market logics, or is it the market and consumerism that perform non-economical, even religious functions?

For most authors, pointing to economics and using economic terminology ends the discussion, as if the very mention of the market and its automatic adjustment of supply and demand were self-explanatory. Yet reality is not so obvious, as we have seen, as consumption does not work in accordance with neoclassical principles.

---

59 See Linda Woodhead and Paul Heelas (eds), *Religion in Modern Times* (Oxford, 2000), 386–423.

60 See Meredith McGuire, *Lived Religion* (Oxford, 2008).

For most authors, the meaning of terms such as marketisation, commoditisation, and branding remain implicit, and usually refer to either the optimistic liberal point of view or its opposite, the pessimistic post-Marxian one. Hence for example the 'commoditisation of religion' often implicates its devaluation and corruption.

An example worthy of discussion is that of Mara Einstein's *Brands of Faith*.[61] Inspired by the US case where these logics are so clearly evident, Einstein, a former marketer herself, describes in some detail the ways in which religious products such as books and films have become a sector of extraordinary growth at the Christian as well as holistic ends of the spectrum. She also describes how marketing specialists and management techniques are applied within religious organisations, sparking significant changes. Religious organisations have started to invest in names and logos in order to be recognisable in an ever more crowded 'marketplace'. By adopting these strategies, the religious 'offer' has evolved towards 'faith brands'. Religious branding exists in order to 'aid consumers in making and maintaining a personal connection to a commodity product. Introducing marketing into a social category, Einstein argues, changes this category into a market of 'products'.[62] The results of this mutation are manifold: religion is made to compete with other cultural products, and is thereby forced to become more convenient, customer-oriented, relevant to everyday life, and entertaining; the divide between the sacred and profane, religious and secular, is blurred; religions can no longer demand 'brand loyalty', in the form of a life-time commitment, but instead must compete to ignite and reignite commitments; for religious organisations, the objective becomes growth and continual expansion, or at least the stabilisation of their 'niche' or 'market share'; a tension is created within faith brands between disseminating their message to the widest audience and preserving their authenticity; complexity is lost as branding signifies the singling out of a very small number of defining characteristics.

For Einstein, religion and marketing are forms of meaning-making (and, we would add, community-making), and both are active in the identity-formations and modifications of both individuals and communities. Yet Einstein does not theorise her findings in this way, and decides to side with rational choice theory's 'supply-side' explanation. According to neoclassical (and neoliberal) economic theory, religion today is like a collection of enterprises operating in an unregulated open market. Religion becomes a product subject to the rational choices of religious consumers according to their preferences, while 'the market' is naturalised and essentialised. From the perspective we offer here, Einstein's intuitions and observations are curtailed by her theoretical choices.

The whole issue appears in a different light if we return to our previous discussion about the social dimensions of consumerism. Markets are *not* the meeting of supply and demand between the self-interested, rational, maximising individuals of the liberal-utilitarian model, abstracted from social determinations,

---

61 Mara Einstein, *Brands of Faith* (New York, 2008).

62 Ibid., xi.

history, and context. Markets are *marketplaces*: loci for complex social interactions and social re-formations. They are socially instituted and socially embedded institutions that are best described as networked and hyper-mediatised arenas of mutual exposure. They are also opportunities for the dissemination of information that can serve as resources for experimentations and interpretations. With respect to religion today as with the whole of consumer societies, 'markets' are where the complex rapports linking identity and recognition occur. If economics certainly structure the social today and all of its spheres, markets remain social institutions in which formal economics actively intersect values, social symbolisms, religion, politics, law, aesthetics, and so on.

Brands, as we have seen, are symbols around which social networks and loose communities can be formed. They function as providers of meaning, identity, and belonging. Consumerism works by instituting relations between people and brands attached to certain lifestyles. Consumerism is about identification, not satisfaction. It is not a product (a running shoe, for example) that is being bought, but a connection to a brand (Nike) and what it symbolises. It is therefore false to affirm that religion has become a product on the market in the neoclassical sense. Consumerism is a symbolic economy. Products refer to brands which are symbols inscribed in social relations. This is why the ideal for a brand is to achieve cult status – that is the maximum degree of recognisability, uniqueness, authenticity, and emotional power, such that it can become the fixture for identification, belonging, community, personal and collective emotion, and rituals. Inversely, religion within consumer culture has been restructured as an arena of choice, reshaped by the subjective revolution into a lifestyle and a resource for life ethics. This perspective significantly changes the understanding of commoditisation. The question therefore is not whether economics have become religious *or* if religion has become an economic product like any other: there is a religious dimension to consumption *at the same time* that religion has become commoditised.

The advantage of the position we are underlining with respect to the understanding of consumption is threefold. First, it moves beyond the highly normative frame of 'critical theory' which has depreciated consumption as being superficial and meaningless at best and constitutively alienating. Second, it also moves beyond the liberal economic interpretation by showing the symbolic dimensions at the very core of consumerism and thus considerably relativising the rationalistic paradigm. Third, while pursuing Charles Taylor's insights on the links between consumerism and the culture of authenticity, we also move beyond a strictly individualist account and highlight the social dimensions of this specific type of individualism and its new modes of sociality and community. Hence speaking of the 'commoditisation' of religion must be understood as meaning a specific way of producing meaning, values, and 'commons' through the circulation of commoditised symbols into social relations supported by the globalising mediasphere.

The fact that religion is now often an element constitutive of lifestyle has been widely critiqued as signifying some kind of degradation of religion in comparison with its 'serious', traditional, male-dominated forms. Yet from our perspective, such value judgements fail to apprehend contemporary religious phenomena with the normative neutrality that science must strive to achieve with regards to its object. From the perspective adopted here, the lifestyling of culture brought on by consumerism does not amount to a degradation of some kind of pure tradition and parish-community based, essentialised brand of religion. Rather, it is one of the specificities of the society of identities that the national, traditional and institutionally-bound type of religion morphs into a symbolic economy of lifestyles.[63] On the other hand, cultural phenomena such as subcultures that were born with the rise of consumer society have been widely interpreted as playing out religious functions and sparking religious types of commitment and experiences. These include youth and music-based subcultures such as hippies, ferals, techno-rave, hip hop, metal, goths, and so on, but also sports, arts, and martial arts for instance. It appears significant that in many cases, those involved in these lifestyles consider their involvement in religious or 'spiritual' terms. For them, world religions and subcultures evolve on the same 'level'. Interestingly, the Catholic Church itself seems to be more aware of this new reality than many sociologists of religion. In the run up to a Catholic World Youth Day which was held a few years ago in Toronto, an advertisement was given mass exposure, being broadcast in mainstream cinemas across Canada in both French and English. Apparently marketers didn't have much trouble convincing the Church that religion nowadays is linked to lifestyle and disseminated through entertainment media rather than the traditional relays of the local church, schools, and even family. The clip consisted in images of youths in undetermined contexts, smiling and embracing, with captions reading 'Community', 'Fun', 'Friends', 'Emotion', and so on. The end of the clip revealed the advertisers' intent, which was to publicise the World Youth Day event with a finale that read: 'Better than a rave[64] …'.

Management and the Ideology of Consumer Capitalism

Consumerism was well installed in the late 1970s when neoliberalism traversed from political economy to governmental policy. Yet this period is also that of the emergence of management as a new 'science' within the universities and the workplace. Management lies at the crux of the economy, politics and polity, society, and culture. Tracking the emergence of management and casting it against the backdrop of the social and economic evolution of the last century, sociologists Luc Boltanski and Eve Chiapello have argued that management acts as today's 'spirit of capitalism', in other words, that it is a set of beliefs associated with the

---

63 See for example Emma Tarlo, *Visibly Muslim: Fashion, Politics, Faith* (Oxford, 2010).

64 Rave is the name for all-night techno music parties since the emergence of the phenomenon in England in the very late 1980s.

current hyper-marketised and financial breed of capitalism, and that it functions as the justification, foundation, and legitimisation of this capitalist order, by sustaining and promoting modes of action and dispositions that are coherent with its logics.[65] Weber had argued that the Protestant religious ethic, with its elective affinity with the capitalist requirements of accumulation and re-investment of profit, had jolted capitalism into being. Only, according to Weber, such ideological and religious legitimisation was believed unnecessary once capitalism was 'well set on its saddle', as if some kind of self-propelled machine, the famous 'iron cage'.[66] Here Boltanski and Chiapello correct and reinterpret Weber within a functionalist frame, arguing that the German sociologist had in fact only described the emergent phase of capitalism, that of the first industrial entrepreneurs typical of the nineteenth century. According to them, a second phase of capitalism succeeded in the twentieth century, one which also required a new legitimising ideology (or 'secular religion', 'sacred canopy', and so forth), allied to Taylorism as a mode of administration and Fordism as a mode of production. This second spirit of capitalism was effective during the heyday of the postwar Welfare State and provided the guarantees of security, motivations, life perspectives, faith, and morality which were required for social and individual investments within the capitalist economy.

The globalisation of the economy which occurred during the 1980s acted as a thrust towards a new social and economic model favouring mobility, adaptation, outsourcing, delocalisation, denationalisation, de-unionised working conditions, network management, and so on, inaugurating a new phase of capitalism: financial and consumer capitalism. According to Boltanski and Chiapello, this transformation of capitalism was in part a reaction towards its critiques, sparking the elaboration of a new, legitimising narrative that coalesced in management and marketing. The underlying argument is that market economics are by no means value-neutral; each phase of capitalism corresponds to a specific ethical content and belief system – an ethos. Although management presents itself as being pragmatic, descriptive, value-neutral, rigorous, and objective, it constitutes an ideology that reinterprets the modern will to control through rational and 'scientific' means.[67] Management literature presents competition as a law of nature, a self-evident reality to which one must adapt – continually. It aims at efficiency, growth, ever-increasing productivity and profitability, and promotes company development regardless of social development. Yet it mobilises positive values and equates success with self-realisation within this entrepreneurial frame and an economically defined reality. It views change as being essentially a good thing, as it is said to open onto 'new possibilities'

---

65 Luc Boltanski and Eve Chiapello, *Le nouvel esprit du capitalisme* (Paris, 1999).

66 Max Weber, *The Protestant Ethic and the Spirit of Capitalism* (London, 2001 [1905]).

67 Vincent de Gaulejac, *La société malade de la gestion. Idéologie gestionnaire, pouvoir managérial et harcèlement social* (Paris, 2005).

and opportunities that 'must be grasped'. The modern project of the self is actualised at growing distance from the Kantian ideal and redefined in terms of participation in the global flows of meaning to which economic success and its technologies provide access. Parallel and complementary to consumerism, management reinforces an economic perspective of human life as it considers individuals as 'human capital', 'human resources' whose – economic – potential needs to be realised. Far from being a neutral vessel directed at maximising rationality and efficiency, management promotes an array of values in tune with neoliberal/consumer age capitalism: self-realisation, enrichment, liberty, autonomy, entrepreneurialism, pragmatism, flexibility, mobility, adaptability, utility, happiness (defined as pleasure, ease, health, and comfort), positivity, desire for progress, power, creativity, confidence, commitment, communication, maximisation, cost-effectiveness, efficiency, competitiveness, self-sufficiency, self-reliance, profitability, success, growth, and action.[68]

Examining the impact of economic factors on religion, we notice that certain kinds of religion are more susceptible to managerialisation than others – namely the 'old', institutional types which had already engaged in bureaucratisation (Peter Berger). After the 1980s these also succumbed to the lure of managerialism. The churches, above all, seek to adopt more managerial structures and procedures. If this is true of established churches, it is even more so with the new Pentecostal and charismatic churches, which promote a prosperity-oriented theology and the very same values that are carried by management.

Holding the subjectivisation/consumerism perspective alongside the management/institutional one allows us to distinguish between two complementary trends affecting religion today. This is both a limitation and an extension of Hervieu-Léger's homogenisation thesis, since the new regulation of religion operates differently with respect to economics whether we look at other-directed ('life as')[69] or autonomous forms of religion. On the one hand we see religious institutions, both established and new, which conform to a (male-dominated) managerial logic, while on the other we have an explosion of 'alternative spiritualities' which reject both traditional and bureaucratic modes of authority (Weber) and favour loose networks of mediated authority, in which the individual can be 'authentic'. In reality though, these two logics often become mixed, as 'holistic spiritualities' have been shown to be increasingly in agreement with neoliberalism, as some of the following contributions demonstrate. Similarly, the study of everyday Islam by scholars shows trends that can be interpreted within the subjectivisation frame, while promoting material affluence and an economic success based on 'Muslim

68 Ibid.

69 Paul Heelas and Linda Woodhead, *The Spiritual Revolution: Why Religion Is Giving Way to Spirituality* (Oxford, 2005).

pride'.[70] As a whole, the highly subjectivised forms of religion serve as a counterweight and alternative to the larger managerial forms of religion.

But in both cases, the massification of consumerism finishes the break with tradition – whether it be by engaging in a more managerial direction or a more 'authentic', individualist direction, or a combination of the two. Such an important change in the most profound dynamics of our societies can only result in equally significant changes in religion. The shift from traditional culture to consumer culture is mirrored by a shift from a type of religion inherited from tradition and ethnicity to a religion that is chosen: from progress on the path to self-realisation to becoming 'born again' within a charismatic trend. One of the results of this shift is the popularity of the term 'spirituality' over that of religion. Thomas Luckmann[71] was perhaps the first to claim that a 'spiritual revolution' was under way that would erode the foundations of traditional religion (namely Christianity) in the West in favour of entirely 'privatised' expressions of religiosity. While Luckmann's interpretation in terms of solipsistic individualisation have been rightly critiqued, more recent accounts have acknowledged the rise of 'spirituality' and 'quest culture'.[72] In *The Spiritual Revolution*, Paul Heelas and Linda Woodhead have tried the spiritual revolution claim against empirical evidence gathered from a survey of the small British town of Kendal, concluding that those forms of religion most in tune with the subjective turn are faring best.[73] We argue that the 'individualization' or 'privatisation' thesis is better recast as one of 'subjectivation', thus emphasizing the inherent social and cultural determinations, dynamics, aspects and effects at work (which go well beyond narrowly defined 'public' implications of religion), as well as stressing we also acknowledge the corresponding modes of sociality that are incurred.

In Conclusion: Opening New Perspectives

If we consider as a whole the discussion forwarded in these two volumes, in our view, the social acceptance of neoliberalism depends on a wider shift within Western societies, one which has to do with the rise of consumerism as a dominant cultural ethos. Both embrace a certain style of individualism and embrace managerialism, as well as reactions against it. Neoliberalism and its assumption of endless growth depends on belief in the endlessness of consumption and that individual liberty is best actualised by consumer choice. Consumerism as an

---

70 See Patrick Haenni, *L'islam de marché. L'autre révolution conservatrice* (Paris, 2005); Roy, *Globalized Islam*.

71 Thomas Luckmann, *The Invisible Religion* (London, 1967).

72 See, specifically, the pioneering work of Raymond Lemieux, for example. Raymond Lemieux and Micheline Milot (eds), *Les croyances des Québécois. Esquisses pour une approche empirique* (Québec, 1992).

73 Heelas and Woodhead, *The Spiritual Revolution*.

ethos and matrix of lifestyles is also inextricably tied to the development and democratisation of communication technologies. Together, they act as vectors for cultural globalisation and a certain degree of homogenisation.

The social sciences have been far from neutral in their treatment of consumption. They have generally understood consumption as either alienating or emancipating. For the liberal tradition, in tune with economic theory, the consumer is a cultural hero who best incarnates the modern ideal of autonomy through self-definition by means of the pursuit of individual interests. The 'consumer is the epitome of the liberal individual', constructing his life 'through the exercise of choice among alternatives'.[74] In sharp opposition, the Marx-inspired school of 'critical theory' and its 'postmodern' forwarders (such as Baudrillard) have denounced consumption as a vehicle for domination, alienation, and conformity. Within this ideologically and normatively drenched *épistémè*, the consumer is either hero or dope, rational or irrational, sovereign or manipulated, autonomous or other-directed, active or passive, creative or conformist, subject or object, with very little space for nuance, complexity, or simply empirical credence.[75] As has been the case with popular culture and mass media, consumption has been deemed trivial, superficial, feminine, and debased, and therefore not a serious and worthy object of scientific interest. Furthermore, dictionary definitions of consumption equate 'to consume' with 'use up', 'discard', 'destroy', and 'make away with'.[76] Thus the challenge with respect to consumption is the avoidance of symmetrical, one-sided reductions to either domination and over-determination by the social structure on the one hand, and the free, autonomous, asocial individual on the other.

While the spreading of consumption goes hand in hand with marketisation and commoditisation within this new type of society – which is henceforth best defined as a 'consumer' or 'market society' – we argue that consumerism is not to be understood analytically as the expansion of meaninglessness, simulacra, and alienation, as neo-Marxist interpretations would lead us to think. Nor is it to be understood as being primarily and essentially emancipatory, as liberalism enthusiasm would like us to believe. One way to explain the appeal of consumerism, its drive, is to see how it provides a formidable vehicle for the massification and radicalisation of the modern individualistic culture of authenticity and expressivity as defined by Charles Taylor. However, we emphasise, against Taylor, the extent to which the market is also social, and how the drive of consumerism, marketisation, and branding creates new forms of sociality (such as virtual and globalised networked communities) even as it destroys old ones.[77] In relation to religion, the essays in this book move far beyond a rational choice approach which merely uses (the classical, liberal conception of) the market as a metaphor for understanding

---

74 Slater, *Consumer Culture and Modernity*, 61.

75 Ibid., 33; Slater, 'The Sociology of Consumption'.

76 Lury, *Consumer Culture*, 10.

77 Eeva Sointu and Linda Woodhead, 'Holistic Spirituality, Gender, and Expressive Selfhood', *Journal for the Scientific Study of Religion*, 47/2 (2008): 259–76.

religious growth and decline, and explores how the very particular and historically contingent features of contemporary consumer culture shape religion – and *vice versa.*

In an attempt to draw together the several, and fragmented, insights about religion and economy, this volume and its sister volume suggest that the transformations of the religious field are best understood in relation to one another and set against the backdrop of wider socio-economic changes, catalysed by the spread of consumerism and the neoliberal ideology. Rather than highlighting the diffuse, disorganised, fragmented and deregulated aspects of contemporary religion, our claim is that recent mutations in the religious field run across other fields such as politics and can often be analysed in similar terms. They are not unregulated, but their modes of regulation differ radically in many respects from earlier more hierarchical, centralised forms of institutional authority, which became naturalised by conceptual tools including secularisation, the public/private division, and implicit methodological nationalism. The intent behind this hypothesis is not the enunciation of a new totalising and uni-factorial, all-encompassing, and uber-explanatory theory pledging the understanding of social reality with respect to economics. This would merely be participating in a reduction to the economic, which is precisely the present cultural and societal trend that needs to be analysed. What this approach stresses is how the present situation in societies across the world and how the development of transnational and global realities have been shaped through the growing impact of economic factors on social life, above all through the coupling of intensified consumerism as a dominant cultural ethos (hand in hand with the growth and development of electronic media) with neoliberalism as a cultural and political ideology (affecting 'governance' at all levels, and increasing the sway of 'management').

PART I
Changing World Religions

This section looks at consumerism and related issues among world religions. The chapters ask how established religious traditions are coping with consumer society and how their message to their contemporaries is changed in the process. The chapters describe varying processes of cultural creativity and conflicts arising from changing customs within some of the world's main religious traditions.

Simon Speck delivers a more theoretical discussion on the role and social place of religion in two recent influential accounts of social theory: Zygmunt Bauman's 'liquid modernity' and Ulrich Beck's 'reflexive modernity'. These authors provide alternative perspectives on the role of consumerism in shaping both cosmopolitan and fundamentalist religious forms. Speck argues that Bauman idealises political citizenship and views consumerism as leading to the impotence and trivialisation of religion. Fundamentalism – cast as a religion of flawed consumers – is here understood as a reaction to postmodernity that aims to resolve the uncertainties into regularities and simple truths. Beck's account differs. For him, religion has become freed from state control and individualised, and has become a potentially important actor along other civil society actors in 'second modernity's' project of validating human dignity. Thereby, religion in its different disguises may become a positive force for a cosmopolitan future. The two theorists have a contrasting view of the power of civil society on religion; for Beck it is revitalising, and for Bauman it is trivialising.

Turning to more empirical case studies, Per Pettersson analyses the Lutheran Church of Sweden's attempts to adapt to consumer pressures in the face of a constantly declining membership. Church members are continuing to shun the Sunday service which is still seen as the core of the Church's identity, yet there is an afflux when it comes to life rituals and other activities offered by the Church. In a move that Pettersson views as typical of contemporary consumer societies in contrast to the standardised logics of industrial society, the Church has gradually responded to these pressures by creating novel types of activities that focus more on interaction between the participants and downplay creed and traditional authority.

Stephen Ellingson's contribution reveals the formula for the success of megachurches in the United States. He argues that megachurches have successfully adapted to consumer society by effectively repackaging Evangelical Christianity into emotionally powerful and constantly changing and adaptable packages. Due to this success, megachurches have become highly significant producers of religious innovations which have circulated far beyond their places and contexts of origin.

Stefania Palmisano's contribution investigates the phenomenon of New Monasticism, which emerged in the aftermath of the Second Vatican Council's attempts to renew Catholic monasticism. Using Italian case studies, Palmisano highlights the manifold paradoxes linking New Monasticism and consumer societies, namely through the simultaneous criticism of success-oriented consumer capitalism and an adaptation to its ambient, highly subjectivised culture. Palmisano exemplifies how monastic commoditisation, eclectic everyday theologies, and emotional regimes focusing on happiness and wellbeing, all of which characterise New Monasticism, are in tune with consumerist culture while steering significantly away from classical asceticism.

Mira Niculescu's chapter examines how American Judaism is transformed by a novel opening up to popular cultural forms and experiential religion, namely in reaction to the appeals of Buddhism for 'cultural Jews'. The dilemma for Judaism as a non-proselyte, 'canned' religion is to keep non-active Jews within Judaism while setting itself in competition within a pluralist and competitive religious sphere. Niculescu identifies three types of strategies adopted by Jewish communities to reach their 'clientele': the appropriation of Eastern spiritualities, the rebranding of Judaism *via* popular culture, and the 'exotericisation' of Kabbalah, Jewish mysticism.

Francesca Montemaggi further discusses the commodification and marketisation of religion, starting with a forceful critique of the rational choice approach to religion. By differentiating between 'formal' (the marketing of religious ideas to consumers) and 'substantial' (loss of value in religion) commoditisation, Montemaggi challenges the rational choice model of commoditisation while suggesting a more comprehensive and nuanced account of the impact of consumerism on religion. The notions discussed are then summoned in a case study of a Christian Evangelical Church in Wales.

Chapter 1

Religion, Individualisation and Consumerism: Constructions of Religiosity in 'Liquid' and 'Reflexive' Modernity

Simon Speck

Introduction

This chapter addresses contrasting accounts of contemporary religiosity in the work of two leading social theorists: Zygmunt Bauman and Ulrich Beck. Their sharply divergent evaluations of religion today are particularly noteworthy in light of their common concerns and shared analytical framework. Bauman and Beck are united in conceiving of the present as constituting a 'second' modernity, marked primarily by the supersession of the powers of the nation state by the effects of free market capitalism, and confidence in techno-scientific rationality by the sobering consequences of its prior implementation. Both highlight the impact of these on subjective experience, describing a process of 'individualisation' whereby a complex of economic, social and cultural forces compel individuals to construct their own biographies without recourse to the socially integrating institutions of 'first' modernity (which are characterised by the nuclear family and its ascribed gender roles, full-time paid employment, and class-communal relations of production and institutions, as well as medico-technocratic expertise with its aura of infallibility, and so on). Beck and Bauman are in concord: with the passing of 'traditional' modernity the authentically modern promise of individual autonomy comes into its own. Where they differ is in their estimation of the prospects for success. As will become clear, their contrasting accounts of both consumerism and religious modernity are consequent upon their differing diagnoses of second modernity's compatibility with authentic self-realisation.

In the course of what follows I trace Bauman's and Beck's distinctive constructions of the prevalent forms of contemporary religiosity and situate these in relation to their contrasting accounts of 'consumerism'. This discloses not only the political stakes in the differing construal of religion but also returns us to the 'founding moment', so to speak, of social and political modernity with which any account of consumerism and religion must, however implicitly, treat: the emancipation of civil society from the state, the emancipation of religion into civil society. My argument is that Bauman's anathematising of both religion and 'consumerism' amounts to an *idealisation of political citizenship* which is at odds with his description of the powerlessness of the contemporary state, whilst Beck's dismissal of 'consumerism' as a 'zombie concept' and his celebration of the 'cosmopolitanising' effects of global flows of cultural goods and information revives *an Enlightenment view of civil society* which downplays its 'uncivil' aspect of inequality, instrumentalisation, and exploitation.

Religion in Liquid Modernity: 'Fundamentalism' and Flawed Consumers

Zygmunt Bauman's construction of religion in the contemporary era is coterminous with his analysis of 'liquid' modernity: the era in which all modes of conduct and belief are patterned after the 'consumerist syndrome',[1] giving rise to a society in which individuals, social relations, norms, and values are rendered market-functional. Individuals are 'interpellated' as consumers and the values of 'solid' modernity undergo a thoroughgoing *reversal*: in place of durability is enshrined the primacy of the transient – evident most emphatically in the rapid degradation and denigration of yesterday's fashions – in place of possession and enjoyment comes appropriation and rapid disposal. Desire is modulated into 'wants' which are momentary, volatile, evanescent; and consumption is no longer the 'conspicuous consumption' of Veblen's – or Bourdieu's – aristocracy of taste, for it lacks the typically modernist 'instrumentalism' of this attitude and is rather *autotelic*; a value in its own right. The consumerist syndrome patterns all social relations and provides the framework for politics, culture, interpersonal relationships, and even 'ideology' itself, such that ideas or beliefs are no longer means of social manipulation and co-ordination but rather means of further boosting consumption. The message is 'everything is or should be handled like a commodity'.[2] Consumer life is one of infinite experimentation, novelty, sensation gathering, all supplied by the market with the result that the life process is 'a succession of "resolvable" problems that however need to be and can be resolved only by such means as are not available anywhere than on the shelves of shops'.[3] The uncertainty of a deregulated, privatised existence robbed of the protective shelter of the welfare state and techno-scientific certainty is ramified by the proliferation of choice among which self-cancelling, commodified solutions are to be sought. Bauman is frank about the distress to which this universe of transience gives rise: no basis for trust in the future or trust in others, abandonment to a multiplicity and perpetuity of choices. This pervasive uncertainty breeds a need for expert guidance, on the one hand, and a transformed experience of social disempowerment, on the other.

---

1 Zygmunt Bauman, *Liquid Life* (Cambridge, 2005), 84.

2 Ibid., 88.

3 Ibid.

In the essay 'Postmodern Religion?',[4] Bauman sets the analysis of religious modernity firmly within the context of consumerism and its consequences. To begin with, the account rests on Bauman's understanding of religion as having been born out of a human sense of finitude and *insufficiency* in the face of mortality. Through an 'ecclesiastical self-legitimation formula',[5] religion gains its institutional and doctrinal reality through the priestly interpellation of human beings as frail, mortal creatures in need of protection and salvation. Yet, as the advent of modernity with its project for the rational-scientific domination of nature effectively dissolves the ecclesiastical power over death, human beings are no longer defined by a constitutional 'insufficiency' – all problems are capable of rational solution. Now the transcendent dimension of life evaporates as the focus of concern falls on the emphatically mundane and inner-worldly and modern culture enacts an 'anti-eschatological revolution'[6] as death comes under the care of medicine, to be specialised, sequestered, domesticated, and banalised. Furthermore, the relationship of individuals to life and death is, under modern conditions, the inverse of those which preceded it: under pre-modernity the regular rhythms of life contrasted with the unexpectedly sudden arrival of death; in modernity (and intensified in 'post' or 'liquid' modernity) the individual life-course is subject to untold disturbance, on the one hand, whilst its terminus can be predicted and foretold thanks to the advances of medical science on the other. Second modernity is the age not of dangers arising from 'transcendent' sources, dwarfing human powers and underscoring human frailty, but of 'man-made' or 'manufactured' risks demanding mundane-pragmatic address and solution.

Yet, if risk is secularising, how is one to explain the concurrent 'resurgence' of religiosity? For Bauman, this is an optical illusion – and, again, because of the basic absence of any sense of constitutional human frailty in these new forms of 'religiosity'. In fact,

> uncertainty postmodern-style begets not the demand for religion; it gestates instead the ever-rising demand for identity experts. Men and women haunted by uncertainty postmodern-style need not preachers telling them about the weakness of man and the insufficiency of human resources. They need reassurance that they *can* do it – and a brief about *how* to do it.[7]

Thus, the limitless energy required of perpetual consumers is at odds with any sense of human finitude – 'consumerist religion', for Bauman, is oxymoronic. The obligation to make choices amidst the ceaseless proliferation and rapid obsolescence of the goods on offer, the consumerist syndrome which suggests that all solutions are available as ready-made commodities, means that individuals need

4 Zygmunt Bauman, *Postmodernity and Its Discontents* (Oxford, 1997).

5 Ibid., 168.

6 Ibid., 173.

7 Ibid., 179.

above all else guidance in their choice-making. As a result, new-style religiosity is a vital support to the act and ethic of consumption – providing encouragement and inspiration – as well as embodying a consumer choice itself: self-realisation and sensation seeking are the keynotes. An example of this is the notion of 'peak experiences', identified by analysts and proponents of the 'new spiritualities' as the contemporary equivalent of the feats of asceticism of the mystics of yesteryear. For Bauman, however, these are not only emphatically mundane but, in addition, exemplary of the quest for ever more refined and rarified experiences which are motivated by a sense of limitless possibility typical of the consumerist ethic. Indeed, what sets consumerism apart from religiosity as it has been traditionally conceived, in Bauman's view, is its refusal to admit of any limits to human capacity – in contrast to the wellspring of religious feeling in an awareness of the existential condition of humanity, its insufficiency and weakness.

However, there *is* a

> … specifically postmodern form of religion, born of the internal contradictions of postmodern life, of the specifically postmodern form in which the insufficiency of man and the vanity of dreams to take human fate under control are revealed. This form has come to be known under the English name of *fundamentalism*, and shows its ever more weighty presence all over the part of the world once dominated by the Christian, Islamic and Judaist religions.[8]

If second modernity is organised within the parameters of the consumerist syndrome, then the sense of insufficiency is most keenly felt by those without the resources to participate. Bauman takes up the analogy, suggested by Gilles Kepel, of such 'fundamentalist' religious movements with the workers' movement of the nineteenth century inasmuch as both reveal the ills of society for which they have their own diagnosis'[9] – yet with the significant difference that, if the labour movement addressed the exploitation of labour, religious fundamentalism identifies the source of distress in the exclusion from consumerism. As such, fundamentalism – the authentic religiosity of post or liquid modernity – speaks to those 'left behind in the scramble for the entry tickets to the consumers' party. The poor of today are first and foremost *flawed consumers*, unable to take advantage of the treasures displayed tantalisingly within their reach, frustrated before the act, disqualified before trying ….'[10] Fundamentalism therefore depicts the individual at the mercy of the world of ceaseless, disorienting and unpredictable change, deracinating and atomising,

> and the message arising from that experience is: no, the human *individual* is not self-sufficient and cannot be self-reliant. One cannot go by one's own judgement;

8 Ibid., 182.

9 Ibid.

10 Ibid., 183.

> one needs to be guided, and directed, and told what to do. This is a message of insufficiency; but, unlike the message carried by premodern religion, it is not the message of the weakness of the human *species* – but of the irreparable weakness of the human *individual*, compared to the human species' omnipotence.[11]

For Bauman, then, 'fundamentalism' is both authentically 'religious' *and* postmodern. It is the expression of the individual's inability to exercise the 'freedom' (and risk) of choice and is marked by the same recourse to 'expert guidance' (as well as the technologies) found elsewhere – with the difference that the counsel sought is one that closes down choice. The expert consumers, picking and choosing among the exhilarating range of spiritual-therapeutic guides, exist in a universe parallel to that of the failed consumers, seeking consolation for their exclusion in literalist dogma's insistence on the vanity of human striving. Thus, as Bauman puts it, 'the allure of fundamentalism stems from its promise to emancipate the converted from the agonies of choice. Here one finds, finally, the indubitably *supreme* authority, an authority to end all other authorities'[12] – as such, this breaks with any notion of religion as a 'personal' matter and declares it 'the nearest thing to a *compleat mappa vitae*. It legislates in no uncertain terms about every aspect of life'[13] and presses towards a totalitarian answer to the dilemmas thrown up by consumer capitalism.

For Bauman, then, the authentically religious expression of consumer capitalism in its current guise is fundamentalism: the poor, unable to choose, excluded from the ceaseless game of consumption, placed in existential jeopardy by this universe of contingency and short-term options, choose not to choose. Instead, they seek the ultimate 'expert' guidance on which certainty can be founded and opt to exchange freedom for security, transience for transcendence. In describing the crisis of individualism of which 'fundamentalism' is emblematic, Bauman favours recourse to the description offered by Ulrich Beck: 'How one lives becomes a *biographical solution to systemic* contradictions.'[14] The predicament of individuals in 'second modernity' is that the arch-modernist value of individual autonomy is realised in such a way that individuals are compelled to its exercise without institutional autonomy *de facto*,[15] largely as a result of the depoliticising effects of the 'consumerist paradigm' with its insistence on the cultivation of the private self at the expense of the citizen – whose retrieval is the chief objective of a critical theory. For Beck, however, Bauman's account is one which falls back into the traditional rejection of individualisation as egoistic individualism, as it fails

---

11 Ibid.

12 Ibid., 184.

13 Ibid., 185.

14 Zygmunt Bauman, 'Introduction' to Ulrich Beck and Elizabeth Beck-Gernsheim, *Individualization: Institutional Individualism and Its Social and Political Consequences* (London, 2002), xvi.

15 Zygmunt Bauman, *Liquid Modernity* (Cambridge, 2000), 40.

to recognise the novelty of the contemporary context. This is the root of Beck's identification of contemporary religiosity with a 'normative cosmopolitanism' which – whilst wary of the faddish superficiality of New Age spiritualities and the danger of reactionary fundamentalisms – is the antithesis of Bauman's.

Religion in Reflexive Modernity: Cosmopolitanism and the 'Citizen Shopper'

Ulrich Beck's theory of a 'second modernity' is first set out fully in his book *Risk Society*[16] which describes the process of reflexive individualisation as the cumulative effect of the 'modernisation of modernity'. The unanticipated consequences of 'successful' modernisation result in the release of individuals from 'ascribed' class and gender identities (fundamental to traditional modernity's key institutions, industrialism and the nuclear family) into the 'freedom' of biographical self-construction, 'achieved' identity, and the imperative to choose 'a life of one's own'.[17] At the same time, the success of traditional modernity's other key institutions – the nation state and the market economy – ushers in the need for international cooperation in the handling of the resultant geopolitical, economic and environmental crises. As a result, sovereignty and citizenship can no longer be exercised solely from within national borders and parliaments as the global movement of goods, 'bads', people, and symbols renders the 'container society' of the nation redundant – analytically and empirically. Furthermore, global risks generate not only problems of governance but also a grassroots political response which confronts these threats on the terrain of global civil society. If Bauman sees individualisation as bringing with it a 'life politics' narcissistically preoccupied with the private self of perpetual consumption, Beck emphasises a 'sub-politics' identified with social movements and NGOs, focused primarily on questions of 'autonomy' and human rights and sensitive to the complex causality and interconnections of a global industrial society. If, for Bauman, individualisation amounts to privatisation effected through the 'transformation of the political citizen into the market consumer',[18] for Beck it is a 'universalisation' evident in the transcending of boundaries of nationality and nation. Beck does not, however, deny the intimate relationship between (reflexive) individualisation and capital – as he baldly states, 'individualization means market dependency in all dimensions of living'.[19] It is simply that the individual, thereby emancipated from the ties of traditional modernity yet inserted into a complex set of social relationships via a global network of production and consumption, can now fully exercise her cosmopolitan autonomy. Thus, the meaning of consumption in second modernity

16 Ulrich Beck, *Risk Society: Towards a New Modernity* (London, 1992).

17 See *inter alia*, Beck and Beck-Gernsheim, *Individualization.*

18 Bauman, *Liquid Modernity*, 78.

19 Beck, *Risk Society*, 32.

is infused with a political potency that makes it an adjunct and aid to the 'realistic cosmopolitanism' which is necessary to the era of world risk society:

> The activity of global corporations and national governments has come under pressure from world public opinion. Individual and collective participation in nexuses of global action is here the remarkable and decisive factor. *Citizens are discovering that the act of purchase can always and everywhere be a direct ballot paper*. The boycott can thus join and combine active consumer society with direct democracy – on a world scale.[20]

For Beck, therefore, 'consumerism' – with its assumptions of a privatised, apolitical and narcissistic self – is another of the 'zombie categories'[21] left over from the analysis of first modernity, now rendered anachronistic by globalisation and reflexive individualisation. In *Risk Society* Beck drew on Simmel to underscore the fact that money both individualises and standardises – abstracting, disembedding, and extending social relationships across time and space[22] – and he returns to Simmel to argue that the concept of consumerism needs to be constructed anew:

> It was Simmel who, in his *Philosophy of Money*, elaborated the deep connection between money and religion. Both are to reconcile differences through abstraction, by separating themselves from every particular time and place. It was also Simmel who made the heretical assertion that consumerism is a worthy replacement for religion. Many have lamented that people seem more concerned with commerce than God but Simmel points out that although consumerism is something you can get lost in this is because, like religion, it enacts a dreamworld with material objects. The cultivation of tastes expresses both our identity and our place in society – our status – just as the practice of religion used to. And it does it – this is my main point – on a cosmopolitan level. So consumer society has to be redefined as an everyday image of cosmopolitan society.[23]

This argument derives in large part from that of Beck's occasional co-author, the Israeli sociologist, Natan Sznaider for whom the affinity between cosmopolitanism and consumerism recommends the abandonment of the classical ideal of citizenship based on ethno-national loyalty to the *polis*. In place of the 'citizen warrior' of ancient Greece Sznaider advocates the 'citizen shopper' as the model suited to an age of global interdependence.[24] In this view, critical social theory's denigration

20 Ulrich Beck, *What Is Globalization?* (Cambridge, 2000), 70.

21 Ulrich Beck, 'Interview with Ulrich Beck', *Journal of Consumer Culture*, 1 (2001): 265.

22 Beck, *Risk Society*, 94.

23 Beck, 'Interview', 265.

24 Natan Sznaider, 'Consumerism as a Civilizing Process: Israel and Judaism in the Second Age of Modernity', *International Journal of Politics, Culture and Society*, 14/2

of 'consumerism' extends the traditional dismissal of material and economic life as fundamentally 'apolitical' and, furthermore, overlooks the xenophobic stripe of antiquity's ideal of citizenship. By contrast, the cosmopolitanism of the 'citizen shopper' is predicated on the fact that 'under an advanced division of labour, every act of production and consumption, from your cup of coffee to your fax machine links to thousands of unseen others. The modern word for what the Greeks meant by economic life [*oikos*] is really social life ....'[25] Thus, that which first modernity 'perceived as counterproductive of citizenship, namely the global market and its features of consumption and indifference'[26] becomes the foundation of citizenship in second modernity. The global rule of money and markets gives to social relations the fundamental feature of abstract equivalence and interdependence which then issues in modes of universal recognition and a discourse of egalitarianism and respect for individual rights.[27] What is more, religion too is a consumer choice available to the citizen shopper via the global market: as Sznaider asserts, "Israeli liberals think that modernity is unalterably secular. But America is the most religious country in the industrialised world. What actually happens during the process of modernisation is that religion is individualised and secularised."[28]

In thereby aligning cosmopolitanism, consumerism, individualisation, and religiosity, Sznaider anticipates Beck's change of view in *A God of One's Own*.[29] Now the 'resurgence of religion' is no longer conceived of as a futile attempt to retrieve certainty in an age of contingency and risk but rather as another expression of the probing, cosmopolitan, autonomy-seeking individualism that is the hallmark of second modernity. What is more, Beck turns his attention to the subject precisely in order to undergird the 'realistic cosmopolitanism' necessary to the present.[30] Whilst acknowledging the immensely destructive capacity of religiously-inspired intolerance and violence, Beck maintains that

> There is no doubt that it is hardly possible to overstate the potential of the religions as cosmopolitan actors – not only because of their ability to mobilize billions of human beings across barriers of nation and class, but because they exercise a powerful influence on the way people see themselves and their

(2000): 297–313; Natan Sznaider, 'From Citizen Warrior to Citizen Shopper and Back Again', in Daniel Levy and Yfaat Weiss (eds), *Challenging Ethnic Citizenship: German and Israeli Perspectives on Immigration* (London, 2002), 253–67.

25 Sznaider, 'From Citizen Warrior', 257.

26 Ibid., 254.

27 Sznaider, 'Consumerism', 307.

28 Ibid., 312.

29 Ulrich Beck, *A God of One's Own: Religion's Capacity for Peace and Potential for Violence*, trans. R Livingstone (Cambridge, 2010).

30 For a fuller account of Beck's 'religious turn' see my 'Ulrich Beck's "Reflecting Faith": Individualization, Religion and the Desecularization of Reflexive Modernity', *Sociology*, 47/1 (2013): 157–72.

> relationship to the world. Above all, they represent a resource of legitimation in a battle for the dignity of human beings in a civilization at risk of destroying itself. Thus, what is on the agenda is the competence and readiness of the world religions to assume the role of spokespeople and champions on issues affecting humankind: climate change, the plight of the poor and excluded and, not least, the *dignity* of ethnic, national and religious others.[31]

As Beck now conceives it, the 'paradox of secularization'[32] is that religion is *emancipated*: no longer obliged to legitimise state policy or lay claim to cognitive-scientific authority but – in the present moment of the reflexivity-inducing crises of techno-science and modern political institutions – ideally positioned to criticise the dehumanising consequences of both. Key to this critical vocation is the fundamental concern with the dignity of the human person which is, Beck maintains, the ethical foundation of the world religions, but which has been compromised by the historical requirement of religious institutions to police their own boundaries, to maintain doctrinal purity and orthodoxy, and in the era of first modernity, to reinforce national identity. Now, with institutional individualisation transforming all aspects of social and cultural life, 'the religiosity of the second, globalized, modernity divides into two worlds – the world of priestly religion and the world of individual faith'.[33] Thus, Beck enthusiastically notes the central feature of contemporary religiosity: analogous to the construction of a life of one's own, it is a matter of constructing a 'God of one's own', a 'bricolage deity' assembled through the encounter with other faith traditions – an essentially open and universalistic view of religiosity as a matter of individual *choice*.[34] In this way,

> [c]osmopolitization and individualization are two aspects of reflexive modernization. Both are (different) forms of de-traditionalization. *Cosmopolitization opens up the outer aspect of religious transformation,indiv idualization, the inner*. Cosmopolitization presupposes stripping the religions of their national and territorial foundations. This means that the religions themselves become individualized since faith now becomes optional and tethered to the authority of the religious self.[35]

Habermas provides Beck with the model for 'translating' religious doctrine into the language of liberal humanism, but more significantly it is Durkheim who 'anticipates the union of individualization and cosmopolitanism'[36] in his assertion that the modern division of labour, in its work of differentiating and integrating

31 Beck, *A God of One's Own*, 198.

32 Ibid., 24.

33 Ibid., 87.

34 Ibid., 62.

35 Ibid., 82.

36 Ibid., 96.

ever greater numbers over ever wider distances, ushers in a *conscience collective* which enshrines as its highest value the dignity of the human individual as such. Beck produces an account of religion in second modernity whose chief feature is, therefore, its validation of human dignity *per se*, whence arises its capacity to provide a moral supplement to the 'cosmopolitan vision' necessary to an age of global interdependency. The individualisation of belief is, emphatically, not its privatisation, for reflexive religiosity attends to the injuries suffered to individual human dignity wherever they are inflicted. Thus, religion is potentially 'an actor in the process of (cosmopolitan) modernization' whereby religions 'join forces with transnational, civil movements to respond to global problems and put them on the world's agenda'.[37]

Consumerism, Religion, and Civil Society

At first blush, it is not difficult to identify shortcomings with both accounts. Bauman's 'fundamentalism' is a misnomer and mistakes the constituency for such movements (not solely the 'flawed consumers' of neoliberalism but – as Bernice Martin shows in her account of the 'second Reformation' in Latin America – also the upwardly-mobile and entrepreneurial: those for whom evangelical forms of religious expression provide an individual means of engagement in the deregulated or informal markets of 'disorganized capitalism').[38] Beck's view, meanwhile, although nicely capturing the paradoxical reflexivity of 'fundamentalism', overplays the ecumenical cast and political orientation of the predominantly 'world-accommodating' religious movements and identities of second modernity.[39] Moreover, both accounts – for all their concern with globalisation – are irrevocably Eurocentric (as Beck ruefully concedes). These are all points of criticism worth pursuing. What the focus on *consumerism* illuminates, however, and what concerns us here is the authors' orientation to the meaning and place of religion and *civil society* in the contemporary conjuncture. This opens up the question of the political agency of religion as it is 'freed' from identification with the state, on the one hand, but 'relocated' to a universe of contractual relations and private choice, on the other. Hence, we confront in these accounts a 'consumerist' religion that is ultimately in conformity with the neoliberal privatisation of all aspects of life (Bauman) *or* newly sensitised to the fundamental values of *individual* human dignity regardless of the particularisms of community, nation, or institutional-religious membership (Beck). As I will seek to show – and with

---

37 Ibid., 91.

38 Bernice Martin, 'From Pre- to Postmodernity in Latin America: The Case of Pentecostalism', in Paul Heelas (ed.), *Religion, Modernity and Postmodernity* (Oxford, 1998), 102–46.

39 Bryan Turner, *Religion and Modern Society: Citizenship, Secularisation and the State* (Cambridge, 2011), 276.

the aid of the 'classical' social theorist absent from the account hitherto – these antithetical evaluations of the progressive-political agency of desecularisation, viewed through the prism of 'consumerism', return us to the central question of social, political and religious modernity ('first' *and* 'second'): the split between common good and private interest.

For both theorists, the depletion of the powers of the nation state is the context for construing political agency, and its space, anew: in both cases, it is the place of religion within this space that the question of consumerism foregrounds. Thus, Bauman argues for a renovated republicanism which appeals to the powers of the autonomous *citoyen* to recover a sense of the common good – in opposition to the asocial and destructive force of commoditised, heteronomous, consumers protected by the negative freedoms of liberalism and acting within the sphere of a civil society identified essentially with the satisfaction of private, material needs. As he states matters:

> Once the state recognizes the priority and superiority of the laws of the market over the laws of the *polis*, the citizen is transmuted into the consumer, and a consumer 'demands more and more protection while accepting less and less the need to participate' in the running of the state. The overall result is the present 'fluid conditions of generalized anomie and rejection of the rules' in all their versions. Between the ideal of liberal democracy and its really existing version the distance is growing, rather than diminishing.[40]

Beck, on the other hand, identifies a global civil society which is emphatically inclusive of the circuits and flows of capital and commercial media. This is the space for individuals' choices and action, transcending the parochial, traditional and para-tribal limitations and affiliations of nationality. As Beck puts it, 'whereas the *citoyen* is still trapped in the framework of the national state, the *bourgeois* acts in a cosmopolitan manner – which means that when his democratic heart throbs, his action no longer has to obey the imperatives of national loyalty'.[41] Between Bauman and Beck, then, we witness the contrasting constructions of 'civil society' *tout court*: on the one hand, it is the arena for the expression of individual autonomy and the enactment of a genuinely non-repressive universality, situated between domestic privacy and the state; on the other, it is the sphere of egoism, self-interest, and materialism, precluding the formation of any authentic general will. On the one side, Bauman confronts directly the depoliticising force of civil society via Ernest Gellner's image of the 'modular man' of civil society[42] – one whose associations and relationships are passing, contingent, and ultimately instrumental – whilst Beck's image of the civilising-cosmopolitanising power of

---

40 Zygmunt Bauman, *In Search of Politics* (Cambridge, 1999), 156–7.

41 Beck, *What Is Globalization?*, 67.

42 Ernest Gellner, *Conditions of Liberty: Civil Society and Its Rivals* (London, 1996) cited in Bauman, *In Search*, 159.

trade echoes Gellner's Enlightenment confidence in the moral and democratising force of the expanded division of labour.[43] These concerns bear on religion and its ethico-political potential because of the ambivalent position and significance of religion in, and for, 'civil society' – whether it should function as the apolitical and private expression of 'faith' or, by stark contrast, demand acknowledgement as the universal and necessarily public witness to truth and justice.

The identification of 'religion' as a sphere, institution, or mode of conduct and belief set apart and, primarily, a matter of individual choice, is of course coeval with the constitution of 'civil society' as such. This is to say that social-political modernity is founded in the 'emancipation' of religion from the state and *into* civil society. What concerns Beck and Bauman in their contrasting evaluations of religion's entanglement with modernity in general and market-mediated relations in particular, are the consequences which continue to arise from modernity's diremption of social subjectivity and substantive communal life – the split between the (public) *citoyen*, on the one side, and the (private) *bourgeois*, on the other. At this point it is instructive to turn to Marx's early essay, 'On the Jewish Question'.[44] Here Marx is responding to the demand of the Young Hegelian, Bruno Bauer that the Jews, to be worthy of citizenship and universal human rights, abandon their adherence to a heteronomous and particularistic Judaism. Marx's reply highlights both the irrelevance of religion to modern political citizenship, on the one hand, and the fact of its very accommodation within the Rights of Man, on the other. Thus, in the first place – pointing to the example of the United States, 'the land of religiosity *par excellence*'[45] – Marx asserts that the truly modern state is the atheist state wherein religion is declared a private, non-political concern, so

> the conflict in which the individual believer in a *particular* religion finds himself with his own citizenship and with other men as members of the community is reduced to the *secular* division between the *political* state and civil society. For man as *bourgeois* 'life in the state is nothing more than an appearance or a momentary exception to the essential nature of things and to the rule'. Of course the *bourgeois*, like the Jew, only takes part in the life of the state in a sophistical way, just as the *citoyen* only remains a Jew or a bourgeois in a sophistical way; but this sophistry is not personal. It is the *sophistry of the political state* itself. The difference between the religious man and the citizen is the difference between the tradesman and the citizen, between the day-labourer and the citizen, between the landowner and the citizen, between the *living individual* and the *citizen*. The contradiction which exists between religious man and political man

43 Gellner, *Conditions*; see also Robert Fine, 'Civil Society Theory, Enlightenment and Critique', *Democratization*, 4/1 (1997): 7–28.

44 Karl Marx, 'On the Jewish Question', in *Early Writings*, ed. and intr. Lucio Colleti and trans. R. Livingstone and G. Benton (Harmondsworth, 1975), 211–41.

45 Ibid., 217.

> is the same as exists between the *bourgeois* and the *citoyen*, between the member of civil society and his *political lion's skin*.[46]

In the second place, Marx maintains that the Rights of Man – as the American and French examples show – far from excluding 'the privilege of faith' (which Bauer claims the Jews must abandon if they are to lay claim to those rights) include the right 'to be religious in whatever way one chooses and to practise one's chosen religion'.[47] Moreover, the fundamental human rights of equality, liberty, security, and property ensure and protect the individual, conceived entirely within the terms of 'negative liberty' and possessive individualism, for

> not one of the so-called rights of man goes beyond egoistic man, man as a member of civil society, namely an individual withdrawn into himself, his private interest and his private desires and separated from the community. In the rights of man it is not man who appears as a species-being; on the contrary, species-life itself, society, appears as a framework extraneous to the individuals, as a limitation of their original independence. The only bond which holds them together is natural necessity, need and private interest, the conservation of their property and their egoistic persons.[48]

In a way that anticipates much of the debate around the paradox of religiosity in a state without an established church – culminating in the 'market model' of US religious pluralism – as well as Beck's 'emancipation' of religion under second modernity, Marx describes this dispensation as one wherein both religion and the state are effectively 'perfected'. In Beck's terms, each is free to be 'nothing but' its authentic self: religion is not instrumentalised by the state and the state is not, in Marx's words, the 'bailiff of the church'.[49] Emancipated into civil society, religion, like trade, becomes a matter of individual freedom, whilst citizenship is cleansed of any contamination by social status. As Marx puts it, 'the perfection of the idealism of the state was at the same time the perfection of the materialism of civil society'.[50] In addition, the 'individualisation' of religion is reflected in the degree to which religious belief and conduct is severed from any identification with the *droits de citoyen* and conceived entirely within the purview of the *droits de l'homme*. As a result, it is made a constituent part of the apolitical 'sphere of needs' – or sphere of circulation (which is to say, the realm of legal-contractual relations and exchange, the realm of *consumption*) – which it falls to the state to preserve

46 Ibid., 220–21.

47 Ibid., 228.

48 Ibid., 230.

49 Ibid., 225.

50 Ibid., 233.

and sustain. Thus, as Sznaider has helpfully shown,[51] Beck's assimilation of an individualised religiosity to a cosmopolitan and 'bourgeois' concern for human rights superseding nationally-bounded citizenship stems from the identification of 'sub-politics' with the processes of civil society. Beck's cosmopolitan religiosity is the image of a universal 'humanity' refined from the abstract equivalence of money, as the citation of Simmel's 'monotheism' makes clear. In this way both religion and consumerism can be happily conjoined in making individual need the basis for communal identification and mutual recognition as far as the market extends.

Yet this blithely ignores the inequality subtending these relations – the exploitation *and* instrumentalisation constitutive of the sphere of production which underpins the formal-legal equality and mutual dependence evident in the sphere of circulation, of 'market relations'. As Luke Martell notes, Beck's cosmopolitanism 'takes commonality and starts off from the point of view of finding community in it'[52] – in other words, like Gellner and (Beck's and Sznaider's preferred versions of) Durkheim and Simmel, the sheer fact of market-mediated interdependency is considered sufficient to generate 'sociality' *per se*. In this happy view consumerism necessarily debouches into cosmopolitanism, global commerce is sublimated into global citizenship. Meanwhile, in contrast to Beck's hopeful utilisation of the 'materialism of civil society', Bauman embraces its corollary, the 'idealism of the state', advancing an argument for republican citizenship albeit in an age when (as Bauman himself emphatically reiterates) the powers of the state have been superseded with little indication as to the means (or even desirability) of their retrieval. For Bauman, as we have seen, religion and material needs, patterned in accord with the consumerist syndrome, are essentially private concerns whose public expression is contaminating and destructive – a force of sheer heteronomy in face of which the recuperation of citizenship is the only hope. Furthermore, the absorption of the state by civil society – the depoliticising force of consumerism – is evident in Bauman's explanation of the hegemonic discourse of human rights, regarded as negative liberty raised to a universal power. In words that sound an echo of Marx's, Bauman argues that

> [t]he lodestar of the first reformation was the individual freedom to enter and traverse the road leading to eternal bliss through his or her own life-work; the catchword of the second reformation is 'human rights', that is, the right of every individual to use her or his choice to decide what the bliss she or he wants

---

51 Sznaider's 'cosmopolitan Judaism' (see Sznaider, 'Consumerism' *passim*) is assimilated to the apolitical sphere of circulation in a way that sees itself as inverting the anti-Semitic stereotyping with which Marx's essay has often been identified: the Jew is the *bourgeois* is the authentic 'global citizen' for Sznaider and Beck.

52 Luke Martell, 'Beck's Cosmopolitan Politics', *Contemporary Politics*, 14/2 (2008): 133.

> ought to be like and to select her or his own track which may (or may not, as it happens) lead to it.[53]

The contamination of religion by consumerism brings out, for Bauman, the extent to which the religion emancipated into civil society is complicit with the asocial, egoistical and nihilistic 'materialism' of the latter and cannot, therefore, be regarded as authentically religious. Whilst the religion that persists under the guise of 'fundamentalism' does so as an index of the degree to which 'civil' society is anything but. For Beck, meanwhile, religion's association with consumerism cannot but be treated as a reflection of the milieu in which it thrives – that of the expanding circuits of commerce understood as the medium of mutual recognition. Global civil society is thus endowed with its civil religion – a normative cosmopolitanism drawn from the 'religion of humanity' that can be abstracted from the world religions and appropriated by means of the deculturating effects of global networks of media and trade.

Bryan Turner has stated in the conclusion of his recent book that '[w]hat is at stake in the revival of interest in religion is the possibility of discovering viable forms of social being in a global world of commercial and commodified sociality'.[54] The question of the relationship of consumerism to religion resolves, then, into whether religions can criticise the social, cultural and ideological forms engendered by neoliberal globalisation. For Beck 'cosmopolitan' religiosity gains its moral power from its immersion in the very processes and networks of global commerce which it seeks to hold to account. Bauman, meanwhile, sees 'fundamentalism', the sole authentic mode of contemporary religion, as the false alternative to the reduction of human beings to total market conformity. As I have tried to show, these differing perspectives reside in their opposing conceptions of the political potentiality of civil society and the ambiguous place of religion therein: simultaneously private *and* 'universal'. Beck's elision of civil society with political society, far from a novel response to a 'second' modernity, appears as an erratic version of the Enlightenment belief in the moral progress inherent in commerce. Bauman's anathematising of consumerism, meanwhile, appears as an idealisation of the state – political citizenship is hymned as the force of salvation even as state sovereignty is pronounced dead. For Beck, the emancipation of religion into civil society is the source of its power – providing the moral sustenance of the reflexive individuals who must, it appears, make the running in averting the catastrophe that constitutes 'world risk society'. For Bauman, the emancipation of religion into civil society is its transformation either into another marketable commodity or into a medium of expression of protest at the dominance of the sphere of (manufactured) needs over all aspects of existence – in either case, obstructing the formation of a genuinely autonomous political society. What the question of religion's relationship to 'consumerism' illuminates, however, is the

---

53 Bauman, *In Search*, 157–8.

54 Turner, *Religion*, 276.

relationship of religion to both state and civil society. If, as Turner asserts, the appeal to religion is motivated by the hollowing out of forms of political agency addressed to the common good as a result of the subordination of the state to global market forces, then neither religion's translation into a deinstitutionalised religion of humanity nor its demonisation as an eruption of lumpen *ressentiment* is likely to comprehend its aptitude for both accommodation with and opposition to the uncivil aspects of civil society.

Chapter 2
From Standardised Offer to Consumer Adaptation: Challenges to the Church of Sweden's Identity

Per Pettersson

Introduction

The transformation of European society from an agrarian economy to the present service-dominated one has entailed a series of social and religious changes. Previous values and views which were linked to the standardised logic of goods production have been replaced by new ones which are linked to the logic of services. Service logic implies a focus on the individual's specific needs and perceptions, which is similar to the idea of the independent individual in the philosophy which is to be found in the new economic liberalism.

The position and function of religion has also changed as part of this general transformation of unitary agricultural societies into differentiated service societies. Rationalisation and functional differentiation have dismantled the traditional power of religious institutions. The historical European Christian churches have become religious specialists rather than, as they were formerly, part of the state management. Relationships between the churches and the people have radically changed from being dominated by the power of the churches over individuals to, in practice, the opposite situation. Presently individuals' personal choices and preferences increasingly form the religious reality, causing problems for the traditional religious authorities.[1] Religious organisations have become more like providers of services responding to people's needs and less like hierarchical and doctrinal authorities. These changed relationships between churches and peoples have implied new challenges to the churches' traditional identities, as defined by the churches' leadership. In the present user-driven religious market environment

---

1 Mark Chaves, 'Secularization as Declining Religious Authority', *Social Forces*, 72/3 (1994): 749–74.

the churches' identities are increasingly being developed in response to the impact of religious consumers.[2]

This chapter discusses the social preconditions and challenges for the formation of religious organisations' identities in the present service-logic-dominated society, using the Church of Sweden as a case study. The core activity which expresses the self-identity of the Church of Sweden, as of most Christian churches, is the liturgical services, especially the Sunday service. Local parishes' and congregations' identities, as well as the measure of their success, is often connected to Sunday worship attendance. Thus a decline in participation rates in Sunday services has been regarded as a significant indicator of Christian religious decline, not only by the churches themselves, but also by sociologists arguing that secularisation in Europe is increasing.

There is, however, simultaneously with declining attendance at Sunday services, a persisting and even sometimes increasing demand for the churches to provide resources in other areas – for example, as providers of rites of passage services, for community building, and as social welfare agents. The Church of Sweden is one of the churches affected by this parallel decline and increase, and its struggle with its identity is closely linked to the decline in Sunday service attendance. While the Church maintains the Sunday service as its core activity, the Church members' choices of activities steer the focus of the Church in a different direction. A question for the Church is whether it should redirect resources towards funding these user attracting activities, thereby accepting the fact of a consumer driven development of the Church which will then indirectly impact on Church identity.

This consumer impact is an external driver which forces the Church to become more market oriented by redirecting its resources according to the members' needs. But there is also a development within the organisation itself towards increased consumer and market orientation. This comes from the implementation of new public management ideas which have been brought in by consultants employed by the Church, as well as by Church personnel who have taken part in management courses. Thus the move towards a market and consumer orientation in the Church of Sweden is driven both by the demands of its members and by new management ideas coming from within the Church's own management structure.

The Identity of the Church of Sweden

The Church of Sweden is one of the historic national churches in Europe. Having been separated from the state in 2000 it nevertheless still dominates the Swedish religious scene with 69 per cent of the population registered as Church members, paying a yearly fee of about 1 per cent of their income. In 2011 this amounted to

2 Peter Berger, *The Sacred Canopy: Elements of a Sociological Theory of Religion* (New York, 1967), 145.

6.5 million Church of Sweden members out of Sweden's 9.5 million inhabitants. Statistical figures show that 53 per cent of all new-born Swedish children are baptised into this church, 32 per cent of all 15 year olds are confirmed, 36 per cent of all weddings and 81 per cent of all funerals are handled by the Church of Sweden.[3]

These figures could be regarded as indicative of a high level of religious involvement. However, when looking at attendance figures for worship among the Church members, they show that on an average Sunday only 1.4 per cent of the members are participating in a main Sunday service.[4] Due to this fact and to the comparatively very low figures regarding people's religious beliefs, Sweden is often regarded as one of the most secularised countries in the world.[5] Thus, depending on the choice of perspective and statistical figures, Sweden can be regarded as either very religious or very secularised. The situation is similar in the other Nordic countries and this is sometimes called 'the Nordic paradox'.[6] People 'believe in belonging', since they stay as members, albeit with low rates of attendance and belief.[7]

This sociological paradox is the cause of an identity crisis in the Church of Sweden, since the Sunday service attendance is in continuous decline. The identity of the Church is strongly linked to liturgical worship; at first hand this is enshrined in the Sunday service, which is emphasised in official policy documents as the most important activity of the Church. In the Swedish Church's main ordinance, it is expressed thus: 'The liturgical service is the centre of Church life, where the congregation meets God in the Word and the sacraments. The day of the main liturgical service is Sunday … '[8] The success or failure of the local congregations or the national Church is often judged by the Church itself, as well as by social scientists, in terms of the Sunday service attendance rate. The Church of Sweden even defines its 'parishes' on the basis that a Sunday service is celebrated in them every week. An implicit consequence is that an individual church member's identity as a 'legitimate' church member, or a 'good' Christian, is also indirectly related to attendance at the Sunday services. Thereby the attendance rate is used by the Church as a measure of its own success, as well as a measure of the strength of individual church members' relationships to the Church.

---

[3] Church of Sweden Statistics (2011), [Online], available at: www.svenskakyrkan.se.

[4] Church of Sweden Statistics.

[5] Phil Zuckerman, *Society Without God: What the Least Religious Nations Can Tell Us About Contentment* (New York, 2001).

[6] Anders Bäckström, Ninna Edgardh and Per Pettersson, *Religious Change in Northern Europe: The Case of Sweden* (Stockholm, 2004).

[7] Anders Bäckström, 'Believing in Belonging: The Swedish Way of Being Religious', in Riikka Ryökäs and Esko Ryökäs (eds), *Urban Faith 2000: Publications of Church Sociology* (Helsinki, 1993), 31–42.

[8] *Kyrkoordningen*, Femte avd. 17 kap. Inledning (Stockholm, 2007).

This focus of identity does not sit easily with the Church members' actual religious practice, since attendance at the Sunday service has continuously declined in numbers while simultaneously other kinds of liturgical services and church activities have maintained their attendance numbers and some of them have even increased in popularity.

Service Attendance

The tension between the focus of the Church of Sweden on the Sunday service and the Church members' preferences is clearly shown by statistics on service attendance. The majority of Church members participate in services irregularly and only on certain occasions, such as the yearly holidays – most likely the Advent-Christmas period – and at major life events when the traditional rites of passage of the Church are used, namely at the birth of children (baptism), the traditional symbolic manifestation of adulthood (confirmation), the constitution of the family (wedding), and death (funeral).

The total number of visits to all kinds of liturgical services in the Church of Sweden in 2010 was 17.2 million. Only 4.6 million of these were visits to Sunday services, which mean that there is a much greater demand for other types of liturgical worship than the traditional Sunday service. Statistical data on the long-term development of attendance at liturgical services over the 20 years between 1990 and 2010 clearly show that the declining interest in service attendance is confined to the Sunday service.[9] Table 2.1 shows the average numbers of visits per Church member and year at the different kinds of services; the Sunday main service, the rite of passage services, and services other than these.

Table 2.1 Average visits at services, per year and Church of Sweden membership, 1990–2010

Year	Sunday main service	Baptism, confirmation, wedding, funeral	Other services	Total visits
1990	1.18	0.81	1.18	3.17
1995	1.00	0.78	1.20	2.99
2000	0.90	0.82	1.19	2.91
2005	0.82	0.88	1.20	2.90
2010	0.70	0.87	1.05	2.62
	-0.48	+0.06	-0.13	-0.55

[9] Church of Sweden Statistics.

The average Sunday service attendance rate per member and year has continuously decreased from 1.18 to 0.70, while the average attendance figures regarding the rite of passage services and the 'other services' category are fairly stable. The average attendance rate at the rite of passage services has even slightly increased during these 20 years, from 0.81 to 0.87 visits per member and year. The level of attendance at the other services seems also to be stable, but shows a slight decrease in recent years. From a level of 1.18 visits in 1990 it decreased to 1.05 visits in 2010. The total number of visits to any kind of liturgical service has decreased from 3.17 in 1990 to 2.62 visits per member in 2010. This is a reduction by 0.55 visits. Almost all of this decrease – 0.48 visits – are related to the decline in Sunday service participation.

Thus the continuous decline in attendance at liturgical services is restricted to the Sunday service and does not reflect a general decrease in service attendance on the whole. This analysis of figures on service attendance is one way of demonstrating the slowly increasing gap between the focus on the Church of Sweden's identity as an organisation and the actual practice of the Church's membership. This development makes it a problem for the Church of Sweden to maintain an exclusive focus on the Sunday service as a foundation for its identity and a measure of its success.

A Mismatch Between the Church and Its Membership

A survey of 10,768 Church of Sweden members aged between 16 and 75 years confirms the low level of priority for all kinds of ordinary liturgical services, as compared to attitudes towards many other church activities.[10] When asked which three church activities they prioritise the following ranked highest; '[h]elp for vulnerable people in Sweden' – 49 per cent agreed that this should be the highest priority. This was followed by '[w]orking with children and young people' at 46 per cent; '[c]reating community for lonely people' (44 per cent), '[w]orking with elderly people' (35 per cent) and '[p]reservation of church buildings' (31 per cent). 'Traditional liturgical services' were ranked among the least prioritised areas with only 9 per cent of the respondents giving them priority.

Data from a general population survey of 2005 in the medium-sized Swedish town of Gävle with 661 respondents of the ages 16–75 years show a similar result.[11] Again the 'liturgical services' ranked lowest in the list of Church-provided activities, with only 6 per cent of respondents viewing them as having great or very great importance. This came out in sharp contrast with the importance of the idea that 'my relatives will get a Church funeral' which was highly rated by 61 per cent, or of 'the Church's care of the elderly and sick' at 60 per cent, or

---

10 Jonas Bromander, *Svenska kyrkans medlemmar* (Stockholm, 2011).

11 In 2005 82 per cent of the Gävle population were members of the Church of Sweden.

that 'mine or my relatives' children are baptised in Church' at 44 per cent; 'the Church buildings' were deemed a high priority by 40 per cent, and the 'Church of Sweden's confirmation teaching' by 31 per cent.

Another question in the Gävle survey was formulated thus; 'If you were to become more involved in the Church of Sweden, in what way would it be?' Again the negative attitude to liturgical services was in evidence as only 7 per cent said they would '[p]articipate more in liturgical services', as compared to '[v]olunteer[ing] in social work for vulnerable people' (38 per cent), '[s]upport[ing] people in mourning/crisis' (34 per cent), or '[s]ing[ing] in a choir' (23 per cent), and '[p]articipat[ing] in discussions on faith and life' (11 per cent). Obviously the liturgical services are not engaging people's willingness to volunteer at a similar level to many other areas of church activity.

These surveys show that people's passive attitudes in relation to the liturgical services do not reflect a similarly negative attitude to church activities as a whole. Many of the Church of Sweden's other activities are regarded as important by a significant number of Church members. Thus there is a mismatch and tension between the Church's official identity and priorities on the one hand, and the Church members' attitudes and practice on the other (Figure 2.1).

Church membership is made up in the main of occasional users of the Church, who attend at the times in their lives when they have personal needs, while the Church organisation primarily aims at promoting regular attendance at a specific activity, the Sunday service. This mismatch constitutes the identity crisis which is the focus of this chapter. In parallel with decreasing demand for the Sunday

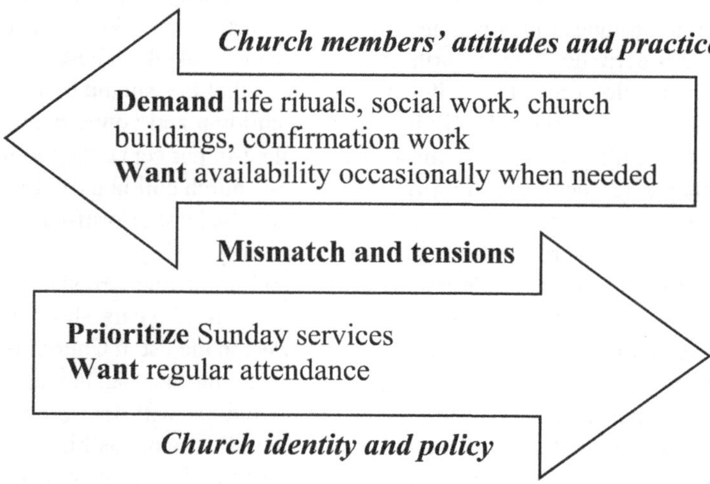

Figure 2.1 Mismatch and tensions between different preferences

services, there is a persistent and even increasing demand for the Church of Sweden in other areas; for example, as a provider of rite of passage services, as provider of social activities for children, young and old people, as a complementary welfare provider, and so on.[12]

Further, since the Church of Sweden is the major organisation in Sweden, second only to the state, most people regard the Church as a part of the Swedish cultural identity. Thereby the Church implicitly has a significant uniting function – for example, in times of crisis – by providing common spaces and rituals for coping with communal trauma.[13] The surveys referred to above, as well as other research have shown that there are expectations from the Church members as well as public authorities that the Church of Sweden should be an active social agent in parallel and cooperation with, for example, schools, social services, hospitals, or the police.[14] Thus the Church is regarded as a kind of welfare service provider similar to other public organisations and is given such an identity by the surrounding society.[15]

Church personnel find themselves often responding to these new demands to meet different social needs, not least since some of the traditional roles of the Church have been reduced or lost. Thereby people's and other organisations' preferences and needs drive the Church to allocate financial and human resources into new areas and to shift its own internal logic towards becoming more 'market oriented'. Consequently Church personnel spend an increasing portion of their working time in other activities than the Sunday service. At the same time they are evaluated as if they are failing in their mission, since they do not succeed in achieving high attendance rates at the activity which is regarded the prime activity according to the official policy documents. Research in environmental health at work has shown that this identity crisis of theological principles combined with hard work, imbued as it is with feelings of failure, is an important factor behind the relatively high figures of sick leave and the increased incidence of burnout symptoms among Church employees.[16]

---

12 Ninna Edgardh and Per Pettersson, 'The Church of Sweden: A Church for All, Especially the Most Vulnerable', in Anders Bäckström, Grace Davie, Ninna Edgardh and Per Pettersson (eds), *Welfare and Religion in 21st Century Europe, Volume 1* (Farnham, 2010), 39–56.

13 Eva Reimers, *Dopet som kult och kultur* (Stockholm, 1995); Per Pettersson, 'The Nordic Paradox: Simultaneously Most Secularised and Most Religious. A Case Study of the Increasing Role of the Church of Sweden in Public Disaster Management', in Hans Georg Ziebertz and Ulrich Riegel (eds), *Europe: Secular or Post-Secular?* (Berlin, 2008), 79–92.

14 Edgardh and Pettersson, 'The Church of Sweden'; Jonas Bromander, *Medlem i Svenska kyrkan* (Stockholm, 2005); Bromander, *Svenska kyrkans medlemmar*.

15 David Martin, *A General Theory of Secularization* (Oxford, 1978).

16 Ann-Sophie Hansson, 'The Psychosocial Work of Environment in the Church of Sweden: An Explorative Study', *Nonprofit Management and Leadership*, 16/3 (2006): 329–43.

The following two sections will provide a theoretical framework to interpret the background of and the challenges to the Church of Sweden in the midst of this identity crisis. The first section builds on traditional secularisation theory; the second section builds on theory from service management, discussing the implications of the implicit social mechanisms of the current service dominated society.

Functional Differentiation Leading to Changed Religious Relationships

The current level of scientific and technological development in our society drives a continuously increasing degree of rationalisation, specialisation, and differentiation of all societal functions.[17] From being relatively uniform in the several-thousand-year-long history of agricultural dominance, society has rapidly become increasingly diversified and pluralistic in the age of the industrial revolution and the subsequent development of a service-dominated society.

The functional differentiation process has also implied changes of relationships in the European religious landscape at societal, organisational, and individual levels. Firstly relationships have changed between traditional religious institutions and society as a whole as a result of the loss of religion's overarching canopy position. Religious institutions have instead become specialised agents in parallel with other specialised organisations.[18] Secondly, this in turn means that the relationships have changed between religious institutions and other societal functions when the latter have developed as separate organisations in parallel with the churches and free from religious control. Thirdly, the relationships have changed between religious institutions and individuals as a consequence of the changed relationships at the two other levels.[19]

From having been authorities of religious regulation, in the present service society religious organisations are appearing as possible resources and service providers in certain areas, for example, rites of passage services, holistic views, values, and social welfare.[20] Thus secularisation as functional differentiation

---

17 Niklas Luhmann, *The Differentiation of Society* (New York, 1982); Max Weber, *Economy and Society, vols 1–2* (Berkeley, CA, 1978); Daniel Bell, *The Coming of Post-Industrial Society: A Venture into Social Forecasting* (New York, 1973); Anthony Giddens, *Modernity and Self-Identity: Self and Society in the Late Modern Age* (Cambridge, 1991).

18 Luhmann, *Differentiation*; Peter Beyer, *Religion and Globalization* (London, 1994).

19 Karel Dobbelaere, *Secularization: An Analysis at Three Levels* (Brussels, 2002); Jackson W. Carroll, *As One with Authority: Reflective Leadership in Ministry* (Louisville, KY, 1991).

20 Per Pettersson, 'Majority Churches as Agents of European Welfare: A Sociological Approach', in Anders Bäckström, Grace Davie, Ninna Edgardh and Per Pettersson (eds), *Welfare and Religion in 21st Century Europe: Volume 2* (Farnham, 2011), 15–59.

does not necessarily mean the disappearance of religion, but rather involves a process of changing relationships between religious organisations and individuals, and other organisations and society as a whole.[21] Some observers even regard this reconfiguration as a religious revival, 'a return of God', or a 'post-secular' development.[22] The declining traditional role of the Church of Sweden and the simultaneously increasing role in new areas can be regarded as the effects of the same general social processes of change, driven by increased functional differentiation and the development of the Church as an agent specialised in certain service functions.[23] The challenges to the Church of Sweden's identity are linked to these social processes of differentiation.

Changes in Dominant Socio-economic Logics

The development of society from an agricultural, via an industrial, to a service-dominated one has meant a change of the dominant form of employment. Swedish figures show that almost 80 per cent of employed people worked in agriculture in the middle of the nineteenth century. In twenty-first-century Sweden the same share, around 80 per cent, now work in the private and public service sectors.[24] Similar development has taken place in Europe generally, as well as in the United States, with today respectively 70 and 80 per cent working in the service sectors.[25]

We don't need to be historical materialists to realise that there are connections between people's daily work and other spheres of life. People's ways of thinking and acting are influenced by their chief form of employment.[26] Consequently there is implicitly a series of links between the form of daily work to which the majority of the population devote themselves and the social patterns, values, and norms which evolve in society as a whole. Thus in parallel with the changed pattern of

21 José Casanova, *Public Religions in the Modern World* (Chicago, IL, 1994).

22 Hans-Georg Ziebertz and Ulrich Riegel (eds), *Europe: Secular or Post-secular?* (Berlin, 2008); Jürgen Habermas, *An Awareness of What Is Missing: Faith and Reason in a Post-secular Age* (Cambridge, 2010).

23 José Casanova, 'Rethinking Secularization: A Global Comparative Perspective', *The Hedgehog Review*, 8/1–2 (2006): 7–22; Peter Berger, Grace Davie and Effie Fokas, *Religious America, Secular Europe? A Theme and Variations* (Farnham, 2008).

24 SCB, Swedish employment statistics (2011), [Online], available at: www.scb.se.

25 Antonello D'Agostino, Roberta Serafini and Melanie Ward-Warmedinger, 'Sectoral Explanations of Employment in Europe: The Role of Services', *European Central Bank, Working paper series*, 625 (May 2006).

26 Karl Marx, *The Poverty of Philosophy* (Moscow, 1975); Peter Berger and Thomas Luckmann, *The Social Construction of Reality* (New York, 1966); Ronald Inglehart, *The Silent Revolution: Changing Values and Political Styles among Western Publics* (Princeton, NJ, 1977).

employment, a series of social mechanisms have changed which can be regarded as symptomatic of a change in society's fundamental logic.[27]

The agricultural, industrial and service-dominated societal forms imply three significantly different forms of social logic. The logic of the agriculturally dominated society was focused on the processes of nature; bound to yearly repeated changes of climate conditions in terms of temperature, sunshine, rainfall, and so on. This meant a focus on repeated and quite standardised processes around which individuals, families, and the whole society found their different roles and occupations. Dependence on a physical piece of land bound people to remain in the same place and promoted stable relationships, social control, and family-based collectivism.

Industrial logic is built on a different type of standardisation, based on mechanical rationalisation. The same processes are continuously repeated in factories, technical chains and processes in order to produce series of standardised products at a lower cost. During the era of industrial dominance society developed a new form of social class collectivism related to people's positions in the industrial production system.

Agricultural as well as industrial societies were based on logics implying standardisation and collectivism which directly and indirectly promoted different forms of unitary culture. Thereby the individual was regarded as coming second to the collective in both types of societies. From the historic European churches' point of view, as being parts of their respective society and located in society's power centre, it was natural to adapt to the logics of the agricultural and industrial eras. Collectivism, standardisation, and subordination of the individual were promoted and tendencies to individualise religion were subdued and even punished by the churches.

The Logic of Services

The logic of the service society is radically different from those of the agricultural and industrial societies. This is primarily determined by the fact that the produced value in agricultural and industrial processes is material, while the outcome of service processes is non-material, intangible value. The value of a service is produced and consumed in one and the same process in which the consumer interacts with the service provider, as for example in healthcare, collective transport or a Sunday service.[28] Unlike goods, services are activities that produce

[27] Ronald Inglehart, *Culture Shift in Advanced Industrial Society* (Princeton, NJ, 1990); Stephen L. Vargo and Robert F. Lusch, 'Evolving to a New Dominant Logic for Marketing', *Journal of Marketing*, 68 (January 2004): 1–17.

[28] Richard Normann, *Service Management: Strategy and Leadership in Service Business* (Chichester, 1991); Christian Grönroos, *Service Management and Marketing: Customer Management in Service Competition* (Chichester, 2007).

value that cannot be stored and used later, independent of the provider. Service processes imply a different organisation compared to goods production, since producer and consumer must in some way cooperate in the process which creates value. Thus human relations and human interactions are often important aspects of the production process itself. This means that services cannot be standardised in the same way as goods, since each service process is more or less unique because of the unique social relations that come into play between the specific individuals involved. Economists in the field of service marketing argue that this 'Service-Dominant Logic' has become the dominant logic of society at large.[29]

The non-material character of services means that there is in practice no way of objectively measuring quality. Service quality is largely dependent on the user's subjective perception and experience, which means that the service provider must adapt to different people's individual needs in order to achieve acceptable service quality.[30] Thus, while the logics of agricultural and industrial societies are characterised by repetition and standardisation, service logic demands flexibility and adaptability. It is not difficult to suggest that this focus of service logic on individuals' subjectively perceived value might contribute to a general and intrinsically subjective turn in the cultural mindset, values, and norms, with consequences also in the religious field.[31]

The Church of Sweden's dilemma with the focus on the Sunday service is a significant example of how the Church struggles with a historic past which is rooted in the agricultural and industrial societies' logic of standardisation, simultaneously trying to adapt to the differentiated and individualised service society. Until the mid-twentieth century all Sunday services were held at the same time – 11 am, and followed exactly the same liturgical order all over the country. Only the songs in the national Swedish hymn book could be used. Today the main Sunday service can be held at any time of the day, there are several optional liturgical orders to be used, and any song can be used alongside a wide range of hymns provided by the Church organisation. In this way the Church has tried to keep the Sunday service as the focus of its identity by renewing its form and content and promoting differentiation within the Sunday service concept, as well as the development of specialised, diverse forms of local Sunday services. This development has been a necessary adaptation to current social conditions and is a kind of market orientation. But the differentiation is also indirectly eroding the idea of one uniform Sunday service as the unifying marker of Church identity, and these reforms have not halted the decline in participation figures.

---

29 Vargo and Lusch, 'Evolving to a New Dominant Logic for Marketing'.

30 Valarie A. Zeithaml, Leonard L. Berry and A. Parasuraman, 'The Nature and Determinants of Customer Expectations of Service', *Journal of the Academy of Marketing Science*, 21/1 (1993): 1–12; Kristina Heinonen, Tore Strandvik, Karl-Jacob Mickelsson, Bo Edvardsson, Erik Sundström and Per Andersson, 'A Customer-dominant Logic of Service', *Journal of Service Management*, 21/4 (2010): 531–48.

31 Linda Woodhead and Paul Heelas, *Religion in Modern Times* (Oxford, 2000).

Discussion

Service Logic Implications for Religious Organisations

When analysing the preconditions for religious organisations in contemporary society, the service theory approach provides useful perspectives. The first interesting idea in this regard is that the focus of religious organisations on non-material values is similar to the focus of service logic, which is also on non-material, intangible values. This means that a service dominated society could be expected to be more open to religious values than a society dominated by goods production which focuses on material value as the outcome. Correspondingly, religious organisations with their non-material spiritual values could be expected to be open to the particular emphasis of service logic.

Secondly, most services are produced and consumed in an interaction process between two or more people. This implies a focus on mutual interaction between individuals, which means that the old hierarchical order in which churches delivered their values no longer fits. The traditional form of one-way religious communication is contradictory to the presently dominant interactive service logic. Thus religious organisations need to reform their ways of relating to their members and interact more on the basis of a symmetrical power relationship rather than on the old asymmetrical one.[32] Such a mutual relationship also means a focus on the individual user of the religious organisation and in that sense a 'consumer orientation'.

Thirdly, in their daily interactions with different service providers people take it for granted that the quality of the services they use should be judged by themselves as the consumers. Studies of the Church of Sweden's membership reveal that similar opinions are held on their relationship and contact with the Church.[33] Thus, there is probably no way forward for religious providers such as the Church of Sweden other than to accept that subjectivity and individual choice is also dominant in the field of religion. But herein lies a challenge for the Church, since when applied in the religious field a focus on individual preferences indirectly implies an acceptance of some kind of religious pluralism, since individuals are different in their needs and perceptions. This is perhaps the most problematic consequence for religious organisations today, also forming the background of the Church of Sweden's hesitancy about changing its focus of identity from the Sunday service as a common unifying activity.

---

32 Carroll, *As One with Authority*.

33 Per Pettersson, *Kvalitet*; Unni Wiig-Sandberg, *Den nödvändiga riten?: om upplevelser av kvalitet i begravningsgudstjänsten* (Uppsala, 2006).

The Church of Sweden's Identity Crisis

The previous investigation of a number of surveys showed that there are tensions between the preferences of the Church of Sweden's members' and the officially prioritised activity of the Church: the Sunday service. Sunday service participation is decreasing, while there is a persistent – and over the last 20 years even an increasing – demand for the Church of Sweden in certain areas: as a provider of rites of passage services, for example, as well as providing holy places and spaces such as church buildings, it is also needed as the guardian of collective memory and tradition and heritage, as an agent of social welfare, expert in death and mourning, provider of values of humanity and care, ethical resources and expertise, and so on.[34] While the identity of the Church is focused on the Sunday service, there are several indicators pointing at the rites of passage services as being the focus of many Church members' implicit Church identity.[35] Figures on attendance to the rites of passage services are relatively stable and a majority of Church members refer to them as a motive for Church membership. Thus Church of Sweden members have a kind of 'service relationship' to the Church, using it as an occasional service provider over the course of a lifetime. The rites of passage services and other Church activities are used only occasionally, but amount to a significant number when counted from birth to death. This individualised consumer behaviour on the part of Church members has developed in parallel to society's changing social logic.

Even the Church of Sweden itself has been affected internally in consequence of the general social change. In recent decades new public management ideas have been implemented by management consultants involved in the reform of the Church organisation. Quality improvement, measurement tools, and general marketing ideas have been introduced into the Church at the national level as well as local parish level when developing new strategies and plans.[36] In this way the change towards consumer orientation is being driven by social forces both from the outside and from inside the Church itself. The Church has become more of a service provider and ideas and values linked to the new public management and to new economic liberalism, which stress the independence of the individual, have been incorporated into the organisation as part of this change.

In relation to the members there is no alternative for the Church of Sweden than to adapt to the members' behaviour if the Church doesn't want to exclude people from being members or from using the Church. It is not possible for the Church to guide people in the way it was possible for the religious authorities of earlier times.

---

34 Bäckström, Edgardh and Pettersson, *Religious Change*; Edgardh and Pettersson, 'The Church of Sweden'.

35 Bromander, *Medlem*; Bromander, *Svenska kyrkans*.

36 Stig Linde, *Församlingen i granskningssamhället* (Lund, 2010); Anneli Öljarstrand, *Den mångtydiga församlingen: organisering, roller och relationer i spänningen mellan sekularisering och desekularisering* (Östersund, 2011).

The Church needs to change its modes of acting and communicating, simply and primarily because the present members have a different mindset from those of the past.[37] Most of them work in service-dominated organisations and apply quality improvement and service management systems in their daily occupations. They are affected by the inherent values of these systems. These systems are inspired by ideas from quality improvement models which focus on the perceived value for the individual user as a prime target for the firm or organisation (for example, TQM, ISO 9000). People applying such user-oriented ideas in their daily work do not find it acceptable that religious organisations appear to be hierarchical authorities. On the contrary they want their individual needs to be taken into account.

Being such a large organisation, involving a majority of the population and so many different kinds of people as members, means that the Church of Sweden has to be, to quite a large extent, inclusive and pluralistic. Thus the identity of the Church will implicitly have many different focuses and the identity will be determined differently among members. This internal diversity might be regarded as a weakness in a religious organisation that has a tradition of maintaining religious control over its members. But internal diversity might also be regarded as a necessary development in an individualised, differentiated society.

Conclusion

The transformation of the social production system to one of service dominance has radically changed the preconditions for religious organisations in relation to their members. When analysing the Church of Sweden's focus of its identity on the Sunday service, it is obvious that this focus is based on a society of an earlier time. The Sunday service and regular collective participation in this activity could be seen as a remnant of the former collectivistic society which can no longer continue to thrive in a more individualised society.

It is no coincidence that the new liberal economic theories have found easy access in many organisational areas, and this includes the religious field. The emphasis of economic liberalism on the strong, independent individual is implicitly supported by the focus of the differentiated service society on the individual, in contrast to the previous agricultural and industrial societies' unitary structures and collective values.

Ongoing rationalisation and functional differentiation processes have implied a specialisation of the religious institutions. From being at the centre of society's power structures, they have become one of a number of potential social resources and service providers.[38] In contemporary European society religious organisations appear and act in parallel with other organisations at a social meso-level. This

---

37 Pettersson, *Kvalitet*.

38 Anders Bäckström, Grace Davie, Ninna Edgardh and Per Pettersson (eds), *Welfare and Religion in 21st Century Europe: Volume 1* (Farnham, 2010); Anders Bäckström,

applies also to those historic Christian churches which have lost their former power, but have re-emerged as potential value-creating resources and are being increasingly evaluated according to their ability to meet the needs of individuals and other organisations. They are increasingly being evaluated in relation to the actually perceived quality of their services and to a reduced extent in relation to their traditional authority and legitimacy.

The development of religious organisations becoming more like service providers, generates new questions about their identities. The former state Church of Sweden is presently in a situation where such questions of identity are high on the agenda since the Church's top priority activity is declining at the same time that members' attendance at other Church activities persists. This persistent and changing role of religion in partially new forms can be regarded as the adaptation of religious organisations to the logic of services and to management ideas which are inspired by new economic liberalism.

Religious organisations are continuously changing since they are part of society as a whole and their members are affected by the general changes in social values and patterns. However, this does not mean that they have to implement all the ideas of the new political economy (neoliberal management). But the former power status of the religious institutions is broken. In practice the individual has power over the Church, in the sense of being free to join and participate or abstain, or leave. It is this power of the Church members, the religious consumers, that is putting pressure on the Church of Sweden's self-identity.

Grace Davie, Ninna Edgardh and Per Pettersson (eds), *Welfare and Religion in 21st Century Europe: Volume 2* (Farnham, 2011).

Chapter 3

Packaging Religious Experience, Selling Modular Religion: Explaining the Emergence and Expansion of Megachurches

Stephen Ellingson

Over the past 30 years megachurches, or churches with at least 2,000 weekly attendees, have come to dominate the religious landscape of American Protestantism. The vast majority of megachurches self-identify as conservative (even among the small number of old mainline megachurches) and often combine orthodox, evangelical theology with practical, therapeutic religious messages. In the United States they tend to be located in the suburbs and exurbs of the southeastern, southwestern and Pacific coast states. Although megachurches represent less than 1 per cent of all congregations in the United States, roughly 7 per cent of all church attendees are at megachurches, or as Thumma and Travis note, megachurches have 'the same number of attendees at weekly services (roughly 4.5 million) as the smallest 35 per cent of churches in the country'.[1] Although there were a handful of large congregations in the late nineteenth and early twentieth centuries, the rapid growth of megachurches is a recent phenomenon. The number of megachurches doubled between 1990 and 2000 (from 310 to 600) and then again from 600 to 1,361 in 2011.[2] Roughly 75 per cent of megachurches reported annual growth rates of more than 20 per cent in a 2008 megachurch survey, while during the same time period every major denomination in the United States reported continuous membership loss.

The power of megachurches not only comes from their sheer size and the number of people who are exposed to their brand of religion on a weekly basis. It also comes from the growing influence that megachurches wield in the religious 'marketplace'.[3] Megachurches have pioneered new forms of worship, church

---

1 Scott Thumma and Dave Travis, *Beyond the Megachurch Myths* (San Francisco, CA, 2007).

2 Hartford Institute for Religion Research, 'Profile of Total U.S. Megachurches' (September 2010), [Online], available at: http://hirr.hartsem.edu/megachurch/megastoday_profile.html [accessed: 21 July 2011].

3 Wade Clark Roof, *Spiritual Marketplace* (Princeton, NJ, 1999).

architecture, religious education, and congregational activities. They also offer a wide variety of religious goods and services – from leadership training seminars and church growth consulting practices, to Sunday school curricula, sermon series, worship music, and leadership models. All of these goods and services are for sale and such sales are a key reason why megachurches collectively bring in over $7 billion annually.[4] Moreover, megachurches are creating new forms of religious associations – proto-denominations – which often function as vehicles for the dissemination and sale of megachurch products. Thumma notes that these new associations, anchored by a megachurch, 'unlike traditional denominations, are loosely-structured, de-centralised, non-hierarchical, and lacking bureaucratic structures'.[5] These associations offer congregational leaders the kinds of resources traditional denominations offer (for example curricula and courses for pastors-in-training), but exercise no organisational power over member churches. Although there is no official count of megachurch networks, three of the most prominent ones highlight the market reach of megachurches. Over 10,000 congregations from around the world have joined the Willow Creek Association (WCA), a proto-denomination, in the past 18 years. This is roughly the same size as two of the largest mainline Protestant denominations and larger than all other mainline denominations except for the United Methodist Church. Over 3,100 US congregations are in the WCA United States and nearly 600 are from mainline Protestant denominations. A second network centres around pastor Rick Warren and the Saddleback Community Church. The 'Purpose Driven Church Network' is a virtual information and resource network that is 'a global coalition of congregations in 162 countries. More than 500,000 ministers and priests have been trained worldwide, and almost 157,000 church leaders subscribe to *Ministry Toolbox*, his weekly newsletter.'[6] Finally, the Potter's House Network, founded by T.D. Jakes, the pastor of a 30,000-member megachurch of the same name, is comprised of nearly 500 (primarily African-American) churches, whose member congregations can purchase Jakes' books, sermons, and other resources.

These examples highlight the extraordinary reach and the potential ability of megachurches to remake American Protestantism in its own image. This size and scope of the megachurches' activities lead Thumma and Travis to argue that they

> are the most influential contemporary dynamic in American religion. They have superseded formerly key influences of denominations, seminaries, and religious presses and publishing. ... [L]eaders of megachurches are defining

---

[4] Thumma and Travis, *Beyond*, 1.

[5] Scott Thumma, 'The Shape of Things to Come: Megachurches, Emerging Churches and Other New Religious Structures', in Charles H. Lippy (ed.), *Faith in America, Volume 1: Organized Religion Today* (Westport, CT and London, 2006), 201.

[6] Saddleback Church: Purpose Driven Life, 'About the Author: Rick Warren', [Online], available at: http://www.purposedrivenlife.com/en-US/AboutUs/AboutTheAuthor/AboutTheAuthor.htm [accessed: 9 August 2011].

> what Protestant America looks like for the foreseeable future. … [B]oth clergy and lay, look to megachurches and their pastors for their cures and direction for the future.[7]

This chapter takes up the question of the megachurches' successful emergence, growth, and reach into American religion, and in particular, asks how megachurches, which still only account for roughly 1,300 of the 335,000 congregations in the United States, have become the creators and purveyors of new religious ideas and practices. The first part of the chapter draws on Weber's explanation of religious change. It argues that megachurches emerged and grew during a period of the widespread membership declines that were caused by the inability of Protestant churches to offer meaningful *experiences* of God. Megachurches offered a new set of religious experiences that re-vivified access to the sacred and satisfied the baby boomers' (and subsequent generations') restless search for meaning and belonging that other forms of Protestantism were unable to offer during the 1980s and 1990s. The second part of the chapter shows how the megachurches have yoked the logics of the market and conversion to gain control over a disparate religious landscape. Megachurches wield inordinate power within American Protestantism by packaging and selling their brand of religious experience in mix and match modules. These packages of sermons, worship services, or small group discussion guides provide church leaders with templates or formulas for transplanting the megachurch experience in their own congregation. At the same time, isomorphic pressures within religious bodies and in local religious economies push congregations to adopt and adapt the megachurch structures and cultures in order to compete and remain viable.

Explaining the Emergence and Growth of Megachurches

Many scholars of megachurches rely on some kind of cultural explanation to address their emergence and success. For example, Thumma and Travis[8] identify three key factors that predict the growth of megachurches: worship services that are experienced as exciting and relevant; non-invasive methods for staying in contact with visitors; and a significant number of members who engage in inviting people they know to attend a service or event. Sargeant shows how new forms of worship pioneered by Willow Creek 'mirror the musical and cultural preferences of contemporary society' and aim to provide therapeutic help for the daily problems confronting middle-class attendees. In this way megachurches embody consumer preferences for innovation and practically relevant worship,

---

7 Thumma and Travis, *Beyond*, 2, 18.

8 Ibid.

both of which are critical for the growth of seeker megachurches.[9] In their ethnographic study of five megachurches, Snow and his colleagues conclude that these churches grow by 'making themselves spiritually relevant to the lives of their current and potential members'. They use several different strategies that hinge on matching the messages and programmes of the congregation with the interests, values and/or lifestyles of their targeted audience. Two congregations tap into 'America's therapeutic self-help culture by offering members assistance in identifying, dealing with, and resolving various individuals' problems', while another incorporates elements from the youth cultures of second and third generation Asian Americans.[10] In particular they show how these megachurches use worship and small groups to attract new members. This finding is consistent with the work of Miller's study[11] of 'post-denominational' Christianity (Calvary Chapel, Hope Chapel, and Vineyard Christian Fellowship) and the megachurches that emerged from these new traditions. He emphasises how the worship services at these churches offer access to an experience of the sacred that is deemed more authentic than the kind of worship experiences offered by mainline Protestant Churches.

In short, these authors all seem to be arguing that megachurches are more adept at making the content of their worship services or programming fit or resonate with the interests, experiences and expectations of a very large portion of the American church-going audience. While these works shed important light on the phenomenon of the megachurch, they tend to emphasise the role of individuals' religious interests and downplay the way in which larger cultural and social forces, especially consumerism and a pervasive economic logic, have been adopted by megachurch leaders as they reshape the meaning and practice of religion.

How and why do megachurch worship services and programmes pull such large numbers of people into participation and membership? Why do their services and goods resonate or articulate with a diverse audience in the ways that they do? Answering these questions requires a close look at the process of articulation, and Weber's explanation of religious change provides a useful starting point.

In 'The Social Psychology of World Religions' Weber offers a model of religious change in which religious elites rework a given belief system in order to make it fit more closely to changes in the social world.[12] Weber's explanation hinges on how religious elites rationalise religion in response to believers'

---

9 Kimon Howland Sargeant, *Seeker Churches: Promoting Traditional Religion in a Non-Traditional Way* (New Brunswick, NJ, 2000), 55.

10 David Snow, James A. Bany, Michelle Peria and James E. Stobaugh, 'A Team Field Study of the Appeal of Megachurches: Identifying, Framing, and Solving Personal Issues', *Ethnography*, 11/1 (2010): 170.

11 Donald E. Miller, *Reinventing American Protestantism* (Berkeley and Los Angeles, CA, 1997).

12 Max Weber, *From Max Weber*, ed. H.H. Gerth and C. Wright Mills (New York, 1958).

questions about suffering. Events such as famines or natural disasters, which increase human suffering, push believers to seek answers from magicians, priests, or other religious leaders. Leaders respond by developing new answers in the form of more generalised or universal salvation myths that provide intellectually and psychologically satisfying answers to typical and recurring problems of human suffering. Weber's model is on target, but incomplete insofar as he overemphasises the cognitive dimensions of religion and the movement towards greater and greater rationalisation, and underestimates the role of ritual and emotion and the demand for authentic experiences of the sacred.

More pointedly, Weber's assumption that questions of suffering drive religious change does not anticipate the questions about religious experience that many church-going Americans are asking. Studies of baby boom religiosity and of the post-Second World War religious environment consistently point out how Americans' questions about religious meaning focus on their restless search for personal fulfilment, novelty, and choice. Miller[13] and Roof[14] argue that a new cultural paradigm emerged post-1960 that profoundly reshaped American religiosity and hence the kinds of religious goods and services being offered. First the rise of a therapeutic approach to the self and an attempt to integrate all of life's varied experiences and emotions have pushed religions towards emphasising the head over the heart in worship and focusing religious teachings on resolving practical daily problems.[15] Roof argues that the baby boomer generation largely rejected rationalised religion which is grounded in an intellectual assent to a set of abstract theological propositions because it turned faith into a static, objective thing – a 'rote religion' – rather than a subjective, lived experience.[16] Americans in search of religious meaning want church to be relevant and to provide answers to the practical problems of daily life; they want practical, biblical or religious rules to organise their lives; they want help addressing everything from conflict at work to home finances, but they want to solve such problems as Christians or as persons of faith.[17]

A second, related shift in American society has been a deepening of the cult of the individual. This is manifest in the way that religion has become a setting where the individual seeks his or her salvation directly, unmediated by a religious community, or in the practice of blending traditions in *bricolage*-fashion, to meet an individual's needs. Within many types of Protestantism, Christianity has been reduced to an imperative for the believer to develop a personal relationship with Jesus. For example, in his study of music and art in contemporary American

---

13 Miller, *Reinventing*.

14 Roof, *Spiritual*.

15 See also Robert Wuthnow, *After Heaven* (Berkeley and Los Angeles, 1998); and Vincent Miller, *Consuming Religion: Christian Faith and Practice in a Consumer Culture* (New York, 2003).

16 Roof, *Spiritual*, 61–2.

17 See Wuthnow, *After Heaven*, 85–93; and Thumma and Travis, *Beyond*, 16–17.

Religion, Robert Wuthnow discusses the way in which contemporary music feeds into an individualised and Jesus-centred faith when he quotes one of his interviewees from a Calvary Chapel church:

> A man who joined the church three years ago says he visualizes Jesus as he sings. By the time the sermon starts he feels, 'laid back,' submissive, and open to whatever God wants to teach him. 'I just feel a connection with the Lord. The music reinforces that feeling of bonding with him.'[18]

A third key cultural shift is the emergence and growing power of consumerism in nearly every sphere of social life, especially religion. While the commodification of religion in the United States is not new,[19] the pace, scope, and willingness to embrace branding and market research, sell sermons, or leadership training seminars online, and even retool Christian theology to legitimate wealth (as in 'prosperity theology') has accelerated since the 1980s.[20] Einstein's recent analysis of church marketing[21] shows how religious bodies (from denominations to megachurches) borrow the marketing practices from the for-profit world and in doing so make the process of selecting a congregation blend seamlessly into the mundane practice of going to the mall. Not only do churches see themselves as purveyors of religious goods and services where the customer is always king, but those who attend and join congregations bring a consumerist mentality to church. The church is seen as a supplier of religious experiences and biblical advice. If a church cannot or will not meet an individual's religious needs and desires, then she or he may very well go 'shopping' for a new church.[22]

The final cultural change is the rise of an anti-establishment ethos, or a generalised mistrust of bureaucracies and organisations. This ethos is manifest at the level of the individual in terms of a willingness to drop out of the religion of one's youth and/or switch religions until one finds a faith that addresses one's needs, or provides a surer and more compelling experience of the sacred. At the

---

18 Robert Wuthnow, *All in Sync: How Music and Art Are Revitalizing American Religion* (Berkeley and Los Angeles, CA, 2003), 160. See also Alan Wolfe, *The Transformation of American Religion* (New York, 2003), 23–35; and Richard Santana and Gregory Erickson, *Religion and Popular Culture* (Jefferson, NC, 2008), 55.

19 See R. Laurence Moore, *Selling God: American Religion in the Marketplace of Culture* (New York, 1994).

20 Miller, *Consuming*; and James B. Twitchell, *Shopping for God: How Christianity Went from In Your Heart to In Your Face* (New York, 2007).

21 Mara Einstein, *Brands of Faith: Marketing Religion in a Commercial Age* (New York, 2008).

22 See Wade Clark Roof, *A Generation of Seekers* (San Francisco, CA, 1993); and Richard Cimino and Don Lattin, *Shopping for Faith: American Religion in the New Millennium* (San Francisco, CA, 1998).

congregational level this ethos is manifest in a rejection of inherited or historic traditions and alignments with denominations.[23]

Megachurch Innovation: Sacralising a Consumer Orientation towards Religion

I argue that megachurches respond to this new religious climate more directly and more completely than mainline and liberal Protestant groups. They create and institutionalise an 'anti-tradition' identity and milieu by offering novel styles of worship and by constantly changing the worship experience. They appeal to the cult of the individual by organising all aspects of megachurch life around the development of a participant's personal relationship with Jesus and orienting sermons, ritual life, and small group experiences to address the kinds of personal problems and lifestyle interests of specific types of participants. They sacralise consumerism through architecture, programming, and theology and effectively create an alternative Christian or church world in which participants live.

Megachurch worship, like other aspects of megachurch life, is largely an organised response to religious consumers' demands for novel, emotionally powerful, and relevant religious experiences. When some of the first megachurches were being developed, their leaders (for example Schuler of the Crystal Cathedral, Hybels of Willow Creek, Warren of Saddleback), did their own market research and they consistently heard complaints that church services were 'lifeless, boring, and predictable' and that sermons were boring, irrelevant, overly judgmental.[24] Hybels noted that the

> average church service [at a traditional church] seems grossly abnormal. … The music we sing, the titles we choose, the way we dress, the language we use, the subjects we discuss, the poor quality of what we do – all of these lead the average unchurched person to say, 'This is definitely not for me'.[25]

Rick Warren concluded while starting Saddleback Community Church that baby boomers in southern California did not have theological objections to church, but rather sociological ones.[26] The church, as these leaders saw it, had a prospective audience that claimed to be facing a crisis of meaning; their church experiences simply failed to make Christianity compelling and meaningful.

---

23 See Miller, *Reinventing*; Roof, *Spiritual*; Sergeant, *Seeker Churches*; and Wolfe, *Transformation*.

24 Lynne Hybels and Bill Hybels, *Rediscovering Church* (Grand Rapids, MI, 1995), 58; and Jeffrey L. Sheler, *Prophet of Purpose: The Life of Rick Warren* (New York, 2009).

25 Hybels and Hybels, *Rediscovering Church*, 32.

26 Sheler, *Prophet of Purpose*, 106.

At the same time, a nascent 'church growth' industry was urging evangelical leaders to think of prospective church attendees as consumers who would join if a church's programmes and messages were tailored to fit the needs, interests, and lifestyles of targeted audiences.[27] A recent content analysis of the websites of the ten largest megachurches reveals how megachurches market themselves as hip, exciting, and relevant. Watson and Scalen[28] find that the majority of those leading megachurches downplay denominational or doctrinal affiliation and positions and instead emphasise their vast array of programmes and in particular highlight their family and child-friendly programmes. They also make available sermons on practical topics such as relationships, and show that they are culturally relevant to lived experiences by underlining their use of technology (such as webcasts and podcasts of services, links to Twitter and Facebook), displaying pictures of their rock bands or their non-churchly campuses, and listing such fun events as the 'Mother/Daughter Chocolate Festival'.[29] In these ways, megachurches offer unique and non-traditional kinds of religious experiences in order to persuade audiences to return to church, and do so by shifting the grounds of participation away from orthodoxy towards ethics or orthopraxy;[30] a move than runs parallel to the underlying logic of consumerism in which the purchase of the right goods will lead one to live correctly.[31]

Megachurch Innovation: Contemporary Worship

In addition to the consumer, or market, orientation, a logic of pragmatic evangelism guides megachurch worship. Megachurch leaders are motivated by the Gospel imperative to convert as many individuals as possible, and they are willing to use a wide variety of means or techniques to achieve their goal. In practice this means cultivating the kind of customer service one might find at Disneyworld; using secular rock and Christian music, professional-grade sound equipment, and non-churchly architecture. New York Times writer Gustav Niebuhr writes that the megachurch movement is driven, 'by a generation of ambitious ministers who

---

27 See Anne C. Loveland and Otis B. Wheeler, *From Meeting House to Megachurch* (Columbia, MO and London, 2003), see Chapter 5 on the early history of megachurch marketing.

28 J.B. Watson, Jr and Walt Scalen, Jr, 'Upsizing Jesus: Megachurches, the Church Growth Movement, and Image Management in a Consumer Society', in Jon K. Loessin and Scott Stripling (eds), *The Year 2011 Annual Proceedings of the Association for the Scientific Study of Religion-Southwest* (Dallas, TX, 2011), 1–12.

29 Ibid., 6.

30 François Gauthier and Jean-Philippe Perreault, 'Jeunes et religion dans la société de consommation: État des lieux et prospective', in François Gauthier and Jean-Philippe Perreault (eds), *Jeunes et religion au Québec* (Québec, 2008), 9–28.

31 Don Slater, *Consumer Culture and Modernity* (Cambridge, 1997); Roof, *Spiritual*; Sargeant, *Seeker Churches*; and Twitchell, *Shopping*.

make it a point, in the name of spreading the Gospel, to know the transient tastes of the middle class and to learn from secular institutions that appeal to it'.[32] In their account of Willow Creek, Lynn and Bill Hybels describe the original goals of worship at the megachurch and illustrate how they were informed by both types of logic:

> We desperately wanted to provide a place where unchurched people with a spiritual hunger – seekers, we called them – could come and hear the truth that could transform their lives both here and in eternity. We wanted to use contemporary Christian music with lyrics that would communicate real-life spiritual experience. Sometimes we used crossover music, secular songs with a message that addressed the frustrations and longings of lost people.[33]

Thumma,[34] among others, likens megachurches to religious Wal-Marts or regional malls that offer something for everyone. In terms of worship services, megachurches commonly offer a variety of different kinds of services that are marketed for distinct audiences (young adults, married couples with children, traditionalists) and anchored in particular musical genres (pop or alternative rock, country, jazz).[35] In this way, megachurches are fully integrated in the consumerist ethos.

The use of contemporary (electronic) pop and rock music is a strategic choice to maximise participant recruitment and retention. Drawing on market research data megachurch leaders learned that many baby boomers and their children found Reformation-based sacred music inaccessible and emotionally barren. This audience claims traditional church music does not prepare them to enter into a prayerful state as much as contemporary praise music does, nor does it leave them exiting the Sunday service joyful and excited to live out the Christian faith.[36] Moreover the use of hymnals and the old fashioned language of classic hymnody discourages participation and limits the theological 'takeaway' of the service. Contemporary worship music solves the problems of irrelevant and lacklustre

---

32 Gustav Niebuhr, 'Megachurches – Second Article of a Series: The Gospels of Management; The Minister as a Marketer; Learning from Business' (18 April 1995), [Online], available at: http://www.nytimes.com/1995/04/18/us/megachurches-second-article-series-gospels-management-minister-marketer-learning.html [accessed: 13 June 2011].

33 Hybels and Hybels, *Rediscovering Church*, 63.

34 Thumma, 'The Shape of Things to Come'.

35 See also John W. Riggs, 'The Megachurch and the Liturgical Renewal Movement' (2002), [Online], available at: http://reformedtheology.org/SiteFiles/PublicLectures/RiggsPL.html [accessed: 13 June 2011].

36 Wuthnow, *All in Sync*, 158–60; and David R. Bains, 'Contemporary Worship: Trends and Patterns in Christian America', in Charles H. Lippy (ed.), *Faith in America, Volume 3: Changes, Challenges, New Directions* (Westport, CT, 2006), 1–23.

worship which plague many mainline Protestant congregations. It does so by creating the expectation that one will meet God or Jesus during the service and that the point of faith is self-fulfilment. For example, in his discussion of contemporary worship at Pentecostal-leaning megachurches Wuthnow argues:

> There is an almost orgiastic quality to the services, an emphasis on having a tactile relationship with Jesus. ... they [the lyrics] are overwhelmingly *relational*, focusing on an intimate, loving relationship between the believer and God. The most common word is *you*, followed in frequency by *I* and *my*. In other words worshipers focus a great deal of attention on their own selves, feelings, desires and needs.[37]

Theologically, megachurch worship emphasises God's immanence, and the experience of contemporary music in the concert hall-like space of the megachurch creates the possibility of a memorable encounter with the sacred. Both Twitchell[38] and Goh[39] make a similar argument about the ability of megachurch worship to create religious spectacles akin to those of rock concerts. They note that worship in the large, sometimes cathedralesque spaces of the megachurch, combining state-of-the-art audio systems, jumbo-trons, light shows, and thousands of bodies swaying and singing with arms upraised, offers a fundamentally different and better experience of the sacred than most small and mainline worship services. Twitchell claims that the genius of megachurch worship lies in its ability to transform the 'sensations of Sunday morning' into the experience of Saturday night. As he notes, '[c]oupling the church experience, which promised rapture to only a select few, with the excitement of the rock concert, which delivered the goods to many, presaged a new kind of church experience'.[40]

Finally the sense of the immanence of God and the ability of megachurches to make religion relevant and personally meaningful via worship is produced in the practical messages offered in sermons. In many megachurches sermons attempt to show how the Bible, or more broadly the Christian faith, provides benefits to the individual. Sergeant chronicles the range of sermon types at Willow Creek and by extension at seeker-oriented megachurches and while he finds that over a third of the sermons have a clear scriptural or theological focus, another 40 per cent of the sermons provide practical, almost 'how-to' advice about relationships and personal growth. He notes:

---

37 Wuthnow, *All in Sync*, 161; italics original. See also Sargeant, *Seeker Churches*, 65–8.

38 Twitchell, *Shopping*.

39 Robbie B.H. Goh, 'Hillsong and "Megachurch" Practice: Semiotics, Spatial Logic and the Embodiment of Contemporary Evangelical Protestantism', *Material Religion*, 4/3 (2008): 285–304.

40 Twitchell, *Shopping*, 229.

> Seeker messages often promote God's therapeutic benefits for the self. … Although the message topics often range widely from discussing the nature of God to improving one's marriage, the pressures of privatization make it likely that these messages will in some way emphasize the personal relevance of Christianity, over any public theology of Christian involvement in the world.[41]

Thus music and message seamlessly work together in worship to deliver a unified message about the relevance of Christianity and offer compelling experiences of the presence of God. The music, as noted above, may create a mood of mindful reflection and the expectation of meeting God, or of joy and the hope that the Christian life will make one's life more fulfilling. Simple praise lyrics, practical sermons, and skits make God personable, caring, and eminently knowable, often by explicitly defining and modelling the primary goal of cultivating a personal relationship with God. The mood of joyful hope coupled with the expectation, often realised, of encountering a God who actually cares about the individual motivates church-goers not only to keep returning to the megachurch, but to get involved more actively. In addition, because worship is organised to cater to the demand for consumer choice and convenience, megachurches are able to meet a very diverse set of needs and interests. This provides them with a distinct advantage in local religious markets, since most smaller congregations cannot offer the same variety of worship services.

Explaining the Reach and Influence of the Megachurches

Although attending to the nature and content of megachurch worship provides insight into the emergence and growth of this new type of congregation, it does not explain their increasing ability to reshape American Protestantism. Historically congregations' abilities to influence other congregations or remake religious life more generally has been limited to national denominations or by the dynamics of a local religious ecology. However, megachurches have begun to extend their reach and influence nationally and internationally. Thumma argues that megachurches have changed the nature of worship and provide both model and incentive for other congregations to adopt contemporary worship practices.[42] More generally megachurches serve as models for how to organise worship, lead congregations, expand ministries, and put theological ideas into contemporary idioms for thousands of congregations. They are pilgrimage sites for hundreds of ministers

---

41 Sargeant, *Seeker Churches*, 79, 83; see also Snow et al., 'A Team Field Study of the Appeal of Megachurches'.

42 Thumma and Travis, *Beyond*, 18; and Jane Lampman, 'Megachurches' Way of Worship on the Rise', *Christian Science Monitor* (6 February 2006), [Online], available at: http://www.csmonitor.com/2006/0206/p13s01-lire.html [accessed: 3 June 2011].

and congregational leaders in the United States.[43] They also exert significant isomorphic pressures in local religious settings, forcing congregations to model themselves after the successful megachurch to remain competitive or to develop alternative church models that will serve distinct niche markets and allow them to survive.[44]

Some megachurches have become purveyors of numerous religious goods and services including Sunday School, Bible study and small group curricula, worship resources, consulting services regarding church growth, and small group or specialised ministries (from home finance to mental health ministries). Many megachurches hold annual conferences and webcasts in which leaders of the megachurch run workshops on such topics as evangelism, creating small group ministries, or organisational restructuring, and even offer ministerial training programmes akin to the kinds of degree programmes offered by theological schools and seminaries. Such practices connect megachurches to large numbers of congregations and individuals from a variety of Protestant traditions and generate significant revenue and exposure. For example, in 2004 the WCA earned $17 million by selling its marketing and management resources to its member congregations.[45] The WCA website claims that it has trained more than one million church leaders from around the world and runs more than 250 leadership training events each year in 50 countries.[46] Similarly, hundreds of congregations, or at least their leaders, are part of the Purpose Driven Church Network which emerged following the publication of *The Purpose Driven Church*, written by Pastor Rick Warren of Saddleback Community Church. Warren has parlayed that book into a national campaign – '40 Days of Purpose' – in which congregations spend 40 days reading and studying the book in order to revitalise and grow their church. 'Purpose driven' has become Saddleback's brand identity, with multiple spin-off campaigns (including '40 Days of Love', '40 Days of Community', '40 Days in the Word') and there is a vast array of resources for sale in order to explore and expand on the purpose driven church.[47] Saddleback now staffs and leads a 'purpose driven' small group ministry network, and a number of denominational purpose driven networks have sprung up among Presbyterian, Methodist, Lutheran, Assembly of God, Nazarene and Seventh-day Adventist churches. Hence megachurches have literally steered religion into behaving like for-profit businesses as they build

---

43 See Stephen Ellingson, *The Megachurch and the Mainline* (Chicago, IL, 2007).

44 See Nancy Eiseland, *A Particular Place* (New York, 1999).

45 William C. Symonds, 'Earthly Empires: How Evangelical Churches Are Borrowing from the Business Playbook' (23 May 2005), [Online], available at: http://www.businessweek.com/magazine/content/05_21/b3934001_mz001.htm [accessed: 13 June 2011].

46 Willow Creek Association, 'Our Story: Who We Are', [Online], available at: www.willowcreek.com/about/ [accessed: 8 August 2011].

47 It should be noted that Warren also offers monthly devotionals and advice for free on the Purpose Driven website.

brand identities and sell their goods and services in pursuit of a market share – something which remains unfathomable to traditional Protestant denominations.

So how have megachurches come to wield such a significant influence within American Protestantism? Although a full answer is beyond the scope of this chapter and will require data from congregational leaders who borrow and use megachurch resources, I suggest the following provisional answer: megachurches exercise extensive influence over religious life in the United States because they have created 'universal' and transposable models of worship and church programmes that promise an end to congregational stagnation and decline. Thus I suggest the answer lies in understanding the form of megachurch models and products and the context in which they are marketed.

One of the hallmarks of modernity has been the rise of 'modularity' in the production of goods and ideas. Goswami points out that modularity refers to 'transposable, dynamic, doubled, and durable' social forms and strategies.[48] Moreover she notes that modular products and ideas have a double nature in conveying both universal and particular meanings (she indicates how 'the universal language of self-determination, for instance, has been routinely mobilized to make claims for a particularized national community'). Similarly, megachurch models of leadership, worship, and small group life are marketed as Biblical or God-ordained and thus universal, but also flexible enough to fit the specific contexts of local congregations. In *The Purpose Driven Church*, Warren posits the book's universal applicability: 'To understand many of the methods in this book, you need to understand the context in which they were developed. Otherwise you might be tempted to copy things we did without considering the context. *Please do not do this!* Instead, look beneath the methods to see the transferable principles on which they are based.'[49] Warren's web page urges visitors interested in transforming their church to adopt the Purpose Driven model and does so along these universal and particular grounds:

> The Purpose Driven paradigm is a church health model to help your church get in shape to live out its God-given purposes. The Purpose Driven model offers leaders in your church a unique, biblically-based approach to help them establish, transform, or maintain a balanced, growing congregation. … And the Purpose Driven model isn't just for mega-churches. It's used by congregations of all sizes, denominational and non-denominational, charismatic and non-charismatic, new plant and well-established, urban and rural.[50]

---

48 Manu Goswami, 'Rethinking the Modular Nation Form: Toward a Sociohistorical Conception of Nationalism', *Comparative Studies in Society and History*, 44/4 (2002): 783.

49 Rick Warren, *The Purpose Driven Church* (Grand Rapids, MI, 1995), 27; emphasis original.

50 Pastors.com, 'About Pastors.com: Rick Warren, Founder', Saddleback Church, [Online], available at: http://pastors.com/about/ [accessed: 13 June 2011].

The double nature of the megachurch model allows it to be transposable. Church leaders do not directly transplant megachurch practices and models, but instead fit them into their specific context. Thus form and function rather than content is critical in modular religion. If a congregation doesn't wish to adopt all of the Baptist theology underlying Warren's model, they can substitute their own denominational commitments. This is evident in the testimonies from and about the Purpose Driven Presbyterian Network. For example, the network's founder, Pastor Michael Carey notes how the tiered discipleship classes from *The Purpose Driven Church* book are 'adapted to reflect Presbyterian rather than Baptist theology'.[51] Another member of the team that attended a Saddleback conference claimed she came away from it, 'convinced the principles are applicable to all churches. It's not a Rick Warren thing or a Southern Baptist thing. It's a biblical thing.'[52]

Goswami also notes that the transposability of modular forms and practices is historically contingent.[53] Borrowing and adapting innovations are more likely under particular market and social conditions in which the innovation comes to be understood as an effective and efficient means of addressing organisational challenges. Megachurch models and products arose nearly 30 years into the ongoing decline of the old mainline Protestantism and the erosion of strong links between congregations and denominations. As church switching and shopping have become commonplace among baby boomers and their children and grandchildren, congregations face increasing competitive pressures and internal demands to grow. Congregations in a local market may experience isomorphic pressures when they see other congregations flourish after successfully implementing megachurch models of worship or education. Megachurch products promise a solution to perennial and persistent membership problems and the weakening loyalty to particular religious traditions in the late twentieth and early twenty-first centuries, and their apparent success across denominational lines heightens the appeal of the megachurch form of Christianity.

---

51 John H. Adams, 'Presbyterian Congregations Use Purpose-Driven Church Model' (8 October 2002), [Online], available at: http://www.faithwebsites.com/sysfiles/site_uploads/pubsartsmeds/pub1756.htm [accessed: 9 December 2011].

52 Sue Washburn, 'Purpose-Driven Presbyterians', [Online], available at: http://www.faithwebsites.com/sysfiles/site_uploads/pubsartsmeds/newsletter2623_2.pdf [accessed: 9 December 2011]; see also Mike McMullen and William Kilgore, 'An Analysis of Rick Warren's 40-Days of Purpose Movement', paper presented to the annual meeting of the Society for the Scientific Study of Religion, Portland, OR, 20 October 2006, [Online], available at: http://hirr.hartsem.edu/megachurch/articles/warren40daysofpurpose.pdf [accessed: 13 June 2011].

53 Goswami, 'Rethinking the Modular Nation Form', 783.

Conclusion

The selling of religious goods is not new, but the way in which megachurches rely on the logic and techniques of consumerism to fuel rapid expansion within as well as an extensive reach into American Protestantism is. In an unprecedented manner, megachurches self-identify as businesses operating in a religious market which grow by correctly reading consumer demand and packaging religious experiences to meet this demand. In particular, they act like Weber's religious virtuosi, who first identify the root causes of religious meaninglessness and then refashion the religion to alleviate suffering. In the case of megachurches, leaders recognise that many prospective church-goers believe that organised religion is boring and disconnected from the practical dilemmas of their lives. In response to market demand (ascertained via systematic market research) megachurches offer emotionally powerful and constantly changing ritual experiences in the idiom of contemporary popular culture, in the milieu of mall and cineplex, and in service of self-development and personal choice. At the same time, megachurches are driven by the evangelistic imperative to spread the good news (both of Christianity and of their particular models of church). They do so by crafting unique brands for a range of products that are then marketed as the answer to the religious malaise of American Protestantism. But the real cause of the growing influence of megachurches is that they market their religious goods and services as theologically and ecclesiologically neutral, and thus inherently transposable across denominations. In effect, megachurches have become important players in the religious sphere because they have been able to sell templates or recipe books that help congregations transform themselves into purveyors of a range of religious choices (in worship, education, and small groups) that promise not just the traditional rewards of Christianity, but the consumer dream of health, wealth, self-realisation, and the perfect life.

Chapter 4
The Paradoxes of New Monasticism in the Consumer Society

Stefania Palmisano

Introduction

The rise of consumerism in the period following the Second World War, which has been accompanied by an ever growing and globalising media sphere, has contributed to a reshaping of religion. This chapter analyses the relationship between New Monasticism – conceived after the Vatican Council II as a new form of traditional monasticism – and contemporary consumer society. It argues that the processes of renewal in monasticism, especially New Monasticism, have been shaped by contemporary social and cultural changes which are driven by the all-pervasive influence of capitalist market dynamics.[1] The chapter discusses particularly how and why New Monasticism stands in a paradoxical relationship with the contemporary social landscape. Through a qualitative study of seven New Catholic Monastic Communities in Italy, this study also shows that if, on one hand, they are an alternative to the accelerated, profit- and success-oriented demands of consumer capitalism, on the other, they affirm and internalise some aspects of the ambient culture.

The apparent incongruence between asceticism and economics is nothing new in the history of monasticism. As Weber observed,[2] monasticism has always had a tendency to fall into contradiction with rational asceticism when it finds itself contributing to the creation of that wealth which it has rejected. This paradox can be explained by the fact that even if monks are practitioners of other-wordly asceticism – a lifestyle which involves contemplative practices to save souls and does not, *a priori*, encourage economic development – they are still not free from

---

[1] Colin Campbell, *The Romantic Ethic and the Spirit of Modern Consumerism* (Oxford, 1987); R. Laurence Moore, *Selling God: American Religion in the Marketplace of Culture* (New York, 1994); François Gauthier, 'Primat de l'authenticité et besoin de reconnaissance. La société de consommation et la nouvelle régulation du religieux', *Studies in Religion / Sciences Religieuses*, 41/1 (2012): 1–19.

[2] Max Weber, *Economia e società* (Torino, 1999), 594. Original edition: *Wirtschaft und Gesellschaft* (Tubingen, 1922).

basic human needs and, in order to be independent of society, they need to work. Moreover, as monastic history has taught, work is an aid to concentration and prayer as it counteracts sloth.

This dialectic reappears in contemporary monasticism, but in comparison with the past the emphasis is currently shifting from the production of goods *per se* to sales and consumption. Convents and monasteries which, until a few decades ago, were afflicted by a decline in vocations, are today full of 'customers' consuming various spiritual and cultural goods and services, including *lectio divina* courses as well as courses in cooking, music, and yoga; spiritual retreats; art exhibitions; concerts and performances; sacred objects; books with spiritual content and Gregorian Chant CDs, as well as cosmetics and pharmaceutical and herbal food products.[3]

The argument in this chapter is that New Monasticism is paradoxical and ambivalent when, reinterpreting and commodifying its traditions, it adapts to the modern consumer society that it reflexively purports to eschew. After having described the object of analysis, the chapter outlines the paradoxical relationship between the New Monastic Communities and the contemporary ambient culture. The conclusion discusses the strategies developed by monks to harmonise their market orientation with the monastic ethic and to reform the apparent incongruence between economics and religion.

New Monastic Communities in Italy: Field Research Findings

The relationship between monasticism, economics, and consumption has recently become a subject of heightened interest in the social sciences.[4] Even if, as this literature demonstrates, contemporary traditional monasticism is not exempt from the influence of consumer culture, in this study the analysis is limited to the phenomenon of New Monasticism.

It is well known that the Second Vatican Council of 1962–65 resulted in widespread conflict between innovative impulses and conservative reactions. In the context of the consecrated life, this conflict cannot be explained by a simplistic opposition between old and new institutions; it is much more complicated. Among both those institutions which predate the Council, as well as those which were founded afterwards, some have instituted processes of renewal and experimental reform, whilst others have chosen to follow more conservative directions. My

---

[3] Danièle Hervieu-Léger, *Vers un nouveau christianisme? Introduction à la sociologie du christianisme occidental* (Paris, 1987); Salvatore Abbruzzese, *La vita religiosa. Per una sociologia della vita consacrata* (Rimini, 1995); Isabelle Jonveaux, *Le monastère au travail. Le royaume de Dieu au défi de l'économie* (Paris, 2011).

[4] Giorgio Agamben, *Altissima povertà. Regola e forma di vita nel monachesimo* (Milano, 2011); Jonveaux, *Le monastère*; Elettra Stimilli, *Il debito del vivente. Ascesi e capitalismo* (Macerata, 2011).

research interest is focused on monastic communities founded after the Second Vatican Council which are renewing monastic life in conformity with its spirit and outside pre-existing orders – although adopting and freely adapting their Rules of Life.[5] New Monastic Communities (NMCs), therefore, are a result of the partial liberalisation of Catholicism which was prompted by the Council, in the sense that they have encouraged liturgical renewal, the no-longer-subordinate role of the laity, and openness towards ecumenical and interreligious dialogue. They were set up by laypeople, members of religious institutes and priests who were attracted by monastic life but critical of classical monasticism. Since their founders are still alive or have only recently died, NMCs are more accurately described as movements than institutions; they are still immersed in their initial effervescence and reluctant to stabilise themselves into canonical forms. Their relative autonomy has enabled them to introduce important innovations which render the organisation of monastic life more flexible and better suited to the contemporary age.[6]

The most innovative characteristic of the NMCs, as distinct from traditional monasticism, is that they are 'mixed' communities, consisting of men and women who may be consecrated or lay (or priests if male), single, married couples, or families.[7] It is well known that neither the cohabitation of monks and nuns, nor the presence of laymen in the monastery is a novelty in monastic history. With regard to cohabitation, while it is true that the dual monasteries of the late Middle Ages already comprised men and women, at that time the male and female branches were largely separate. But in the mixed NMCs of today, monks and nuns pray, eat, and work together. The novelty also concerns the question of authority because the community may be led by a nun, a layman, or a laywoman who is in the peculiar position, not envisaged by canonical law, of being in charge of monks or priests. With regard to the admission of laypeople, if one examines the oblate system in traditional institutions, one realises that the phenomenon of laypersons flexibly affiliated with monastic communities has been around for a long time. Nevertheless, they have little influence on the core of the institution, and their role is recognised by everybody, themselves included, as being secondary to that of the monks. In the NMCs, by contrast, the weight of the lay members

---

[5] Thus neither traditional monastic communities (even if they have renewed themselves according to the teachings of Vatican II) nor conservatively-oriented (that is, those rejecting Vatican II and harking back to previous forms and traditions such as the Lefebvreans and the Tridentine liturgy) new communities have been taken into consideration.

[6] Lluis T. Oviedo, 'Approccio alla realtà delle nuove fondazioni', in Roberto Fusco and Giancarlo Rocca (eds), *Nuove forme di vita consacrata* (Roma, 2010), 163–76.

[7] Patricia Wittberg, 'Real Religious Communities: A Study of Authentication in New Roman Catholic Religious Orders', *Religion and the Social Order*, 6 (1996): 149–74; Olivier Landron, *Les communautés nouvelles. Nouveaux visages du catholicisme français* (Paris, 2004); Stefania Palmisano, 'Moving Forward in Catholicism: New Monastic Organizations, Innovation, Recognition, Legitimation', *International Journal for the Study of New Religions*, 1/2 (2010): 49–64.

can be preponderant, not only because they are sometimes more numerous than the monks (in many Italian NMCs they may constitute up to 80 per cent of the membership), but also because they usually play an active role in the community. Finally, these are 'mixed' communities also in the sense that their ecumenical commitment has induced some of them to institute the cohabitation of different Christian denominations: Catholic, Protestant, and Orthodox.

However, these innovations often provoke distrust among ecclesiastical authorities.[8] Even if in their religious commitment they behave like religious orders (taking on the three vows, committing to lifelong involvement, submitting to collective rule), none of them is recognised by the Apostolic See as a religious order; at best they are recognised by the bishops of their dioceses as Private or Public Associations of the Faithful – the lowest levels of canonical approval.

In spite of the fact that there is no global census supplying statistical data, some mapping[9] shows how widespread these communities are on the international stage – especially in France, the United States, Spain, and Italy – revealing a more modest, steady growth up to today following the immediate post-Conciliar peak. Although NMCs have gained considerable ground in the Catholic world, the international scientific community has so far devoted limited attention to the phenomenon[10] as well as to the renewal processes which they inspire in traditional orders and in the Catholic Church.[11] In Italy, where there are about 40 NMCs,[12] the literature on the subject consists mainly of surveys conducted in ecclesiastical circles for practical purposes, while sociological research is rare. In order to help fill the gap, since NMCs are a largely unexplored world yet a marginal phenomenon, I have chosen to conduct qualitative research on a limited number in a specific region: Piedmont in Northern Italy, where preliminary mapping enabled me to identify seven communities.[13]

---

8 Palmisano, 'Moving Forward in Catholicism'; Stefania Palmisano, 'Ambiguous Legitimation: Grassroots Roman Catholic Communities in Italy and Ecclesiastical Hierarchies', *Temenos*, 47/1 (2011): 31–60.

9 Fusco and Rocca, *Nuove forme*.

10 Wittberg, 'Real Religious Communities; Landron, *Les communautés nouvelles*; Oviedo, 'Approccio alla realtà delle nuove fondazioni'.

11 Patricia Wittberg, 'Orders and Schisms on the Sacred Periphery', in James Beckford and N.J. Demerath III (eds), *The Sage Handbook of the Sociology of Religion* (London, 2007), 323–44.

12 Mario Torcivia, *Guida alle nuove comunità monastiche italiane* (Casale Monferrato, 2001).

13 Palmisano, 'Moving Forward in Catholicism'.

An Alternative to the Consumer Society?

This section examines some of the distinctive elements which make up the life of NMCs – ascesis, ecology, *stabilitas* and *memorare* – which, according to the statements of both monks and their guests during my fieldwork, reject or oppose contemporary social processes and mainstream consumer tendencies, making them a viable alternative to the ambient culture.

Ascesis

Ascesis – because of its self-limiting nature – is the monastic value which the monks interviewed contrasted most sharply with the logic of consumerism. Although in our NMCs the concept of ascesis is grounded in the original practice of limiting food intake and sleep and observing total abstinence from sex, a greater emphasis is now placed on a sense of renouncing the world as it is defined by its comforts, symbols, and contemporary trends. If ascesis, according to Weber's definition,[14] emerges as 'a method, systematically developed, of rational conduct of life with the aim of overcoming *status naturae*, of tearing man away from the power of irrational impulses and slavery to the world', then today, in the society of abundance, it needs to be adopted in the struggle against the spirit of consumer capitalism. The monks and nuns who were interviewed on the subject of vocations reported various problems in recruiting novices as a result of the scant inclination of young people today to commit themselves to the sacrifices implied by monastic life:

> Whereas fifty years ago a boy who entered a Trappist monastery had to choose between cleaning out stables and stirring cheese, so he chose the latter, today's young man who arrives … as a novice has grown up with a car, a computer and a cellphone, all of which he has to give up, so it is like going into mourning (interview no. 1).

The danger of distorting the value of renunciation in order to make monastic life more attractive to modern youth is particularly noted by elderly monks and nuns who, although now members of NMCs, were educated in traditional orders:

> When we start talking about fulfilment, poverty goes out of the window … It is very easy to allow oneself first one comfort, then another, then yet another; but a monk's life is based on austerity. In my day we ate in silence, with iron tables and plates, while sacred scriptures were read from the *collatio* (interview no. 4).

This raises the crucial question of how the perception of ascesis in religious life has changed in recent decades. Although it is still included in the monks' lives as a

14 Weber, *Economia e società*.

reference point, it is assuming new forms in conformity with the areas of plausibility of the modern age.[15] Specifically, according to the interviewees' statements, ascesis is no longer seen in terms of mortification, hardship, and penance: these are archaisms which are incompatible with general social transformations. On the contrary, it is reinterpreted as an ethos of simplicity, whose aim it is to guarantee the monks' physical, psychological and spiritual wellbeing – that is harmony – so that they can be God's hardworking instruments.

Therefore, far from having vanished today, ascesis appears as a means of access to spiritual self-fulfilment: it is not an end in itself, but an aid towards achieving the main goal of moving closer to God. Not only is ascesis socially determined – having significance connected with a specific cultural context – but it is also given subjective value by the person who chooses it: although some NMCs appear to be more conservative than others, we may say that, as a general rule, the idea that ascesis is achieved as a personal programme which does not necessarily coincide with a handed-down doctrine is widespread. Most of the interviewees do not feel obliged to accept a preordained quantity and quality of ascesis, viewing it as commensurate with individual needs and inclinations:

> Ascesis is neither mortification of the flesh nor idealisation of the spirit, but a drill which everyone works out for himself. In the morning we have individual *lectio divina*, everyone in his own cell. The time indicated for this is between 4.30 and 5 but if I need to sleep an extra half hour I do it later (interview no. 2).

Even fasting is reinterpreted in the same way. In all the NMCs surveyed – with one exception, where the members have chosen to 'depend on Divine Providence' and are therefore forced to fast – regular fasting is observed only on particular anniversaries and on the eves of holy days. And where prolonged fasting is advised, it is carried out selectively by the omission of certain foods. What is more, in two NMCs fasting is optional. This is how a monk explains why his community has made this choice:

> Fasting contains at least three dangers. The first is pride. The second is that you have more time for work and thus may overwork and, in extreme cases, enslave the brother who is working with you. The third is that when not eating you will vent your aggression on your brother, since orality and aggression are closely linked (interview no. 2).

As a general rule, therefore, fasting is reappraised as a balanced diet, the aim of which is the monks' good health. If, as the Fathers of the Desert affirmed, ascesis limits the body for the good of the soul, in the monasticism of the consumer

---

15 Jean Séguy, 'Les sociétés imaginées: monachisme et utopie', *Annales. Économie, Sociétés, Civilisation*, 26/2 (1971): 336.

society, paradoxically, ascesis limits the body not only for the good of the soul but also for the good of the body itself.

Finally, although it has acquired new meanings, ascesis today still informs monastic criticism of mundane logic. However, as the second part of this chapter will make clear, we can recognise in this change not only the role played by the reforming of religious life which has been prompted by post-Conciliar theology, but also the influence of contemporary consumer culture which, as Taylor notes,[16] cannot be dissociated from an underlying quest for the self and which has allowed the idea of choice to become a manifestation of individuality – a process of subjectivisation.

Ecology

NMCs constitute an alternative to the consumer society not only by virtue of the monastic life's ascetic system but also its commitment to protecting the environment. The monks interviewed share the opinion that this commitment may not be further delayed because in the consumer society industrial and technologically driven modes of profit-oriented production are fighting ruthlessly for available natural resources, thereby encouraging waste:

> In the name of growth, of an open market, of an insatiable demand for enrichment, Mother Earth is ever more desolate and devastated. We monks must guard her and work her without exploiting or raping her, thereby setting good example (interview no. 5).

The bond between monasticism and ecology has a long history. Danièle Léger and Bertrand Hervieu[17] showed how monasticism has always cultivated an ecological dimension within its religious utopia and identified an elective affinity between ecology and religious eschatology. If the monastery, by virtue of the utopian project which it embodies, reproduces here and now a paradise of the future in memory of paradise lost, then the monks are guardians of a continuity between the glorious past – the golden age – and the long-awaited future when utopia will become reality. Today in Europe, in order to guarantee this continuity, monks look after Mother Earth through the use of organic agriculture and the production of green energy, earning an income by selling the products of these activities.[18]

Italian NMCs, however, are usually of modest dimensions and lack the financial resources to undertake such activities: if they produce green energy or cultivate organic products, it is mostly for their own use. Only three of our NMCs sell the products of their gardens and orchards in the form of juices, jams, herbal infusions,

---

[16] Charles Taylor, *The Ethics of Authenticity* (Cambridge, MA, 1991).

[17] Danièle Hervieu-Léger and Bertrand Hervieu, *Le retour à la nature: au fond de la foret* (Paris, 1979).

[18] Jonveaux, *Le monastère*.

and liqueurs, while many more have tried to step up their commercial activities. Nevertheless, two of these three, although limiting their use of pesticides and fertilisers, do not practice organic agriculture, which they consider to be another trend of the consumer society. More commonly, involvement in protecting the environment is interpreted as fidelity to a sustainable way of life, promoted in the outside world by awareness campaigns. Three examples are useful in order to understand the NMCs' commitment to this aim. One NMC, situated in an ecological oasis and benefitting from its location, runs environmental education courses for schools and families. In addition, it has marked out a part of its land for the cultivation of an experimental orchard which, thanks to the voluntary work of a group of farmers, gathers together various fruit species threatened with extinction. Another NMC which produces ceramics using only raw materials from the surrounding countryside (clay and natural dyes) sells them kitted out with a spiritual-ecological *vademecum*. Even more interesting is a third NMC where ecological involvement is part of a wider utopian project which is critical of the consumer society: these monks have chosen a hermitic life and fight consumerism by means of 'non-activity', that is to say by not offering anything except liturgical services to the public and selling no products. Consequently they have a strategy of gift-giving:

> The honey from our bees is important because, since we receive plenty although our hives are few, it is the gesture by which we thank the people who help us, even bringing us food. ... We don't sell it: we want to instil a sense of gratitude in the people who come to us (interview no. 6).

Stabilitas and Memorare

In consumer capitalism, where the labour market has uprooted the family by forcing its members to grow up, work, retire, and die in different places, sweeping away whatever remained of a collective memory,[19] the monastic values of *stabilitas loci* and of *memorare* preserve a dream which has become increasingly impracticable on the outside. NMCs, in the process of reinventing tradition, reinterpret the meaning of those archetypes, aiming to preserve and reassess them in the light of the concept of a cloistered life which, according to the monks interviewed, is a more suitable response to the needs of the times. Thus, the *stabilitas loci* of Benedictine memory – the monks' permanent lifelong residence in the same monastery, continues to be a pillar of the NMCs, but it is perceived of as a bond more with the community rather than with the monastery as a place. The liturgy too – the site of choice of *memorare* – has been reappraised. Almost all the NMCs examined here have chosen to give precedence to private prayer by reducing the amount of community liturgy, and, even more importantly, in some of these the

[19] Danièle Hervieu-Léger, *La religion pour mémoire* (Paris, 1993); Maurice Halbwachs, *La mémoire collective* (Paris, 1997).

prayers themselves have been modified to make them more meaningful to today's believers:

> We have simplified the daily liturgy. The seven traditional offices have been reduced to three because we wanted to favour personal prayer. Even the texts of the prayers we use are not those handed down by tradition. The Prior has updated them, asking himself how to accept what is new while not losing sight of what is old (interview no. 2).

Although in their efforts to re-invent monasticim, the NMCs have accepted some features of modern culture – such as the simplification of ritual and liturgy, opening up to the lay world, abandoning the cloister and directing more attention towards individual wellbeing – the fidelity to their utopian monastic *mandatum* makes them a real alternative to contemporary consumer society. 'Modernisation' does not deprive monasticism of its authenticity; on the contrary, it allows it to preserve cultural and spiritual relevance for twenty-first-century pilgrims who find in the new communities, to quote one interviewee, a spiritual offer which is 'rendered comprehensible for men of our time', and not usually available in traditional monasteries. The factors inducing the interviewees to stay in the NCMs indicate that they are searching for another world, different and distant from the one in which they live and they also reveal what they value most in this flight from everyday life. Some of them are looking for a secularised and therapeutic variant of a religious retreat, in response to the physiological need for rest, rendered more urgent by the struggle for personal fulfilment in a competitive, capitalist society. Some other pilgrims need continuity: in a universe dominated by the imperative of change, where they have lost their memorial points of reference, they feel the need to join up with tradition once more, to root themselves in an ancient history. Yet others, finally, are seeking someone who knows how to listen to them: in contrast with a society where everything is up for sale, here they find monks who give their time freely to listen to them if and when they want to speak. Thus enclosed spaces are paradoxically the most open which can be found in consumer society. Not only is it possible to stay over without making a reservation or explaining one's motives, but in some NCMs hospitality is repaid by means of 'offerings' where the individual's financial contribution to the monastery is left to his or her own discretion.

… or a Product of the Consumer Society?

Our analysis hitherto has shown that NMCs are places in which an alternative life can be lived which comprises a reflexively orchestrated rejection of the contemporary, consumer-oriented society. However, at the same time, it also shows that in their reinterpretation of monasticism they have been modelled by the ambient culture, incorporating the widely-held view in postmodern consumer society that life and society are arenas of choice rather than places dedicated to the transmission of traditions and possessions.[20] Indeed, the transformations which we have described reveal a monastic institution which, in tune with modern culture's 'subjectivist turn', is less and less interested in imposing its authority on its members and more and more willing to contribute to their fulfilment as 'utopian professionals'.

The remaining analysis examines some of the elements of NMCs – the Rule of Life, monastic commodification, and their associated emotional regime – which more strongly reveal the influence of the ambient culture. I particularly want to show that NMCs, in their attempts to satisfy society's needs end up – as do many other religious organisations today – adapting to consumer capitalism and fulfilling the function of service providers.

Monastic Commodification

Today traditional monastic communities – numerically still considerable and living in historic buildings – are facing up to the problem of economic survival by selling their own produce and services. I argue that, working ascetically with the best intentions for the prosperity of their own communities, while at the same time adapting their production to market demand, monks are involuntarily contributing to the transformation of monastic tradition into consumable and marketable goods. In accordance with Einstein and Kitiarsa,[21] I refer to the process of commercialisation of the monastic tradition as 'monastic commodification'. Although this does not usually result in capitalist profit-making ventures, it nevertheless reveals the influence of market logic and consumer culture on monastic life today.

On the basis of previous research into contemporary European monasteries,[22] monastic commodification is clearly visible from two main activities. The first is tourism. Since monasteries are sites not only of religion but also of culture and memory, they attract a vast public for spiritual, cultural and folkloric reasons. Abbeys – already well known as part of historical and cultural heritage – regularly offer guided tours to visitors who are increasingly accompanied by tour operators specialised in monastic routes (for example Vacances de l'Esprit and Tra terra e cielo). Although these activities disturb the monastic silence, the pilgrims' offerings, in addition to their purchases, are an indispensable source of income, to the extent that, as Jonveaux[23] reports, there are quite a few cases where communities

20 Gauthier, 'Primat de l'authenticité'.

21 Mara Einstein, *Brands of Faith: Marketing Religion in a Commercial Age* (London, 2008); Pattana Kitiarsa, *Religious Commodifications in Asia: Marketing Gods* (London, 2008).

22 Jonveaux, *Le monastère*.

23 Isabelle Jonveaux, 'La cultura rivisitata. I beni culturali monastici tra tradizione e modernità', *Proceedings of the III International Symposium of Pontificio Ateneo di S.*

have fenced off their houses (an example of this is Praglia Abbey in Italy), or have moved elsewhere, leaving the historic sites free for the tourist market (as with Hautecombe in France). The second is commercial diversification. The monastic tradition is put up for sale by means of a broad selection of products and services. For the last 20 years some products can also be bought outside the monasteries in food shops, herbalists, boutiques, and – more recently – from specialised websites (for example holyart.it). Nor should we forget business activities connected with the French Monastique association which, born in 1989 and today including 250 monastic enterprises, distributes their products, trains monk-managers, and attempts to catch consumer tastes and trends.[24]

Yet this tendency also interests NMCs. Although some of them emerged from polemical opposition to the accumulated wealth of certain monasteries, they too – at least the larger ones – have developed a market in monastic products. In our research sample, St Patrick's,[25] the biggest Italian NMC, with 80 members divided among the mother house and three fraternities, is an informative case for the study of monastic commodification because, even if it has been in existence for only about 40 years, it demonstrates the very characteristics which compete to make the monastic tradition a market good – the founders' media visibility, the international importance of the community, and the volume of business.

Although lacking historical architectural goods, St Patrick's is the destination of a remarkable religious pilgrimage, with around 12,000 guests a year staying in the monastery for day retreats, bible courses, and spiritual exercises, as well as the same number of visitors who attend the Divine Office and stay for meals. The community survives solely on the proceeds of hospitality – for which the guest-house has been greatly enlarged – and the sales to visitors of its products and services. Indeed, various market-oriented activities are carried out within the monastery's walls: the garden, vineyard, and orchard supply raw materials for various herbal infusions, sweets, sauces, preserves, and wines; the publishing house, with more than 300 titles, specialises in biblical exegesis, patristics, and liturgy, as well as interreligious and ecumenical matters; beekeeping provides 11 varieties of honey; the candle factory and the ceramics laboratory produce objects for the liturgy and the home; the icon studio, besides reproducing traditional Russian, Coptic, Byzantine and Greek images, offers innovative icons inspired

---

Anselmo (Roma, St. Ottilien, 2013-in press), 131–49.

24 See the article 'Undicesimo: Produci e fai soldi' [The Eleventh Commandment: Produce and Make Money] in a well-known Italian newspaper which cited French monasteries' volume of business, as well as Luxembourgois, Portuguese, and Italians engaged in the production of beer, liqueurs, cheese, perfumes, jewels, toys, and lingerie (*La Stampa*, 28 July 2006).

25 Respecting the privacy of the monastic community, I have used a pseudonym. The empirical documentation which concerns this NMC was collected by means of interviews and documentary analysis of the rule of the community, the diary of the founder, and the books of prayer and those on spirituality produced by him and his collaborators.

by the Italian thirteenth- and fourteenth-century pictorial tradition; the bakery; the carpenter's shop; the production of CDs and audiocassettes recording meetings, concerts, and monastic offices; courses on lyre playing, ancient languages, and the study of monasticism and the Bible. In all of these fields the monks and nuns – many of whom have benefitted from studying abroad at prestigious monasteries, universities, and academies – aim to create handcrafted, 'one-off' pieces. This objective coincides with today's Italian fashion, driven by the 'Slow Food' phenomenon, of rediscovering tastes of the past, to the extent that monks have incorporated into their production ancient local recipes which were in danger of being lost. This quest for the beautiful, the ancient, the authentic, the sustainable, and the new embodies a distinctive style – upon which the community's identity has been built – attracting both sacral and secular markets.

Einstein[26] coins the term 'faith brand' to argue that, in a society overrun by commercial clutter, in order to compete effectively, faiths have had to become brands – with easily recognisable symbols and spokespeople with whom those with religious prospects can make immediate connections. I argue that St Patrick's is a case study of a successful faith brand, whose fame and visibility exceeds that of many millenary monasteries. One determining element in this success has been the high volume of business achieved by taking advantage of their familiarity with marketing tools. Following the logic of primitive benchmarking, as a result of a succession of visits to various European monasteries, St Patrick's monks have imported into Italy not only technical production know-how, but also entrepreneurial management skills. This has encouraged them to invest in commercial development aiming at the production of a wide range of products competing with the secular market. Although these products are labelled as being produced according to an 'ancient traditional formula', they have little or nothing to do with tradition because, as the interviewees have stated, the ingredients and processes have been changed in order to satisfy commercial demand, legal requirements, and the fashions of the moment.

To this can be added the decisions of the monks' chapter to advertise the community on the internet (the first website dates from 1998) and, in 2000, to put their products up for sale online. The latter decision was consequent upon the employment of a marketing consultant who, in addition to updating the site, created a logo which established the community's brand image. Today we can find on the website a detailed introduction to the community and its activities, materials for prayer, and cultural and spiritual development, a catalogue of all the products on sale, and a monthly downloadable newsletter informing friends, benefactors, and sympathisers – the 'brand community'[27] – about the monastery's activities.

If public assent and economic success have contributed to its reputation, being a 'credit of trust' giving room for manoeuvre on the national stage, then among the

---

26 Einstein, *Brands of Faith.*

27 Ibid., 116.

determining factors which have allowed the Prior to assume political importance, the management of external relations – conducted over the years with ever increasing deliberation and skill – predominates. Today he is one of the laymen most wooed by reporters and publishers, most sought-after by ecclesiastical authorities for sermons and spiritual exercises, and most appreciated by the hierarchies of other churches. His public speeches, his writings, his television appearances, public relations, and contact with the press contribute daily to consolidating the value of the 'faith brand'. By collaborating with him, Catholic institutions seem to be seeking legitimation and new appeal. Of particular interest here is the case of a weekly magazine which sold for two months with one of the Prior's books accompanying each issue, increasing sales all round. Subscribers to the website also received personalised short messages throughout Advent, signed by the Prior himself and giving the references for that day's liturgy; they could also converse with him on Facebook.

Monastic commodification thus demonstrates that to continue to exist in a secularised consumer society, where believers professing a faith – no longer the majority faith – are on the wane, and where fewer visitors to monasteries are seeking only eschatological salvation, monks increase their chances of survival if, alongside their religious mission, they manufacture a cultural one and agree to work as dispensers of services to different publics. To this end, they need to accept that their own religious life – in the form of products, courses, events, visitors' stays, CDs, films, and postcards – will become a cultural product to be bought and sold for reasons which have nothing to do with religion.

The Rule of Life

Within the consumer society, human nature is defined by the ability to choose: *homo sapiens* becomes *homo eligens*[28] or *homo optionis*.[29] Sociologists of religion claim that beyond emerging and existing religious markets, individual religiosity is increasingly following the logic of consumerism as the individual behaves as a buyer, choosing from the assortment of 'ultimate' meanings as she sees fit.[30]

The Rules of NMCs generally reflect this 'consumer orientation'. Traditionally, every monastic rule draws on different sources because it incorporates prior teachings and experience, usually selected from within the same theological-spiritual tradition. But the rules of the NMCs, as Landron notes,[31] can be called 'composite' or '*à la carte*' because their founders often combine Catholic sources (monastic rules, writings of the saints, teachings of the Desert Fathers) with non-Catholic ones (Judaism, the Eastern Churches, Pentecostal Charismatics, yoga,

[28] Zygmunt Bauman, *Liquid Life* (Cambridge, 2005), 33.

[29] Ulrich Beck and Elizabeth Beck-Gernsheim, *Individualization: Institutionalized Individualism and Its Social and Political Consequences* (London, 2002), 5.

[30] Andrew Dawson, *Sociology of Religion* (London, 2011), 136.

[31] Landron, *Les communautés*.

Transcendental Meditation), neglecting the theological dissonance that springs from mingling such different versions of the world, mankind, and God. This bricolage has been orchestrated by the goal of self-expression or, as the NMCs' founders would say, by virtue of the distinctiveness of their 'charisma'.

In the rules of one NMC that I have studied – whose mission is interreligious dialogue and where it is possible to practise yoga together with the monks – we find Saint Benedict's teachings alongside some suggestions from Oriental religions and spiritualities. The rules of another NMC take their organisation of the Liturgy of the Hours from The Rule of Saint Benedict, their style of *fraternitas* in the community's relations from the Franciscan tradition, and their love of solitude from the teachings of Saint Bruno. Then too the life of the Holy Family of Nazareth has been chosen as the model that inspires the life of the community, along with the life of Saint Therese of Lisieux, chosen by the community as its patron saint.

Therefore, in contrast with the theological-spiritual exclusivity of traditional monastic rules, the rules of the NMCs range freely among a heterogeneous medley of – mainly Christian – sources. Picking and choosing according to subjective spiritual tastes and idiosyncratic concerns, their founders construct 'eclectic' and '*ad hoc*' rules whose thematic heterogeneity legitimate the affectively determined personal priorities and preferences.

Emotional Regime

A further confirmation of new monasticism's interiorisation of certain aspects of consumer society can be found in an analysis of the NMCs' 'emotional regime', a concept developed by Riis and Woodhead[32] to designate the way that emotions are integral to the structured social and material relations which constitute a particular social unit or setting – whether a business, a family, or a religious community. Contrary to the view that religious emotion is a purely private matter, this notion offers a new framework showing how religious emotions arise in the varied interactions between human agents and communities, objects of devotion, and sacred symbols. According to these scholars, in late modern society some religious emotional regimes, particularly those connected with historical forms of a once mainstream religion – for example, Christianity – clash with the contemporary emotional agenda and adapt to wider emotional developments. In addition, under the influence of consumer capitalism, religious emotions and their associated symbols may float free of religious communities and enter the embrace of the market.

The NMCs offer an example of these dynamics. In their processes of monastic renewal, they have distanced themselves from the 'emotional programme' associated with the pre-Vatican II religious life, which stressed shame, guilt, remorse, and duty – which today are considered to be unacceptable, a source of embarrassment and emotional contradictions. These emotions have been replaced

---

32 Ole Riis and Linda Woodhead, *A Sociology of Religious Emotion* (Oxford, 2010).

by others more in tune with late modern society, such as pleasure, happiness, and wellbeing. The monks' reassessment of the emotional tones relating to 'pleasure' is particularly evident in the monastic *milieu*. The slogans used to sell their food products echo those of the consumer society, recalling emotional hints from that very environment: 'delights for the palate', 'divine goodness', which invites us to 'enjoy the pleasure of life'. The 'pleasure' stimulated by 'the palate' assumes a positive connotation, in contrast with the medieval Catholic tradition which saw 'gluttony' as one of the seven deadly sins. Furthermore, the search for pleasure is associated with the demand from visitors for psycho-physical wellbeing to which the monks respond, as we have seen, by offering therapeutical variants of the monastic retreat as well as herbal products and cosmetics – all of which indicate the importance of personal regeneration understood as healing *here and now*. How is this change possible? Post-conciliar theological *updating*, rejecting both dietetic regimes which aim at spiritual purification and the 'palate = sin' equation, helps to explain, but it is still incomprehensible without considering the influence of the consumer society which has legitimated hedonistic values in marketing monastic wares. Thus the influence of the consumer society can be seen in the dedication of the monastic appeal more to aesthetic than to ascetic ideals; health, long life, and slimness – promises implicit in the monks' good food – are the rewards of physical rather than spiritual salvation. As Hervieu-Léger observes,[33] if the monasteries have gone from being places of other-worldly salvation to privileged places for seeking individual, this-worldly salvation, the emotional regime associated with them has also changed, and on the basis of the analysis in this study – findings from new meanings attached to ascesis and to monastic hedonism – we can argue that the new regime revolves around the 'feel-good factor', described by Davie,[34] which today characterises the religions attracting most converts.

Conclusion

My analysis so far demonstrates that the logic and idioms of consumer capitalism and late modern culture permeate the NMCs not only in their dealings with the outside world – as the commodification process proves – but also in ways that are below the surface, in that the 'emotional regime' and the 'Rule of Life' practices which inhabit bodies on an unconsciousness level are affected. Moreover, NMCs exhibit a recalibration in the relationship between community and individuals in favour of the latter. The empirical data collected shows that, while the ideal-type characteristics of the new monks are similar to those of traditional monks – with a commitment to the Rule of Life, assiduous prayer, a more or less radical separation from the world, and the taking of vows – what is new in sociological terms is that, if in previously constituted orders the management of these aspects is entrusted

[33] Danièle Hervieu-Léger, *Vers un nouveau christianisme?* (Paris, 1986), 22.

[34] Grace Davie, *The Sociology of Religion* (London, 2007), 146.

to an institution which guarantees a respect for tradition, in the NMCs they are controlled by founders who have elaborated them creatively with inspiration from the tradition which grants them legitimation.

In any case, it must be noted that new monks are aware of the paradox between the ascetic lifestyle and consumer culture and strive to limit the impact of the market and prevailing cultural trends by conferring on their economic activities characteristics from the religious field. The resulting strategies are not unlike those now used by traditional monasteries,[35] with the difference that, as a rule, the income of NMCs is not very substantial due to their limited commercial activity. All the monks interviewed stressed that in any case economic activity must needs be contained and serve monastic life. These statements reflect decisions essential for the community's survival, such as suspending activities which though successful nevertheless risk compromising the monks' primary object of contemplation. The monks thus refuse to undertake economic production which is over-demanding in terms of commitment, or will hire lay employees for the more burdensome tasks – such as gardening – which would distract the monks from regular participation in the 'Divine Office'. Another strategy for developing 'divine' economies is the application of religious values to economic activity. The monks try to recover the ethics of the fraternity by allowing more space for personal relations in commercial exchanges – an antidote, in their opinion, to the anonymity of contemporary capitalist economics. The monk working in the shop is well placed to receive spiritual requests; and in the case of online purchases, the community's answering mail usually contains an invitation to the purchasers to come in to the monastery in order to choose the objects they desire in person – in this way attracting people who might otherwise not come. Finally, the monks try to place their economy at the service of the Church and the world – first of all by performing acts of charity which aim at purifying, in retrospect, the money earned. A typical example of this is the balancing of the community's annual budget – running expenses having been detracted – by devoting what remains to missionary work.

35 Jonveaux, *Le monastère*.

Chapter 5

'Find your Inner God and Breathe': Buddhism, Pop Culture, and Contemporary Metamorphoses in American Judaism

Mira Niculescu

In January 2004, an issue of the American Jewish magazine *Sh'ma*[1] gathered educational leaders, journalists, academics, and Rabbis from all denominations to reflect on the question of 'Marketing Judaism'. This question is a relatively new one for Jewish institutions: Judaism, as a nation-religion, is automatically transmitted by birth. Why, then, is it necessary to 'market' it to natural-born Jews?

The premise of the following reflection is that the achievement of modernisation processes in Western societies has weakened Jewish adhesions, threatening the continuity of Jewish communities in new ways: over the preceding centuries of diaspora and persecution, the main concern for Jewish institutions was the survival of Jewish bodies. However, secularisation, brought about by the modernisation of European societies, and the more recent trend of adhesions to Eastern 'spiritualities', have caused growing numbers of disaffiliations from Judaism. But how can religious disengagements affect an identity that is inerasable?

The problem for the Jewish community, as an 'ethnic religion', is the frequent causality chain between secularisation and assimilation: religious disengagements can lead to the extinction of Jewish lineages. This is why maintaining 'religiously Jewish' Jews is a priority for Jewish institutions. Hence the dilemma currently facing Rabbis, educators, and community leaders can be summarised as follows: in the competitive religious field of today's pluralist and secularised Western societies, how can a non-proselyte group secure its continuity if it is losing its own members?

Through concrete examples from an ongoing ethnographic fieldwork study which began in America (San Francisco and New York), Western Europe (France and England), and Israel in 2009, I will show that a general institutional reaction is visible in the form of competitive attempts to renovate the image, and also the contents, of Judaism as a viable religious option. This is mostly expressed through

1 *Sh'ma*, 34/607 (January 2004), [Online], available at: http://www.Sh'ma.com/archives/web-edition/ [accessed: 3 October 2011]. *Sh'ma* means 'listen' in Hebrew.

endeavours of repackaging, rebranding, and marketing of Jewish 'salvation goods' (to borrow Weber's terminology), so as to attract disaffiliated Jews. More specifically, these initiatives are being implemented through mirroring, or borrowing, elements from Western popular and Zen cultures – Jewish religious culture's main competitors today. Hence this phenomenon represents a particularly interesting case study in which to observe the impact of contemporary consumer and popular cultures on a tradition-based religious group.

The American Jewish community – the largest of the Jewish communities until a few years ago and certainly still the most influential – is the main site of such transformations. This is why this chapter will focus mainly on the American scene – and especially, for the most recent examples, on New York. The first section will propose an explanatory scheme of how Judaism found itself 'on the market' in the context of the trajectory of modernisation and the counterculture of the 1960s. The second section will offer a comparative, thematic typology of institutional innovations all along the spectrum of Jewish denominations, divided mainly between 'progressive' and 'traditional' Judaism.[2]

How the Modernisation and Globalisation of the West Have Affected the Jewish Tradition

Because of the structural definition of Judaism as a matrilineal nation-religion, the expression 'marketing Judaism' – the title of the aforementioned issue of *Sh'ma* magazine – sounds like an oxymoron. Yet, with the progressive loss of an institutional hold on individuals and with increased competition in the globalised religious field, Judaism has found itself to be 'on the market' too.

Marketing Judaism?

Most contemporary reflections on the penetration of consumer culture into religious groups focus mainly on three types of religious phenomena: the 'New Religious Movements'[3] including the 'New Age' nebula;[4] Eastern spiritualities in the West, especially yoga and neo-Hindu movements;[5] and, as far as 'historical Western religions' are concerned, Christianity, with the development of megachurches and

---

2 With the exception of ultra-orthodox or *Haredi* groups.

3 Eileen Barker, 'New Religious Movements', in George Ritzer (ed.), *Blackwell Encyclopedia of Sociology* (Blackwell Publishing, Blackwell Reference Online, 2007).

4 Hildegarde Van Hove, 'L'emergence d'un marché spirituel', *Social Compass*, 46/2 (1999): 161–72; Grace Davie, Linda Woodhead and Paul Heelas, *Predicting Religion: Christian, Secular, and Alternative Futures* (Aldershot, 2003); François Mayer, 'Biens de salut et marché religieux dans le cultic milieu', *Social Compass*, 53/1 (2006): 97–108.

5 Veronique Altglas, 'Indian Gurus and the Quest for Self-perfection Among the Educated Middle Class', in Jörg Stolz (ed.), *Salvation Goods and Religious Markets* (New

church counselling.[6] Contributions from Jewish fieldwork[7] remain marginal – and are in any case limited to the field of Jewish studies.[8]

Yet consumer culture and its marketing rules have also entered the Jewish world: the Central Conference for American Rabbis (CCAR)[9] of Reform Judaism hires marketers to improve their communication and branding skills; philanthropic societies and think tanks conduct surveys and offer marketing strategies to Jewish institutions, especially those aimed at the young;[10] and the orthodox Student's Union group, Hillel, described by one of its leaders as a 'dying brand'[11] a few decades ago, has now started using 'popular culture' visuals to rebrand itself.[12] The marketing terminology has also entered common parlance: 'We are a family business', says, most naturally, a venerable *Loubavitch* Rabbi[13] at the opening of his Manhattan weekly class;[14] 'we've been in the business for almost 6,000 years'. At the same time, the post-denominational cultural association, Limmud New York,[15] welcomes visitors 'to the Jewish marketplace of ideas', while the

York, 2008), 211–34; Maya Burger, 'What Price Salvation? The Exchange of Salvation Goods between India and the West', *Social Compass*, 53/1 (2006): 81–95.

6 Robert L. Moore, *Selling God: American Religion in the Marketplace of Culture* (New York, 1994); Mara Einstein, *Brands of Faith: Marketing Religion in a Commercial Age* (London, 2008).

7 Ayala Fader, 'Jewish Spirituality and Late Capitalism', in Celia Rothenberg and Anne Vallely (eds), *New Age Judaism* (London, 2008), 34–51; Maya Katz, 'Trademarks of Faith: Chabad and Chanukah in America', *Modern Judaism*, 29/2 (2009): 239–67.

8 Mikel Koven, '"Cool Jewz": Contemporary Jewish Identity in Popular Culture', special issue of *Shofar: An Interdisciplinary Journal of Jewish Studies*, 25/4 (2007).

9 See http://ccarnet.org/ last [accessed: 20 March 2012].

10 Frank Luntz, 'Israel in the Age of Eminem', Report for the Combined Jewish Philanthropies (CJP), Boston (2003), [Online], available at: http://www.bjpa.org/Publications/details.cfm?PublicationID=3157 [accessed: 17 February 2012]; Sylvia Barak Fishman and Shlomo Fischer, 'Learning Jewishness, Jewish Education, and Jewish Identity', Report for the Jewish People Policy Institute (JPPI), Jerusalem (2012), [Online], available at: http://jppi.org.il/uploads/Learning_Jewishness,Jewish_education_and_Jewish_Identity.pdf [accessed: 17 February 2013].

11 Interview, February 2012, New York.

12 Steve Cohen, 'Cultural (Con)fusion', *Sh'ma*, 34/607 (January 2004): 8, [Online], available at: http://www.shma.com/archives/web-edition/ [accessed: 3 October 2011].

13 *Chabad* is a Chassidic (pietistic) group started in the eighteenth century in the Polish town of Loubavitch. The group is today commonly defined as 'ultra-orthodox' and is famous for its inner proselytism.

14 January 2012.

15 In Hebrew 'learning', see http://limmudny.org/conference/ [accessed: 20 March 2012].

'Conservadox'[16] founder of the *Chai Mitzvah* organisation[17] defines his initiative as a strategy to 'create demand for the existing supply in Jewish learning'.[18]

Religion and marketing are thus being merged in today's Jewish institutions' discourses and actions, across the entire scope of its denominations. However, this trend is the subject of a keenly argued debate: while some Rabbis are opposed to encouraging consumerist approaches to synagogue membership,[19] contrasting opinions in the aforementioned *Sh'ma* issue have ranged from those who are pro to those who oppose themselves the most to the marketing of Judaism, all in the name of its very 'survival' in a 'competitive secular culture'[20]; others showed weary of 'taking the means for the goal' and turning 'Judaism into a commodity'.[21] But only one contributor was entirely opposed to applying the logic of consumer culture to the promotion of Jewish goods, in the name of the preservation of the 'holiness' of religion from the rules and drives of the secular world.[22]

Such an insistence on the separation between the sacred and profane echoes the founding dichotomy of Judaism, which is also the founding sociological definition of religion by Emile Durkheim.[23] Yet a century later, the penetration of market logic and consumer culture into the religious field seems to contradict this definition.

From Judaism's Closure on Tradition to the Challenges of Secularisation and Globalisation

While Jewish theology is built on the principle of a constant reinterpretation of sacred texts, to ensure that the Torah be a 'lively' experience for each individual, historical circumstances have made it a rigid canon. What is known as the Jewish rabbinical canon – the Torah and Talmud – was written down and sealed as

---

16 American Judaism is said to have entered a 'postdenominational' era. 'Conservadox' Judaism, a term taken from common parlance, refers to a blending of conservative (interpretative) and orthodox (literal) approaches to *Halakha* (Jewish law).

17 http://www.chaimitzvah.org.

18 Interview, January 2012, New York.

19 Fader, 'Jewish Spirituality and Late Capitalism'.

20 David Nelson, 'Advertising Judaism', *Sh'ma*, 34/607 (January 2004): 3–4, [Online], available at: http://www.shma.com/archives/web-edition/ [accessed: 3 October 2011].

21 Chava Weissler, 'The Jewish Marketplace', *Sh'ma*, 34/607 (January 2004): 1, [Online], available at: http://www.shma.com/archives/web-edition/ [accessed: 3 October 2011]; Cohen, 'Cultural (Con)fusion', 8.

22 Jay Michaelson, 'Marketing Undermines Judaism', *Sh'ma*, 34/607 (January 2004): 4–5, [Online], available at: http://www.shma.com/archives/web-edition/ [accessed: 3 October 2011].

23 Émile Durkheim, *Les formes élémentaires de la vie religieuse* (Paris, 2007 [1912]), 8. Durkheim was born into a rabbinical family.

early as the first centuries of this era for the pragmatic reasons of maintaining the community's identity in the context of the diaspora and in the face of the domination of other religious systems: successively Greek, Roman, and Christian. For Jacob Neusner,[24] as the term 'creative responses' in the subtitle of his book suggests, the multi-phased process constituting 'Rabbinical Judaism' from the fifth century BCE to the sixth century CE, should be seen as *ad hoc* religious responses to the successive political and social turmoil – namely the destruction of the two successive Jerusalem temples, the subsequent exiles, and the final takeover by Christianity. Taking a more sociological perspective, Philip Davies sees Jewish scriptures as an 'exercise in self-definition, in a conscious attempt to invent an "Israel" that had an ancient history, a constitution, a land, and a wisdom ethic'.[25]

This movement of encasing the *ortho-doxa* (legitimate doctrine) into a written canon can be associated with Roger Bastide's concept of 'cultural canning'. Comparing, in the Americas' post-colonial context, the syncretistic turn taken by religious groups in Haiti to the 'closure' of Brazilian religions, the French anthropologist distinguished two opposing survival strategies for religious institutions in competitive pluralist contexts. 'Canned religions' had fossilized their tradition into 'cultural cans' so as to avoid the dissolution of their integrity into pluralism. For Bastide, this closure process is 'the expression, for a threatened culture, of the will to resist and to maintain its ethnic identity, by crystallizing tradition and uncoupling it from the flow of history'.[26] 'Lively' religions, by contrast, opt for blending and flexibility, adapting to whatever cultural mould in which they are embedded in (?). The spread of Buddhism throughout the world, blending with Daoism in China, Shintoism in Japan, and more recently, Judeo-Christian faiths in the West, is a typical example of a 'lively' reaction to pluralism.

On the contrary, and notably in comparison with its two 'lively' offspring, Christianity and Islam, which have kept diversifying fissiparously throughout history, Judaism has evolved for two millennia, as culturally diverse as it was staying theologically monolithic.

The modernisation of European societies was to explode this safely sealed can: in the wake of eighteenth-century Enlightenment philosophy and the propagation of a universalist human rights ethos, European countries progressively started granting civil rights to the Jews. This sparked the desire for assimilation amongst Jewish intellectuals. Thus began the *Haskalah* (Jewish Enlightenment), an internal secularisation movement in Jewish thought and scriptures which aimed at attuning Judaism to its times and to the 'external' context of the secular society. From this stems the new trend of 'Reform Judaism', which regards the Torah as a human

---

24 Jacob Neusner, *Transformations in Ancient Judaism: Textual Evidence for Creative Responses to Crisis* (Peabody, MA, 2004).

25 Philip R. Davis, 'Judaism and the Hebrew Scriptures', in Jacob Neusner and Alan J. Avery-Peck (eds), *The Blackwell Companion to Judaism* (Malden, MA, 2000), 45.

26 Roger Bastide, *Les amériques noires. Les civilisations africaines dans le nouveau monde* (Paris, 1967), 136. My translation from the French.

production to be constantly reinterpreted and adapted into a more liberal and inclusivist view vis à vis the world of the gentiles. A counter-trend duly emerged as a reaction, in order to preserve traditional Judaism. It was soon termed 'orthodox' by the liberals. Thus resumed Jewish theological diversification which had been interrupted for two millennia by its canonisation in the Torah. And it was only to spread further in the second half of the 20th century.

In sum, European modernisation has impacted on the Jewish world in two main respects: first, secularisation has enacted a dichotomy between Jewish identity and Jewish religion; second, religious subjectivity has led to an inner diversification within Judaism. Hence, Jewish institutions have found themselves to be suddenly confronted with both internal and external competition.

At first, Judaism's external competitors were only secular: philosophy and politics were seen as ethical alternatives to the path of the Torah and *Mitzvot* (commandments) – as the development of political Zionism and of a Jewish secular thought demonstrates. But in the second half of the twentieth century, additional competitors appeared; these were purveying spiritual systems. These competitors can be named broadly as "eastern spiritualities", mainly Hindu and Buddhist practices, which entered western culture especially after the Second World War. Indeed, for the post-Holocaust baby boomers of Western Europe and America, these 'Eastern spiritualities' had become the spiritual supports of a general Western countercultural movement they were massively part of.

In the aftermath of the *Shoah* and the atomic bomb, and in a context of new international conflicts (the war in Vietnam and the Cold War), and of domestic tensions due to enduring racial, gender, and economic inequalities, the counterculture considered the ideals of progress and justice in Western modernity to have failed. They especially resented its ethical basis: the Judeo-Christian system, which was felt to be dualistic and intolerant, and was held responsible for most of the bloodshed of the past. By contrast, 'the East', which the romantic orientalists had started unveiling through a western bias in the late nineteenth century, was seen as offering accessible, empirical paths leading to individual-universal liberation from physical and emotional suffering. In their Western versions, these exotic salvation goods insisted on intuition rather than theology, compassion rather than guilt, and on the experience of the body and feelings rather than their repression. In short, they seemed to be the perfect alternative meaning-making and practice systems for a youth movement which was rebellious, but nonetheless in need of spiritual guidance.

Jewish baby boomers had additional reasons for being countercultural: they were not only rejecting, like their Christian counterparts, the negative image of a paternalist, coercive and materialist ethos of Western culture. They were also reacting to a post-traumatic, post-*Shoah* Jewish culture. Hence, their turn to Eastern spiritualities can be seen as enacting several specific needs: to find alternative meaning systems to replace the 'failing' God of the Deuteronomy; to form alternative communities to replace the uninspiring parochial bonds imprinted by materialism, conformism, and fear of 'a religion of survival';[27] and finally, to enact constant desires of assimilation, in a social context where Jews were still being discriminated against.[28]

American Jews soon became leading figures in the massive Western turn towards Eastern spiritualities. In addition to their involvement in the blossoming new Buddhist groups in America, such as the Japanese Zen schools of Suzuki and Maezumi Roshi and the Tibetan Shambala school of Chogyam Trungpa, Jews became leading figures in the constitution of a 'Western Buddhism': the first American centre of Vipassana Buddhism, the Insight Meditation Society (IMS), was founded by four American Jews who had trained in Asia in the 1960s. Although difficult to measure, this phenomenon was visibly remarkable.[29] In the mid-1990s, Jews were estimated to represent about a third of American Buddhists – less than 3 per cent of American society.[30] No update of these assessments – for which no source was indicated – has been provided, but my own fieldwork observations suggest that this proportion may have decreased – in great part because of the development since then of similar practices labeled 'Jewish meditation'. However, a look at the teaching staff of American Buddhist centres still shows a remarkable proportion of Jewish names.

Such a massive turn to Eastern spiritualities was soon seen as a new, albeit indirect threat to Jewish continuity. Hence it provoked at first very negative reactions within the community.[31] It still does, but to a much lesser extent. Today, Buddhist and Hindu-based practices have become 'legitimate' (in a Bourdieusian sense), in Western culture as Eastern spiritualities have become recognised as effective tools for wellbeing and self-actualisation[32] and have been appropriated by corporate and consumer cultures.[33] There is nothing countercultural anymore about doing

---

27 Nathan Glazer, *American Jewry or American Judaism?* (Cambridge, MA, 1988); Anne Vallely, 'Jewish Redemption by Way of the Buddha', in Celia Rothenberg and Anne Vallely (eds), *New Age Judaism* (London, 2008), 24.

28 Denis Lacorne, *La crise de l'identité américaine: du melting pot au multiculturalisme* (Paris, 2003).

29 Charles Prebish and Kenneth Tanaka (eds), *The Faces of Buddhism in America* (Berkeley, CA, 1998), 2.

30 Rodger Kamenetz, *The Jew in the Lotus* (San Francisco, CA, 1994), 7; Judith Linzer, *Torah and Dharma* (San Francisco, CA, 1996), xxii.

31 Linzer, *Torah and Dharma*, xviii.

32 Charles S. Prebish and Martin Baumann (eds), *Westward Dharma: Buddhism Beyond Asia* (Berkeley, CA, 2002), 51; Davie, Woodhead and Heelas, *Predicting Religion*, 235.

33 Altglas, 'Indian Gurus and the Quest for Self-perfection Among the Educated Middle Class'; François Gauthier, 'Religion in Contemporary Consumer Societies: In Search of a Global Comprehensive Analytic', *Revue du MAUSS permanente* (1 September 2009), [Online], available at: http://www.journaldumauss.net/spip.php?article539 [accessed: 2 February 2013].

yoga during the week and attending the synagogue on the *Shabbat*.[34] In fact, many mainstream synagogues in the large American urban centres, including orthodox ones, now offer yoga and Tai Chi[35] classes: exclusion not being an option, it seems that Jewish institutions have opted for incorporation and competition.

The Jewish Institutional Response: Embracing Western Popular and Consumer Cultures

The proportion of mainstream Jews practising yoga and meditation has kept growing since the countercultural *avant-garde* of the 1970s. So has the number of secular Jews. Ten years ago, according to the American National Jewish Population Survey, nearly 50 per cent of marriages were exogamic.[36] Disaffiliated Jews, if they respect or take pride in their identity, nevertheless feel less attached to their inherited religion.[37] They have no scruples in attending a *Zendo*,[38] or a nightclub, rather than the synagogue on a Friday night.[39] For them, the consumption of Jewish goods, if there is any, is motivated by desire more than by duty.

Jewish institutions have therefore found themselves to be facing an unforeseen challenge: In secular and cosmopolitan societies characterised by individualism, choice, and hybridisation, how can Judaism, which is built on traditional values such as community, obedience, and separation, adapt and stay relevant to individuals, without jeopardising its own identity?

The two classical means of attracting an audience – money (in the form of stipends for Torah study and trips to Israel) and matchmaking (for which the aforementioned study and trips are often a side agenda) – are still widely used. But they have proved to be insufficient. Once it is understood that the driving force of consumer society is 'attraction', or desire, as opposed to 'need'—or in other words, once the search for symbolic fulfilment is enacted through material satisfaction—, it is easy to see why religious groups at large are turning towards *bona fide* marketing strategies.

To the extent that it focuses on Jewish institutional efforts to seduce its own members who are thereby turned into 'customers', such an analysis could be seen as following the rational choice theory's explanation of 'top down' religious

34 The seventh and holy day of rest in Jewish theology.

35 A Chinese martial art.

36 *National Jewish Population Survey 2000–2001: Strength, Challenge and Diversity in the American Jewish Population* (New York, 2004), 16, [Online], available at: http://www.jewishdatabank.org/NJPS2000.asp [accessed: 17 February 2013].

37 Luntz, 'Israel in the Age of Eminem'.

38 A meditation hall in the Zen tradition.

39 The beginning of *Shabbat*.

change. Its proponents[40] have proposed an analysis in terms of economic laws of 'supply and demand', 'naturally regulated' by the competition of the free market.

However this explanation is limited in its scope and therefore doomed to be inaccurate. I do not abide by its premises that individuals choose neither rationally, nor freely from inherited belongings, or that religious innovation comes from the supply side. The current changes in contemporary Judaism appear, on the contrary, to be a direct response to the 'Jewish Buddhist' phenomenon: it is an institutional adaptation to the enacted desires of individuals. Hence the contemporary institutional changes are really speaking of a bottom-up dynamics.

This is why I will rather develop here the thesis of institutional appropriation of religious *autopoiesis*[41] as expressed by Enzo Pace.[42] Indeed, this type of competitive response is best explained through considering 'religious marketing' as institutional attempts at annexing individual heterodoxies:

> It often happens that the religious *autopoiesis* of salvation goods produced by spontaneous movements is perceived by a religious institution as an interesting new niche on the market. As such, the niche has to be occupied to achieve greater control of a socio-religious environment which is increasingly varied and where there is a real risk of losing 'customers'.[43]

The 'Jewish Buddhist' phenomenon, and more broadly what has become a 'Zen culture' in the West, applies very well to Pace's definition of contemporary 'popular religion' as individual mysticism.[44] Zen, from the Chinese *Chan*, or 'silent meditation', is only one school of Japanese Buddhism; but in the West it has become an adjective in itself, a synonym for 'quiet coolness'; and it is massively used in the marketing world. This is why, using this mainstream stereotype, I call the composite subculture of Eastern-based wellbeing practices, the 'Western Zen culture'. As the following examples will show, this 'Zen culture' has clearly become a 'niche' for Jewish institutions. The same goes for the secular entertainment world, specifically in visual and musical popular culture and the movie industry.

---

40 Rodney Stark and William S. Bainbridge, 'Towards a Theory of Religion: Religious Commitment', *Journal for the Scientific Study of Religion*, 19/2 (June 1980): 114–28, published by Blackwell Publishing on behalf of Society for the Scientific Study of Religion; Roger Finke, and Lawrence Iannacone, 'Supply-Side Explanations for Religious Change', *Annals of the American Academy of Political and Social Science*, 527, 'Religion in the Nineties' (May 1993): 27–39.

41 Self-creation.

42 Enzo Pace, 'Salvation Goods, the Gift Economy and Charismatic Concern', in Jörg Stolz (ed.), *Salvation Goods and Religious Markets: Theory and Application* (Bern, 2008), 150.

43 Ibid.

44 Enzo Pace, 'New Paradigms of Popular Religion', *Archives de Sciences Sociales des Religions*, 64/1 (July–September 1987): 7–14.

This is why I argue that contemporary changes in the morphology and contents of the Jewish supply in America have to be examined specifically in the light of these subcultures. The result is the offering by Jewish groups of similar 'goods' as those found in the 'outside world', only within the Jewish context. Hence 'kosher' versions of 'wellbeing', 'spirituality', and 'entertainment' are blooming. These changes have resulted in developing three themes traditionally neglected in Judaism for theological reasons:[45] the body, the image, and music.

The New Faces of Judaism: Body, Pop Music, and Mysticism

Three main types of competitive strategies and cultural adaptations to make Judaism more attractive can be identified.: 1) appropriating 'Eastern spiritualities' within the Jewish mould; 2) rebranding Judaism with the tools of popular culture; 3) launching a 'counter-attack' by re-introducing Judaism's own supply in mysticism: Kabbalah.

From 'Jewish Renewal' to 'Down-to-Earth Judaism': A New Care for Body and Soul

In the 1970s, Lubavitch Rabbi Zalman Schachter-Shalomi was given a mandate by *Chabbad* to 'bring back' Jewish individuals who had gone over to Buddhism. Instead, however, he implemented what was later to be called a 'paradigm shift',[46] opting for blending Jewish spirituality (mainly Chassidism and Kabbalah) with elements from selected world spiritualities (Buddhism, Hinduism, Sufism, and shamanism), while downplaying the role of *Halakha*. What mattered to him was that Judaism would be inspiring and meaningful, so that Jews would come (back) to it not because they 'have to', but because they 'want to'.[47] He founded the Jewish Renewal Movement,[48] today the umbrella of independent progressive groups all around the Jewish diaspora, but mainly in America.

In addition, as a result of the dual practices of Jews who were embracing Eastern and other alternative "spiritualities", have entered on the Jewish scene

---

45 Mainly the prohibition of idolatry, or *Avodah Zara*, applied to visual representations of the Divine, as well as the prohibition of playing instruments on the *Shabbat* and holidays.

46 Ellen Singer (ed.), *Paradigm Shift: From the Jewish Renewal Teachings of Reb Zalman Schachter-Shalomi* (New York, 1993).

47 Ibid., 40.

48 Jeffrey K. Salkin, 'New Age Judaism', in *The Blackwell Companion to Judaism* (Oxford, 2003), 354–69.

since the nineties new hybrid trends such as 'New Age Judaism', 'Jewish shamanism',[49] 'Jewish mindfulness', and 'Jewish yoga'.[50]

These trends have been mostly developed in America and in Israel – but also, in the case of Jewish yoga, in England. The French community remains remarkably detached from such hybridisation tendencies. Apart from the 'language barrier', this may be explained by a cultural reluctance for hybridisation, as well as the greater conservatism of a French Jewish community which is mainly composed of traditionalist *sepharadim*[51] and still dominated in its religious expression by orthodoxy.[52]

These new hybrid trends have in common a combination of three themes: 'exotic' spiritualities; the Jewish tradition; and a holistic concern to heal the body and soul. This concern for the 'body and soul' reflects the dominant culture of western societies in the beginning of the 21st century, of which it has become a central element of. Hence the 'body-soul' label is a pattern which circulates through different worlds of American urban life. For instance, in the New York Upper West Side, the Renewal affiliated Romemu Synagogue offers a 'Judaism for mind, body and spirit',[53] while a few blocks downtown, a martial arts Tai Kwon Do school promises 'the ultimate workout for body, mind, and spirit'. The similarity of slogans in these two very different centres of practice is a striking example of today's generalisation of a 'body, mind, and spirit' practices paradigm.[54]

One could argue that the body has always been central in Judaism. But it has been so only as a theological allegory, and as a tool with which to perform *Mitzvot* (commandments). By contrast, in late modern Western culture, the body is the site of display of a self for whom personal 'wellbeing' is of primary importance. It is therefore not surprising that renewal movements would tackle this issue, and sometimes in the most prosaic ways, as is indicated in the title of a book by Rabbi Waskow: *Down-to-Earth Judaism: Food, Sex, Money and the Rest of Life*.[55]

Without opting for blending with other traditions, more traditional Jewish currents are catching up with this trend. On the New York scene for instance,

---

49 Ibid.

50 Celia Rothenberg, 'New Age Jews: Jewish Shamanism and Jewish Yoga', in Celia Rothenberg and Anne Vallely (eds), *New Age Judaism* (London, 2008), 1–18.

51 In Hebrew 'Spanish', refers metonymically to the Mediterranean Jews.

52 Mira Niculescu, 'Juif-bouddhiste? Conflictualités internes et intracommunautaires autour des adhésions au bouddhisme par des juifs français', in Anne-Sophie Lamine and Nathalie Luca (eds), *Quand le religieux fait conflit. Désaccords, négociations ou arrangements* (2013, forthcoming).

53 http://romemu.org/ [accessed: 17 February 2013].

54 Paul Heelas and Benjamin Seel, 'An Ageing New Age?', in Grace Davie, Linda Woodhead and Paul Heelas (eds), *Predicting Religion: Christian, Secular, and Alternative Futures* (Aldershot, 2003), 229–47.

55 Arthur Waskow, *Down-to-Earth Judaism: Food, Sex, Money and the Rest of Life* (New York, 1995).

if proof were still needed for the thesis of the mainstreaming/neutralisation of Eastern spiritualities within Western culture, some orthodox Synagogues offer weekly Tai Chi or yoga classes, as well as 'standing posture' classes to improve one's experience in the recitation of the *Amidah*,[56] while the orthodox website 'Bang it out' advertises 'Yoga for Jewish spirit' and 'Jewish prayer dance'.[57]

On a didactic level, egalitarian Yeshiva 'Mechon Hadar' has recently addressed the topic of 'the body and emotions in the world of *Mitzvot*',[58] while the orthodox Rabbi Shmuley Boteach became famous with the publication of 'Kosher' books on 'hot topics' regarding sexuality such as *Kosher Sex*,[59] *Kosher Adultery*, and even, alluding to the famous Hindu book on sexuality, the *Kama Sutra*, his version of a *Kosher Sutra*.[60] In France, the orthodox Rabbi Elie Lemmel wrote a book on *Self-development According to Jewish Tradition*,[61] and gives lectures on 'Judaism and sexuality'.[62]

However, what attracts the largest audiences remains the entertainment world. This secular competition for Jewish observance is also a more easily accessible universe for orthodox institutions, as it is more neutral than 'Zen culture'.

Introducing 'Jewish Coolness': Pop Culture, Role Models, and Rebranding Judaism

Music plays a large part in popular culture, and therefore in the success of religious groups who bet on it, as is illustrated in the contemporary developments of Christian rock music. A similar phenomenon has appeared in Judaism since the 1970s: by touring American campuses with his guitar, the late Rabbi Shlomo Carlebach, then part of the orthodox 'Chabbad Loubavitch' movement, 'brought' many young Jews 'back' to their religion by making prayer charismatic and entertaining. Since then, popular music has been continuously expanding in Jewish religious culture, apparently liberating a popular hunger for merging entertainment and prayer. Today, one of the distinctive features of the Jewish Renewal Movement – and one of the secrets of its fast-spreading success, is musical *Shabbat* services.[63] But this

---

56 A central prayer in Jewish liturgy, which is said standing up.

57 http://www.bangitout.com/events/index.php [accessed: 20 March 2012].

58 http://www.mechonhadar.org/c/journal/view_article_content?groupId=10488&articleId=1191472&version=1.0 [accessed: 4 March 2012].

59 Shmuley Boteach, *Kosher Sex: A Recipe for Passion and Intimacy* (New York, 1999).

60 Shmuley Boteach, *The Kosher Sutra: Eight Sacred Secrets for Reigniting Desire and Restoring Passion for Life* (New York, 2009).

61 Elie Lemmel, *Les quatre coupes de lait: le développement personnel selon la tradition juive* (Paris, 2010).

62 Conference Limoud France, March 2011.

63 Salkin, 'New Age Judaism', 360.

trend has also expanded to more traditional denominations, such as conservative Synagogue 'Benei Jeshurun' in New York.[64]

This general dynamic has encouraged the development of religious musical bands. In the Jewish Renewal world, their names clearly show affinities with 'the East', such as the New York band *Darshan*[65] which fuses prayer, jazz, and rap, or the '*Kirtan* Rabbi'[66] Andrew Khan, who offers 'Jewish mystical chant'. In the orthodox world, 'the Maccabeats',[67] an American choir of *yeshiva*[68] boys, sing religious songs to electronic tunes, providing 'legitimate' alternatives to secular pop music. But most famously, a new spokesman of the Chabad movement[69] has been very influential in providing Jewish youth since 2005 with a 'kosher' version of entertainment: the 'Chassidic reggae superstar'[70] Matisyahu lights *Chanukah*[71] candles during his concerts, sings Hebrew prayers, and praises God to the sounds of reggae-rap and beat-boxing. More than his music, it is his personality that has made him so charismatic. The journalist Lisa Klug, author of *Cool Jew*,[72] a tribute to the (re)conciliation of Jewish identity with Western culture, notes that until the arrival of Matisyahu, Jews who were part of the entertainment industry would either downplay their Jewishness, or, like Woody Allen, deride it. By contrast, the inspirational power of Matisyahu comes from the fact that not only he own up to his Jewish identity, but he uses his religious observance as spiritual and musical inspiration and makes it a major part of his marketing image.[73] This new form of

---

64 Fader, 'Jewish Spirituality and Late Capitalism'.

65 In Sanskrit 'seeing the divinity', referring also to the apparition of a guru to his disciples in Hinduism.

66 http://kirtanrabbi.com/ [accessed: 19 March 2012]. *Kirtan* or *Bhajan* is a Hindu devotional ceremony implemented with call and response chanting.

67 http://www.maccabeats.com/ [accessed: 19 March 2012].

68 A *yeshiva* is a religious school.

69 A French counterpart has recently appeared: Shmoolik, the *chassid* rapper, 'trained', like Matisyahu, with the Chabbad Loubavitch of Brooklyn, see http://shmoolik.com/ [accessed: 20 March 2012].

70 Taken from his own expression on Twitter: 'no more Chassidic reggae superstar' [13 December 2011].

71 A Jewish holiday celebrated in the darkest month of the year celebrating, according to Jewish mythology, the miracle of a candle burning for eight days in the Temple during the Maccabean revolt around the second century BCE.

72 Lisa Alcalay Klug, *Cool Jew: The Ultimate Guide for Every Member of the Tribe* (Kansas City, MO, 2008).

73 However, in December 2011, in a radical symbolic gesture of personal emancipation, Matisyahu posted on Twitter a photo of his shaved face, letting go for good of the 'Chabbad look': black suit, white shirt, long beard. He said he was still religious but no longer 'afraid to be himself'. This episode has been widely commented on in the Jewish world, and many Jews, religious and non-religious alike, felt personally betrayed by the fact that he had abandoned his traditional religious image: http://thespiritualityproject.org/uncategorized/matisyahu-i-forgive-you/ [accessed: 29 May 2012].

charisma, almost 'countercultural' in a secular culture, is enhanced by the fact that it is a conscious choice: Matthew Miller grew up secular and decided, like many *Chozerei Tshuva* (returnees to religion) of his generation, that a religious life was more fulfilling to him. Renamed after a biblical character, Matisyahu therefore appears as a genuine role model for both religious and non-religious Jews: owning up to his religiousness while becoming a 'Chassidic reggae superstar star', who appears on mainstream TV shows, Matisyahu represents both a new 'Jewish pride', and a new image of Judaism to be projected on to the non-Jewish world.

For the Jewish community, this issue of the Jewish 'image' is more than anecdotal: over centuries of persecution and pogroms, culminating with the *Shoah*, the Jewish image has long been displayed in the form of a negative stereotyping called anti-Semitism. But according to a recent issue of *Shofar*, an interdisciplinary review of Jewish studies, popular Jewish characters from the entertainment industry have been in recent decades turning the Jewish stigma into a proper 'brand'. In a whole issue dedicated to the theme of 'Jewish coolness' within American entertainment culture, the metamorphosis in the Jewishness of movie and TV show characters are being interpreted as a paradigmatic shift in the perception of Jewish identity: through the charisma of openly Jewish celebrities, perceptions of Jewish identity have become more positive as it is not only being owned up for , but also displayed as 'cool'.[74]

The topic of 'coolness' seems to be of particular interest for the orthodox milieu, perhaps because they don't benefit from the post-hippie 'Yogic-Zen' aura of the more progressive trends. As a result, while Jewish Renewal groups invest massively in yoga and 'mindfulness', orthodox trends focus on 'coolness': two orthodox blogs are entitled 'Cool Jew';[75] a former Hillel member, preoccupied with revitalising American Jewish adhesions, has published a book entitled *Getting our Groove Back*;[76] and a Hillel director relates how the organisation, 'struggling to shake the stigma of "uncool"'[77] had used for the promotion of its *Purim* party[78] a fashionable brand of alcohol, Absolut Vodka and advertised the event as 'Absolute Purim'.

However, such marketing approaches are being denounced, especially by progressive Jews. The media critic Donald Rushkoff 'criticizes Jewish organizations for trying to increase their numbers by attempting to make Judaism

---

74 Koven, 'Cool Jewz'.

75 http://www.thecoolJew.net, and http://thecoolJewshow.blogspot.com/ [accessed: 19 March 2012].

76 Scott A. Shay, *Getting Our Groove Back: How to Energize American Jewry* (Jerusalem, 2007).

77 Cohen, 'Cultural (Con)fusion', 8.

78 A Jewish holiday taking place around February and celebrating the mythical history of 'Queen Esther' against the evil 'Haman' who wanted to exterminate all Jews. In remembrance of the queen's concealed Jewishness, Jews wear costumes, and in celebration of the victory, are invited to drink abundantly.

"cool", using marketing techniques rather than inspiring people'.[79] More severely, the scholar, journalist, and gay activist Jay Michaelson considers that 'Judaism cannot use power/sexiness/fun as tools to sell itself. We undermine Judaism by (...) dressing it up as "cool".'[80] This unorthodox advocate of Jewish spirituality particularly criticises today's widespread commodification of Kabbalah, Judaism's highest mystical path.

From the Unearthing of Kabbalah to the Emergence of Kabbalah-based Spiritual Businesses

While the two main transformations we have just described are being implemented through appropriating or imitating other spiritual or secular worlds, the last one represents the only endogenous institutional response to compete with Eastern spiritualities and the Western culture of self-actualisation. Indeed, today's unseen unearthing of Jewish mysticism represents the third type of competitive creativity by Jewish Institutions: a counter-attack with a 'home supply'. I have called elsewhere such a tactic the 'Buitoni strategy':[81] In the 1990s in France, a TV advertisement showed a man running outside of his house to jump on a passing boat full of cans of his favourite raviolis, while his dismayed wife was chasing after him and shouting 'Honey, come back! I have the same at home!'

In a similar movement, Kabbalah, the most esoteric and elitist of Jewish practices, has been exhumed from the depths of Jewish tradition as the domestic tool to compete with the exotic appeal of Buddhist esotericism and Hindu Tantra. Both progressive and orthodox trends are betting on this niche, but from different perspectives and with different agendas: while Jewish Progressive groups dwell on the 'similarities' between Kabbalah and Eastern mysticisms, orthodox trends use Kabbalah precisely to prevent Jews from crossing over to Eastern mysticism. In contemporary orthodox discourses, Kabbalah is presented as the 'legitimate' version of spirituality, so that Jews can stop looking outside for what they 'already have in their own tradition'.[82] Hence, what was once reserved for 40-year-olds and above *Halakha*-observant scholars and patriarchs in an exclusive context of oral transmission from master to disciple is today unearthed, democratised, and translated beyond recognition. Hence, following the commodification trajectory of Buddhism and yoga in the West a few decades earlier, Jewish mysticism has been refashioned as a tool for self-actualisation. Today, a plethora of goods in 'kosher' mysticism and meditation have bloomed on the Jewish scene, under the form

---

79 In Gary Rosenblatt, 'Eminem Jews Rap Establishment', *The Jewish Week* (2 May 2003), [Online], available at: http://www.jewishfederations.org/page.aspx?id=42782 [accessed: 17 February 2013].

80 Michelson, 'Marketing Undermines Judaism', 4–5.

81 Niculescu, 'Juif Bouddhiste'.

82 Rifat Sonsino, *Six Jewish Spiritual Paths: A Rationalist Looks at Spirituality* (Woodstock, VT, 2000), 7.

of publications of 'practical' and 'everyday' Kabbalah, crash courses, seminars, websites, weekly teachings, and so on.

For Michaelson, these developments have 'distorted the Jewish mystical tradition to cater to the desires of "customers"', so that 'instead of offering a pathway to higher awareness, Kabbalah is being peddled as self-help'.[83]

As a consequence, Kabbalah, once the most elitist and exclusive of practices, has become a way in to Judaism. Today, not only can non-religious Jews who ignore all of *kasherut* (dietary laws) become familiar with the esoteric *sphirot* (attributes of the kabbalistic 'tree of life'); non-Jews can too, in particular with the emergence of new religious movements which are universalising elements of Judaism and Kabbalah on the Western 'spiritual market',[84] sometimes in controversial ways. In America, for instance, the ex-orthodox rabbi and charismatic 'Master of World spirituality', Marc Gafni, links Kabbalah and sexuality.[85] But while his movement remains limited in scope, a very powerful spiritually-based business has developed in recent decades, exploiting the image of Jewish esotericism and offering it to the whole world – in exchange for significant amounts of money. Presenting Kabbalah as a self-actualisation tool, the 'Kabbalah Center', ruled by a former real estate agent 'Rav Berg' and his sons, distorts Jewish and Kabbalistic concepts and mixes them with classical self-help discourses and Zen culture visuals, promising to uncover the 'best kept secrets of the universe', so that one's life will be 'changed forever'.[86] A recent advertisement campaign displays a young woman meditating in the lotus position on a beach and praising the 'power of Kabbalah', hence mixing all cultural codes. This type of hybrid 'catch-all' discourse is supported by massive advertisement campaigns, in the streets, on the internet, and even on the radio. All these elements shows the universal reach of the recruitment of 'students' into the Kabbalah Center, a strategy which goes diametrically against the particularistic Jewish agenda. Students-clients of the Kabbalah Center are particularly encouraged to acquire the centre's self-published literature, including the 'mini *Zohar*', a 'pocket' version of the thirteenth-century Kabbalah text, the *Book of Splendour*. But this product, prefaced in holistic, Universalist terms in all languages -including Arabic, simply displays a weekly *Parasha* (portion) of the Torah. Of course its owner, obviously presumably a non-Jew (or a disaffiliated one), will never know, since it is 'written in Aramaic' and in letters 'too small to be read'[87] anyway, says the Center. Indeed, this book is designed not to be read but to be carried as a talisman, a 'tool for healing and protection',[88] says the website. It is used like the 'red thread' proudly worn on the wrists of Hollywood stars who follow the example of Madonna. Indeed, the American pop star, a very

83 Michelson, 'Marketing Undermines Judaism', 6.

84 Van Hove, 'L'emergence d'un marché spirituel'.

85 http://www.marcgafni.com/ [accessed: 10 April 2012].

86 http://www.kabbalah.com/node/3119 [accessed: 20 April 2012].

87 http://www.newthoughtkabbalah.com/minizohar.htm [accessed: 2 April 2012].

88 Ibid.

generous donor to the centre, has become, according to Mara Einstein, the centre's 'brand icon'.[89] As a non-Jewish Hollywood idol oscillating between pop culture and 'spiritual searching', toying alternately with Catholic, Hindu, and Kabbalistic symbols, Madonna represents the ultimate popular universal icon; not only can she gather fans from all quarters; she incarnates a popular culture which merges the star system and spiritual materialism, which is the aim of the Kabbalah Center.

All these features clearly show that the centre is not targeting Jews. Indeed, unlike all the marketing, branding, and repackaging efforts of the Jewish institutions examined in this article, the Kabbalah Center's agenda includes everything but bringing Jews back to Judaism. The centre, as Einstein's thorough examination reveals,[90] only seeks its own corporate development. However, by registering Kabbalah as a trademark, uncoupling it from Judaism, and promoting it through aggressive radio, internet and poster campaigns, the Kabbalah Center has paradoxically made world famous the most exclusive dimension of Judaism, kabbalah, as a brand. Hence, confusion often arises with respect to contemporary practices of 'Kabbalah', even on the part of scholars: in his article on 'Kabbalism' for Partridge's *New Religions: A Guide*,[91] Christianson doesn't distinguish between this Judaism-based business which has completely exited Judaism, and the contemporary developments of Kabbalah within Judaism. Hence the importance of distinguishing between different salvation goods which nonetheless bear the same 'brand-name', and of focusing on the practices and agendas lying behind the marketing discourses.

Hybridisation and Standardisation: The Contrasting Faces of Late Modern Judaism

From this survey of the image and content changes on the contemporary Jewish scene, a few conclusions can be drawn. First, the influence and incorporation of elements from Zen and popular cultures are testaments to the contemporary hybridisations which define today's Western cultures as cosmopolitan. The instance of orthodox groups proposing yoga is the most blatant sign of such dynamics, be they celebrated or denied.

Second, the thematic comparison between progressive and traditional trends in Judaism clearly shows a levelling of the Jewish offer. As a result, individuals not strictly affiliated to a particular trend can pray in a Jewish renewal group, dance at a Matisyahu concert, and learn Kabbalah in a *Chabad* group. This creates a continuum between Jewish 'salvation goods so that one can circulate more easily among the different groups according to what is being sought at a particular time.

[89] Einstein, *Brands of Faith*, 165.

[90] Ibid., 93, 147.

[91] Eric Christianson, in Christopher Partridge (ed.), *New Religions: A Guide* (New York, 2004), 114.

This also confirms the contemporary thesis of an American 'post-denominational' Judaism.

Hence, thirdly, while the different Jewish trends had emerged in contradiction to each other with the rise of Western modernity in the nineteenth century, their recent thematic *rapprochement* contradicts the mechanical assumption that religious pluralisation leads to diversification. On the contrary, this phenomenon confirms French sociologist Danièle Hervieu-Léger's suggestion,[92] developed by François Gauthier,[93] that the subjectivisation of beliefs and practices doesn't necessarily cause an anomic atomisation of the religious field, but really leads to a standardisation of practices.

Of course these dynamics are still characteristic of the American scene, and, one could say, of a New York/San Francisco urban middle-upper-class network having digested the counterculture, while symbolic boundaries would remain stronger in the rest of world Jewry. However, in Europe and in Israel, even if the subcultures of yoga and Buddhism still mainly concern secular Jews, contemporary, marketing-style attempts at attracting the disaffiliated Jewish youth are becoming increasingly visible.

While time will be the only judge, the ongoing influence of American Judaism as well as the mainstreaming and the gentrification of the 'Zen culture' in the West lead me to think that the homogenisation dynamics described above can be generalised outside of America. At the expense, maybe, of each subculture's specificities: the price to pay for a 'lively' religious idiom.

92 Danièle Hervieu-Léger, 'Quelques paradoxes de la modernité religieuse. Crise de l'universel, planétarisation culturelle et renforcements communautaires', *Futuribles*, 260 (2001): 99–109.

93 François Gauthier, 'Primat de l'authenticité et besoin de reconnaissance. La société de consommation et la nouvelle régulation du religieux', *Studies in Religion / Sciences religieuses*, 41/1 (2012): 93–111. See also the introduction to this volume.

Chapter 6
Shopping for a Church? Choice and Commitment in Religious Behaviour

Francesca E.S. Montemaggi

Introduction

In the neoliberal world, religious organisations, as much as other organisations, face competition for 'customers'. This marketisation of religion turns the 'goods' of religion into commodities and religions into either the agents or victims of commodification.[1] The 'silent takeover of all aspects of life by the corporate world'[2] leads to 'the colonisation of our collective cultural heritage by individualist and capitalist forms of spirituality',[3] which needs to be resisted. Religious symbols and practices are in danger of being stripped of their intangible value. Thus goes the theory. As I sat in the steam room of the gym recently, I noticed that the music in the background was a Gregorian chant. There goes 'sacred music', I thought. However, I also pondered whether the playing of a Gregorian chant in a steam room of a gym necessarily devalued it. The following day, Grieg's *Morning Mood* was playing, and the commodification claim seemed even less persuasive. Listening to Grieg or Gregorian chanting in the gym does not preclude one from appreciating music and devoting one's entire attention to it when at the 'appropriate' venue. Arguably, music in non-conventional venues reaches a wider audience which might not otherwise experience it.[4]

The feeling of discomfort at the twin processes of the marketisation and commodification of religion implies that consumer choice eschews considerations of value, and that, more worryingly, left to our own devices, we neglect what is

---

1 Michael York, 'New Age Commodification and Appropriation of Spirituality', *Journal of Contemporary Religion*, 16/3 (2001): 361–72; Vincent J. Miller, *Consuming Religion: Christian Faith and Practice in a Consumer Culture* (New York, 2004).

2 Jeremy Carrette and Richard King, *Selling Spirituality: The Silent Takeover of Religion* (London, 2005), 170.

3 Ibid., 171.

4 Tia DeNora, *Music in Everyday Life* (Cambridge, 2000).

considered 'authentic' or 'valuable' in the religious life. This normative judgement obfuscates the reality of the choices religious people make. I thus propose a distinction between 'formal commodification', which indicates the marketisation of religious goods to consumers, and 'substantial commodification', which identifies a decrease in the value of religious life. Accordingly, the 'formal commodification' of Gregorian chant means that it can be 'back in fashion', and its 'purchasing power' is not limited to a religious audience, or that Hillsong Christian music is a successful music enterprise among Christian evangelicals and beyond. 'Substantial commodification', by contrast, reduces the value of religious practices, beliefs, and symbols to being simply merely of commodities. 'Substantial commodification' describes a situation where, to paraphrase Oscar Wilde, we know the price of religious practices, beliefs, and symbols, whilst ignoring their value. I pose that 'substantial commodification' is not the inevitable consequence of marketisation. By contrast, an example of 'substantial commodification' is the application of a market-oriented logic to the study of religion, as pursued by rational choice theorists. Rational choice theory, instead of explaining the effects of marketisation on religion, imposes a reductive perspective, which ignores the actors' motives and devalues their actions.

This chapter presents a critique of the market-derived logic of rational choice theory and raises the question of the complexity of 'choice' on the basis of an analysis of primary data from a Christian evangelical church. It is argued that rational choice theory (RCT), by reducing choice to 'rational self-interest' and thus adopting a utilitarian and instrumentalist ethic, misinterprets the intentions of religious actors. RCT, far from being neutral, ascribes an instrumentalist system of values to religious behaviour, ignoring subjective motivations based on value. This is not to dispute that there are no market dynamics in religious life. Religious establishments and groups do not live in isolation from the rest of society. Churches often engage in activities that are designed to attract people and to compete with other providers of non-religious activities or, even, other religious establishments and initiatives. Religious practices can indeed be seen as 'commodities' to be advertised and 'enjoyed'. However, this does not necessarily lead to a devaluation of substance, as those who lament marketisation claim, nor does it turn subjects into 'rational' calculating agents, choosing merely what 'suits them most', as RCT proponents suppose. Indeed, self-interested rationality discounts the increasing relevance of moral values in the markets.[5]

The chapter focuses on the assumptions of rational choice theory in relation to self-interest, choice, and rationality, which underpin what I term 'substantial

---

[5] Nico Stehr, *Moral Markets: How Knowledge and Affluence Change Consumers and Producers* (Boulder, CO, 2008); Nico Stehr and Marian Adolf, 'Consumption Between Market and Morals: A Socio-cultural Consideration of Moralized Markets', *European Journal of Social Theory*, 13/2 (2010): 213–28.

commodification'. It includes an analysis of an alternative formulation of RCT,[6] which is more closely connected to Weber's idea of rationality. It then reflects on the dynamics of choice on the basis of the findings from my own ethnographic research in 'Bethlehem', a Christian Evangelical church in Wales. The fieldwork included participant observation and interviews which took place between 2009 and 2011. The selected data consists primarily of public and private speech. This is to underline the actors' reflections on their faith and how they relate faith to their everyday lives. The section on the findings is divided into two parts: the first part interrogates the data which exhibits features that might conform to a rational choice interpretation, and the second part presents data which highlights the meanings of their choices for the actors. The latter proposes a reflection on the relationship between choice and commitment, which takes into consideration how values shape forms of behaviour which override self-interest.

Having provided a critique elsewhere[7] of 'religious capital' or 'spiritual capital, as developed by Iannaccone[8] on the basis of RCT, my reflection here focuses on the notions of choice and commitment as they emerge from the data. By paying closer attention to the actor's intentions, we can begin to appreciate the multidimensional nature of choice. Accordingly, choice cannot be reduced to a mechanical calculation, as espoused by rational choice theorists; rather it is suffused with the actor's cognitive and emotional processes. Thus, the 'voices' of religious actors are here employed to open the door to a deeper understanding of decision-making and faith.

A Critique of Rational Choice Theory

Rational choice theory provides a neat and simple conception of the basic rationale and process of decision-making which human beings apply in their daily lives. The framework seemingly offers a way of understanding behaviour, in particular organisational behaviour, and claims to predict changes in and outcomes of the decision-making of the actors. It is predicated on actors choosing freely an optimal course of action in order to maximise their gain. The essential element of 'maximising behaviour' imputes to actors the fundamental rationale of self-

---

[6] Peter Hedström and Richard Swedberg, 'Rational Choice, Empirical Research and the Sociological Tradition', *European Sociological Review*, 12/2 (1996): 127–46.

[7] Francesca E.S. Montemaggi, 'Misunderstanding Faith: When "Capital" Does Not Fit the "Spiritual"', *International Journal of Interdisciplinary Social Sciences*, 5/5 (2010): 179–92.

[8] Lawrence R. Iannaccone, 'Religious Practice: A Human Capital Approach', *Journal for the Scientific Study of Religion*, 29/3 (1990): 297–314; Lawrence R. Iannaccone, 'The Consequences of Religious Market Structure: Adam Smith and the Economics of Religion', *Rationality and Society*, 3/2 (1991): 156–77; Lawrence R. Iannaccone, 'Introduction to the Economics of Religion', *Journal of Economic Literature*, 36 (1998): 1465–96.

interest. The actor chooses between a set of alternatives. Lack of information does not invalidate the model, as 'an actor will act on the basis of his or her *beliefs* about possible action opportunities and their effects'.[9] The theory is, therefore, aimed at predicting trends resulting from the choices made by a group of individuals.

Rational choice theory assumes that the logic of self-interest applies to all individuals, where differences in values and cultures only count as variables. Accordingly, what an individual values is a mere preference which is to be pursued as a goal within a framework dominated by self-interest. Satz and Ferejohn[10] explain that profit maximisation is 'an externally derived theory of interests',[11] which supplements RCT. Kiser and Hechter,[12] drawing on Weber,[13] recognise that there are non-instrumental orientations, such as 'value-oriented action', 'emotional action' and, also, habitual action. However, when faced with lack of evidence on the action orientation, the assumption is that 'actors are instrumentally oriented. Instrumental action is least ambiguous and therefore most understandable to the analyst, who may not share an emic perspective with her subjects.'[14] The rationale of instrumentality is assumed to be present in all human beings.

There are several problems with these conceptions of choice, instrumentality, and self-interest. In reference to choice, this is reduced to outcome-driven behaviour, which dismisses any other concern of the actor, any dynamic of the group, and any environmental and circumstantial influence. It is a mechanical conception of choice as the outcome of a calculation. Social relations seem to count only as a cultural reference impinging on one's preferences, rather than a continuous dynamic interaction. In reference to instrumentality, rational choice theorists claim that instrumental actions are based on the assumption of the shared 'pursuit of wealth, power, and prestige'.[15] However, the 'pursuit of wealth, power, and prestige' is not a goal-orienting action, but a value.

Consequently, rational choice theorists are not as 'instrumentalist' as they think they are; rather they are disingenuous about the underlying values informing the theory. The self-interest assumed by RCT is not informed by a theory of value. Therefore, it is difficult to understand how actors seek to maximise profit when profit does not equate with money. Further, rational choice theorists, by isolating individuals, prevent any reflection on what can be deemed 'efficient' or 'rational'. Even a consideration of costs and benefits requires an explanation as to what the agent considers a cost and a benefit and how these are balanced. Indeed, actors

---

9 Hedström and Swedberg, 'Rational Choice', 128 (emphasis in the original).

10 Debra Satz and John Ferejohn, 'Rational Choice and Social Theory', *The Journal of Philosophy*, 91/2 (1994): 71–87.

11 Ibid., 87.

12 Edgar Kiser and Michael Hechter, 'The Debate on Historical Sociology: Rational Choice Theory and Its Critics', *The American Journal of Sociology*, 104/3 (1998): 785–816.

13 Max Weber, *The Sociology of Religion* (London: Methuen, 1965 [1922]).

14 Ibid., 801.

15 Ibid., 802.

may choose very destructive and 'irrational' behaviour in order to pursue 'wealth, power, and prestige'.

More significantly, the logic of economic self-interest, here implied, is generalised to all and in all circumstances, given the claims rational choice theorists make to explain the most diverse behaviour in the most disparate situations.[16] Money might make the world go round, but the logic of economic self-interest is but one of many and is not necessarily the dominant logic in human behaviour. It is thus arbitrary to assume that self-interest is the most fundamental motivation in all human beings. Arguably, an actor's pursuit of wealth, power, and prestige could be determined by a deep-seated need for love and longing for human relationships, meaning and purpose in life. Whilst it is difficult and often impossible to establish the underlying motivation for the pursuit of wealth, it is likely to impact on the actors' choices much more than an external and mechanical understanding of rationality.

This is not to dismiss self-interest as a powerful orientation in action; rather it is to appreciate that there are overarching 'logics', including faith, which inform human decision-making. Thus, the sense of belonging to a group will engender a particular type of logic that will affect our interaction with members of the group and our identity. Even instrumental action will be directed by the logic of place, culture, identity, and belief, to name just a few of the possible factors. This is not to be intended in a particularistic fashion, but to include the many factors that will shape how that logic will work in a situation, including psychological mechanisms. For example, the logic of love is not to be thought solely in a sense of rosy, positive and altruistic feeling. Love engenders a logic leading to various dynamics, such as attachment and a diminished self, which can bring out constructive or destructive behaviours. 'Out of love' people kill even the objects of their love. 'Out of love' people endanger or destroy their livelihoods. Actions might still be deemed instrumental, although in a very superficial sense of the word, but not self-interested.

Rational choice theory is heavily biased towards an assumption of self-interest. This is partly mitigated by the consideration of the context of the action. However, an adequate understanding of the societal, cultural and psychological constraints is prevented by the logic of a very narrow rationality. One's identity is not irrational, neither are one's feelings, rather they construct their own logic, rendering the RCT approach hollow. This is not to say that identity and emotions do away with choice; rather that they actively create a worldview in which meaning is ascribed according to values, experience, and individual cognitive processes, not according to utilitarian standards of behaviour. Thus, the French sociologist and rational choice theorist, Raymond Boudon, rejects any idea of RCT providing an explanation for behaviours motivated by beliefs, in particular, non-common place beliefs, non-consequentialist beliefs; and behaviour that is not dictated by self-

---

16 Michael Hechter and Satoshi Kanazawa, 'Sociological Rational Choice Theory', *Annual Review of Sociology*, 23 (1997): 191–214.

interest.[17] Boudon[18] proposes a model of cognitive rationality which includes non-instrumental action; however, such rationality is still deprived of the 'rational' role of emotions[19] and their multifaceted nature.[20]

Finally, rational choice neglects altruistic motivations by giving primacy to self-interested behaviour. Many rational choice theorists seem reluctant to recognise that not all behaviour is motivated by self-interest and adduce the excuse that self-interest should not be confused with selfish interest.[21] However, such a distinction fails to acknowledge altruism, which is by definition not self-interested, let alone selfish. Altruism is simply denied and transformed into 'deferred self-interest',[22] where the altruistic act is performed with the aim of achieving one's own personal gratification. On the contrary, altruism is 'behaviour intended to benefit another, even when doing so may risk or entail some sacrifice to the welfare of the actor'.[23] Monroe stresses the importance of the intentions over the consequences. If an action results in benefit to another, regardless of the actor's motivation, it cannot be considered altruistic.

The Actors' Meaning Making

A perhaps more fundamental problem with RCT is, as mentioned previously, the way in which it effectively insulates the actor from reality whilst claiming superior knowledge of the actor's motives. The theory removes actors from everyday reality, imposing motivations on them that are alien to their way of thinking. It is, of course, reasonable that a social theory should shed light on the mechanisms behind behaviour which might not be fully acknowledged by actors. However, it is difficult to see how this can be applied to allegedly self-interested action and, in particular, motivation. By definition, motivation needs to impel the subject to act in a certain way. Thus, one needs to be aware of one's motivations in order to make a 'choice'. Whilst there may be unconscious or subconscious influences on one's actions, these do not count as 'rational', in RCT terms, for the subject is not aware of them, nor can the subject make a free choice on how to act. After all, the theory is of rational 'choice', but if actors ignore the reasons why they act

---

17 Raymond Boudon, 'Limitations of Rational Choice Theory', *The American Journal of Sociology*, 104/3 (1998): 817–28.

18 Raymond Boudon, 'Beyond Rational Choice Theory', *Annual Review of Sociology*, 29 (2003): 1–21.

19 Martha C. Nussbaum, *Upheavals of Thought: The Intelligence of Emotions* (Cambridge, 2001).

20 Jerome Kagan, *What Is Emotion?* (New Haven, CT, 2007).

21 Hechter and Kanazawa, 'Sociological Rational Choice Theory'.

22 Kristen R. Monroe, 'A Fat Lady in a Corset: Altruism and Social Theory', *American Journal of Political Science*, 38/4 (1994): 861–93.

23 Ibid., 862.

in a certain way, can they still be said to be pursuing profit? Are they exercising choice? Is it still rational behaviour or just 'chance' behaviour? RCT imputes the wrong motives to actors and exercises guesswork rather than analysing the data.

Hedström and Swedberg[24] present an alternative version of rational choice theory that is heavily reliant on Weber's sociology. Here, actors' meanings are factors to compute rather than understand (*Verstehen*). Accordingly, for Hedström and Swedberg, RCT is a mechanism of 'ideal-typical action', based on methodological individualism, to explain 'aggregate social systems'.[25] The ideal type is an abstracted construction modelling action. The interests, beliefs, and opportunities of an actor are elements of the mechanism. They are factors carrying what appears to be the same weight in the 'final calculation' producing action. Such interests, beliefs, and opportunities are decontextualised in the ideal-typical framework.

Hedström and Swedberg refer to situational analysis to 'explicate mechanisms that make individual action *social*, in the Weberian sense of the term. Actions are social when the choice of one actor influences or is influenced by the choices of other actors.'[26] It is true that Weber privileged a rationalistic approach to *Verstehen* that reflected 'purposive-rational action'. However, he recognised the epistemic value of psychological and emotional understanding. Thus, 'the "recapturing"' of an experience (*die Nacherlebbarkeit eines Erlebnisses*) is important for accurate understanding (*Evidenz*), but not an absolute precondition for its interpretation'.[27] Thus, as noted by Harrington, the 'psychological acts of sympathy and imagination could be used to grasp the "artistic" or "emotional" context of action'.[28] This aspect was pivotal to Weber's *Protestant Ethic and the Spirit of Capitalism*.[29] In the *Ethic*, Weber explored the individual subjective processes which are not confined to purposive rationality, as will be examined below.

Finally, this version of rational choice theory, whilst leaving out self-interest as the paramount logic, takes typologies in a non-problematic fashion. Typologies are abstract constructs, which have less to do with the empirical reality they try to explain than with the mind of the social scientist creating them. Yet there is no acknowledgement of the bias and context of rational choice theorists and how these play out on the framework. Indeed, it can be argued that Weber too showed a strong tendency to read phenomena through the lenses of rationalisation. As

---

24 Hedström and Swedberg, 'Rational Choice'.

25 Ibid., 129.

26 Ibid., 134.

27 Max Weber, cited in Austin Harrington, 'Dilthey, Empathy and Verstehen', *European Journal of Social Theory*, 4/3 (2001): 314.

28 Austin Harrington, 'Dilthey', 314.

29 Max Weber, *The Protestant Ethic and the Spirit of Capitalism* (London, 2001 [1905]).

noted by Vandenberghe,[30] for Weber the sociologist has no access to the mind of individuals; therefore, it is necessary to construct an ideal-type of possible meanings that can explain action. However, as the ideal-type stops being a construct for the understanding of motivations and becomes an explanatory device for rational action, meanings are lost and utilitarian logic prevails.

> … [I]t is necessary to construct an ideal-type of the hypothetical meanings or motivations that would explain the observed course of action. … [T]he problem arises when Weber subsequently tends to reduce this understanding of motives to the understanding of purposively rational action (*zweckrationales Handeln*), sliding thus from a hermeneutically sensitive methodological individualism to the purely utilitarian one which is nowadays advocated and promoted by the world-wide movement of the rational choice theorists.[31]

The *Ethic* and *The Sociology of Religion*[32] are far more focused on the actors' subjective processes, including their emotions. The *Ethic* is a classic example, which is often cited and often misunderstood by rational choice theorists. RCT scholars seem to be under the impression that the Protestant believers, Weber discusses in the *Ethic*, are seeking salvation and, thus, engaging in productive work in order to secure it. This understanding turns on its head not only Weber's analysis, but also the fundamental tenet of the Protestant theology of *sola fide*. Protestantism was a reaction to the use of good works and indulgences to secure a place in heaven. The purchase of indulgences and the pursuit of 'good works' would have been much more 'rational' in obtaining salvation. Instead, Potestants believed that they were saved by faith alone, which could not be proven. For Weber, this caused 'salvation anxiety', which influenced the systematic activity in which they engaged.

Rationality, here, clearly does not equate with profit maximisation or even with choosing the course of action that would most likely guarantee a certain outcome, as supposed by rational choice theory; rather it is a methodical procedure. Further, it must be stressed that Weber considered such systematic behaviour to be the unintended consequence of the doctrine of *sola fide*, rather than the result of the intentional, let alone instrumental, action of rational choice theory. Salvation anxiety is thus the unintended consequence which generates systematic behaviour. Such systematic behaviour has an affinity with, but is not parallel to, and certainly has no correspondence in, capitalist activity. It can be argued that Weber's reflections in the *Ethic* and his sociology of world religions do not fit neatly with his wider sociology, especially ideal types. There is undoubtedly room for misunderstanding and picking and choosing according to one's preference and intention. However,

---

[30] Frédéric Vandenberghe, 'Simmel and Weber as Ideal-Typical Founders of Sociology', *Philosophy and Social Criticism*, 25/4 (1999): 57–80.

[31] Ibid., 73.

[32] Weber, *Sociology*.

the brief analysis provided here has highlighted the fundamental distortion of Weber's thesis by rational choice theorists, which no amount of theorising could possibly legitimise.

Weber's approach to the study of religion, and society in general, is ground-breaking for recognising the importance of how individuals interpret and live culture. The diversity of religious behaviour warrants an investigation of the actors' sensings (*Sinn*) of their religious ideas and practices. The *Ethic*, despite its focus on economic behaviour, is a testament to the importance of the meaning-making processes the individual activates. As expressed by Talcott Parsons in his introduction to Weber's *The Sociology of Religion*:

> [t]he central problem was whether men's conceptions of the cosmic universe, including those of Divinity and men's religious interests within such a conceptual framework could influence or shape their concrete actions and social relationships, particularly in the very mundane field of economic action.[33]

Weber highlights the inner dimension of the actor and how this is translated into 'rational', in the sense of methodical, behaviour. His famous method of *Verstehen* – the understanding of human subjectivity and its interpretative role – is central in order to identify what shapes behaviour. Human beings interact with their environments and attribute different meanings to every aspect of life. Therefore, individual consciousness plays an important role in 'translating' ideas about the world into one's relationship to them and one's resulting actions. Weber's attention to subjective processes has been mechanised in rational choice theory, depriving the subject of meaning. Rational choice theory is the best example of what Weber lamented of the modern era: the disenchantment of the world.

For Weber reason had succumbed to mechanistic rationalisation, thus denying freedom. It is, therefore, clear that, contrary to rational choice theorists, Weber was lamenting rationalisation rather than celebrating it. Undoubtedly, he employed an excessively rationalistic methodology; yet, he saw in the disenchantment of the world the demise of ethics, to be confronted and not accepted as inevitable.

> The fate of our times is characterized by rationalization and intellectualization and, above all, by the 'disenchantment of the world'. Precisely the ultimate and most sublime values have retreated from public life either into the transcendental realm of mystic life or into the brotherliness of direct and personal human relations.[34]

---

33 Talcott Parsons, 'Introduction', in Weber, *Sociology* (1965), xxi.

34 Max Weber, 'Science as a Vocation', in Hans Gerth and Charles W. Mills (eds), *From Max Weber: Essays in Sociology* (New York, 1958 [1918]), 155.

Bethlehem Church: Commodification or Commitment?

According to RCT, believers pursue their own self-interest, engaging in religious activities in order to get something back, so to speak. In the words of Iannaccone, believers invest in religious activities to accumulate 'one's stock of religious human capital'.[35] Religious actors spend time and money to increase their familiarity with the religious environment and customs. Below, I present examples from my informants that could be interpreted within the framework of RCT, which is then examined critically. As mentioned previously, the selected data consists of public and private speech collected during participant observation and interviews, as specified in parenthesis at the end of every quote.

Bethlehem Church was established nearly 30 years ago with the intention of giving a community feel to a newly developed area of a city in Wales. The church adheres to a conservative Protestant Trinitarian theology, loosely affiliated to the Baptist tradition, although it requires no strict behavioural codes. When it was first established, the Sunday services were 'seeker services', seeking to communicate the message of Christianity in simple terms to 'non-Christians'. The overarching philosophy was and still is to be a 'welcoming and caring' church. Thus, the 'vision' of the church, as often described by its founding and current Elders, is to provide a community centre to 'meet people's needs', both spiritual and practical. To that end, the church leadership has sought to provide non-religious activities for the local community, including parent and toddler groups, groups for people suffering from a chronic illness, for the elderly, for young people and prayer groups.

'A Church That Fits'

The church has a nursery and a café, where the staff are friendly and always willing to 'have a chat' with customers. Most of the church members live locally, although some choose to travel to Bethlehem from further away. Some of the informants had attended other churches in the past before choosing Bethlehem. Some had even decided to move house to be closer to the church. Many church members had been attracted to the church because of its welcoming atmosphere. Some had developed friendships through making contact with the people in the nursery and the parent and toddler group and later became Christians and joined the church. Dorothea, one informant, said that when her husband went to Bethlehem, he told her that he knew that they would 'fit in this church' (7 August 2009, interview). She added that she felt that it was 'the right place' for her. In interviews and informal conversations, informants described the church as welcoming and that they felt it was their 'home'. Selina, who is a regular attendant of the 'women's prayer group', told me that she likes it because she feels free to share with other women what goes on in her life.

35 Iannaccone, 'Religious Practice', 299.

Rational choice theorists argue that actors choose to 'maximise behaviour'. 'Profit', in this sense, is not necessarily pecuniary; rather it can be emotional. It could thus be argued that members of Bethlehem church are involved in the religious and social activities because they perceive that they will get something in 'return'. Accordingly, 'feeling at home' and friendships are the 'goods' people gain by attending church. In this vein, we could interpret Dorothea's thinking that 'there's a God out there that really cares about me' (7 August 2009, interview), as an emotional 'good', which provides comfort and reassurance. Further, Dorothea, in her interview, contrasted Bethlehem Church with other churches she had attended previously and stated that she felt Bethlehem was the church for her as she felt accepted for who she is. Thus, Bethlehem, by being a 'spiritual home' where everybody is welcomed and where people care for one another, provides a comforting physical and emotional place.

During Nicholas' interview, I asked him – in a spirit of provocation, adopting marketing terms – 'if you were to sell Christianity to non-Christians, what would it be that Christianity offered?' In his reply, he joked about the 'benefits' of Christianity 'from a sales and marketing perspective'. He thought they were 'pretty major'. He said:

> [i]f you do a SWOT analysis, there are pretty major ones, some of them are faith based, like heaven … but also there's the here and now aspect of that as well. There's the whole aspect of quality of life … the characteristics that we would describe as the fruit of the [Holy] Spirit: love, joy and peace, patience and kindness, and goodness and humility, and self-control. (Nicholas, 13 December 2010, interview)

Arguably, Bethlehem 'fits', it is 'the right place' and 'meets people's needs'. It undoubtedly satisfies many of its members' needs. It does not simply provide services but also relationships. The guiding philosophy of the church is explicitly oriented towards meeting the physical and emotional needs of a person.

'Choosing Faith'

Church members, as mentioned previously, have chosen Bethlehem and often preferred it to other churches. They choose to attend without necessarily feeling compelled to do so. They will occasionally miss services, study groups, and social activities with no reproach from the leadership. Further, conscious choice is also believed to be fundamental to embracing a religious life here. Thus, believers are not generally baptised before they reach their teenage years. For my informants, faith is not culture, or something one grows up with, but a conscious decision. Dorothea explained that it is not sufficient to grow up in a culturally Christian country in order to be a Christian.

> I was brought up in a non-Christian home, but my parents sort of thought that to be a Christian you just have to be brought up in a Christian country, 'cos in a lot of faiths that seems to … sometimes it's the case. It seems to be that it's not a conscious decision, but it's like you're brought up with it. (Dorothea, 7 August 2009, interview)

Arguably, the prominence of choice makes 'shopping for a church' more likely in the search for the environment which stimulates one's spiritual development, and emotional and physical needs. Rational choice theorists might argue that Bethlehem members choose the church for its multiple benefits, including a caring community, friendships, and groups for all ages. However, the image of Christian identity that emerges from my fieldwork is multifaceted and does not lend itself to such simplistic interpretations. Accordingly, Dorothea told me how she became a Christian and how she 'realised that it was all about Jesus' and felt that there needed to be a commitment to 'follow Jesus'. Accepting Christianity thus requires a conscious decision, from which commitment arises.

Christianity as Countercultural

My informants contrast the Christian life with 'the world outside' and its 'rationality', which is centred on self-interest. The world outside is experienced as lonely and cold, competitive and harsh. Contemporary society is perceived as, at times, a hostile place, characterised by a loss of morality. Being a Christian, therefore, means challenging the dominant culture. Bethlehem seeks to be the refuge that goes against selfish and empty consumerism. Informants, however, do not withdraw from the 'world'. On the contrary, they are fully and, to an extent, painfully aware that they are part of a materialistic world. Being a follower of Jesus is thus an admonition against selfish and materialistic pursuits and an exhortation to be 'counter what normally happens, the way we normally are' (Arthur, 9 June 2010, home group evening).

> We tend to think that we own what we have … the culture around us tells us so. Materialism is a fundamental part of our society, we are part of society so it affects us … The challenge of the bible is how we deal with our possessions and money. (Arthur, 7 October 2009, home group evening)

> In Western society it's 'what's in it for me?' We move into the upside-down Kingdom [of God] with its upside down values about what I can give back. Society is focused on comfort. (Arthur, 8 July 2009, home group evening)

Religious life is the fruit of a 'personal relationship' with God, which requires a deep commitment and a different way of living. Such way of living is 'countercultural' for it is centred on God and God's will, rather than one's own will. Informants, especially those who became Christians in their teenage years or adulthood, such as Nicholas and Lucy, compared how they used to see religious people as 'loonies' or as members of the 'flat-earth society' when they were non-Christians. Following their conversion, both Nicholas and Lucy came to see reality in a different light and learnt that religious life involved 'listening to God' even when what they heard was in opposition to what they wanted. Christians choose to 'follow Jesus', and this choice engenders a duty. Choice is thus not opposed to duty, but is the source of duty.

The duty of 'being a Christian', in Bethlehem, is understood as being 'countercultural'. The Christianity, my informants espouse, is primarily a challenge to contemporary culture, a challenge to themselves in their daily lives, and also to the 'world-friendly church' and to the 'traditional church'. Churches which do not challenge the cultural norms outside their doors, or that do not demand commitment are seen as 'world-friendly' for they provide comfort but lack obligation. However, churches that are not inclusive are disparaged as a 'holy huddle', which erects barriers separating church members from the outside. Bethlehem church is not 'strict', yet core members feel that being a Christian requires a continuous effort to make 'the presence of God' felt. As Nicholas also put it:

> We try to live our lives almost as if we weren't Christians, you know, not really following Christ, not really living as his disciples, where belief is almost second-hand. 'I believe you for my heaven, but I'm not sure about finding you down here', you know (Nicholas laughs). That's where we've done a disservice to the gospel. (Nicholas, 13 December 2010, interview).

Choosing Commitment

The believer chooses God. This choice engenders commitment and, consequently, duty. By choosing God, the believer establishes a 'personal relationship' with God, which, in turn, calls on the believer to 'answer' God. In this case study, believers respond by seeking to 'be like Jesus', to live differently, the way Jesus would live. This relationship and this response create a religious perspective from which the believer views the world. The initial choice thus becomes a commitment to 'live differently' and be in accordance with 'God's will' by following the 'upside down' logic of faith as it is understood by the community of believers. However, whilst commitment might have originated in an autonomous choice, the 'personal relationship with God' transforms that choice into dependence on God. In other words, believers choose to commit, but in doing so, they create a bond with the overarching authority of God.

During the 'women's prayer group', one of the participants commented that prayer is about 'handing it over to God rather than clinging onto the problem'. Prayer is asking God to manifest God's will. This requires trust in God and, therefore, acceptance of God's will, even when it seems to be against one's own perceived interests or what is considered 'rational' in the general culture one inhabits.

> When we ask for revelation from God, we need to be prepared to deal with what comes from it. (3 July 2009, women's prayer group).

> Will: make yourself open to the answer you don't want. (25 November 2009, home group evening)

This dependence on God does not mean that the person abdicates any responsibility over her actions; rather action is seen as evidence of the relationship with God. Believers are also conscious of finding difficult to understand what God 'says' and of 'getting it wrong'. More importantly, 'following Jesus' does not simply mean leading a moral life, but listening to God's voice, doing what one is called to do, serving even when one does not realise that one is serving, as in the example given by Dorothea (7 August 2009, interview) recounting how she helped someone in difficulty 'just by being there'. At that time, she 'did not realise' that she was serving, and that her being there for her friend was part of God's plan. She felt surprised that God could 'really use someone who is so insignificant in the grand scheme of things' and 'has so little life experience'. In viewing one's life as meaningful, even 'in the grand scheme of things', one stresses the relationship with God. This could be interpreted as a hierarchical relationship imposing set duties and requiring the submission of the believer. However, my informants suggest a much more volitional approach. One's behaviour is not the result of a moral injunction, but it is the response of serving 'out of love', rather than looking to 'earn points'.

Behind choice and commitment is religiosity. To be able to choose God, one needs faith. However, religiosity needs to be understood not as a specific belief or dogma, but as an attitude, a feeling of trust towards God and dependence on God. This conceptualisation of religiosity cannot be explored here. It suffices to note that it is not an adjunct or a preference, but an overarching logic, which has a cognitive and affective dimension. Religiosity is relational, linking the believer to God and to other believers, and colouring the believers' relationship with the world around. Accordingly, religiosity engenders a logic which affects thinking and behaviour.

Most importantly, religiosity imposes a degree of heteronomy. It does not necessarily do away with autonomy, but it makes autonomy dependent on a higher authority and enmeshes it with other believers and other relationships. Thus, the religious actor is never 'alone'. In deciding what to do, the religious actors' estimation of 'costs and benefits' does not simply rely on an 'objective' and external assessment of actions, even if the decision is based on theology rather than self-interest, but a constant battle within themselves trying to discern what God requires of them. The role of sacrifice, no matter its degree, is something of importance in religious life, although, as Nicholas comments, 'most of us shy away from ultimately carrying around the cross' (13 December 2010, interview).

In conclusion, the data show that choice is fundamental to the pursuit of a committed religious life. Indeed, it is from choice that commitment arises. Such commitment imposes an element of heteronomy, of an external authority (God) as sovereign over one's life; or, at least, of a diminished autonomy. God is seen as being in relationship with believers. Thus, God's authority, whilst supreme, requires believers to exercise their cognitive and affective faculties in order to discern God's will. It is this committed relationship that is 'salvation'; 'that is the eternal life today … the result of the [Holy] Spirit living in your life' (Nicholas, 13 December 2010, interview).

Conclusions

It has been argued that the marketisation and commodification of religious practices, beliefs, and symbols does not necessarily lead to a loss of their value or 'authenticity'. It is to be acknowledged that some people will engage in religious practices superficially: however, this is a personal response. It is, by contrast, the application of a narrow utilitarian logic that trivialises and devalues religious life. Thus, the assumption made by rational choice theorists that religious actors choose out of 'rational self-interest' to 'maximise their benefits' commodifies religion by imposing a utilitarian value-system on actors. RCT seeks to stress the notion of the individual as a free agent, choosing rationally. However, by reducing actors to calculating subjects seeking profit, it embraces the unquestioned mentality of the 'money economy'.[36] Thus, far from being neutral, it projects its own assumptions about being human and about social relations onto social reality. This interpretation of human beings as calculating machines ultimately fails to grasp the complexity of human nature and human behaviour.

Paradoxically, RCT can interpret religious action, as the rational pursuit of self-interest by freely choosing actors, only by discounting the actors' rationales for their choices. It theorises on the 'product' in terms of its outside package rather than its content. Judging from 'the outside', looking at the package, religious forms might look like commodities. However, the 'formal commodification' of religion does not imply 'substantial commodification', or loss of value. Miller[37] argues that the marketisation of religion is turning religious forms into products, detached from their original religious meanings. This account of neoliberalism is rather mechanistic and deterministic. It presumes, rather dubiously, that nothing like this ever happened before industrialisation. More importantly it suggests that changes in form affect the substance irremediably and inevitably. Thus, the marketisation

[36] Georg Simmel, *The Philosophy of Money* (3rd enlarged edition, London, 2004 [1900]).

[37] Miller, *Consuming Religion.*

of religion is bound to devalue substance, making it empty and 'inauthentic'. This 'alarmism' about religious symbols and practices being used and 'abused' through the 'profane' process of marketisation highlights the assumption that there are 'authentic' and inauthentic' forms for the expression or worship of the 'sacred'. Should Gregorian chant thus be confined strictly to a religious setting in order for it not to be devalued? Or should we not be asking, instead, whether Gregorian chant is still relevant to the twenty-first century's religious life?

The distinction proposed between 'formal commodification' and 'substantial commodification' questions the inevitability of the devaluation of substance by marketisation. Intangible values and human emotions are not quantifiable; they need to be attended to and understood within their framework of values. They will thus give the observer a glimpse into the substance. The attractiveness of rational choice theory lies in the importance that it gives to choice. In liberal Western democracies, choice lies at the basis of religiosity, including traditional religiosity.[38] However, choice is not the simple notion rational choice theorists expound, but a complex, meaning-making process. The case study presented here shows that religious people choose, but they choose commitment. Commitment is not a mere preference, but depends on value.[39] Religion seeks to go to the heart of what it means to be human. Accordingly, salvation is not just about heaven, or reward and punishment; rather it is 'what life is about'. Religious people seek the 'meaning of life', the 'purpose of life', something that is 'authentic' in the sense of capturing the essence of life and of being human. So, as I walked out of a supermarket, a Muslim man was handing out leaflets and 'advertising' his faith inviting the passer-by to 'know the purpose of life'.

---

38 Stuart Z. Charmé, 'Varieties of Authenticity in Contemporary Jewish Identity', *Jewish Social Studies*, 6/2 (2000): 133–55.

39 Charles Taylor, *Sources of the Self: The Making of the Modern Identity* (Cambridge, 1989).

PART II
Commoditised Spiritualities

New Religious Movements, New Age and many new, not-so-new and alternative spiritualities have commonly been viewed as more related to consumer society than the traditional religions discussed in the previous section. This section continues to discuss the relationship of spiritualities to consumerism, by adding to the conceptualisation of commoditisation begun in the previous section and by highlighting more of the paradoxical and complex rapports between consumerism and religious phenomena.

Andrew Dawson tackles the issue from the perspective of a particularly well-developed and synthetic account of the individualisation thesis by discussing the commoditisation of religion in 'entangled' modernity within the 'new, globalised middle class', showing how the logics hinted at in this volume are affecting not only Western but also Westernised countries through a focus on the Brazilian case, where the individual-centred life of the new middle class appears to be shaped by consumption and aesthetic experiences within an array of customised, yet constantly changing lifestyles. The merging of the roles of the consumer and the producer into that of a 'prosumer' creates a type of personhood in which an individual becomes the product of his own making through the consumption of religious symbols, practices, and experiences.

François Gauthier adds to the discussion initiated in the introduction on the processes of commoditisation and the ways in which consumerism enacts a new form of cultural regulation. Through the case study of the annual Burning Man Festival, which coalesces many strands of Western counter-cultures in a vibrant, gift-economy-fuelled potlatch of self-expression, community, and self-reliance, Gauthier challenges neoclassical economic theoretical accounts of consumption and shows the multiple and paradoxical ways in which religion is shaped by consumerism and how consumerism in turn strives to turn brands into religious cults. Religion does not sprout out of the cracks of a disenchanted world, nor is it reified through a commoditisation process that comes from without. Rather, consumer capitalism thrives on its enchantments, while religious forms are increasingly, and inherently, commoditised in consumer societies.

John S. McKenzie studies the commoditisation of Rokpa, a Tibetan Buddhist organisation, in Scotland. McKenzie argues that Rokpa has reacted to the pressures of consumer society through the institutionalisation of differentiated levels of membership. Only the most committed, core members have full access to all the teachings and traditions, whereas the more occasional visitor is set to encounter a more customer-friendly, religio-spiritual movement which caters to the ambient quest and wellbeing culture through a host of courses, therapies, and other services. The example of Rokpa shows the strenuous exigencies of contemporary spirituality, which must find a balance between the need to attract a wider public and survive financially while maintaining authenticity.

Lars Ahlin discusses the *a priori* surprising place given to New Age practices and ideologies in the course of the 1980s in the pages of the Swedish newspaper *Svenska Dagsbladet*, which was at that time also the voice calling for neoliberalism-inspired economic reforms. While the early New Age movement espoused non-materialistic values and worldviews, Ahlin argues that the mainstreaming of the movement annulled the anti-consumer capitalist critique of New Age while allowing for a more radically individualised, prosperity-oriented nebula to develop. This possibility, Ahlin argues, existed inchoately within New Age, through its emphasis on the individual, its critique of hierarchical authority, its calls for personal responsibility, and so forth, all of which are largely in tune with neoliberal principles. As the ethics of Protestantism functioned to legitimise the birth of industrial capitalism, so did those of New Age function to legitimise neoliberalism and consumerism in the pages of this influential newspaper.

Anne-Christine Hornborg extends the previous case study by looking at the more contemporary successes of neospiritual therapies and personal coaching in Sweden. Hornborg argues that therapy and coaching are to an extent relocating traditional religious services into a new framework which is oriented towards personal wellbeing and success. The therapists and coaches aim at empowering the individuals by helping their clients 'reach their full potential'. These phenomena which lie at the intersection between religion, economics, and wellbeing promote ideologies that are founded in a neoliberal anthropology (that of a *homo oeconomicus*) whose finalities are described in terms of personal success and entrepreneurialism. Yet the bottom line of these practices is profitability rather than true personal accomplishment, as responsibility for an eventual failure is that of the individual, not that of the coach, therapist, or technique.

Marion Bowman discusses the processes of commoditisation and consumption in the English town of Glastonbury. The complex history of Glastonbury as Christian pilgrimage locus, then its rise as the heartland of New Age spiritualities in England, provides a formidable case study in which to analyse the effects of spiritualities and religion on the economies of the high street, as well as the impact of marketisation on those very spiritualities and the tensions between authenticity and financial sustainability in consumer capitalist societies. Describing the historical formation of Glastonbury's spiritual service economy and presenting the views of entrepreneurs, citizens, and spiritual 'consumers', Bowman concludes that for many service providers their work is part of a spiritual path by which they contribute to the value of Glastonbury as a religious centre.

Chapter 7

Entangled Modernity and Commodified Religion: Alternative Spirituality and the 'New Middle Class'

Andrew Dawson

Introduction

Although noted by various studies, the prevalence of the urban-industrial professional classes within contemporary non-mainstream and alternative religiosities has remained relatively undeveloped.[1] This chapter goes some way to rectifying this oversight by drawing upon research with non-mainstream religions and alternative spiritualities in Brazil, Europe, and North America.[2] While so doing, this chapter also engages a problematic which concerns the manner and extent to which theories and concepts used to explicate social (and, by extension, religious) change in one part of the world might be considered relevant to elucidating socio-religious transformations in other regions of the globe. As will be evident in what follows, my response to this issue is qualifiedly positive, assuming that one speaks only of particular (here, 'modern') regions which, by virtue of their shared ('entangled') modernities, allow theories and concepts originating in one socio-cultural domain to be applied to other areas of the world.

What follows unites a response to this particular problematic with an exploration of the implications of the urban professional character of many new religious phenomena. As such, this chapter combines the following three arguments. First, it is argued, irrespective of nationality or regional status, the majority of those involved in non-mainstream and alternative religiosities share – by virtue of their late modern, urban professional character – a similar ('entangled') life experience.

1 For example, Lorne Dawson, *Comprehending Cults: The Sociology of New Religious Movements* (Toronto, 1998); Paul Heelas, *The New Age Movement: The Celebration of the Self and the Sacralization of Modernity* (Oxford, 1996); José Magnani, *O Brasil da Nova Era* (Rio de Janeiro, 2000).

2 For example, Andrew Dawson, *New Era – New Religions: Religious Transformation in Contemporary Brazil* (Aldershot, 2007) and *Santo Daime: A New World Religion* (London, 2013).

Second, the shared life experience of the majority of those involved in non-mainstream and alternative religiosity permits a meaningful degree of common analysis and collective theorisation which applies to the group as a whole (as a single unit of analysis). Third, this chapter argues that the contemporary dynamics of commodification are a central component of the shared repertoire of beliefs and practices to which the common life experience of urban professional, non-mainstream religionists gives rise.

Whose Modernity?

Recent debates around secularisation have perhaps done most within the sociology of religion to problematise the relevance of theories formulated in one socio-cultural context for explicating developments in another. Sensitised to the dangers of uncritical theoretical generalisation from one modern context to another, it is increasingly commonplace for academics of religion to mobilise the concept of 'multiple modernities'.[3] Popularised by Shmuel Eisenstadt, the 'multiple modernities' thesis rejects what it regards as the argument for 'the convergence of industrial societies' implicit within 'classical theories of modernisation' and 'sociological analysis'.[4] Subsequent to the mid-twentieth century, Eisenstadt argues, the globalisation of modern processes and dynamics has engendered 'multiple institutional and ideological patterns' in a manner which refutes 'the homogenising and hegemonic assumptions' of classical approaches along with their theoretical association of modernisation with Westernisation. Consequently, while Western modes of modernity both 'enjoy historical precedence and continue to be a basic reference point for others … [o]ne of the most important implications of the term "multiple modernities" is that modernity and Westernization are not identical'. In sum, 'Western patterns of modernity are not the only "authentic" modernities' available for concrete societal expression.[5]

Seeking to highlight the theoretical implications of the inherent variegation of modern social formations for academic understandings of religion, the intentions of those employing the 'multiple modernities' thesis are unqualifiedly laudable. Unfortunately, however, while the emphasis upon socio-cultural difference has successfully hit its mark, an unintended consequence has been the now pervasive failure to pay serious attention to the theoretical implications of the structural processes, institutional dynamics, and socio-cultural characteristics which modern

---

3 For example, Willfried Spohn, 'Multiple Modernity, Nationalism and Religion: A Global Perspective', *Current Sociology*, 51/3–4 (2003): 265–86; Serif Mardin, *Religion, Society and Modernity in Turkey* (Syracuse, NY, 2006); Peter Berger, Grace Davie and Effie Fokas, *Religious America, Secular Europe? A Theme and Variations* (Aldershot, 2008), 1–7.

4 Shmuel Eisenstadt, 'Multiple Modernities', *Daedalus*, 129/1 (2000): 1–29.

5 Ibid., 1–29.

societies, by virtue of being 'modern', hold in common. In effect, both within and outwith the academic study of religion, there has been too much emphasis upon the differences implied by the 'multiple' and insufficient attention to the shared features implicated in the 'modern'.

The erosion of the analytical purchase of the concept of modernity inherent within the 'multiple modernities' paradigm and the work of those who employ it to treat religion can be rectified without returning to the kind of problematical universalising mentioned above. While the 'alternative modernities'[6] and 'varieties of modernity'[7] approaches offer constructive alternatives, I wish here to use the notion of 'entangled modernity' formulated by those articulating the 'cosmopolitan modernities' paradigm.[8] The 'cosmopolitan modernities' approach, it is argued, avoids the dual dangers of methodological 'nationalism' (also termed 'provincialism') – of which the 'multiple modernities' thesis is commonly accused – and methodological 'universalism'. On the one hand, the traditionally dominant methodological universalism has involved the uncritical transposition of Eurocentric theories and concepts which has resulted in the imposition of analytical models and critiques unsuited to non-European contexts. On the other hand, however, the unqualified avowal of socio-cultural difference espoused by methodological provincialism underwrites an assumed incommensurability between different societal contexts which unduly delimits proper consideration of actual shared processes and dynamics.

'Methodological cosmopolitanism' avoids the theoretical pitfalls of these two extremes by distinguishing between what it calls the 'basic principles' and the 'basic institutions' of modernity. The former term refers to the range of 'structural and organisational' processes and dynamics which, by virtue of its definition, are foundational characteristics of modern society. Where these basic principles are in evidence, 'modern' society – as opposed to 'traditional', 'pre-modern', or 'post-modern' forms – can be said to exist. As noted below, the processes of structural differentiation, socio-cultural pluralisation, and individualisation may be considered among the 'basic principles' of modernity and thereby among the defining features of modern society. Whereas these macro-processes are to be found in every modern society, the ways in which they are institutionally realised may differ from one modern society to another. The 'basic institutions' of modernity are thereby varied as different modern societies actualise foundational processes such as individualisation through a variety of – sometimes contrasting

[6] For example, Dilip P. Gaonkar, 'On Alternative Modernities', in Dilip P. Gaonkar (ed.), *Alternative Modernities* (London, 2001), 1–23.

[7] Volker H. Schmidt, 'Multiple Modernities or Varieties of Modernity?', *Current Sociology*, 54/1 (2006): 77–97.

[8] Ulrich Beck and Natan Sznaider, 'Unpacking Cosmopolitanism for the Social Sciences: A Research Agenda', *British Journal of Sociology*, 57/1 (2006): 1–23; Ulrich Beck and Edgar Grande, 'Varieties of Second Modernity: The Cosmopolitan Turn in Social and Political Theory and Research', *British Journal of Sociology*, 61/3 (2010): 409–43.

– political, legal and economic institutional arrangements. While the foundational processes of modernity (for example, individualisation) remain the same from one modern society to another, the manner of their institutional configuration (in the field of political and legal rights for example) may differ from one social context to the next.

The notion of 'entangled modernity' involves three assertions of immediate relevance to this chapter. First, it is asserted that many of the processes of modernisation currently at play across the globe are – owing both to historical origins and more recent formations – of a 'transnational' or 'border transcending' character. In so being, the cosmopolitan dynamics of existing modernisation processes comprise a 'dynamic intermingling and interaction between societies', the 'interconnectedness' of which constitutes a form of 'entanglement'. Such entanglement plays out across established national borders and traditional cultural boundaries through shared ('entangled') modern processes which manifest in every dimension of society. Second, while the degree of interconnectedness and extent of any entanglement inevitably differs from one group of societies to the next, it is argued that some modern societies share intertwined historical paths or intermingling contemporary relations which result in a heightened level of both structural and socio-cultural embroilment. By virtue of their intensified interrelations and greater degrees of modern entanglement, those societies in the latter group most easily allow for an inclusive theorisation which aims to identify, analyse, and interpret shared features and common transformations which, allowing for caveats and qualifications, transcend traditional societal boundaries.

Third, it is argued that – typically since the 1950s – a radicalised form of modernity has been emerging at various points across the globe. In recent decades, the notion that modernity has entered a new phase of its existence has become increasingly prevalent through the application of prefixes such as 'late', 'hyper', 'liquid', and 'second'.[9] By talking of 'second' (Beck), 'liquid' (Bauman) or 'late' (Giddens) modernity, social theorists argue that certain modern societies have, over the course of recent decades, experienced a significant radicalisation of their overarching macro-structural dynamics, mid-range institutional processes, and everyday micro-social interactions. While the 'basic principles' of modernity remain in force, their transformation has resulted in a radicalised form of society which remains thoroughly modern, but even more so.[10]

Bringing these three assertions together – and allowing for varied historical trajectories – I wish to argue that the societies of Brazil, North America, and Western Europe (or, more accurately, sections thereof) today share an entangled, late modernity which has proved particularly conducive to the emergence, consolidation, and spread of non-mainstream and alternative religiosities.

[9] For example, Zygmunt Bauman, *Liquid Life* (Cambridge, 2005); Ulrich Beck, Anthony Giddens and Scott Lash, *Reflexive Modernization: Politics, Tradition and Aesthetics in the Modern Social Order* (Cambridge, 1994).

[10] Beck and Grande, 'Varieties of Second Modernity'.

Furthermore, I also wish to assert that these particular religious phenomena are overwhelmingly populated by urban professionals whose origins and ethos are intimately connected with that of entangled late modernity. In addition, I wish to assert that as a consequence of their entangled, late modern, urban professional existence – and irrespective of nationality or regional status – the majority of those involved in alternative and non-mainstream religiosities share a range of common concerns and aspirations which both permits a meaningful degree of inclusive theorisation and exhibits a steadfastly commodified character.

Entangled Late Modernity and the 'New Middle Class'

Prior to engaging the religio-spiritual repertoire of the urban professional classes who make up the bulk of alternative religious practitioners – and not least by way of contextualisation – something will now be said of the entangled, late modern, socio-cultural terrain within which this repertoire was first seeded and subsequently took root. Through a series of broad brushstrokes, this section outlines what are here regarded as the foundational processes ('basic principles', if you will) and attendant socio-cultural dynamics of the entangled, late modern, urban professional context within which alternative religiosity has made its home.

The entangled late modernity addressed here is constituted, first and foremost, by a *market-orchestrated*, *urban-industrial* and *techno-scientific* complex underwritten by structural and social *integration*. Orchestrated by the imperatives of a market economy, modern society typically concentrates a substantial majority of its population (or 'workforce') within urban environments facilitating industrial and technologically driven modes of profit-oriented and competition-driven production. Though characterised by agricultural production, even rural parts of the modern landscape are oriented to meeting the needs of the conurbations they serve. The linkage of urban and rural production is characteristic of modernity's integrative tenor. In structural terms, modern societies are characterised by the universal, and usually centralised, application of political, legal, economic, educational and, at times, linguistic processes which impact upon all aspects of life. Structural integration is facilitated through infrastructural networks of transport (including road, rail, and air) and communication (for example mail, telephone, and satellite). The social integration characteristic of modernity arises directly from the processes and networks of structural integration. Catalysed by the dynamics of urbanisation and modern economic production, social integration is further enhanced by virtue of the modern individual's increased interaction with and mutual reliance upon an extended web of other human beings – both known and unknown. From basic goods (food, clothing, and shelter), through institutional encounters (such as education, work, and leisure) to mediated interaction (for example radio, television, and the internet), the average member of modern society both interacts with and relies upon a vast array of integrated networks and those who populate them. In socio-cultural terms, the shared ('common') knowledge which underwrites this diffuse interdependence is infused by a sense of the world and its nature as mutable and thereby pliant to human endeavour. Furthermore, the techno-scientific developments upon which late modern society rests enable the enjoyment and cultivation of lifestyles whose practices and values transcend pre-modern preoccupations with the pursuit and securing of the basic goods of material survival.

Realised through the process of *differentiation*, the typically complex nature of late modern society is characterised by *structural variegation* and *socio-cultural plurality*. In structural terms, modern society has an almost vertiginous number of processes, mechanisms, and institutions through which the day-to-day activities of its members occur. Be they economic, political, legal, employment-related, educational, recreational, communal, or familial, the structures of modern society are numerous, variegated, and highly specialised. At the same time, modern society exhibits a socio-cultural variety unprecedented in human history. On the one hand, social pluralisation occurs in response to structural differentiation, as the variegated kinds of societal structures engender progressively diverse life experiences for the different groups who populate the increasingly varied parts of the social system. The increased number of 'social categories', 'status groups', or 'classes' evident in modern society reflects its structural complexity. On the other hand, social differentiation occurs through domestic and transnational migration, as different socio-cultural groups move – or are moved – from one place to another. The subsequent interaction of different social, racial, ethnic and linguistic groups further enhances the socially plural character of modern society. Although its implications are disputed, most social scientists agree that the process of societal differentiation involves the *relativisation* of established knowledge, belief and value systems. Coupled with the increased presence of previously unavailable practices and symbols, the relativisation of existing repertoires wrought by socio-cultural pluralisation facilitates the construction of new and hybrid forms of practical knowledge.

The process and consequences of societal differentiation are reinforced by late modern society's characteristically *constant*, *rapid* and *far-reaching transformation* at both structural and social levels. In combination, the imperatives of urban-industrial and techno-scientific development involve ongoing revisions of economic, political, legal and educational structures to manage, if not keep pace with, the scale and rapidity of contemporary change. In socio-cultural terms, the swift and widespread transformation typical of modernity fundamentally alters the hold which established traditions and practices are able to exert. Exacerbated by the rapid, large-scale and continued uprooting (*disembedding*) and formation (*re-embedding*) of practical knowledge systems, the process of *detraditionalisation* undermines the authority and hold of inherited forms of practice, knowledge, belief, and morality. At the same time, the flipside of the erosive dynamics of detraditionalisation involves the formation of new traditions (*retraditionalisation*), albeit ones of a less permanent and all-embracing nature.

In contrast to what has gone before, late modern society is typically *oriented to the individual*. Comprising a diverse range of collective institutions and identities through which human life plays out (for example family, class, religion, sex, and race), modern society is characterised by a weakening of the influence they have traditionally exerted over the individual. Born through the combination of aforementioned dynamics, the limitation of collective determination wrought by the modern process of *individualisation* furnishes the individual with an enhanced degree of personal choice and expression. On the one hand, the erosion of collective determination manifests through an increased level of socio-cultural *mobility*, as the late modern individual enjoys newfound latitude in, for example, matters of education, employment, leisure, and personal relationships. On the other hand, the dynamics of individualisation engender enhanced degrees of *subjective expression*, exhibited through broadened repertoires of, for example, sexuality, belief, and lifestyle (for example self-presentation, diet, and patterns of consumption).

Among the processes which perhaps best express and contribute to the emergence of late modernity, those of *globalisation* and *commoditisation* are in the fore. While the growth of international exchange has been integral to the rise of modern society – not least in respect of trade and workforce migration – the recent intensification of transnational processes is such that the term *globalisation* has been coined to signal a hyper-modern step change. The techno-scientific advances of the late modern period (including travel, communications, and information technology) enable the rapid and large-scale circulation of material goods, people, information, tastes, values, and beliefs. Exemplified by recent financial crises and subsequent global slumps, such is the nature of this worldwide circulation that domestic structures and socio-cultural dynamics are now inextricably interwoven within a highly integrated network of transnational processes and flows. In the same vein, whereas market-orchestrated consumption has long been an important component of modern society, recent developments – not least the dominance and spread of the late capitalist, neoliberal paradigm – have radicalised established commercial processes and consumerist tendencies. Within late modern society, consumption is no less – indeed, in some contexts it is more – important than production. As Zygmunt Bauman argues, the *commoditisation* of modernity has produced a 'society of consumers' in which 'consumerism' dominates as 'the *principal propelling and operating force*' through which 'systemic reproduction, social integration, social stratification and the formation of individuals … and group self-identification' are coordinated. As society is commoditised, human existence is *commodified* to the extent that '*everyone* needs to be, ought to be, must be a consumer-by-vocation'.[11]

The globalising structures and commoditising dynamics which combine with established processes to constitute the contemporary realities of entangled late modernity are perhaps best conceptualised as forming a worldwide and rapidly

[11] Zygmunt Bauman, *Consuming Life* (Cambridge, 2008), 28, 53–5.

evolving network characterised by rapid and large-scale flows. On the one hand, entangled late modernity unfolds through the establishment of economic, legal, political, ethical and aesthetic structures and institutions which connect localities and regions to a seemingly limitless number of otherwise disparate locations. On the other hand, this increasingly worldwide network enables the flow of goods, people, information, power, tastes, and values, the transmission of which occurs at a scale and speed bordering on the vertiginous. In combination, the global connections and the worldwide flows they enable both reflect and contribute to the ongoing radicalisation of entangled late modernity and the human subjects whose behaviour, beliefs, and values it encompasses.

The 'New Middle Class'

As noted above, I contend that the urban middle-classes who populate non-mainstream and alternative religiosities are of a quintessentially entangled, late modern provenance. Born of aforementioned processes and their radicalisation under late modern conditions, the urban professional classes of which I speak have been variously designated as the 'new professions', 'new *petite bourgeoisie*', and 'new cultural intermediaries',[12] 'new class',[13] 'knowledge class',[14] 'emergent' and 'service class',[15] '(new) new middle', 'transformed' and 'post-industrial middle class',[16] and, most popularly, the 'new middle class'.[17] Allied to the post-1950s' expansion of the state apparatus, the technologisation of private commerce, the growth of the culture industry, and rise of the service sector, the new middle class is chiefly employed in administrative bureaucracy and management, communications

---

12 For example, Pierre Bourdieu, *Distinction: A Social Critique of the Judgement of Taste* (London, 1984).

13 For example, Ronald Inglehart, *Culture Shift in Advanced Industrial Society* (Princeton, NJ, 1990).

14 For example, Peter Berger, *The Capitalist Revolution: Fifty Propositions about Prosperity, Equality, and Liberty* (New York, 1988).

15 For example, Scott Lash and John Urry, *The End of Organized Capitalism* (Cambridge, 1987).

16 Scott Lash, 'Reflexivity and Its Doubles: Structure, Aesthetics, Community', in Ulrich Beck, Anthony Giddens and Scott Lash, *Reflexive Modernization: Politics, Tradition and Aesthetics in the Modern Social Order* (Cambridge, 1994), 110–73.

17 For example, Hans-Georg Betz, 'Postmodernism and the New Middle Class', *Theory, Culture and Society*, 9 (1992): 93–114; Michael Featherstone, *Consumer Culture and Postmodernism* (2nd edition, London, 2007); Alexandre Guerra, Marcio Pochmann, Ricardo Amorim and Ronnie Silva, *Classe Média: Desenvolvimento e Crise. Atlas da Nova Estratificação Social no Brasil* (São Paulo, 2006), vol. 1; Martyn Lee, *Consumer Culture Reborn: The Cultural Politics of Consumption* (London, 1993).

and information technology, education, health and research, and sundry provision of cultural goods, capital services, and immaterial commodities.[18]

Perhaps embodying the archetypal late modern experience, the repertoire of those belonging to the new middle class exhibits a range of practices, beliefs, and values which reflect the conditions of radicalised modernity under which it has been forged. Virtually inseparable from the late modern culture industry with which it has grown up, the worldview of the new middle class is imbued with a liberal-capitalist mindset and its commoditised articulation of aspirational and meritocratic preoccupations. Assured of its place in the late modern firmament, the new middle class is expectant of its share of the benefits of modernity and by no means shy of complaining when they do not prove forthcoming. Late modernity's natural and social environment is perceived as pliant to human endeavour and – all being as it should – amenable to giving up at least the equivalent of the energies expended in mastery and extraction. This expectation extends as much to the self and the human body as it does to the world outside.

A scion of societal differentiation and the informational age, socio-cultural pluralism and value relativity come naturally to the new middle class. Difference and ambiguity are likewise well tolerated. Formed in the midst of rapid and widespread social transformations, subjective identity is fluid and decentred, and likewise marked by a tendency to eclecticism and openness to, if not a penchant for, the exotic. Although fluid and decentred, the sensibility of the new middle class is by no means directionless or haphazard. Not least owing to its socio-economic status, enhanced educational capital, and informed worldview, this sensibility is endowed with a highly reflexive character.[19] For the new middle class, reflexivity comprises a strategic and self-aware instrumentality through which its practical and symbolic repertoire is enacted. On the one hand, this well-honed reflexivity informs a collective positional awareness *vis-à-vis* other groups occupying the late modern landscape and is characterised by the comparative dynamics of association, dissociation, and 'distinction'.[20] On the other hand, reflexivity manifests through the subjective dynamics of strategic self-presentation through which practical and symbolic resources are appropriated in the cause of personal development (*ad intra*) and individual advancement (*ad extra*) – these often being regarded as two sides of the same coin.

The individualised character of the new middle class engenders a mobile, expressive and self-oriented demeanour. Informed by the above, the combination of these individualistic characteristics is actualised through the unremitting and eclectic pursuit of aesthetic satisfaction, intellectual gratification, and psychophysical stimulation which finds its greatest pleasures in the new, different,

---

18 For a detailed examination of the history and treatment of the term 'new middle class', see Arthur Vidich (ed.), *The New Middle Classes: Life-Styles, Status Claims and Political Orientations* (New York, 1995).

19 Beck, Giddens and Lash, *Reflexive Modernization.*

20 Bourdieu, *Distinction.*

and exotic. Relativising long-term relationships, exclusive commitments and extrinsic authorities, the new middle-class is a late modern transient *par excellence*. Permanently under construction, new middle-class identity is forged as a customised lifestyle and stage-managed presentation. This understanding of the self as project is manifest through a 'stylistic self-consciousness' and 'aestheticisation of the body'[21] which valorises inner feelings and emotions, yet demands outer expression and public exhibition. By no means averse to social agitation or collective action, the 'politics of the first person' is that which most readily stirs the innards of the new middle class.[22]

Indicative of its commodified worldview, the act of consumption serves as a fundamental marker of the identity and self-esteem of the new middle class.[23] The culture of consumption central to new-middle-class identity denotes, according to Slater, 'a social arrangement in which the relation between lived culture and social resources, between meaningful ways of life and the symbolic and material resources on which they depend, is mediated through markets'.[24] Indeed, argues Slater, the all-embracing character of the late modern market entails that 'values from the realm of consumption spill over into other domains of social action, such that modern society is *in toto* a consumer culture, and not just in its specifically consuming activities'.[25] Echoing Slater's view on the all-embracing nature of consumer culture, Lury maintains that its infiltration of the 'economic', 'social', 'domestic' and 'psychological' levels of everyday life is such that 'it affects the construction of identities, the formation of relationships and the framing of events'.[26]

The 'consumer', Sassatelli argues, functions within late modern society as a '*normative cultural identity*'.[27] As such, consumer culture is about more than 'commoditization and affluence' or 'conspicuous consumption and the democratization of luxuries'.[28] It is, perhaps most fundamentally, about the production of commodified selves. In terms of its relationship with the world at large, the commodified subject merges with the commodities furnished by its given socio-cultural environment to the extent that the objects provided 'often function as dynamic elements of an extended self'.[29] In effect, the commodified self understands and values itself relative to the manner and extent of its ability to

21 Featherstone, *Consumer Culture*.

22 Betz, 'Postmodernism'.

23 Lash and Urry, *Organized Capitalism*; Lee, *Consumer Culture*; Bernardo Sorj, *A Nova Sociedade Brasileira* (3rd revised edition, Rio de Janeiro, 2006).

24 Don Slater, *Consumer Culture and Modernity* (Cambridge, 1997), 8.

25 Ibid., 25.

26 Celia Lury, *Consumer Culture* (2nd edition, Cambridge, 2011), 193.

27 Roberta Sassatelli, *Consumer Culture: History, Theory and Politics* (London, 2007), 149.

28 Ibid., 6.

29 Lee, *Consumer Culture Reborn*, 26.

consume that which its external context makes available. *To be is to consume*. At the same time, however, the commodified self engendered by consumer culture looks also upon itself as something amenable to being consumed. As Bauman observes, 'the most prominent feature of the society of consumers – however carefully concealed and most thoroughly covered up – is the *transformation of consumers into commodities*'.[30] In effect, the commodified self understands and values itself relative to the manner and extent of its ability to serve as a commodity for the extraction of value. *To be consumed is to be*.

The concluding section of this chapter engages the ritual and discursive repertoire of non-mainstream and alternative religiosity by drawing together the various threads of what has gone before. Taking as its principal theme the commodified identity of the late modern self, what follows identifies the dynamic of 'spiritual prosumption' as central to the shared repertoire of beliefs and practices to which the entangled, late modern life experience of urban professional, non-mainstream religionists gives rise. While by no means encompassing all that the alternative religious repertoire embodies, the notion of spiritual prosumption is nevertheless a useful means of explicating a range of characteristics, tendencies, and dynamics which combine to manifest and reproduce much that is typical of late modernity as a whole.[31]

Commodified Religion as Spiritual Prosumption

The term 'prosumption' was coined to describe the late modern tendency to collapse the acts of production and consumption into a singular process through which commodity value is both extracted and generated at one and the same time. Positioning the late modern subject as a 'prosumer' (that is, both a producer and consumer), the act of prosumption optimises capital efficiency by harnessing the creative energies of the consumer to an act of production which makes the process of consumption possible and, by way of adding value to it, more profitable. From self-service restaurants, petrol stations, and banks, through self-assembly furniture and do-it-yourself health checks, to radio call-ins and user-generated websites such as Facebook, Second Life, and YouTube, the prosumptive process merges the value-generative act of production with the traditionally value-extractive act of consumption.[32] The act of prosumption is an archetypal neoliberal process in that its fusion of consumption and production maximises profit through the

---

30 Bauman, *Consuming Life*, 12.

31 I treat another central dynamic of spiritual prosumption, which I label 'commodicy', in Andrew Dawson, 'Consuming the Self: New Spirituality as "Mystified Consumption"', *Social Compass*, 58/3 (2011): 309–15.

32 Detlev Zwick, Samuel Bonsu and Aron Darmody, 'Putting Consumers to Work: "Co-creation" and New Marketing Govern-mentality', *Journal of Consumer Culture*, 8/2 (2008): 163–96.

minimisation of corporate outlays and business overheads. Strange as it first may appear, the prosumptive process is actually perceived as enhancing rather than diminishing the status of the late modern self.[33] Such is the case because the notion of the prosumer is paradigmatically late modern in that its merger of producer and consumer plays to the contemporary valorisation of the individual as the central axis around which all else is held to revolve. Treating the individual as 'product, producer and consumer' in one, the act of prosumption embodies a typically late modern modality of selfhood which both extols and exploits contemporary understandings of the subject as 'entrepreneur of the self' (du Gay) and 'virtuoso' of 'self-(re)creation' (Lazaretto).[34]

The process of spiritual prosumption comprises five aspects relevant to this current discussion; they are agency, site, benefit, repertoire, and modality. In respect of *agency*, the act of spiritual prosumption has at its core contemporary understandings of the 'sovereign self'. While the individual subject inevitably draws upon externally furnished components of a material and immaterial kind (for example ritual artefacts and supernatural energies), such appropriation is mediated through an individualised understanding of the self as the ultimate arbiter of authority and principal agent of transformation. Reflecting aforementioned notions of the late modern individual as entrepreneur and virtuoso of the self, the alternative religionist is both master of the prosumptive act and artisan of the technical processes involved. Although variously construed as, for example, 'enlightenment', 'healing', 'release', and 'transformation', the *benefits* inherent to spiritual prosumption always involve some form of direct (physical and emotional) or indirect (employment and living conditions) betterment to the spiritual prosumer. Whatever the benefit accrued, however, its acquisition is posited as a spiritual good obtained as the outcome (product) of a transitional process through which the individual has moved from point *a* to point *b*. As indicated below, what makes this transformative process truly prosumptive is the self's role in effecting (as producer) and experiencing (as consumer) the transition (as product) from *a* to *b*.

The *site* in which the act of spiritual prosumption occurs is that of the human body understood as an integrated psychophysical unit. Similar to the aforementioned aspect of agency, although the prosumptive act is undertaken *via* the body's relationship with its physical environment (for example religious paraphernalia and ritual co-participants), the external relational dynamic is relativised through emphasis upon the constitutive role of internal psychophysical processes and the individual's management of them. What happens without is but a means to effecting what happens within. Building upon a presumed metaphysical continuity (connaturality) between the human subject and the universe at large

[33] George Ritzer and Nathan Jurgenson, 'Production, Consumption, Prosumption: The Nature of Capitalism in the Age of the Digital "Prosumer"', *Journal of Consumer Culture*, 10/1 (2010): 13–36.

[34] Alison Hearn, '"Meat, Mask, Burden": Probing the Contours of the "Branded Self"', *Journal of Consumer Culture*, 8/2 (2008): 197–217.

(such as the body as *mundus minor* or the self as divine spark), the body is posited as a medium through which cosmic energies and universal forces can be accessed and ultimately harnessed by the self for the benefit of the self. It is here that the fourth aspect of spiritual prosumption makes its contribution. The *ritual repertoire* of alternative religiosity is important because its form and content are central to enabling the prosumptive process. Positing the body as the site of self-betterment, the alternative repertoire furnishes the individual with the practical knowledge necessary to accessing and appropriating the cosmic forces which, by virtue of its spiritual connaturality, reside deep within the subject. Although dependent upon an individual's successful acquisition and correct application of the requisite knowledge and skills, self-betterment is nevertheless reliant upon elements of instruction and practice culled from, or situated within an existing ritual repertoire. While the variation of alternative repertoires is as numerous as the non-mainstream religious spectrum is diverse, a number of the most enabling and generic reportorial features are worthy of note.

Underwritten by the avowal of a holistic worldview, alternative religious repertoires tend to be hybrid and flexible.[35] In the first instance, the relativising effects of the holistic paradigm facilitate the conspicuous appropriation and concomitant hybridisation of formerly diverse – if not objectively discordant – beliefs and practices. In the second, the epistemological contingency born of holistic relativism renders existing articulations of the sacred as provisional (thereby perpetually revisable) and ambiguous (so open to multiple interpretations). By maximising optionality and enhancing polysemy, the combination of hybridism and flexibility caters directly for aforementioned late modern preoccupations with increased choice and subjective determination. Personal choice and determination are further reinforced through the individualised character of alternative religious repertoires. Orchestrated by self-oriented and mobile selves, alternative repertoires allow for the religious transit and spiritual *bricolage* integral to the reflexive biographical quest of the late modern 'seeker'. Comprising consecutive membership of, or concurrent participation within different groups, religious transit optimises individual 'freedom' while feeding the eclectic, if not flitting, appetite of the spiritual *bricoleur*. While collective participation remains an important component of alternative religious expression, the enervation of communal commitment wrought by late modern individualisation gives rise to qualified notions of membership and ephemeral forms of belonging which might best be rendered through the concept of 'associational individualism'.

The subjectivised character of alternative religious repertoires is further manifest through their expressive and meritocratic-egalitarian nature. The tendency to expressivity reflects two complementary dynamics. On the one hand, ritual facilitation of subjective expression permits the externalisation of otherwise

---

[35] Religious holism espouses a universal force or energy which underlies and unites every individual component of existence, such that particular beliefs and practices are treated as relative and thereby interchangeable expressions of the cosmic whole.

inner experiences which – by virtue of publicly broadcasting what was formerly private – serves to enhance personal gratification by expanding the perceived reach of the self. On the other hand, the ritual space allowed for increased expressivity permits greater self-assertion which – as the purported objectification of actual subjective conditions – manifests as a form of status claim or demand upon others for such things as acceptance, recognition, or reward. In both instances, then, expressivity involves some form of perceived expansion to the reach of individual subjectivity, inherent to which is an assumed enhancement of the self's purchase upon its external environment. The meritocratic ethos implicit in the dynamics of subjective expression is further manifest in reciprocal understandings of agency whereby the ritual practitioner assumes an equivalence of fair return for the psychophysical labours expended. Coupled with an egalitarianism born of the holistic belief that we all have access to the same universal forces, the spiritual work ethic – although wary of established pecking orders – is ultimately accepting of hierarchy *on the condition that* it can be climbed by those who are willing and able to make the necessary exertions. On the one hand, then, hierarchy is understood as a purely functional – and thereby contingent – arrangement, the graduated structure of which remains relative to the individual endeavours of subjective agency. On the other hand, hierarchy – or rather the individual's place in it – exists as an objective measure of the expenditure of subjective agency and the authority and status thereby accrued.

The spiritual enchantment of the world effected by the combination of these repertorial features is further complemented by an immanentist tendency through which the 'things of this world' are regarded as material manifestations of otherwise immaterial dynamics. Regarded as differentiated components of the same overarching ubiquity, the material and spiritual domains are understood to be mutually implicating such that what pertains to one pertains to the other. In effect, the material world is sacralised while the spiritual realm is immanentised. Importantly, just as the spiritual sphere is rendered immanent by its grounding in material processes, so the material realm is supernaturalised as a means to absolute self-betterment. Among other things, the elision of the material and spiritual informs an increased estimation of the body and its physical environment as principal loci of spiritual fulfilment. This, in turn, entails that the material aspects of life which nurture and allow the body to flourish become significant means of spiritual expression.

In his critique of the culture of new capitalism, Sennett cites Erving Goffman's notion of 'half finished frames' through which the advertising industry increases the allure of products by offering an incomplete scenario which the consumer is asked to complete by way of 'filling in the picture'.[36] In so doing, the 'half finished' advertisement both energises the consumer by calling upon her consumptive imagination and mobilises him to action by asking that he put himself in the frame

---

[36] Richard Sennett, *The Culture of the New Capitalism* (New Haven, CT, 2006), 148–9.

(as purchaser) and thereby complete the picture. This concept, I think, lends itself to explicating something of the attraction of alternative religious repertoires as modes of spiritual prosumption. Such is the case because the benefits offered by alternative repertoires are predicated on the rectification of an absence or realisation of unfulfilled potential by which the subject moves from point *a* (where one is now) to point *b* (where one should be). In the first instance, the individual is energised through her representation as a half-finished frame in need of completion. In the second, the subject is mobilised through the promise of tangible benefits which accrue once the picture has been completed.

The half-finished framing of the individual as a product in need of completion is complemented by two other key prosumptive dynamics. On the one hand, alternative religious repertoires posit the self as the primary agent through which the act of self-completion is achieved. Fundamentally reliant upon the productive agency of the self, the transition from *a* to *b* is, first and foremost, a process of *autopoiesis*. Self-betterment is thereby not simply an end state to be achieved, but also a productive process by which the self produces itself through the concerted application of the practical knowledge furnished by the alternative religious repertoire. The representation of the individual as both outcome (product) and agent (producer) of the prosumptive spiritual process is further nuanced by an understanding of the self as a reflexive consumer of all that it does and experiences. In and of itself, neither the act of moving (as producer) nor being moved (as product) from *a* to *b* is sufficient to satisfy the aestheticised demands of the reflexive self. Implicated by the aforementioned aestheticisation of the body and stylistic self-consciousness, the act of spiritual prosumption is only fully consummated by the self's consumptive experience of itself as that which both produces and is produced through the transformative dynamics of the alternative religious repertoire.

Modifying Max Weber's famous term, and by way of conclusion, the *modality* of the act of spiritual prosumption might best be described as an 'inner-worldly aestheticism'.[37] In respect of the 'inner-worldly' aspect of this term, aforementioned characteristics and features underline the manner and extent to which the alternative religiosity of the urban middle classes is oriented to and by engagement with the entangled, late modern world. Although its version of new-middle-class identity politics is more that of an 'apolitics of identity',[38] the self-project orchestrated by alternative religious repertoires is nevertheless thoroughly saturated by an inner-worldly attitude which both seeks and expects some form of material return for the subjective labours expended. Concerning the dynamics of 'aestheticism', and perhaps in contrast to the Protestant ethic of

[37] The original term is 'inner-worldly asceticism' (*innerweltliche Askese*) and is used as part of Max Weber's ideal typology of religious attitudes to the world. See *The Sociology of Religion* (Boston, MA, 1963).

[38] See Andrew Dawson, 'New Era Millenarianism in Brazil', *Journal of Contemporary Religion*, 23/3 (2008): 269–83.

which Weber speaks, it is not simply the expenditure of labour (asceticism) which matters to late modern alternative religionists but also the self's experience of itself (aestheticism) as the expender and recipient of the labours being spent. It is this combination of self as agent (producer), beneficiary (product), and aesthete (consumer) which marks the alternative religious repertoire of the new middle class as a quintessentially prosumptive process.

Chapter 8

The Enchantments of Consumer Capitalism: Beyond Belief at the Burning Man Festival

François Gauthier

For Raymond Lemieux[1]

Every year[2], tens of thousands[3] make the long journey out to the harsh environment of Nevada's Black Rock Desert at the end of the summer for a week of 'radical self-expression', 'radical self-reliance' and effervescent community at what is one of the most vibrant subcultural phenomena today; the Burning Man Festival. After months of preparation, 'burners', be they first time 'virgins' or long-standing 'veterans', arrive on the flat and lifeless desert playa to participate in this 'no spectator' event that calls on the creativity of everyone so that the utopian 'ephemeropolis'[4] of Black Rock City can materialise as a three-mile-wide open circle at the centre of which stands a forty-foot-tall wood, metal and neon figure called 'the Man'. Dominating the city from atop its three-storey-high pedestal, the 'Man' is the symbolic and physical icon of the festival (its 'axis mundi' as

---

1 My debt to Raymond Lemieux in problematising religious reconfigurations of religion with respect to the cultural and social influence of the market is enormous. His insightful and avant-garde work as well as his teachings have been an illumination and an inspiration.

2 Many thanks to Graham St John, Linda Woodhead and Tuomas Martikainen for their critical insights on this text. I am of course the sole responsible for the final content. The research that I have been conducting on the Burning Man festival since 2002 has benefited of the financial support of the Social Sciences and Humanities Research Council of Canada (SSHRC) and the Fond québécois pour la recherche sur la société et la culture (FQRSC) through various funding programs.

3 Participation has risen, initially exponentially, thereafter constantly from 1990 onwards. For example, there were 30,000 participants in 2003 and 55,000 in 2011.

4 D.S. Black, 'Burning Man as Ephemeropolis and the Refusal of Meaning', paper presented at the North American Interdisciplinary Conference on Environment and Community, University of Nevada, Reno (1998). For a history and general information on the event, see Brian Doherty, *This Is Burning Man* (New York, 2004).

the city plan indicates),[5] yet is devoid of any affixed or explicit meaning, thereby offering itself to a wide array of variously enunciated interpretations, associations and appropriations. Designed as a space of discovery and experimentation of otherness and for emancipation from the constraints of the 'default world', Burning Man's community builds up to a crescendo until Saturday evening when the Man is set alight in a feverish frenzy of music, drum pounding, fire swirling, shouts, dances, pyrotechnics and delirium before toppling over and continuing to consume itself well into the cold desert night. The 'sacrifice' by fire of many of the year's gigantic sculptural artworks follow that of the Man until the following evening when the 'Temple', Black Rock City's second symbolic centre, set at the frontier with the '(W)hol(l)y Other' (city plan) of the open 'Playa', is also consumed – this time in a surprisingly hushed and contemplative ambience.

Burning Man's most striking and certainly most structurally significant characteristic is its ban on vending, advertisement, and any form of commercial activity in favour of a thriving gift economy in tune with the festival's ethos of do-it-yourself creative entrepreneurship, participation, and involvement in the fostering of community.[6] This radicalises a defining trait of subcultural phenomena in that it claims to be a haven of authenticity set against the conformist and alienating superficiality of media-saturated and consumerism-fuelled, corporate capitalist mainstream culture.[7] In addition, and while Burning Man avoids most attempts at defining its ultimate meaning and does not present itself as an overtly religious event, it is underwritten by a profuse cosmology and self-consciously offers innumerable ritual settings and opportunities for one-time or spontaneous religious and spiritual investments. For many participants, the experience of Burning Man has strong religious dimensions.[8] As a consequence, this utopian

---

[5] See http://www.burningman.com. The organisation's website is a gold mine of information on the event.

[6] The entrance fee for participating in this gift economy presently ranges between $250 and $450 per ticket (which covers the organiser's costs in addition to contributing to the Black Rock Arts Foundation which provides funding for some of the authorised installations and art work), and at least another $1,500 in getting there and purchasing all that might be needed over the time of the festival (and much more depending on what one intends to give to the community).

[7] See Sarah Thornton, *Club Cultures: Music, Media and Subcultural Capital* (Middletown, CT, 1996).

[8] Most prefer the term spiritual. It is interesting to note that claiming spiritual or religious dimensions has little connection with the actual content of the interviews. The testimonies of those who shun such qualifiers still hold very rich material from a religious socio-anthropological perspective. The Burning Man experience widely functions as a rite of passage founding identity and belonging, is central to life narratives, is transformative, links with the cosmos, provides 'peak experiences' and experiences of *communitas* (Victor Turner), etc. See namely François Gauthier, 'Le Temple de l'Honneur. Rituels et deuils dans le désert au Festival Burning Man', *Frontières*, 17/1 (2004): 87–90; Lee Gilmore and Mark Van Proyen (eds), *Afterburn: Reflections on Burning Man* (Albuquerque, NM, 2005); Lee

experiment is readily interpreted as a vivid example of postmodern re-enchantment in an otherwise commoditised and disenchanted world.

It has become common within the social sciences to understand contemporary religiosities as examples of re-enchantment, be they novel and Dionysian forms (such as those found in subcultures) or more traditional ones. In this chapter, Burning Man provides a case study to contest the interpretation according to which its religiosity is the expression of re-enchantment effected by the transgression of a disenchanted, commoditised world. It rather develops the argument that such an interpretation rests on an erroneous comprehension of consumer societies and their constitutive enchantments. This in turn opens onto a more paradoxical and complex analysis of the rapports between consumerism and religion.

Burning Man as a Subcultural Phenomenon

Subcultures are cultural ensembles composed of a matrix of styles, codes, meanings, values, aesthetics, music, modes, and networks of communication and so on, constructed around claims of authenticity in opposition to mainstream values of conformity (and thus *in*-authenticity).[9] Born out of the consumer society of the 1950s and 1960s, subcultures construct specific identities expressed as a lifestyle with their own overarching mythology and rituals such as gatherings, festivals, and shows. Born in *the* subcultural capital of the US, San Francisco in the late 1980s prior to moving to the desert in 1990, the Burning Man Festival is not so much a subculture in itself as an annual meeting place for subcultures and marginal (and not-so-marginal) identities; a 'meeting of the (neo)tribes'.[10] As such, Burning Man has grown to become a year-long cultural and social phenomenon which includes regional associations in most Western countries and a growing number of smaller annual regional burns occurring everywhere from the US to Australia, South Africa, and Spain.

Gilmore, *Theater in a Crowded Fire. Ritual and Spirituality at Burning Man* (Berkeley, 2010); François Gauthier, 'Les HeeBeeGeeBee Healers au Festival Burning Man. Trois récits de guérison', *Ethnologies*, 33/1 (2011): 191–215.

9 On authenticity as the crux of subcultural phenomena, see Graham St John, 'Going Feral: *Authentica* on the Edge of Australian Culture', *Australian Journal of Anthropology*, 8/2 (1997): 167–89.

10 Burning Man as a meeting of the tribes is an idea borrowed from Graham St John, who, while at Burning Man 2003, formulated it during a discussion held in the midst of a severe dust storm. See Steven T. Jones, *The Tribes of Burning Man* (San Francisco, 2011). While subcultures are often born as youth phenomena and coalesce within similar age groups thereafter, Burning Man has a varied population age-wise, ranging from newborns (with their parents) to 70 year-olds. 'Subculture' and 'tribe' are each contested concepts, and do not overlap as I seem to be suggesting here, but this is not a very important debate in my view with respect to the aims of the present discussion.

The population growth of the 1990s sparked the institutionalisation of its present form and the adoption of a small set of rules.[11] Voices were quick to arise, warning against what subcultures fear most: institutionalisation, recuperation and commoditisation. Two sets of narratives have since competed within the Burning Man community. On the one hand, it is said that the event allows for emancipation from the market. As one participant confided: 'So much of what you are is made by media: which products you buy, which groups you associate with. Burning Man crosses out all that.' On the other, some regret the good old days when there were no rules at Burning Man and fewer people, and lament the fact that 'Burning Man is now packaging meaning and selling community'; in other words that it has 'sold out' to media attention and mainstream consumer culture. Hence the question: does Burning Man's authenticity and religiosity stem from its opposition to a disenchanted consumer society?

Re-enchantment and the Myth of Rationality

The re-enchantment narrative emanated from postmodernists like Michel Maffesoli before spreading through the social sciences. It appeared to be particularly relevant from the 1990s onwards as the notion of the decline of religion, which had been announced by the most popular brands of secularisation theory, was increasingly recognised as being of limited help in understanding the complexities of religious realities and emerging phenomena such as subcultures. Re-enchantment seemed an adequate term, especially on account of the emergence of phenomena exhibiting explicit or implicit religious dimensions in politics, culture, arts, and sports. Yet re-enchantment presupposes a prior disenchantment, and thus carries forward what it initially aims to critique. Re-enchantment occurs at the margins of an otherwise disenchanted whole, like resilient weeds growing in the cracks of modern rationalisation.

This narrative equates the modernisation process (and modernity itself) with rationalisation, as in Weber's evolutionist account of the progressive unbridling of instrumental, formal rationality. This process, the story goes, marginalises the (supposedly) irrational basis of magic and religion (disenchantment is *Entzauberung*, 'demagification'), thus allowing modern capitalist societies to function without metaphysical foundations, and without a 'sacred canopy'. From this perspective, the capitalist market economy and consumerism are heralded as being governed by the laws of formal rationality and self-interest, and are held to be inherently secularising (in the sense of shaking religion from the 'symbolic economies' of modern societies). Yet, as some observers have noted, the capitalist

---

[11] The 'Ten Principles' are Radical Inclusion, Gifting, Decommodification, Radical Self-reliance, Radical Self-expression, Communal Effort, Civic Responsibility, Leave No Trace, Participation, and Immediacy. See the 'Survival Guide' at http://www.burningman.com.

economy is not a sphere of reason but a 'theatre of emotions',[12] starting with the irrational desire to accumulate power in the form of wealth. As such, this perspective fails to understand the specific 'enchantments of capitalism'.[13]

One widespread mistake is to understand modernity as essentially characterised by rationality, and thus equating 'postmodernity' with the rise of emotionality. Against this belief Charles Taylor has forcefully argued[14] that both reason and emotion (or passion, or irrationality) are constitutive of modernity, that they are two sides of the same coin – that they are, to use Foucault's terminology, modernity's *epistémè*.[15] In sum, modernity is defined by a tension between Reason and Emotion, incarnated in the opposition between techno-science and Romanticism, or the works of Descartes and Rousseau, and so on. Thus objectified, Reason and the wild fluxes of Interiority complement and presuppose each other. The disenchantment and rationalisation narratives are, incidentally, but truncated and partial graspings of modern (and late modern) culture.

Authenticity as Romantic Truth for the Late Modern Self

As cultural theorist and economist Don Slater has argued, Romanticism and the idea of culture that it 'produced were in many respects reactions against industrial, commercial, consumer society from Rousseau in the 1750s through revolutionary and nationalist romanticism up to the mid-nineteenth century. It has therefore provided probably the most enduring source of critiques of consumer culture, which it sees as part of a materialistic modernity that lacks authentic collective values and truths.'[16] Yet at the same time, 'paradoxically Romanticism also bequeathed to consumer culture many of the themes that we consider most modern or even postmodern', promoting ideas of 'personal authenticity … derived from what was "natural", emotional, irrational, sensual and imaginative in the self'.[17]

The modern period hosted a shift away from a Christian, other-determined morality towards individualism and the autonomous ethics of authenticity. Authenticity can be aptly defined with Taylor as

---

12 André Orléan, *L'empire de la valeur. Refonder l'économie* (Paris, 2011).

13 Peter van der Veer, 'Market and Money: A Critique of Rational Choice Theory', *Social Compass*, 59/2 (2011): 183–92.

14 Charles Taylor, *Sources of the Self: The Making of the Modern Identity* (Cambridge, 1989).

15 An *épistémè* (literally 'I believe') refers to the conditions of discourse, the belief structure underlying the very processes of thought (and thus analysis) in a particular society at a given time, its grammar one might say. See Michel Foucault, *Les mots et les choses* (Paris, 1966).

16 Don Slater, *Consumer Culture and Modernity* (Cambridge, 1997), 15.

17 Ibid., 16.

> the understanding of life that emerged with the Romantic expressivism of the late eighteenth century, that each of us has his or her own way of realizing one's own humanity, and that it is important to find and live out one's own, as against surrendering to conformity with a model imposed from outside, by society, or the previous generation, or religious or political authority.[18]

For Taylor, the extension of post-war consumerism in the second half of the twentieth century and the development of mass media have been a powerful force in the massification, dissemination and radicalisation of a modern culture of authenticity and expressivism, which until then was mostly the affair of the bourgeoisie and the élite. To push things slightly further, it is in a way *because* consumerism became a vehicle for the expression of individual authenticity that it was able to penetrate and shape culture to the extent that it has. In other words, the rise of consumption as a desirable social ethos has less to do with the spread of instrumental rationality than we commonly think, and a lot to do with the fact that it provided a powerful vehicle for the modern ideology of authentic and autonomous individualism.

Taylor's perspective is reinforced if we consider the history of marketing and consumerism in the last century. In the 1950s, marketing pioneers in the US initiated a trend which propagated throughout the West, in which products became conceived of as vehicles for individual self-expression in accordance with a new standard of self-realisation.[19] Consumption is driven by the socially constructed imperative to create oneself in order to be recognised, and the act of consuming aims not so much at the satisfaction of needs as the construction of an authentic self, much like that promoted by Romanticism:

> [t]he very idea that acts of consuming are seriously consequential for the authenticity of the self (as opposed to mere physical survival or social climbing) is an unintentional consequence of these early [Romantic] developments, as are many of the 'authentic values' in which modern consumer goods come wrapped: naturalness, emotional gratification, ethnic and national cultural values ….[20]

One of the consequences of such a consumption-driven culture of authenticity is the need to express the symbols of this authenticity for it to be recognised – and therefore socially grounded and legitimised. Hence the development and popularity of increasingly sophisticated and personalised electronic media interfaces such as the internet, email and more recently social networks and their public *mise en scène* of private life. While the rationalistic pull of the modern project strove to

---

[18] Charles Taylor, *Varieties of Religion Today: William James Revisited* (Boston, MA, 2002), 83.

[19] See the introduction to this volume.

[20] Slater, *Consumer Culture*, 16.

separate the individual sphere from the public and the influence of the state,[21] Romanticism symmetrically encouraged the outward expression of interiority and the merging of public and private.[22] Through late twentieth-century consumerism, such Romantic values were given a powerful voice to the extent that the public and private divide, which had been foundational of our modern political systems (in both republican and liberal models), has become seriously challenged by what some have called the 'de-privatisation of religion'.[23]

This discussion highlights the ways in which consumer culture is founded on the perpetuation of cycles of enchantment linked to the Romantic ethos. Contemporary consumer societies are not disenchanted and rationalised barren lands in the cracks of which resilient phenomena such as the Burning Man Festival constitute isolated and pure arenas of resistance and re-enchantment. The reality is more complex, as are the rapports between religion and consumerism.

The religious landscape has been profoundly modified as a result of the cultural changes brought on by the multifarious and variegated processes of modernisation leading to today's globalising consumerism. Yet very few scholars to date have acknowledged the importance of consumerism and economic ideologies (such as neoliberalism) with respect to these changes. While many have written about the incidences and dynamics of the individualisation of religion, the idea that this individualisation might be intimately tied to the consumer nature of our societies is an idea that has passed well under the radar. Similarly, noting the erosion of traditional, institutional regulations is commonplace, yet almost inevitably leads scholars to conclude that religion today is fragmented and diffused, since 'deregulated'. In concordance with the perspective sketched out in this volume's introduction, I would like to argue the contrary: that the contemporary religious landscape reveals not so much a state of un-regulation as a coherent system in which the values, ethics, worldviews, and eschatologies of consumerism are structural.[24] If religion has shifted away from a traditional type of culture, it is because it has become re-embedded (to use Karl Polanyi's expression)[25] in a globalising consumer culture. In other words, consumerism defines (in part at least) the backdrop for the re-configurations of religion, and the thorough understanding of its nature and dynamics can help us seize the *grammar* of a significant portion

---

21 See Jeff Weintraub, 'The Theory and Politics of the Public/Private Distinction', in Jeff Weintraub and Krishan Kumar (eds), *Public and Private in Thought and Practice* (Chicago, IL, 1997), 1–41.

22 Slater, *Consumer Culture*, 95.

23 Philippe Portier, 'Les mutations du religieux dans la France contemporaine', *Social Compass*, 59/3 (2012): 193–207.

24 See also François Gauthier, 'Primat de l'authenticité et besoin de reconnaissance. La société de consommation et la nouvelle régulation du religieux', *Studies in Religion/Sciences religieuses*, 41/1 (2012): 93–111.

25 Karl Polanyi, *The Great Transformation: The Political and Economic Origins of Our Time* (Boston, MA, 2001).

of religious reconfigurations today. The remainder of this chapter discusses the different levels linking religion and consumerism at Burning Man.

Rituals without Dogma @ Burning Man™

The 2003 Burning Man theme 'Beyond Belief' was meant to bring the religious aspects of the event to the fore.[26] In an interview, the founder of Burning Man, Larry Harvey, explained that he had wanted to propose this theme for years but had waited to feel that the community was ready for it. Harvey is a reader of anthropology and the philosophy of religion, and it is quite knowingly that the layout and geography of Burning Man makes such an abundant and purposeful use of religious functionalities and symbolisms: 'The city planning has always been a form of sacred geometry.' For example, the Man's situation at the centre of an open circle is directly inspired by his readings of Mircea Eliade on the construction of sacred time and space, and the Man's 2003 pedestal was inspired by Meso-American pyramids. His youthful reading of William James' *Varieties of Religious Experience* and the idea that beliefs were secondary to experience especially moved Harvey. 'Belief is thought at rest' was indeed the first quote that one could read on the signs aligned along the dusty desert path leading to the Black Rock City gates that year. Accordingly for Harvey, only the resort to experience can help avoid a situation where objects of beliefs, which is to say, particular metaphysical assertions, become 'idols one could kill for'.[27]

In such an environment, says Harvey, 'Spontaneously, rituals sprout'. From the Temple to the sacrifice of the Man, from the lamplighters' ritual at dusk to the meditation classes and sweat lodges, Black Rock City's offers, scattered across its 'sacred geometry', act as an invitation for all burners to participate in and create rituals. Burning Man's 'ritual without dogma'[28] type of religiosity radicalises the trend towards experiential and emotional religion in consumer societies. For Harvey, the religious investment of Burning Man is a direct product of the gift economy created by the vending and advertising ban. He sees culture as a naturally occurring phenomenon which is inhibited by consumerism. It is because Burning Man thwarts the reifying logics of consumer capitalism that rituals happen all over Black Rock City. For example, the San Francisco artist David Best has overseen the construction of the Temple for over a decade, and it has become indispensable

---

[26] Themes have been part of Burning Man since 1996. The themes are invitations to reflect on certain dimensions of the Burning Man experience and experiment with certain meanings and symbols. Each year a certain fraction of activities, theme camps, and artwork resonates with the theme, often in an ironic and playful fashion.

[27] This interview was realised two years after 9/11.

[28] See Lee Gilmore, 'Fires of the Heart: Ritual, Pilgrimage, and Transformation at Burning Man', in Lee Gilmore and Mark Van Proyen (eds), *Afterburn: Reflections on Burning Man* (Albuquerque, NM, 2005), 43–64.

to the Burning Man experience. Innumerable rituals occur within and around its lavish and intricate structure, made of recycled materials: from marriages to funerals, in addition to a host of personalised rituals of mourning, loss, joy, forgiveness, longing, hope, wish, and love. According to Harvey, these are the types of rituals one will not see happening in a consumer society. Rather, culture is

> actively exploited and extirpated and strip lined and destroyed before it can elaborate itself into anything beyond primitive forms. … The culture scouts seek authenticity, the most valuable commodity of them all, remove it as a bearer of identity, and then sell it as a lifestyle. We live in a situation where the economic forces are generally hostile to the generation of culture … that is one reason we are in the desert and why we need to be very vigilant. … Late twentieth-century capitalism concentrated on the marketing end, the manufacture of desire, the creation of spectacle, leaves the consumer isolated from inner resources, to others and to a greater world.

Larry Harvey's perspective is interesting because it is both right and wrong. It is right because consumerism indeed seeks to harness authenticity, yet it is wrong if it implies that consumerism is not itself involved in the production of culture. Returning to the mechanisms of consumer culture, Roberta Sassatelli argues that it relies on the two fundamental processes of commoditisation and de-commoditisation. Consumer culture does indeed seek to harness authenticity and meaning in order to derive a profit. Yet it relies at the same time on the circulation of brands within social relations. Consumer culture does not so much isolate individuals as it encourages them to express their identities with its products: 'All in all, modern consumers are asked to actively participate in the process of de-commoditization, producing themselves as the source of value.'[29] Goods are not so much material objects as symbols that must be appropriated by individuals and used to produce subjectivity:

> Consumption is a sphere of social action regulated according to the *cultural principle of individual expression*. This is not to say that the subject is absolutely free; on the contrary, the subjectivity required by consumption is a binding individuality. To consume in appropriate ways people must be masters of their will and signal their difference from commodities.[30]

Consumer culture is not a vampire that thrives by sucking the meaning out of otherwise spontaneous productions of culture. *It is the means of production of culture in a globalising world.* Hence one never escapes consumer culture, even when side-stepping profit-making. As was discussed in the introduction to this

---

[29] Roberta Sassatelli, *Consumer Culture: History, Theory and Politics* (London, 2007), 149. Emphasis in text.

[30] Ibid., 161.

volume, brands were the result of the self-realisation turn in marketing. They were conceived to fill 'the great gaps of meaning that exist in people's lives' and propose 'ideas that people can live by',[31] in the words of UK marketer John Grant. While goods can fill a variety of functions, 'brands are primarily to be understood as resources for the construction of the self and its social moorings'.[32] 'For consumers, brands are means of production. They function as a pre-established context of consumption that anticipates a certain style, mood or experience.'[33] Brands are promises that are intended as media for the 'construction of a common social world'.[34] As one loyal 'supporter' of a soft drink (!) confides: 'Because things are so crazy out there, people like to find out if they see the world the same way as other people. People will believe in anything – from a chocolate bar to a political view – if it makes them feel that they belong to something bigger than themselves.'[35] For the marketing guru Douglas Atkin, a brand is a meaning system, 'a unifying structure for the community' which separates those who identify with this meaning system from others. Brands allow for identification and differentiation. Brands are symbols, and the economy of consumerism is a 'spiritual' and 'symbolic economy'. As a consequence, the ideal of branding is the making (and sustaining) of a 'cult brand'.[36] Atkin even argues that 'the same dynamics are at play behind the attraction to brands and cults. They may vary in degree of strength (although not always), but not in type.'[37] Quoting Eileen Barker's empirical work in addition to his own interviews with Harley riders, Marines, Mormons, and Krishna followers among others, Atkin writes that cults and brands answer similar 'urges' for meaning, identity, community, belonging, security, and intelligibility. In other words, the branding ideal is to create a nexus of religiosity.

As a consequence, one can no longer oppose Burning Man's religiosity and authenticity to the reified disenchantment of consumer culture. From this perspective, Burning Man is a (successful) brand in its own right. The Burning Man logo, which depicts the figure of the Man in a minimalist design with arms raised and ready to burn (see Figure 8.1), has been appropriated by thousands

---

[31] Quoted in Celia Lury, *Brands: The Logos of the Global Economy* (New York and London, 2004), 38.

[32] Adam Arvidsson, *Brands: Meaning and Value in Media Culture* (London and New York, 2006), 81.

[33] Ibid., 93.

[34] Ibid., 3.

[35] Douglas Atkin, *The Culting of Brands: When Customers Become True Believers* (New York, 2004), 95.

[36] Atkin defines a cult brand as: 'a brand for which a group of customers exhibit a great devotion or dedication. Its ideology is distinctive and it has a well-defined and committed community. It enjoys exclusive devotion … and its members often become voluntary advocates' (Atkin, *Culting of Brands*, xix).

[37] Ibid., xiii.

Figure 8.1 Examples of the Burning Man as re-appropriated by participants

of burners and appears on self-made T-shirts, bumper stickers, jewellery, even tattoos – just like other successful logos. It is an immediately recognisable symbol for those in the know and it sparks enthusiastic conversations with like-minded spirits across the globe. It is the marker of a tribe, the expression of a certain set of values, meanings, and commitment that readily confers identity. It is also, within its own territory, exclusive, as all other logos from the outside world are banned within Black Rock City.

From such an anthropological perspective, concerned with the symbolic (and religious) aspects of branding, one can indeed say that Burning Man is selling community and meaningful experiences. Yet selling access to community and possibilities of self-exploration and self-expression does not taint the authenticity of Burning Man. In the dynamic process of commoditisation/de-commoditisation, Burning Man generates authenticity for as long as it is considered to do so by participants, that is, as long as it maintains a delicate balance between financial, legal and political sustainability on the one hand and a sense of resistance to the pressures of outside sponsorship and commercialism on the other. It is interesting to note that the Burning Man organisation is constituted as a limited liability corporation, which is to say that it has a for-profit structure that allows the organisation to have full decision-making power over the event. Yet, the very existence of Burning Man depends upon the volunteer work of several hundreds of people over the course of a year, and upon the participation and gifts of all burners during the event. This is how the sale of tickets at a moderate price still makes the event possible, while allowing for significant amounts of money to be redirected to the Black Rock Arts foundation which subsidises projects on (and off) Playa.[38] Gift and market economies are not opposed, but complementary and necessary to each other, certainly at Burning Man, but also elsewhere in consumer culture. The difference lies perhaps in the finalities: Burning Man does not sell community in order to make a profit (which is what a stock exchange inscribed company like Nike does), but for the sake of a certain ideal of community, to support the creation of culture for its own sake and, as is evident in Larry Harvey's discourse, to change the world by promoting and producing non-materialistic experiences.

Burning Man and the Rituals of Consumer Capitalism

Burning Man certainly attracts a good deal of people who are disenchanted, wary or simply critical of the consumer capitalist culture in which they live. Such testimonies as that quoted earlier in this chapter are easy to come by. Yet the important thing to note is that they do not differ in nature from what one would hear associated with other brands that successfully generate authenticity. This perspective allows us to make sense of a series of facts that are otherwise problematic from the idealist perspective according to which Burning Man's authenticity and religiosity depend on its opposition to and subtraction from consumerism. This is summed up by one participant who happens to be happily involved in the capitalist economy *and* a prominent member of one of Burning Man's longest standing theme camps: 'I love capitalism, just not at Burning Man.'

Burning Man rose to subcultural fame during the 1990s at the same time that the expansion of the internet and electronic communications were developed. It is well known that, alongside more bohemian, hippie, artsy, spiritualist and marginal burners, a significant fraction of burners are also professionally involved in the Silicon Valley. A 1996 article in *Wired* – the 'geek' magazine *par excellence* – heralded Burning Man as the 'New American Holiday',[39] publicising the event within tech-savvy networks. The network sociality of Burning Man was seen by many as the materialisation of the horizontally networked, radically inclusive utopia of the internet, as developed in open sourcing and common-based peer

---

38 See http://blackrockarts.org.

39 Bruce Sterling, 'Greetings from Burning Man!', *Wired*, 4/11 (1997), [Online], available at: http://www.wired.com/wired/archive/4.11/burningman.html [accessed: 20 July 2011].

production (such as Wikis). The very idea for Google was allegedly born at Burning Man (the name itself is supposed by some to be derived from 'goggles', a piece of equipment made indispensable by the frequent desert windstorms that sweep the Playa), and this company, along with many others involved in the dot-com sector, design conception, programming, and marketing, has been encouraging cultural creatives to go to Burning Man for inspiration and team-building.[40] Burning Man experiences such as organising theme camps and putting up some of the giant interactive art projects also appear on CVs. Yet if Black Rock City is a place where new relationships are intensively created, talking about one's professional activities in the 'default world', making business propositions and acting in an interested manner are taboo there. Participants widely take on pseudonyms, called Playa names (often given by others rather than self-appointed), and it is not uncommon that one will have no idea of a person's true identity or professional activity, even after spending a lot of time together over the course of the festival. The gift economy of Burning Man ensures that social relations are not the product of pure self-interest and thus guarantees authenticity.

As such, it is undeniable that Burning Man serves a social function with respect to wider society. Fred Turner has documented how Burning Man's bohemian ethos supports new forms of production which are emerging in Silicon Valley by showing 'how elements of the Burning Man world – including the building of a socio-technical commons, participation in project-based artistic labour, and the fusion of social and professional interaction – help shape and legitimize the collaborative manufacturing processes driving the growth of Google and other firms', and thereby act as a 'key cultural infrastructure'[41] for new media industries and consumer capitalism at large.

A similar case could be made for participants linked to sectors such as education, social work, bars, restaurants, and entertainment arts (such as music and circus). The whole array of alternative and Eastern spiritualities and holistic therapeutics can also be found at Black Rock City. While the 'alternative' offered by these spiritualities often involves a critique of capitalism, their primary actors (yoga teachers, *reiki* practitioners, meditation coaches, and so on), contrary to traditional church structures, completely rely on practices that are wholly integrated in a personal-care market for their income and livelihood.[42]

---

40 Clément Baudet, 'Les chaleurs du festival Burning Man', *OWNI* (6 September 2011), [Online], available at: owni.fr/2011/09/06/dans-la-chaleur-du-festival-burning-man [accessed: 20 July 2012].

41 Fred Turner, 'Burning Man at Google: A Cultural Infrastructure for New Media Production', *New Media and Society*, 11/1–2 (2009): 73–94. Quotations are drawn from the abstract.

42 See Marion Bowman's contribution to this volume.

Catering for the Lifestyles of the Culture of Authenticity

One of the main tropes of the personal narratives collected on Playa is personal transformation.[43] One could even say that self-transformation is Burning Man's *raison d'être*. The typical (and idealised) first experience is recalled in terms of being 'blown away', shocked, humbled, and so on, often with profound and lasting consequences. Participants discover another way of being, interacting, and belonging. They are revealed to themselves. Not only are participants transformed at Burning Man, but they also use its context for rituals that involve transformation.

As a theatre for radical self-expression, immediate experience, radical self-reliance, participation, and individual responsibility, Burning Man is a remarkable and radical example of the culture of authenticity that has emerged out of the modern subjective turn and which has been diffused throughout society with consumerism. Burning Man's religiosity is therefore entirely on the side of what Linda Woodhead and Paul Heelas have called subjective spirituality, in opposition to 'life as' forms of religion that depend on tradition and an outside authority.[44] Accordingly, the socio-demographics of Burning Man, in spite of its call for radical inclusion, are massively middle class, white, and highly educated – in other words, the social strata most affected by the subjective turn.

The introduction to this volume stresses how the ethos of consumerism is inseparable from the dissemination of the culture of authenticity and how this has favoured the crystallisation of identities around recognisable lifestyles. The underlying issues are that of identity (who I am in my own life?) and ethics (how to live this unique life?). This cultural shift has affected religion, whose lived forms can often be assimilated to lifestyles.[45] My own research on subcultures has tended to show how for many people, subcultures and 'religions' coexist on the same 'level' in consumer societies – which is one way of understanding why these phenomena make such an explicit use of ritual structures and why they are infused with so many religious symbols.

While outside observers have tried to define the meaning of the festival, the organisation has successfully evaded any limiting definition (for example, as a 'Woodstock remake', or as a resurgence of *Wicker Man*). Rather, Burning Man attracts *because* of the indeterminacy of its ultimate meaning, which allows for personal investment and appropriation.[46] It is because the Man has no defined

---

[43] See Lee Gilmore, 'Fires of the Heart: Ritual, Pilgrimage, and Transformation at Burning Man', in Lee Gilmore and Mark Van Proyen (eds), *Afterburn: Reflections on Burning Man* (Albuquerque, NM, 2005), 43–62; Gauthier, 'HeeBeeGeeBee Healers'.

[44] Paul Heelas and Linda Woodhead, *The Spiritual Revolution: Why Religion Is Giving Way to Spirituality* (Oxford, 2005).

[45] See François Gauthier and Jean-Philippe Perreault (eds), *Jeunes et religion au Québec* (Québec: Presses de l'Université Laval, 2008).

[46] For holistic spiritualities, the indeterminacy of meaning is the very condition for religious meaning and communalisation.

meaning that it can coalesce a community made of autonomy- and authenticity-seeking individuals. One often hears that the Man has as many meanings as there are burners. Yet this is only correct to the extent that everyone's experience is irreducible by definition. In reality, interviews and informal conversations on this matter tend to revolve around a limited set of themes. The following statement collected from a burner onsite reflects the opinion of a quite significant majority: 'For me, the Man is the symbol of my experience here. I think it's also the symbol of the community', before hurrying to add: 'But that's just me, I'm sure everybody else has a different answer.' The paradox that lies in the massive dissemination of this opinion coalesces the two sides of the 'religion of the individual' (Durkheim) in the era of authenticity: personal experience, and interactive, voluntary-based (versus organic) community. Here is a vivid illustration of how a radically unregulated space in the guise of the indeterminate meaning of the Man leads to homogeneous appropriations. While the meaning of the Man is not defined by any cultural, political or religious exteriority, the predictable and highly homogeneous meanings uncovered by empirical research serve the socially constructed imperatives of self-realisation and authenticity.[47]

Conclusion

This chapter has shown some of the complex and somewhat paradoxical ways in which the religiosity of Burning Man is intimately tied to consumerism and the dynamics of consumer culture. If the interdiction on vending and advertising allows for a thriving and extravagant gift economy (in which the community, symbolised by the Man, is implicitly the intended receiver) that catalyses its religiosity and is foundational of its authenticity and community, these dynamics do not break with those of consumerism, understood as a symbolic economy aiming at providing (more or less profitable) building blocks for self-realisation, identity, and belonging. Furthermore, this late modern potlatch supposes an abundance only made possible by consumer society. Consumers do not escape the market when they participate in Burning Man, but find a refreshing and catalysing frame outside the overt finality of utilitarian profit.[48] While participants speak abundantly of personal transformation, and while many lives are rerouted in the wake of this experience into less standardised, materially-oriented and corporate lifestyles, Burning Man is not confrontational with respect to consumer capitalism. Rather, for the economies linked to new media and the holistic spiritualities milieu for example, the ephemeral incandescence of Burning Man's religiosity can even be said to be foundational.

---

[47] Gauthier, 'Primat de l'authenticité'.

[48] See Robert V. Kozinets, 'Can Consumers Escape the Market? Emancipatory Illuminations from Burning Man', *Journal of Consumer Research*, 29/1 (2002): 20–38.

The Burning Man Festival, as many subcultural gatherings, can perhaps best be defined as an 'alternative cultural heterotopia'.[49] Heterotopias are places of otherness, as the Latin signifies. Yet heterotopias, unlike utopias (u-topia: non-place), are not idealised and suspended time-places but rather embodied, socially embedded and heterogeneous liminal social worlds with paradoxical, ambivalent, ambiguous and contested meanings. As an alternative cultural heterotopia, Burning Man actualises, legitimises, and defers the dynamics of consumer culture at the same time as it contests certain of its contradictions (such as the *telos* of profit versus the imperatives of individual authenticity outside any pre-determined frame) by proposing cultural 'alternatives' and new possibilities. This chapter has argued that a subcultural phenomenon such as Burning Man is not a haven of religiosity because it manages to escape consumer culture, but rather because it is a radical example of its most profound symbolic dynamics. As an alternative cultural heterotopia, Burning Man is not so much an array of enchantments and resistances in rupture with the disenchantments of consumer capitalism as it is a blazing and colourful example of its enchantments.

---

49 See Graham St John, 'Alternative Cultural Heterotopia and the Liminoid Body: Beyond Turner at Confest', *Australian Journal of Anthropology*, 12/1 (2001): 47–66.

Chapter 9

Buddha for Sale! The Commoditisation of Tibetan Buddhism in Scotland

John S. McKenzie

Introduction

'Consumer culture uses images and symbolic products which summon up desires and fantasies which suggest that romantic authenticity and emotional fulfilment is achieved in narcissistically pleasing oneself instead of others. Contemporary consumer culture is widening the range of contexts in which such behaviour is deemed to be appropriate'.[1] Everything within such a culture can be commoditised. This results in a society which 'promotes, encourages or enforces the choice of consumerist lifestyle and life strategy and dislikes all alternative cultural options'.[2] This consumer culture is often presented as being destructive of religion in terms of its emphasis on hedonism, the cultivation of expressive lifestyles, and the development of narcissistic and egotistical personality types. Indeed it is often alleged that consumer culture has led to the spiritual impoverishment and selfishness which runs counter to the ascetic regimes which religion teaches.[3]

In *Consuming Religion* Vincent J. Miller[4] explores the effect of consumer culture on Christianity. He argues that the commoditisation of culture has untethered religious meanings from their sources and that symbologies are consumed without reference to the religious traditions that produced them. In other words, the 'corporate cultural production' – the range of media used to present ideas on a global scale – can have the effect of fragmenting religious traditions as they are lifted from their traditional contexts and thrown into 'a cultural marketplace where they can be embraced enthusiastically but not put into practice'.[5] For

1 Mike Featherstone, *Consumer Culture and Postmodernism* (London, 1992), 22.

2 Zygmunt Bauman, *Consuming Life* (Cambridge, 2008), 53.

3 Featherstone, *Consumer Culture.*

4 Vincent J. Miller, *Consuming Religion: Christian Faith and Practice in a Consumer Culture* (New York, 2005).

5 Ibid.

Jeremy Carrette and Richard King[6] this kind of marketing allows companies and their consumers to pay lip-service to the historically significant religions of the world while at the same time distancing themselves from any engagement with the worldviews and forms of life they represent. This has resulted in what they call *The Silent Takeover of Religion* by large businesses which 'use the positive gloss of spirituality to support its corporate interests and work practices'.[7]

However, religion does not disappear in the consumer society. Featherstone[8] compares the ethos of consumerism with that of religion and argues that the focus of the sacred has changed. This is a society in which 'Capital' is God and theology derives its values from the questionable ethical foundations of neoliberalism and corporate capitalism.[9] This has led many theorists, including Carrette and King and Miller to lament the continuing demise of 'authentic' religion. However, Adam Possamai argues that whilst religion cannot escape consumer culture, resistance is not futile.[10] Carrette and King and Miller also acknowledge that religious organisations can resist the corrosive effects of consumer culture on their traditions. Urging that we escape such oppositional and highly normative perspectives, Gauthier et al. argue that more attention needs to be given to the sophisticated ways in which religious organisations negotiate consumer culture.[11] The aim of this chapter is therefore to explore these negotiations through a case study of the Tibetan Buddhist organisation, Rokpa, in Scotland.

The chapter will begin by outlining the significant developments of Rokpa, both in Scotland and worldwide and the research undertaken for this study. Some of the ways in which Buddhism has been adapted for Western consumer culture and the consequences of such adaptations will be identified. However, it will be argued that Tibetan Buddhism has not been passively corroded. Rokpa has responded to the effects of adapting to a consumer culture by limiting the effects of exogenous commoditisation through restricting access to the fundamentals of the tradition whilst embracing the principles of consumption – which are rampant in the consumer culture in which it is situated – bringing them in to the organisation and commoditising Tibetan Buddhism for a Western audience. It will then be demonstrated that this allows Rokpa in Scotland to provide the cultural resources for participants to pursue their religious goals whilst satisfying their consumerist desires within the limits of the organisation. Furthermore it will also be argued that this commoditisation provides the organisation with the resources to pursue religious goals which remain consistent with Tibetan Buddhist philosophy.

---

6 Jeremy Carrette and Richard King, *Selling Spirituality: The Silent Takeover of Religion* (London, 2005).

7 Ibid., 171.

8 Featherstone, *Consumer Culture*.

9 Carrette and King, *Selling Spirituality*.

10 Adam Possamai, *Sociology of Religion for Generations X and Y* (London, 2009).

11 Francois Gauthier, Tuomas Martikainen and Linda Woodhead, 'Introduction: Religion in Consumer Society', *Social Compass*, 58/3 (2011): 291–301.

Research Site and Methodology

Rokpa Scotland

The focus of this chapter is on the Tibetan Buddhist centres in Scotland: the Kagyu Samye Ling Monastery at Eskdalemuir, Dumfriesshire and the other centres that have originated therefrom. Samye Ling was founded in 1967 by Dr Akong Tulku Rinpoche and Chogyam Trungpa Rinpoche.[12] Oliver has illustrated the further development of the monastery: 'Samye Ling … has been with us for over 10 years – a decade in which this hitherto unknown entity has blossomed into an international Tibetan Buddhist Centre.'[13] This expansion has continued. A retreat centre has been built a short walk away from the monastery, alongside a nunnery and the abbot's house. Work is constantly being done to expand Samye Ling and to establish groups throughout Scotland.

There is now a centre in Dundee and group meetings in Edinburgh, Glasgow, Aberdeen, and the Highlands. Rokpa has also become the guardians of the Holy Isle Project, a conservation and retreat centre off the west coast of Scotland. Furthermore, Samye Ling is now the mother institution for establishments in Europe and Africa and has been incorporated into Rokpa International, known in Britain as the Rokpa Trust, a charity organisation founded by Akong in 1980. Rokpa International has central headquarters in Zurich and national headquarters and branches in 18 countries. It is the groups and centres of Rokpa International in Scotland that I refer to as Rokpa Scotland (RS). The website for Samye Ling explains the purpose of the organisation: 'It is a centre for wisdom and learning within the Karma Kagyu tradition of Tibetan Buddhism and is open to people of all faiths and none. You are welcome to come for day visits, short stays or to participate in our meditation retreats and courses available throughout the year.'[14]

Tibetan Buddhism

Up until the second century AD there were two main schools of thought in Buddhism: *Hinayana*, the 'lesser vehicle', which only provides salvation for a select few, and *Mahayana*, meaning 'great vehicle', which provides salvation for all. However, a third form, *Vajrayana*, meaning 'adamantine vehicle', subsequently developed in Tibet.[15] Tibetan Buddhism, with its use of mystical diagrams, or mandalas, and magic formulas, or mantras, to which only initiates have access, came into being as Buddhist teachings from various sources

---

12 Jeremy Paine, *Re-Enchantment: Tibetan Buddhism Comes to the West* (New York, 2004), 85.

13 Ian P. Oliver, *Buddhism in Britain* (London, 1979), 105.

14 http://www.samyeling.org [accessed: 15 September 2008].

15 Emma M. Layman, *Buddhism in America* (Chicago, IL, 1978).

combined with the Bon tradition.[16] Bon, the indigenous religion of Tibet, is a form of shamanism centred on a cult of dead kings, spirit possession, magic, and the exorcism of demons and vampires.[17] Bon, combined with Tantric Buddhism, which emphasises the importance of guru guidance and may utilise sexual yogic techniques, produced a unique path which claims to provide a more rapid way to enlightenment for all. Powers (1995) explains that the *tantras* – 'practices derived from esoteric texts stressing cognitive transformation through visualisations, symbols and rituals'[18] and practised by the Tibetan Schools – differ from other Mahayana practices. These *tantras* are believed by Tibetans to be more powerful and effective in completing the path to enlightenment and are known as 'skilful means', or *upaya*. These skilful means also allow lamas to adapt the philosophy and 'to pitch their teaching according to the particular proclivities and attainment levels of their audience'.[19] This has allowed the lamas in RS to adapt Tibetan Buddhism for the audience in Scotland and still maintain that a traditional form of Tibetan Buddhism is practised by the participants within the organisation.[20] There are four main schools of Tibetan Buddhism – Nyingmapa, Gelugpa, Sakyapa, and Kagyupa. The Nyingmapas place emphasis on the shamanic approach and the Gelugpas, the clerical. The Sakyapas and Kagyupas fall somewhere in between.[21] RS is affiliated with the Kagyu School.

However, it is also important to note that as a form of Mahayana Buddhism, Tibetan Buddhism accepts the basics of both the Hinayana and Mahayana teachings. These include the importance of the 'Three Jewels' of Buddhism – the *Buddha*, the *Dharma*, and the *Sangha*. The term *Buddha* here simply refers to the teacher, *Dharma* to the teachings, and *Sangha* to the community of believers. Tibetan Buddhists also lay great emphasis upon the highest ideal of Mahayana Buddhism – a life dedicated to the wellbeing of others. This is exemplified in the ideal of the *bodhisattva*, a being who takes a vow to work over countless lifetimes for the salvation of others.[22]

---

16 John Powers, *Introduction to Tibetan Buddhism* (New York, 1995).

17 Peter Harvey, *An Introduction to Buddhism: Teachings, History and Practices* (Cambridge, 2005), 145.

18 Powers, *Introduction*, 119–20.

19 Richard King, *Indian Philosophy: An Introduction to Hindu and Buddhist Thought* (Edinburgh, 1999), 95.

20 John McKenzie, 'Keeping It Real!: Constructing and Maintaining Traditional Authenticity in a Tibetan Buddhist Organisation in Scotland', *Sociological Research Online*, 16/3 (31 August 2011), [Online], available at: http://www.socresonline.org.uk/16/3/7.html [accessed: 15 September 2011].

21 Geoffrey Samuel, *Civilised Shamans: Buddhism in Tibetan Societies* (London, 1993).

22 Herbert V. Guenther, *Tibetan Buddhism in Western Perspective* (Berkeley, CA, 1989).

Research Methods

This chapter is based on research which took place in the branches of the Tibetan Buddhist organisation, Rokpa International, in Scotland between June 2004 and September 2009. The study employed a combination of ethnographic methods, including participant observations, document analysis, and qualitative interviews.

Overt participant observations took place in Aberdeen at weekly meetings over the research period, in Dundee at two weekend workshops, in Samye Ling at two weekend workshops, and at a week-long retreat on the Holy Isle Project. Participation involved taking part in teachings, prayers, and socialising and helping with chores. I also carried out 20 formal interviews and my overt status allowed me to conduct further informal interviews whilst participating. In addition I also carried out an analysis of the literature and promotional material produced by RS.

RS provides an ideal site to research the effects of consumer culture on a religious organisation for a number of reasons. First, Samye Ling was one of the first Buddhist organisations to open in the West and it has thus been exposed to the effects of consumer culture for a considerable period of time. Consequently, RS has had time to develop strategies for negotiating consumer culture. Second, the expansion of Rokpa throughout the world allows the researcher to address both the effects of global consumer culture on religion and the negotiation of these effects on a global scale, through a localised study.

Rokpa Scotland (RS) and Consumer Culture

In moving to the West, Rokpa had to adapt Tibetan Buddhism for a Western audience if they were to gain any foothold.[23] At the same time RS also had to construct and maintain plausible links with the historical practice of Tibetan Buddhism.[24] One aspect of this transplantation process involved adapting to the consumer culture by providing a range of services and commodities for a Western consumerist audience. That is, within the West, there is a more compelling pressure to commoditise Buddhism than is the case in the East. As Turner (2011) says, 'Globalized religions are constantly and inevitably drawn into the global circuits of capital insofar as they are themselves converted into lifestyles and into agencies offering commodities and services that cater for the needs of their clients.'[25]

One of the dominant ways that RS has adapted Tibetan Buddhism is through the commoditisation of a range of Tibetan Buddhist teachings for a given fee. Teachings vary from lectures in public places such as the University of Aberdeen, to

---

23 David Kay, *Tibetan and Zen Buddhism in Britain: Transplantation, Development and Adaptation* (London, 2004).

24 McKenzie, 'Keeping It Real!'.

25 Bryan S. Turner, *Religion and Modern Society: Citizenship, Secularisation and the State* (Cambridge, 2011), 277.

weekly *dharma* and prayer sessions at the various groups and centres, introductory courses to advanced *dharmas*, and short- to long-term retreats at the various centres. Tibetan Buddhism is particularly well suited for this because the teachings are very diverse and traditionally taught on three levels, or *yanas*.[26] In addition to these Tibetan Buddhist *dharmas*, RS hosts a range of non-Buddhist courses in subjects such as yoga, Reiki, cookery, and gardening. RS also provides a range of holistic therapies for a given fee. The therapy providers are typically participants who are more deeply involved with the organisation and the clients range from those at the centre of the organisation to those on the periphery. Anyone who wants to take part has to pay a corresponding fee ranging from £5 for public lectures to hundreds of pounds for retreats (for the full range see www.samyeling.org).

Furthermore RS is also open to the general public who can come along to the centres for refreshments in the teashops and to buy products from the shop. Tibetan Buddhism may be particularly suited to this kind of commoditisation due to the exotic nature of the traditional architecture and the range of paraphernalia – including such items as bells, whistles, and mats – that goes along with it.[27] This also provides an outlet for RS to sell *dharma*-based literature to practitioners and the wider public. Many of these goods are also made available to the public via the online shops, at mobile shops at public events, and in retail outlets outside the organisation.

This kind of service provision for a fee is reminiscent of the highly consumerist client and audience cults typically associated with New Age.[28] Several studies have recognised this kind of peripheral consumerist involvement in their studies of Buddhist organisations[29] and others point to the role that New Age played in the development of Buddhism in the West.[30] However, in this case, it is important to note that it is not only the peripheral participants who consume the products and services produced by RS, but also those with deeper degrees of involvement.

Similar forms of adaptation to consumer culture can be found in other Buddhist organisations. This can lead to some claims that Buddhism is being adapted too far and selling out to the materialistic culture of the West. For example Deirdre Green questions whether chanting for material gain represents a selling

---

26 Paine, *Re-Enchantment*.

27 Ibid.

28 Paul Heelas and Linda Woodhead, *The Spiritual Revolution: Why Religion Is Giving Way to Spirituality* (London, 2005); Steve Bruce, *Religion in the Modern World: From Cults to Cathedrals* (Oxford, 1996).

29 See for example, James Coleman, *The New Buddhism: The Western Transformation of an Ancient Tradition* (Oxford, 2001); Layman, *Buddhism in America*; Jan Nattier, 'Who Is a Buddhist?: Charting the Landscape of Buddhist America', in Charles S. Prebish and Kenneth K. Tanaka (eds), *The Faces of Buddhism in America* (Berkeley and Los Angeles, CA, 1998), 183–95.

30 Denise Cush, 'British Buddhism and the New Age', *Journal of Contemporary Religion*, 11 (1996): 195–208.

out of Tibetan Buddhist philosophy to Western consumerism,[31] whilst Coleman reported dissatisfaction amongst Zen students when they felt that centres were more concerned with profit-making than personal growth.[32] Adapting to consumer culture can also lead to the kind of superficial involvement where participants can utilise the resources and symbologies of the religion whilst only paying lip-service to the tradition.[33] For example, figures of the Buddha have become popular as household ornaments amongst people who know little about Buddhism.

Furthermore, external organisations such as the media and global corporations can plunder these symbologies and utilise them to forward their own materialistic ends.[34] For example the media circus surrounding the Dalai Lama turned Buddhism into a fashion, known as 'Buddhist chic', which involved little more than considering the Dalai Lama to be 'cute'.[35] In addition many retailers now sell much of the paraphernalia associated with Buddhism and its symbols have been used in brands such as the Buddha Bar Hotel chain. In this instance the religious symbology of the Buddha has been used to promote a product (alcohol) which runs contrary to one of the five golden rules of Buddhism: specifically, that adherents should not consume intoxicants. In this instance a sacred symbol has been untethered from its religious meaning and commoditised without reference to the religious tradition that produced it. This demonstrates that in our global consumer society 'Cultural commodities become more susceptible to manipulation and misappropriation, free-floating signifiers that can be put to uses unrelated, indeed contrary, to the meanings that they bear'.[36]

This kind of superficial consumption and the corporate takeover of religion have led many to argue that commoditisation erodes religions. Indeed Lorentz argues that Buddhism cannot be adapted for a society in which values of consumerism dominate and at the same time retain plausible links with the Buddhism of the East.[37] Harris elaborates:

> Religious traditions like Buddhism may only remain true to their early canonical purity by continuing their long sleep, oblivious to the realities of the post-traditional order. Only then, assuming that this is even possible, can the imprimatur authenticity be convincingly given. Deviation from this basic

---

31 Deirdre Green, 'Buddhism in Britain: "'Skilful Means" or Selling Out?', in Paul Badham (ed.), *Religion, State, and Society in Modern Britain* (New York, 1989), 277–91.

32 Coleman, *The New Buddhism*, 99.

33 Carrette and King, *Selling Spirituality*, 17.

34 Ibid.

35 Paine, *Re-Enchantment*.

36 Miller, *Consuming Religion*, 72.

37 Todd Lorentz, 'The Dharma and the West: Can Buddhism Survive Consumerism', *Contemporary Buddhism*, 2/2 (2001): 191–9.

> ground of tradition must inevitably result in a state of affairs that is traditional in nothing more than in name.[38]

At the same time others point to modes of negotiation, and the purpose of this chapter is to illustrate how RS negotiates compliance with *and* resistance to commoditisation.

Negotiating the Effects of Commoditisation

It is well documented that there are ways in which religious organisations can resist the corrosive effects of consumer culture.[39] Within the literature surrounding Buddhism it is recognised that the Buddhist liturgy advocates practices that run counter to the values of consumer culture. For example Prebish points out that Buddhist principles urge practitioners not to 'accumulate wealth whilst millions remain hungry'.[40] At the same time McMahan points out that socially engaged Buddhism 'extends to include the interdependence brought about by the globalization of trade and the part that western consumers play in the structural violence and suffering brought about when industry destroys natural resources or exploits labour in developing countries'.[41]

However, during my research, it seemed that RS has also adopted a less confrontational means of resistance and in fact required a group of consumers to facilitate its development. The following sections demonstrate how RS resists consumer culture by limiting access to the higher levels of Tibetan Buddhist teaching and keeping control of commoditisation within the organisation.

Limiting Access

One of the ways in which RS protects Tibetan Buddhism from Western consumer culture is by limiting access to the different levels of teaching.[42] Access to higher levels of teaching is controlled by the lamas and the advanced *dharmas* are chiefly passed down orally to the most dedicated practitioners, in accordance

---

38 Ian Harris, 'Buddhist Environmental Ethics and Detraditionalization: The Case of EcoBuddhism', *Religion*, 25/3 (1995): 199–211.

39 Carrette and King, *Selling Spirituality*; Heelas and Woodhead, *Spiritual Revolution*; Miller, *Consuming Religion*.

40 Charles Prebish, *Luminous Passage: The Practice and Study of Buddhism in America* (Berkeley, CA, 1999), 84.

41 David L. McMahan, 'Repackaging Zen for the West', in Charles S. Prebish and Martin Baumann (eds), *Westward Dharma: Buddhism Beyond Asia* (Berkeley, CA, 2002), 224.

42 McKenzie, 'Keeping It Real!'.

with traditional practice.[43] In this case the lamas therefore act as guardians of the tradition;[44] traditional communications structures are utilised to preserve it.[45] Limiting access to the core of Tibetan Buddhism also helps to limit the effects of commoditisation of Tibetan Buddhism by external organisations. Thus, because external corporations only have access to the periphery of the philosophy, the commoditisation remains superficial. In this case then the superficial consumption of religious symbologies does not corrode the tradition, but instead provides plausibility structures which give RS the opportunity to ensure that the central practices retain authentic links with traditional Tibetan Buddhist practice.[46] In addition to limiting the access of external agencies, RS further resists the effects of exogenous commoditisation by keeping it within the organisation.

Controlling Commoditisation

Rather than passively allowing the corporate takeover of its religious philosophy, RS actively commoditises Tibetan Buddhism for a Western audience. Firstly, RS provides a range of Tibetan Buddhist teachings, other courses and health therapies, and opens tearooms and shops to the public. For example, during a visit to Samye Ling for a course I met a family in the tearoom who had just dropped in for refreshments. As one of the visitors explained:

> I was visiting my family and went for a run in the countryside. We needed to stop for tea and thought it looked really nice here so we decided to come in. I do not really know anything about what they do here but it seems nice and peaceful and the grounds are nice.

RS also welcomes visitors to come on holiday to Samye Ling and the Holy Isle Project. Whilst on retreat on the Holy Isle Project I met a couple from Edinburgh who explained their presence on the Isle:

> We come to the Holy Island every year for a walking holiday. It is so beautiful and peaceful here and there is a great hill to climb running across the middle of the island. We do not get involved with the Buddhists though. I mean we chat and things but we don't participate.

RS sells a wide range of Tibetan literature and paraphernalia via the various retail outlets associated with the organisation. Indeed, it seemed during my participation that making money was a high priority. For example, whilst on retreat at the Holy Isle Project one participant was receiving an Indian head massage from another

---

43 Coleman, *The New Buddhism*, 104.

44 McKenzie, 'Keeping It Real!'.

45 Miller, *Consuming Religion*, 178.

46 McKenzie, 'Keeping It Real!'.

participant. When the group leader observed this he suggested that the receiver of the treatment should make a donation to the Holy Isle in return for the treatment. In addition, after the retreat, I asked the photographer if he could email me a photograph of the retreat participants. He agreed but was immediately reminded that a charge for the photograph had not yet been set.

This emphasis on making money may persist because Samye Ling has been developed along a business model. For example, the current abbot or lama of Samye Ling first became involved with Rokpa in his capacity as a business graduate and only took ordination vows later.[47] There are also a whole host of professionals such as doctors and lawyers involved with the administration of Rokpa International and developments tend to follow a clear and structured plan. Evidence of global branding also emerged when all the Rokpa centres in Europe changed their name so they all begin with 'Samye Dzong'. Lama Yeshe explained that this allowed the centres to be recognisable no matter where in the world they are located.

This commoditisation of Tibetan Buddhism can result in superficial levels of involvement. This is exemplified in a brutally frank manner by Isaac, an occasional attendee at Rokpa Aberdeen:

> I sometimes like to go to Rokpa meetings but it is just for a bit of a laugh. I mean it's quite trendy so I have made a little shrine in my bedroom and give the Buddha a kiss every now and then and do my own kind of chanting. It's just a fashion accessory. I have no real conviction, or any intention in taking my involvement any further. I will probably move on to the next trend soon.

Furthermore there is evidence that some participants feel discouraged from continuing their involvement due to what they see as the commercial nature of the organisation. For example, Jacob, a university lecturer in optometry, explained why he did not further his involvement:

> I do not mind going to the occasional class, but I am always suspicious when things start to cost so much money. It seems wrong that a religious organisation should charge so much and I do not think it is fair that some are excluded because they cannot afford it.

However, such adaptation to consumer culture allows RS to resist the takeover of their religious symbology and its corrosion, by commoditising Tibetan Buddhism within the organisation. In so doing RS can protect the heart of Tibetan Buddhism from corrosion by reinforcing the interconnections between doctrinal symbols and practice at the various classes and by strengthening and facilitating the cultural agency that has accompanied the rise of consumer culture by providing authorisation practices and spaces in which believers can act as agents of the

[47] Ani Rinchen Khandro, *Kagyu Samye Ling: The Story* (Dumfriesshire, 2007).

tradition.[48] For example, many participants explained that they only bought the Buddhist literature and went to teachings that were recommended by their gurus, as this ensured that they were learning from the 'right sources'. Indeed, the kind of pick and mix consumption associated with the New Age[49] was actively discouraged in the teaching sessions. This is well illustrated by the teacher in Aberdeen:

> I heard on the radio that Buddhism is New Age. No it is not. It is a very ancient practice. You should not just play around with meditation or come and go when you please. Try a bit of this and a bit of that. Pick what suits you and leave the rest. This is a very serious matter.

Many of the more involved practitioners also showed some disapproval of superficial involvement. This is well demonstrated by schoolteacher Kathleen's attitude to Isaac, discussed above:

> Isaac has come and gone over the years and there are many others like him. I am not sure why they bother really. I guess they might think it's fashionable. It's not a game. I guess we are open to everyone, but I do not particularly want to be surrounded by people who come here because it's trendy.

This kind of superficial involvement encourages some to deepen their involvement. Judy, a scientist, explained her involvement:

> I am not here just for fun. It takes up most of my time when I am not at work. I volunteer at Rokpa Dundee so I am there every night and there at the weekends. … In fact there is a group of us who get up early in the morning and come into the centre to practise before going to work.

Similar levels of commitment can be found in the Aberdeen group, despite conflicting demands. For example Stewart, an environmental officer, spoke of his practice:

> I like to do as much as I can. I go to meetings regularly and on workshops and to retreats. I even went on a pilgrimage to Nepal last year. However, I cannot always get out of work. Sometimes I have to work late and at weekends and sometimes I run out of annual leave or sometimes I cannot afford it.

It is also fairly common for participants who have been absent for a period of time to pay more for classes on return. For example, after a couple of months of attending meetings at Rokpa Aberdeen, Sarah, a schoolteacher, appeared for the first time. When she paid for the class she handed over 20 pounds and said

48 Miller, *Consuming Religion*, 11.

49 Bruce, *Religion in the Modern World.*

'Keep the change. I have not made a contribution for a while'. Others enjoyed going for some of the health treatments whilst at the same time making a financial contribution to the organisation. For example Ian, a retired headmaster, explained why he liked to go for treatments: 'Rokpa do a lot of good work so I do like to support the centre and the therapists. So I keep regular contact with the centre and like to put more money in the coffers.'

Furthermore studies suggest that the general trend amongst Buddhist organisations has been to disassociate with the New Age in recent years,[50] in order to protect the philosophy. Such association can result in the 'cannibalisation' of Buddhism by 'any number of New Age or quasi-Buddhists groups … taking key Buddhist teachings and practices out of cultural and institutional context as if acquired on a shopping spree'.[51] However, in this study, it appeared that this did not result in less consumption, but a consumption that was more directed by the authority structures, such as the teachers and their literature, within the organisation. That is to say, RS provides both the cultural space and the authoritative guidance for practitioners to achieve religious goals within the consumer culture, within the limits of the organisation. This is recognisable in RS as participants are encouraged to spend their money in the organisation so that they know that the produce has come from an ethical source. By stocking crafts from Tibet and providing food grown in their own gardens, RS can remind people of where products come from. For example, after a trip to Tibet, the teacher reported that he sourced traditionally-crafted Tibetan wares that were now available at the Rokpa Dundee shop. This combats the commoditisation of culture and religion by training our imagination to consider the connections between 'cultural objects and their originating traditions'.[52] This is recognised by Kathleen, a long-term member of the Aberdeen group:

> I like to buy as much as I can from Rokpa in terms of books and crafts. At least when you buy it here you know that your money is reaching the people who produced the stuff and that the money you spend will be put to good use. Besides you never know what you are buying from other places, who made it and where it came from. So if Rokpa do it then I get it here.

Furthermore, considering the origins of the beliefs and products of foreign traditions simultaneously calls attention to the relationship among symbols, beliefs, and practices in one's own and thus serves as a challenge to the commoditisation of culture.[53]

---

50 Cush, 'British Buddhism and the New Age'.

51 Bruce Matthews, 'Buddhism in Canada', in Charles S. Prebish and Martin Baumann (eds), *Westward Dharma: Buddhism Beyond Asia* (Berkeley, CA, 2002), 132.

52 Miller, *Consuming Religion*, 194.

53 Ibid.

Further Religious Goals

In order to transplant Tibetan Buddhism to Scotland, RS had to raise funds by commoditising Tibetan Buddhism for a Western audience. As Baumann says 'All studies of Buddhist groups in Britain emphasize the importance of material conditions to their successful transplantation and growth. At its most basic level this refers to a group's ability to attract committed supporters who will become financial sponsors.'[54] Whilst many studies such as those of Layman and Prebish highlight the provision of a variety of teachings, little is said about the financial contribution participants make to the development of the organisation. As has been shown here, attending the various courses provided by RS involves paying a corresponding fee. Such commoditisation may seem to dilute the religious tradition as the objectives of profit-making may seem to obscure religious goals.[55] However, such enterprise has also provided RS with the financial and institutional resources to further its religious goals. In other words, RS can use profits to put into action the bodhisattva vow to alleviate suffering of all sentient beings by promoting Tibetan Buddhist practice, forging environmental conservation programmes, and establishing welfare projects, both in Scotland and throughout the world. As the website for Samye Ling explains:

> Samye Ling is part of Rokpa Trust, a registered charity which has three main areas of activity: spiritual, humanitarian aid, and Tibetan medicine and therapy. Our activity extends around the world through an international network of Dharma centres.[56]

In the first instance, by providing a range of teachings and therapies RS can address the spiritual needs and promote the health of the participants in Scotland. For example, the Rokpa Dundee Healthy Living Centre provides a range of *dharmas* and therapies that claim to reduce stress and promote good health, both mental and physical. Many respondents also reported the health benefits of the *dharmas* and therapies. For example, Dot, a social worker from Dundee, explained:

> I was looking for help with my own personal problems. I have an anxiety neurosis and clinical depression and an attachment disorder. I have tried hypnotherapy, aromatherapy, reflexology, psychotherapy, psychology and my mental health problems still persist. I have been on medication for ten years and have put on five stone in weight. So I have tried all these things and nothing has worked. Going to Rokpa seems to be helping.

---

54 Kay, *Tibetan and Zen Buddhism in Britain*, 12.

55 Coleman, *The New Buddhism*, 99.

56 http://www.samyeling.org [accessed: 15 September 2008].

The monies raised through these and other service provisions can then be used to provide further teaching facilities and develop them. For example, a college for Buddhist Studies is currently being built at Samye Ling. Reliance on the consumer activities of participants for such RS developments is well illustrated in an email sent out to RS participants by the teacher:

> It has been brought to my attention that Rokpa Dundee lost £4,000 last year. Rokpa Dundee is the foundation of all the other meditation groups. If it fails then all the other groups fail too. It is noticeable that many in the groups are willing to let Jiga travel, but are unwilling to attend workshops and those that do only come at the last minute. You need to make a commitment to the classes and workshops as they are the foundation for the future.

Funds raised are also used to support welfare projects. For example, RS has run Lochlorien, a therapeutic community in Dumfriesshire for people with mental health problems since 1989.[57] On a global level Rokpa International also runs welfare projects. The website explains 'We support around 150 projects whose primary goal is to help the very poorest of the poor in the most remote regions of the world.'[58] Projects in these areas include promoting the welfare and safety of children, helping the homeless, and providing health care.

RS is also involved in environmental projects. The Holy Isle is dedicated to wildlife preservation and thousands of trees have been planted there as part of a conservation project.[59] Likewise Rokpa International is committed to planting trees in environmentally critical areas and protecting endangered habitats throughout the world.[60]

Thus by commoditising Tibetan Buddhism in the ways it does, RS can raise the resources to fund spiritual, humanitarian and environmental projects on a local and global level. In this case then, commoditisation does not undermine religious values, but rather provides the financial resources to promote them.

Conclusion

The purpose of this chapter is to explore the effects of consumer culture on religion through a case study of the branches of the Tibetan Buddhist organisation, Rokpa International, in Scotland. In so doing this chapter aims to extend the study of the relationship between consumer society and religion beyond the Christian context, and, more particularly, to explore the sophisticated and complex ways in which religious organisations can both adapt to and resist the effects of consumer

57 http://www.lochlorien.tc [accessed: 21 September 2007].

58 http://www.rokpa.org [accessed: 20 January 2010].

59 http://www.holyisland.org [accessed: 15 September 2008].

60 http://www.rokpa.org [accessed: 20 January 2010].

culture. In other words, rather than allowing the corporate takeover of Tibetan Buddhism, RS adopts active strategies to preserve the fundamentals of Tibetan Buddhism by limiting access to the higher levels of teaching. Thus any exogenous commoditisation of the philosophy remains superficial and thus provides the plausibility structures for RS to claim that the organisation retains credible links with a historical practice. In addition RS actively commoditises Tibetan Buddhism by providing a range of courses, therapies, and services for participants to consume. This allows participants to satisfy consumerist desires within the organisation whilst providing RS with the resources to further its religious goals via global humanitarian, spiritual and ecological programmes. Thus RS provides a subcultural space where the organisation and its participants can 'accomplish politically and religiously significant things through their consumption'.[61] Furthermore, by commoditising Tibetan Buddhism, RS can remind participants of both the origins of their products and the interdependence of a globalised society. Thus RS can resist the effects of exogenous commoditisation by 'engaging consumerism on the level of practices and structures rather than meaning'.[62]

However, it is important to remember that tactics for re-embedding a tradition must swim against a massive cultural tide of commoditisation. To resist the corrosive effects of commoditisation organisations must have a robust institutional and communications structure. Nonetheless, it must also be accepted that these structures are still dwarfed by the corporate culture industries.[63] Therefore RS needs to be constantly vigilant as to the effects of consumer culture, while being profoundly shaped by its negotiation within a globalising consumer culture.

---

[61] Miller, *Consuming Religion*, 145.

[62] Ibid., 145.

[63] Ibid., 223.

Chapter 10

Mutual Interests? Neoliberalism and New Age During the 1980s

Lars Ahlin

Among scholars New Age is almost unanimously considered to have its origin in the counterculture of the 1960s and 1970s[1] and the view is also that this cultural movement was from the beginning strongly opposed to capitalism and materialism. To a large extent this is true, but for essential parts of the New Age movement the latter aspect had changed by the 1980s. This was the decade during which, due to the success of neoliberalism, the whole socio-economic agenda in most parts of the Western world changed radically. In Sweden, until 1976, the Social Democratic Party had held an almost hegemonic position for more than 40 years. This changed during the 1980s, however, when a liberal agenda gained momentum. One forum in which neoliberal ideas were propagated and the old Keynesian ideas were challenged during this period was one of Sweden's largest daily newspapers, *Svenska Dagbladet* (*SvD*). Simultaneously, in the same paper, New Age ideas were propagated to such an extent that one section of the paper received a prize for its dissemination of New Age ideas to a wider public audience. How is this seemingly paradoxical situation to be interpreted? Is it a question of coincidence, or is it possible to find other, more sociologically based explanations?

Historical and Economic Background

In the late 1960s and in the 1970s the left set the agenda in Sweden. Demonstrations were held against the capitalist system, the US as the capitalist superpower, and the war in Vietnam. The Swedish Employer's Association (SAF) decided on a counterattack. Their information-gathering activities would be given more resources with the objective, as expressed in an SAF newsletter of 1972, to counteract 'the increasingly anti-corporate and subversive tendencies in the formation of public opinion, particularly as manifested in the so-called left-wing

---

1 Wouter J. Hanegraaff, *New Age Religion and Western Culture: Esotericism in the Mirror of Secular Thought* (Leiden and Albany, NY, 1998). Olav Hammer, *På spaning efter helheten: New Age, en ny folktro?* (Stockholm, 1997).

skewing of the media'.[2] Sture Eskilsson, head of the information department of the SAF, was requested to make this aspiration a reality. He later became the strategist behind the construction of the liberal think tank, Timbro 1978, and numerous other specialised organisations.[3] Timbro was designed 'to originate, promote and disseminate ideas and issues supporting the principles of free markets, free enterprise, individual liberty and a free society'.[4] Timbro's influence was not just a result of its financial strength, but also its ability to change 'the thinking of academic economists, endorsing their agenda with expert authority'.[5] These initiatives were inspired by examples in the US, but probably also in the UK, where similar think tanks had been founded in the early 1970s with the aim of influencing the intellectual and ideological landscape in such a way that it would lead to social and economic changes in the country. The stated objective was to create an 'enterprise culture'.[6]

However, from an employers' perspective, the situation in Sweden during the 1970s did not improve. Not only did they find themselves in an antagonistic relationship with the extreme left, but tensions also increased in relation to the Social Democrats and the trade unions. The following quote from Mauricio Rojas, taken from *Paradoxen SAF: och den svenska modellens uppgång och fall* (SAF: A Paradox), a historical review of the SAF published by the think tank Timbro in 2001, portrays how the SAF experienced the 1970s:

> The 1970s is the era during which Sweden went wrong. The Swedish growth-oriented consensus model was abandoned by an increasingly militant labour movement in interaction with a social democracy that was completely out of touch with 'reality' – that is, the forces and not least the values that once made Sweden into a prosperous nation. Ideological polarisation, political confrontation, and recurring labour disputes replaced the consensus, cooperation, and peace in the labour market that had been characteristic of the previous three decades. Growth slowed significantly, inflation accelerated, Swedish industry lost market shares in the global economy, government finances came increasingly chaotic, and public debt increased massively.[7]

---

2 All translations by the author.

3 Sven Ove Hanson and Anna-Lena Lodenius, *Operation Högervridning* (Stockholm, 1988).

4 http://www.timbro.se/innehall/?art=about-timbro [accessed: 4 September 2011].

5 Desmond King and Fiona Ross, 'Critics and Beyond', in Francis G. Castles, Stephan Leibfried, Jane Lewis, Herbert Obinger and Christopher Pierson (eds), *The Oxford Handbook of the Welfare State* (Oxford and New York, 2010), 48.

6 Paul Morris, 'Freeing the Spirit of Enterprise: The Genesis and Development of the Concept of Enterprise Culture', in Russell Keat and Nicholas Abercrombie (eds), *Enterprise Culture* (Chatham, 1991), 22–3.

7 Mauricio Rojas, *Paradoxen SAF och den svenska modellens uppgång och fall* (Stockholm, 2001), 68.

This outlook resulted in the SAF becoming more active in an increasingly information-intensive effort that came to affect all of society. In a retrospective view of events of the 1980s, moral philosopher Per Bauhn states:

> The neoliberal message was spread by Timbro in two phases. The first was in the form of the 1980's discussion about freedom and talk about the liberation of the individual from what is called state paternalism: that is, tax-funded social security and welfare institutions, from welfare payments to healthcare. These institutions, the neoliberals argued, prevented the individual from taking responsibility for his life. Individual initiative was stifled by the welfare state. People were rendered passive. Why should you work when you could live on welfare benefits?[8]

What was at stake in Sweden during the 1980s was what Noam Chomsky has called 'the control of the public mind'[9] and essential in achieving this is 'the power to set the agenda'. Violence is not an option in undertaking such endeavours in democratic societies; the new agenda 'must be instilled into the public mind by more subtle means',[10] one of which, naturally, is via the media.

What was happening in Sweden was not unique to this small, northern European country; quite the contrary. John Kenneth Galbraith states in *The World Economy since the Wars* (1994) that during both the Kennedy and Johnson administrations, the public considered the federal government to be a positive force for the achievement of national prosperity. This attitude changed, however, during the Nixon administration, especially after Nixon's re-election in 1972. After the Watergate scandal of 1972–74 and Carter's inauguration in 1976, the attitude towards the federal government became even more negative and during the Reagan administration this negativity intensified further.[11] The federal government's role was then said to have become too prominent and many argued the need for the market to regain its former dominance.[12]

By the end of the 1970s 'the swing to the right' in Sweden was generally considered to be the manifestation of a reassessment of the Keynesian Welfare State policy, which had been the ideal for decades in much of the Western world. The above developments in the United States were particularly important to Sweden, not only because the country was so financially dependent on the United States, but also due to the fact that the neoliberals in Sweden were inspired by American

---

8 Per Bauhn and Jan Svensson, 'Retoriken ändrade välfärdssamhället', *LUM: Lunds Universitet Meddelar*, 11 (1996).

9 Noam Chomsky, *Profits over People: Neoliberalism and Global Order* (New York, 1999), 45.

10 Noam Chomsky, *Necessary Illusions* (Boston, MA, 1989), 48.

11 John Kenneth Galbraith, *The World Economy since the Wars* (London, 1994), 206.

12 Ibid., 211.

scholars and economists.[13] In this context, it is worth mentioning that 'the two founding fathers of neoliberalism', Friedrich von Hayek and Milton Friedman, were awarded the Nobel Prize in economics in 1974 and 1976 respectively, and that their ideas thus gained a foothold in Sweden. Furthermore, the new economic doctrines gained a political platform, first as a result of Margaret Thatcher's victory in the elections of 1979 in Great Britain and then through Reagan's victory in the United States the following year.

In 1976 the Swedish Social Democrats lost the election for the first time in 44 years and the breakthrough of neoliberal ideas into Swedish government policy followed in 1980. Swedish political scientist Rune Premfors (1984) links this change to the then current economic crisis and believes that neoliberal ideas were expressed directly for the first time in the bourgeois government's supplementary Budget Bill, passed in the spring of 1980. In summary, the background to neoliberal ideas gaining a foothold 'in Sweden, where Keynesian ideas were more embedded than in Britain or America' was the existence of 'right-wing think tanks with critical legitimization by the social democratic economist Assar Lindbeck'.[14]

Svenska Dagbladet: Sounding the Neoliberal Charge

In 1980, as previously mentioned, efforts increased to bring neoliberal ideas to a wider public. Part of this strategy was the direct and significantly increased participation of SAF and the Swedish National Federation of Industry in the public debate being held in the metropolitan press – namely in *SvD* and *Dagens Nyheter* – at the beginning of the 1980s.[15] A study shows that *SvD* constituted the main arena in this regard.[16] Indeed from 1980 and throughout the decade *SvD* was the primary mouthpiece among the press in promoting the neoliberal ideology. This newspaper can be characterised by its closeness to the liberal-conservative party (*Moderata samlingspartiet*) and its positive attitude towards and close relations with the private business world. Its readers were in general highly educated and highly paid.

What ideas then did the SAF (and the Federation of Industry) try to disseminate via the pages of *SvD*? Kristina Boréus' (1994) investigation of this question revealed the cornerstones of the neoliberal ideology as presented in the paper to be: a) state control of society should be minimised; b) the market should be allowed to operate freely; c) support for the individualistic postulate: anything that violates an individual's rights is unfair – the individual is inviolable and only under special conditions may the individual's interests be sacrificed for

---

13 Kristina Boréus, *Högervåg. Nyliberalismen och kampen om språket i svensk debatt 1969–1989* (Stockholm, 1994), 42.

14 King and Ross, 'Critics and Beyond', 48.

15 Boréus, *Högervåg*, 157.

16 Ibid., 390.

the collective; d) people tend to choose rationally and with self-interest; e) the freedom ideal is negatively defined, that is, freedom is the absence of coercion, and the ideals of rights are also negatively defined – this is, the individual will receive protection (mainly in relation to the state) so that nobody will be hindered from doing what they already do; f) the individual's rights in relation to majorities are emphasised; and g) capitalist society is basically harmonious, thus no fundamental conflicts of interest exist. One of the main harmonic relationships is that between capital and labour.[17]

Svenska Dagbladet: A Mouthpiece for New Age Ideas

The same newspaper, *SvD*, which was characterised above as a propagator of neoliberal ideas in the 1980s has also been described as the most important among the mainstream media when it came to spreading New Age ideas during the same period.[18] This evaluation is made in *Sökaren* (The Seeker), for many years Sweden's dominant New Age magazine. This evaluation, however, does not apply to *SvD* as a whole, but to the daily women's page 'Idag' (Today), described by *Sökaren* as *SvD*'s 'New Age Page'.[19]

What ideas then, in this context, are characteristically New Age? An investigation of this was one of the aims of the PhD thesis *New Age: Consumer Goods or Values Worth Fighting For?*[20] For this purpose articles from the 'Idag' page whose content could be described as New Age were collected, amounting to, in total, about 800 articles published between 1974 and 1995. These articles naturally fell into five categories according to content: psychology, medicine, economics/business, religion, and physics.

The largest category, in terms of number of articles, was religion, followed by psychology, medicine, economics, and physics. One pervading theme, regardless of category of content, which comes across particularly clearly during the 1980s, is the principle of the individual's unique value; the primacy of the individual. From this, virtually all other detectable New Age-related viewpoints can be derived.

Of course the idea of the individual's primacy appears and is constructed differently in different contexts, but it can be summarised in a few statements: an individual decides his/her own reality; an individual should rely only on his/her own authority; an individual has full responsibility for his/her own life; the individual has enormous capacity/potential/force just waiting to be fully expressed, and so on. This positive attitude towards the primacy of the individual is contrasted with its negative counterpart – the attitude of established institutions that *do not* recognise the primacy of the individual, but instead seek to limit and

17 Ibid., 72–96.

18 *Sökaren*, 1 (1985); *Sökaren*, 6 (1994).

19 *Sökaren*, 2 (1981).

20 Lars Ahlin, *New Age: konsumtionsvara eller värden att kämpa för?* (Lund, 2001).

suppress the individual. Society is just one of these institutions, each with their own hierarchy, dogma, tradition, and authority.

In terms of the sometimes ambiguous concept 'New Age', it seems reasonable to differentiate between three types: one which has a spiritual/religious focus, such as that which David Spangler (1984) considers to be essential, since it deals with 'the birth of the sacred and a resacralizing of life on earth'; a second, which has an intellectual character, preoccupied with a change in the basic values of society, that is to say, shifts of paradigms; and the third, the 'popular New Age', which provisionally can be defined as the one on which the media focuses.[21] The first type is in all likelihood of small numeric importance and therefore also of small societal importance. The intellectual type is important, not due to its numeric size, but to the fact that to a large extent it has been integrated into mainstream society. Lastly, the popular type has acquired societal importance due to its numeric size. It is also the one most associated with the concept of 'New Age', both among scholars and in the public perception. In the Swedish context a similar differentiation is applicable. Sven Magnusson (2000), the founder and editor of *Sökaren*, differentiates between '*folklig* New Age' (popular New Age) and '*klok* New Age' (wise/intelligent New Age). In *SvD* we are dealing with the intellectual type of New Age.

New Age Articles Related to Economics and Business

Firstly, it must be noted that until 1980 the 'Idag' page only published a few articles in which New Age ideas related to economics and business emerged. This, however, changed rather dramatically with the advent of the new decade. During the early 1980s this type of article was in one way or another related to the conference 'Living Business in a New Age', which was held between 1980 and 1983 and arranged by the Swedish Personnel Administration Association. In 1980 the annual conference was heralded, according to the 'Idag' page, as being launched 'in the sign of the New Age', which was supposedly reflected in its representation of the environmental movement, the women's liberation movement, the new spirituality, and general interest in personal development and new businesses.[22] Another recurring point of departure for many articles related to economics and business, was the New Age community Findhorn, in Scotland. Such articles might take the form of interviews with representatives of the Findhorn community, or 'Idag' journalists reporting on their impressions of courses held there.

New approaches in business and economics were often accompanied by a belief that 'the New Age' was advancing. Indeed, descriptions of 'the New Age' at that time envisioned a new kind of society, completely different from that of the

---

21 James R. Lewis and J. Gordon Melton, *Perspectives on the New Age* (Albany, NY, 1992); Richard Kyle, *The New Age Movement in American Culture* (Lanham, MD, 1995); Hanegraaff, *New Age Religion.*

22 *Svenska Dagbladet*, 5 October 1980.

1970s. To make this vision a reality required paradigm shifts in economics and business, which were afoot as a result of a paradigm shift that had already taken place in psychology. What was hinted at was the view, taken from humanistic psychology, that human beings have within themselves incredibly large untapped resources through which they can achieve anything they want. However, before these resources can be accessed, all obstacles to growth, creativity, and development must be eliminated; although ultimately it is the individual who is solely responsible for his or her development. As an American interviewee expressed it: 'the only limits we have are those we have created ourselves in our unconsciousness.'[23]

The new society, which would materialise after the paradigm shift, was in no way a socialist system, but a transformed and humanistic, yet still capitalist society. In the business world of the New Age, everyone would have the opportunity to take responsibility and grow; work would be the life-goal for the individual and the lines between work and leisure would become blurred. The destructive, conflictual thinking that characterised the 'old' time would not have a place in this new society. Instead, consensus would come to characterise both economics and politics.

However, in 1983 a radical change in attitude towards the concept of 'New Age' occurred on the 'Idag' page. Until then, the concept had been extremely positive and closely associated with new approaches in several areas, not least in economics and business. Now the paper distanced itself from the concept since it had become, as it expressed, increasingly associated with trickery and commercialism. However, despite the disappearance of 'New Age' as a concept, the views that had previously been described as New Age did not disappear. They were still given a great deal of space and some were focused on and developed even more than they had been previously.

One such view was the development of individual potential, which continued to receive wide coverage until 1987. Others that were focused on in the second half of the 1980s involved the ideas of 'good business' and 'good investment'. These themes were concerned with the extent to which businesses in various substantial respects were moral. However, clearly this was not a question of how altruistic they were. Repeatedly it was stressed that good business in a moral sense was also good business in an economic sense.

Another motif to be given coverage, in particular from the late 1980s onwards, was consensus. The idea was that consensus rather than conflict should characterise society. Decisions should be taken by consensus, within companies as well as in politics and the labour market, without the polarisation that characterised the 1970s. The common good was supposedly hidden behind all the surface conflicts between, for example, employees and management.

---

23 *Svenska Dagbladet*, 17 December 1986.

Neoliberal Ideology and New Age: A Comparison

It was stated above that one view was dominant in the 'Idag' page throughout the 1980s – the principle of the primacy of the individual – and that it was possible to derive virtually all other New Age views from this. The individualistic postulate has similar importance and weight in neoliberal ideology. Moreover similarities between the two notions are striking and indeed almost totally overlapping.

A pregnant expression of this postulate can be found in Margaret Thatcher's statement: 'There is no such thing as society, only individuals and their families.'[24] Most of the other cornerstones of neoliberalism, as described above, are also capable of being derived from this. For example, it is believed that the market should be allowed to operate freely, as individuals and their freedom of choice is decisive for the market to function, which is also directly related to the idea that people tend to act rationally and be self-serving. The individualistic postulate is also directly related to neoliberal views about rights and freedom, both of which are negatively defined: the individual should not be deterred from acting as he or she thinks is right. Furthermore, the idea of individual rights *vis-à-vis* the majority (the view on democracy) is another expression of the individualistic postulate.

In their respective views of the individual one therefore finds the crucial point at which the two systems of ideas, neoliberalism and New Age, coincide. However, among basic neoliberal ideas, two cannot be directly traced to the individualistic postulate: the view that state influence over society should be minimised and the view that there is a fundamental harmony in capitalism. The former idea – the state and its negative role – is not explicitly discussed on the 'Idag' page. However, the negative role played both by 'society' and by various established institutions – since they do not recognise the individual's primacy – is frequently discussed. Nevertheless, parallels are clearly made between the perception of the state and that of established institutions and that a negative view of all sorts of oppressive institutions and collectives are easily transferred to apply to the state. The latter idea – the basic harmony of capitalism – on the other hand, is something strongly supported on the 'Idag' page. When commenting on the dawning of a New Age, this is highly contrasted to the 1970s which were said to be dominated by strong conflicts, especially between employees and corporate managements.

New Age and Neoliberalism Side by Side in Svenska Dagbladet

'New Age' and 'neoliberalism' were, and are, seemingly extremely different concepts, belonging to very different societal spheres. The former is something that the public presumably associates with 'slightly weird people', 'green people', and bizarre religious beliefs; the latter is associated with the business world and

---

[24] Quote from Michael Thompson, 'The Dynamics of Cultural Theory and Their Implications for the Enterprise Culture', in S.H. Heap and A. Ross (eds), *Understanding the Enterprise Culture: Themes in the Work of Mary Douglas* (Edinburgh, 1992), 182–202.

right-wing political parties. Despite this, the two concepts, at least the intellectual type of New Age and neoliberalism, have, as we have seen, quite a lot in common. *SvD* provides a good indication of this, and both New Age and neoliberal ideology were given considerable space during the same period of time. How can this be explained?

It is unreasonable to imagine that the corporate world wanted to create 'a centre of light that through dedicated work will create a global network of light – Christ's living body on earth. A theocracy that attempts to incarnate the world soul'[25] in which neoliberalism would flourish. This was how the New Age community Findhorn in the late 1970s was described in *SvD*. In spite of the fact that Findhorn was also known during the following decade as a spiritual centre, spirituality was not an issue discussed in the paper in regard to Findhorn. Instead Findhorn was described as a conference and training centre to which representatives of Swedish businesses made pilgrimages. On the whole, the spiritual aspects of New Age were not highlighted in relation to economics and business. What was focused on was rather that New Age views, especially those related to economy and industry, were fully in line with certain economic interests. This meant that these views acquired legitimacy among many of *SvD*'s readers, who to a large degree belonged to an elite with both high levels of education and high incomes,[26] and most likely were also supporters of the right-wing party which from 1980 embarked on the neoliberal path.

This legitimacy can be assumed, then, to have been transferred to New Age views in other areas of society. The long series, entitled 'Positive Expectations', published in 1980 may have worked exactly in this way. New views in psychology were here given legitimacy since it was stressed that these functioned as guiding principles for representatives from the corporate world. The same psychological viewpoints were used to justify the need for new views in both medicine and religion. The legitimacy applied to new views in relation to these areas may in turn have given legitimacy to new approaches in business and economics.

But how to explain the coexistence of New Age and neoliberalism in *SvD*? One explanation is that this tended to result in a continuous, reciprocal process of legitimising. Most important in this context was of course the view of the individual and its right to accountability, development, and freedom from coercion. The negative mirror image – that various institutions oppressed and restricted individuals – was also of importance. The fact that these views to a great extent were worded similarly, and simultaneously but in different parts of the paper, both in an economic/political context and in that part of the paper primarily viewed as the women's page, meant mutual legitimisation.

---

25 *Svenska Dagbladet*, 22 October 1978.

26 Ahlin, *New Age*, 104–10.

An Affinity between New Age and Neoliberalism?

This phenomenon of New Age and neoliberalism flourishing side by side in the Swedish newspaper *SvD* was later observable on a more general level. As shown above, there are considerable overlaps between the basic ideas of neoliberal ideology and those of the New Age movement. There is a clear affinity, a kinship between the two, especially in regard to perceptions of the individual. This provides an example of a special economic ideology fitting well with a particular religious view at a certain point in history; this can also be seen as a parallel to the affinity Max Weber (1978) saw between the 'Spirit of Capitalism' and the Protestant ethic. These two interacted, according to Weber, in the emergence of modern capitalism, although they had completely different goals. For capitalists, the goal was increased efficiency and profits, while for the Calvinists, the goal was salvation. Despite its completely different motives the Protestant ethic could, according to Weber, when the necessary material conditions were in place, contribute to the rise of capitalism. The interaction between the emerging neoliberalism and New Age can be interpreted in a similar way.

Neoliberals fought for the establishment of a radically new economic agenda, while favourable material conditions were at hand in the form of the IT revolution and a massive increase in globalisation.[27] But a prerequisite for complete success was that the mode of thinking which had been firmly established in Swedish society during the previous 20–30 years should be changed. This mode had its basis in the idea of 'the people's home', which is to say the Swedish Social Democratic Welfare State, which was characterised by, on the one hand, a strong state and strong collectives and on the other hand, a collaboration between the Social Democrats and the main export companies. Social security and equality had been the hallmarks of this discourse. However, instead of being, as previously, honourable concepts, the aim of the neoliberalist endeavour was to change radically the connotations of these notions from something generally seen as positive into something interpreted negatively, as an expression of a 'dependency culture' in which individuals were rendered passive and were hindered in the self-development that they were meant to be achieving.

When in 1975 the SAF went from being primarily an organisation that made agreements with the trade unions to being a creator of public opinion, it was precisely the changing of such patterns of thinking that was the final objective. They certainly wanted to win an intellectual and academic struggle, but a further aim was to change the whole mode of thinking, the entire climate of opinion.[28] Or to paraphrase Chomsky, they wanted to set the agenda and thereby acquire control over the public mind. To this end, they made efforts in various fields and at multiple levels.[29] That the intellectual battle was won is evident in how the new

27 Rojas, *Paradoxen SAF*, 85.

28 Hans de Geer, *Arbetsgivarna. SAF i tio decennier* (Stockholm, 1992).

29 Ibid., 81–2.

views were established in the mass media during the first half of the 1980s. In both of the two news programmes that aired on TV and radio, neoliberal ideas acquired more and more airtime during this period.[30]

This undoubtedly helped to change thinking in purely economic terms, but what was at stake was a change in the basic mindset of the individual. This might be one reason why New Age ideas were allowed space in *SvD*. The religious or spiritual aspects of New Age must have been obvious to the economic establishment, but they were clearly willing to accept these since other ideas associated with New Age were consistent with neoliberal ones. A willingness to accept the spiritual element prevailed because the basic ideas with regard to the primacy of the individual were part of New Age thinking, and by association, the negative perception of oppressive institutions and collectives. Through the New Age movement, a wider dissemination of basic neoliberal ideas could be expected because of the affinity between the two systems. Thus New Age ideas propagated in *SvD* could be used to influence certain groups in society towards a more positive attitude to neoliberal ideas. The target groups here were women and people of the post-war generations who had come to adopt post-materialistic values of freedom.[31] However, the background for this co-existence of New Age and neoliberalism should be regarded as only one small part of a much more broadly laid-out strategy to bring about a change in the climate of opinion as a whole.

The Protestant ethic had played an essential role, according to Weber, in the beginnings of capitalism, but when the capitalist machinery began to move, driven entirely by its own force, there was no longer a need for it. New Age ideas in relation to neoliberalism seemed to be headed towards the same destiny. During the 1980s struggle for the public mind there was a need for, among many other things, New Age ideas. Once neoliberal ideas had gained the upper hand, the need for New Age ideas vanished. They were stripped of their spiritual content and only the instrumental elements remained.

New Age: Support for Capitalism?

The New Age movement is considered to have its origin in the counterculture of the 1960s and 1970s, and was comprised mainly of young people from the middle classes who had grown up with material wealth and had been brought up in an environment where the importance of the individual and its wellbeing was emphasised. They went to a school where individual creativity was rewarded and at which one of the goals was to see the individual's inner self come to full

---

30 Johan Lönnroth, 'Nyliberalismens genombrott i massmedia', *Socialistisk Debatt*, 1/88 (1988), 14–27.

31 See Ronald Inglehart, *The Silent Revolution: Changing Values and Political Styles among Western Publics* (Princeton, NJ, 1977); and Ronald Inglehart, *Culture Shift in Advanced Industrial Society* (Princeton, NJ, 1990).

expression.[32] Furthermore, this culture was characterised by a rejection, or at least a questioning, of the capitalist system and its materialistic values.

Matters changed, however, with the advent of the 1970s. The economic crises of the new decade had the effect not only of ushering in the propagation of new economic ideas and creating opportunities for those in powerful circles to implement a fundamental change in the economic system, but also of forcing the counterculture into the mainstream. According to Robert Wuthnow a worsened economic situation will force people from the counterculture into conventional life, while simultaneously preventing others from looking beyond this.[33] This change in behaviour would have been reinforced by the political decisions taken in the US in the 1980s. Galbraith says that mainly two goals were in evidence during Reagan's presidency: on the one hand, to reduce taxes for the rich so they had an incentive to invest, and on the other, to reduce benefits to the poor so they had an incentive to work.[34] This neoliberal policy affected the young people in the counterculture and New Age in such a way that they adapted themselves and their ideas to the mainstream society in order to make a career, and thereby hopefully achieve individual affluence in economically troubled times. Indeed the dominant values of the 1980s fitted very well with the values of the New Age movement.[35] One goal of the movement had been to free human beings from the constraints placed upon them by society, thereby making it possible for individuals to evolve according to intrinsic conditions. This and other prominent objectives in the counterculture and New Age were in various ways transformed to fit into mainstream society and into mainstream activities.

Thus, New Age, or at least parts of it, became part of mainstream culture. Hence the prominent position of New Age in *SvD* during the final years of the 1970s and onwards. The New Age movement had aligned itself with prevailing cultural values and no longer evaluated capitalism and materialism so negatively. One explanation for this change in attitude may have been the emergence of a 'soft capitalism'. This could be seen as an alternative to 'harsh' capitalism since work was presented as a way of life and since employees felt that the company was interested in them as human beings and not just as tools for increasing profits. Here one had the opportunity to work with oneself, to learn, grow and become more efficient as a human being.[36]

As an effect of this, many New Agers came to work in the capitalist world. As Paul Heelas says, '[i]t looks as though an alliance has been forged, bridging the chasm which previously existed between counterculturists questing within for Self

---

[32] Theodore Roszak, *The Making of a Counter Culture* (London, 1970), 27–31.

[33] Robert Wuthnow, *The Consciousness Reformation* (Berkeley, CA, 1976).

[34] Galbraith, *The World Economy*, 230–33.

[35] Kyle, *The New Age Movement*, 53–4.

[36] Paul Heelas and Linda Woodhead, 'Homeless Minds Today?', in Paul Heelas, David A. Martin and Linda Woodhead (eds), *Peter Berger and the Study of Religion* (London, 2001), 54–7.

and business people questing without for commercial glory.' Heelas also points to evidence that in England alone at that time there were hundreds of organisations providing staff development courses on 'self-spirituality'.[37] He also comments that a substantial part of the New Age, 'the Prosperity wing', had come to a positive attitude in relation to material wealth, evident in developments of the two large classical New Age centres, Findhorn in Scotland and Esalen in California, one sign of the change of attitude being the explosive growth in course offerings directly appealing to the world of business.[38] Moreover, Heelas points to the many books that spread the message that the previous incompatibility between the outer and the inner had been suspended and that the internal search could have a positive impact on how the external world, not least work, developed.[39]

This development may explain why New Agers agreed to join the capitalist mainstream, although it is also possible to see more idealistic motives for doing so. By allying with the powerful economic forces the movement saw an opportunity to get its ideas distributed to parts of society from which it had previously been cut off. One must be aware, however, that it is idealistic to have such hopes; clearly the economic system sets limits and New Age representatives are forced to adapt to them.

Conclusion

The point of departure for this chapter was the fact that New Age ideas and neoliberal ideas were propagated simultaneously in the same Swedish newspaper, a liberal-conservative paper with close connections to the corporate world. At first it appeared as if this paradox was the result of sheer chance. How else would it be possible to explain the concurrence of ideas normally associated with a new type of soft spirituality with ideas normally associated with the harsh business world?

To obtain an alternative understanding of this ostensible paradox, one must first establish which of the two entities is the most powerful and therefore the one setting the agenda. The answer to this appears to be obvious: the corporate world. In the Swedish context it has been shown above that the corporate world in the 1970s formulated an ambition to transform the mental landscape in Sweden – to change it from having values originating in classical social democratic ideas to values that constitute and support neoliberal ideas. In this endeavour proponents for the neoliberal ideas needed supporters. This demand was fulfilled by the intellectual type of New Age thinking due to the fact that the two systems shared

37 Paul Heelas, 'The Sacralization of the Self and New Age Capitalism', in Nicholas Abercrombie and Alan Warde (eds), *Social Change in Contemporary Britain* (Cornwall, 1993), 153–4.

38 Paul Heelas, *The New Age Movement: The Celebration of the Self and Sacralization of Modernity* (Bodmin, 1996), 65.

39 Heelas, 'The Sacralization of the Self and New Age Capitalism', 154.

one view, constitutive for both – that is, freedom of the individual, from which several other views in each system can be derived. An effect of this is that in many respects, the same terms are used in both systems, superficially expressing the same view, but with a basic meaning that is essentially different.

Clearly New Age had something to offer the corporate world. Firstly as an ally, promoting a view of the individual and society which converged with views essential for neoliberalism. Secondly as something that could promote efficiency and growth. This was not, however, the spiritual worldview upon which New Age was fundamentally based. What the corporate world wanted were the techniques used in New Age to stimulate the individual's spiritual development. Specifically, these techniques could also serve as useful tools in the quest for greater efficiency, increased performance, and hence increased growth in the highly competitive world of which the corporate world was and is a part.

Chapter 11

Healing or Dealing? Neospiritual Therapies and Coaching as Individual Meaning and Social Discipline in Late Modern Swedish Society

Anne-Christine Hornborg

In 2003–2007 I held a research fellowship in the cross-disciplinary subject Ritual Studies at Lund University, Sweden. My research field had up to then been in the anthropology of religion, mainly based on field work which documented and investigated the history and life worlds of Mi'kmaq, a First Nation people of Nova Scotia, Canada. Reserve life has created and is still generating a community feeling which is clearly observable in the form of traditions, the building up of personhood, and healing rituals. But studying these rituals made me consider what might be said about the Swedes in this field? What rites or ritualised practices are promoted and generate meaning in contemporary Sweden, a country with one of the highest living standards in the world?

When I started to look into the field of Swedish rituals, I found many practitioners who offered and sold a variety of healing rites, and I observed how these rites had rapidly expanded on the market. Therefore, this chapter will discuss the various neospiritual and science-like practices which are currently being mobilised in late modern Swedish pursuits of identity, meaning-making, and health. The focus is on the emergence and marketing of new entrepreneurs who have established themselves as 'therapists' or 'coaches' promoting personal development, and how they organise their own systems of training and certification. Publicly financed institutions at local, regional, and national levels increasingly purchase such services for the benefit of their clients and personnel. Sweden, a country formerly well known for being a centralised welfare state, has in recent years embraced a neoliberal agenda, encouraging private entrepreneurs to be involved in the business of curing individual shortcomings as well as societal problems. The development of a new outlook on the self is thus the focus, as individuals are invited to create new ways of self-presentation (self-branding). In this construction of a new self, or at least an image of an eligible self, 'life coaches' (or neospiritual therapists) are offering their supporting services on the market. More often than not, the discourse of such advisers incorporates spiritual and/or scientific terminology and tonalities.[1]

This chapter discusses how these new discourses and practices are marketed and applied in Swedish society, how they cater to individual pursuits of meaning and prosperity, and how they contribute to socially acceptable expressions of discontent. The term 'neospiritual' refers in this context to the image of a universal, spiritual essence, embedded in the deep self. The characteristic of this immanent power is usually defined by practitioners as opposing religion, the latter being depicted as ritualistic, dogmatic, and something which hinders humanity from transcending contextual borders. The term 'science-like' refers to Olav Hammer's definition: 'to appropriate parts of the external characteristics of science, without adopting – or even fully understanding – its meaning content'.[2] Since the new practices are sold on the market, marketing strategies are also analysed.

'I'm Spiritual – Not Religious'

As Paul Heelas has stated, late modernity in some countries has caused a decline in institutionalised religious traditions: 'In Sweden, regular attendance in traditional religion is on the point of total collapse', having fallen as low as 2 per cent.[3] But does the decline of traditional religion and traditions (in this case, in Swedish Lutheran Protestantism) indicate the emergence of a secular climate in society? The number of people who define themselves as atheists and agnostics is also low and does not seem to be increasing. The move in Sweden is thus not from religion to secularism, but rather a move by the practitioners towards defining their religiosity under the concept of spirituality, which Heelas defines as the 'experience of the divine as immanent in life'.[4] Eva Hamberg draws a similar conclusion in her discussion of unchurched religions and spirituality in Sweden: 'religiousness

---

1 Anne-Christine Hornborg, 'I coachningland – på spaning efter den inre potentialen', *Chaos: Skandinavisk tidsskrift for religionshistoriske studier*, 53/1 (2010): 1–16, Anne-Christine Hornborg *Coaching och lekmannaterapi – en modern väckelse?* (Stockholm, 2012).

2 Olav Hammer, *På spaning efter helheten: New Age en ny folktro?* (revised edition, Stockholm, 2004 [1997]), 242.

3 Paul Heelas, 'The Spiritual Revolution: From Religion to Spirituality', in Linda Woodhead (ed.), *Religions in the Modern World* (London and New York, 2002), 360; see Paul Heelas and Linda Woodhead, *The Spiritual Revolution: Why Religion Is Giving Way to Spirituality* (Oxford, 2005).

4 Heelas, 'The Spiritual Revolution', 368; see Peter Berger, 'Epistemological Modesty: An Interview with Peter Berger', *Christian Century*, 114 (1997): 972–5, 978; Rodney Stark, 'Secularization, R.I.P.', *Sociology of Religion*, 60/3 (1999): 249–73.

has not disappeared in Sweden, it is simply not to be found in church.'[5] Faith has become synonymous with a privatised, unchurched spirituality or the Swedes have become, as Grace Davie would say: 'believing non-belongers'.[6]

Reports published in 2007 by the Swedish Council for Working Life and Social Research (FAS) also show that the use of complementary and alternative medicine (CAM) is high in Sweden (higher than it is for example in Denmark, Norway, or the US).[7] There hasn't been an extensive survey of the Swedish population, but one conducted in Stockholm showed that the use of CAM had more than doubled from 22 per cent (1980) to 49 per cent (2001).[8] Many of these new practices would be referred to as New Age, and especially a number of hybrid forms of East-West practices are popular and marketed as Ayurveda, Qi Gong, Mindfulness, Reiki, and so on. These East-West hybrid practices are often classified by the practitioners as a 'technique', said to be detached from religious dogma, and marketed as such. Mindfulness, with roots in the Asian *vipassana* tradition (*sati*), has become very popular in Sweden and is also promoted by some psychiatrists or psychologists in clinical therapy. But we primarily find the practice in the context of self-certified private entrepreneurs, who are marketing their courses to individuals or in workplaces as a way of reducing stress, anxiety and increasing working capacity. Defined as a 'technique' or 'spirituality', the context-bound melts down into one common sign, like currency, and as such the practices can be marketed more easily across borders and even in secular contexts. Or as one representative of neospiritual therapy states: 'Journeywork is clearly cross-cultural and appeals to people from all religions, creeds, and walks of life.'[9] However, even if the practices are marketed as cross-cultural, they are clearly products of the Western, consumer society.[10]

How can we classify these practices which are rapidly becoming established and which could be said to be representing the spirituality of late modernity? Some of these practices are still commonly recognised as New Age, but if asked, most Swedes would probably consider the forms of spirituality which are associated with New Age to be flaky or 'mumbo-jumbo'. There would surely be protests

---

5 Rodney Stark, Eva Hamberg and Alan S. Miller, 'Exploring Spirituality and Unchurched Religions in America, Sweden, and Japan', *Journal of Contemporary Religion*, 20/1 (2005): 3–23.

6 Grace Davie, *Religion in Britain since 1945: Believing Without Belonging* (Oxford, 1994).

7 FAS, *Complementary and Alternative Medicine (CAM): A Systematic Review of Intervention Research in Sweden* (Stockholm, 2007).

8 Ibid., 3.

9 Brandon Bays, *The Journey: A Practical Guide to Healing Your Life and Setting Yourself Free* (New York and London, 2008 [1999]), vii.

10 Karen Lisa Goldschmidt Salamon, 'Going Global from the Inside Out: Spiritual Globalism in the Workplace', in Mikael Rothstein (ed.), *New Age Religion and Globalisation* (Aarhus, 2001), 150–72.

if crystal healing were offered as a healing technique in hospitals, or tarot cards introduced as a means of improving working capacity. The idea of a universal spirituality, often marketed as a way to bring 'flow' and prosperity to life, is found to be more attractive in contemporary Sweden than the 'old' New Age, which was introduced in the 1960s and was embedded in the counter-culture movement. The attraction of 'flow' and prosperity correlates with the ideology of the neoliberalist state, since the practices offer means by which individuals may enchant their daily lives according to this ideology.[11] Introvigne discusses this shift as a second stage of New Age – the 'Next Age', in which individual happiness, self-development and prosperity are mainly in focus.[12]

Enchanted Practices

What creates the climate for the introduction of these new practices? Why are they attractive to individuals in contemporary Sweden, a modern, welfare state in which there is no lack of treatment available at hospitals and public institutions?

We can read in reports from studies conducted in the early 2000s how various forms of illness in Sweden have increased.[13] The need for different kinds of treatments, including courses in dealing with stress and difficulties in private and working life, opened up this market for new entrepreneurial activities. Several of these rapidly expanding activities were influenced by the mind-body therapy, which has been classified as a form of complementary and alternative medicine (CAM) and defined as 'a variety of techniques designed to enhance the mind's capacity to affect bodily functions and symptoms'.[14] At first the new entrepreneurs offered neospiritual or science-like therapy, or courses to become therapists, but to these activities were later added coaching and coaching training. These educational systems or healing treatments developed outside the formal Swedish education system, but were introduced as science-based. The entrepreneurs succeeded in selling courses both for private use as well as to publicly financed institutions.[15]

---

11 Jeremy Carrette and Richard King, *Selling Spirituality: The Silent Takeover of Religion* (London, 2005).

12 Massimo Introvigne, 'After the New Age: Is There a Next Age?', in Mikael Rothstein (ed.), *New Age Religion and Globalization* (Aarhus, 2001), 59.

13 SCB, Statens offentliga utredningar, *Sjukfrånvaro och ohälsa i Sverige – en belysning utifrån SCB:s statistik 2004:3* (Örebro, 2004).

14 FAS, *Complementary and Alternative Medicine*, 5.

15 Anne-Christine Hornborg, 'Selling Nature, Selling Health: The Commodification of Ritual Healing in Late Modern Sweden', in Sigurd Bergmann and Yong-Bock Kim (eds), *Religion, Ecology and Gender: Contributions from Korea, Canada and Scandinavia*, Studies in Religion and the Environment, 1 (Münster, Hamburg, Berlin, Wien, London and Zürich, 2009), 109–29; Anne-Christine Hornborg, 'Arbetslösa erbjuds kosmisk energi', *Aftonbladet*, Debatt, 19 February 2009; Anne-Christine Hornborg, 'Rites for Modern Man:

One case of this occurred during the Swedish surge in unemployment, which was met by national investments in 2009 when the Swedish government allocated 300 million euros to the Swedish Employment Service (*Arbetsförmedlingen*) in order to buy the services of coaches to help approximately 250,000 unemployed Swedes by encouraging them to search for their inner potential, boost self-confidence, and find a job.[16]

The expansion of layman therapy and coaching could partly be explained by the fact that it clearly responds to the focus on the individual and self-realisation. Questions arise such as 'How can I manage in life?' – or better, 'succeed in life' – or as one of the slogans marketed by a coaching enterprise said in one of its brochures: 'Are you content with being just ordinary? Or do you wish to move along and be outstanding?'[17] This focus on the inner self and the formation of a new, late modern selfhood requires, according to Catherine Bell, new, individual-centred practices, responding to the longing for intense experiences of personal transformations on the way to finding the authentic self:

> In this newer model, ritual is a medium of expression, a special language suited to what it is there to express, namely, internal spiritual-emotional resources tied to our true identities but frequently unknown and undeveloped. ... The new paradigm is directed more inward than outward, apt to define community and society in terms of the self rather than the self in terms of the community.[18]

In order to display structural similarities between coaching and neospiritual therapy, I have chosen the coaching enterprise CoachCompanion and a Swedish layman therapist, who uses Brandon Bays's *The Journey*,[19] a version of neospiritual therapy. One reason for choosing these two enterprises is their aim to offer their services to public institutions, and they add neospiritual messages to the scientific agenda which has been said to be the hallmark of the secularised state. I will

---

New Practices in Sweden', in Lina Midholm, Annika Nordström and Maria T. Agozzino (eds), *The Ritual Year and Ritual Diversity: Proceedings of the Second International Conference of the SIEF Working Group on the Ritual Year, Gothenburg June 7–11, 2006* (Gothenburg, 2007), 83–92; Anne-Christine Hornborg, 'Att återförtrolla det sekulariserade samhället: Är Sverige på väg in i Vattumannens tidsålder?', *Svensk religionshistorisk årsskrift* (2007): 33–59.

16 Hornborg, 'Arbetslösa erbjuds'.

17 Hälsoakademin Europa, *Certifierad Coach med kognitiv inriktning*, Brochure (2010), [Online], available at: http://www.haeu.se/ha/blanketter/coach.pdf [accessed: 8 August 2011].

18 Catherine Bell, *Ritual: Perspectives and Dimensions* (New York and Oxford, 1997), 241.

19 *The Journey* is the book, a 'therapy manual', written by Brandon Bays, and also the name of the practices sold as therapy. In Swedish The Journey (therapy) is translated as *Resan (terapi)*.

start introducing 'the Journey' therapy and from now on refer to this and similar therapies as layman therapy, as distinct from the treatments that are part of the public Swedish health care system, including training programmes.

Brandon Bays's bestseller *The Journey* is marketed as a book on therapy, and a network of initiated persons in Sweden (and worldwide) is currently working under her guidance. In Sweden about 60 persons, mainly women, market themselves as accredited or authorised therapists. The Journey layman therapy is Bays's specific and personally constructed hybrid between a popular interpretation of Freudian psychoanalysis, cellular healing, neospirituality, and Asian philosophy. The 'client' starts the healing process by sitting on a chair with their eyes closed and the layman therapist will guide this client in making an inner journey (visualising herself or himself as travelling bodily in a UFO with a personally chosen mentor as guide). The mission is to find the little child within, who once was injured, and to connect with the 'Source'. They arrive at a campfire and with help from the layman therapist, as well as the visualised mentor, the 'client' meets and forgives the perpetrator of distant times, often a parent.

The Journey tells modern stories of miracles, but in a science-like way, referring to cellular healing. Bays refers to Deepak Chopra, who is often quoted in New Age literature:

> I knew what Dr. Chopra was saying was not just scientific theory – it was demonstrable fact. … Dr. Chopra went on to explain that stored inside our cells are old memories – he called them 'phantom memories'. These old memories can eventually cause degenerative disease patterns within the cells. And before a diseased cell dies, it passes its memory onto the next cell being born. … He intimated that in order to interrupt the programming, and uncover the cell memories and let them go, you would need to get in touch with the same part of you that had created the programming in the first place – the infinite intelligence, the body wisdom.[20]

According to Bays, participants using the Journey are said to have been cured of 'heart disease, breast cancer, chronic fatigue, debilitating arthritis, Crohn's disease …'.[21] Bays says she suffered from cancer; a 'tumor the size of a basketball',[22] but after she made an inner journey it disappeared and in six weeks she was healed. This is how the Swedish layman therapist introduces the Journey:

> The Journey therapy is a deep conversational therapy, based on a guided visualisation within the inner part of your self, where you can find the basic causes of your emotional, physical and psychological problem, deep down to the cell level, in order to be cured of their negative influence on your life.

20 Bays, *The Journey*, 46–7.

21 Ibid., viii.

22 Ibid., 3.

> Many clients have said it is like 'clearing the hard disk' and one said there is so much 'shit' saved on hidden files, which unconsciously influence us and that the Journey therapy really can find it and delete all of it.[23]

This computer metaphor for the body is taken from Bays's autobiography, in which she refers to Deepak Chopra: 'He likened the human body to a computer, saying it was possible to interrupt the "programming", and that once the programming was interrupted, the possibility for healing existed.'[24] This Swedish layman therapist offers instant relief for a variety of problems: 'healed from, amongst other things, stress, feeling worried, anger, guilt, anxiety, depressions, low self-esteem, but also various physical problems.'[25] She offers Higher Mindfulness meditation and life coaching, a technique which she describes as supporting the healing process and reducing the number of healing 'journeys' to be made.[26]

As for coaching, the enterprise CoachCompanion is marketing practices to improve life for the individual and develop skills for better working capacity. It is one of the enterprises the Swedish Employment Service (*Arbetsförmedlingen*) hired in 2009 to coach unemployed people.[27] The advertising slogan on the website gives very ambitious visions, 'We Change the World', describing this change as:

> our *mission*. We are fully convinced that we are able to change the world – in ways large and small. Our ambition is to change the world for the individual, at workplaces and thus also society by incorporating the coaching approach.[28]

Coaching as a 'win-win' concept has moved in recent years from sports to a variety of other societal practices. CoachCompanion defines coaching as 'a powerful tool at work between people, based on a profound respect for the capacity and knowledge within each individual. Coaching is a positive process which leads development forward to the goal.'[29]

I will now examine the Journey and CoachCompanion further in order to display the more general construction of these and similar practices: the concept of inner

---

23 Resanterapi, http://www.resanterapi.com/resanterapi.htm [accessed: 8 August 2011], my translation.

24 Bays, *The Journey*, 46.

25 Resanterapi, http://www.resanterapi.com/jag.htm [accessed: 8 August 2011], my translation.

26 Resanterapi, http://www.resanterapi.com/utveckling.htm [accessed: 8 August 2011].

27 CoachCompanion, http://www.coachcompanion.se/?p=887 [accessed: 8 August 2011], my translation.

28 CoachCompanion, http://www.coachcompanion.se/?p=66 [accessed: 8 August 2011], my translation.

29 CoachCompanion, http://www.coachcompanion.se/pages/utbildnings_arrangor.html [accessed: 8 August 2011], my translation.

potential; leadership, education, the commercialisation, and commodification of personal development; and the aim to offer services to public institutions.

The Concept of Inner Potential

When, in 2005, Hamberg described how representatives of supernaturalism in Sweden are about as sceptical of science as they are of organised religion,[30] this statement required some modification, at least concerning the new practices for healing or self-development. Science is a powerful discourse in contemporary society, and thus many of the new enterprises refer to science in order to legitimise their methods; either they refer to their practices as being scientific, or the practices are said to be powerful antidotes to the shortcomings of science.

One way to promote a scientific approach has been to avoid a language which gives connotations of the religious sphere, and instead transform the idea of a 'spirituality of humanity' – the notion of an 'inner' self in every human – into the more science-like concept of 'inner potential'.[31] The 'inner potential' concept encapsulates the transcendental forces inside every person, presupposing a concealed realm, larger than the daily and ordinary life of the individual. It has become the key word, found in nearly all layman therapy and coaching practices, and the mission is to transform individuals by giving them the means to find this 'inner potential'.[32] Although the enterprises commonly refer to this inner potential concept, some of these practitioners might also explicitly use the word 'spirituality'. But they clearly distinguish between spirituality as an inner essence in every individual, and religion, which they define as the external form spirituality may take. Defined as a human essence, the concept of spirituality becomes seemingly harmless for public institutions to handle, since references to a common, 'cozy' and empowering essence, embedded in the nature of humanity, is not imagined to provoke conflicts in workplaces.

Brandon Bays's offering to the Journey participants is to awaken the healing forces in the inner potential of each: 'Deep inside a huge potential beckons, waiting to open us up to the infinite wisdom, freedom, and love within. This presence is calling you home *right now*, longing to set you free.'[33] Bays commonly uses the concept of inner potential, including inner wisdom and something called 'the Source': 'setting yourself free to live your life at your highest potential, as a

---

[30] Stark, Hamberg and Miller, 'Exploring Spirituality', 16.

[31] Heelas, 'The Spiritual Revolution'; see Liselotte Frisk, 'Vad är New Age? Centrala begrepp och historiska rötter', *Svensk religionshistorisk årsskrift*, 6 (1997): 87–97; Lars Ahlin, *New Age: konsumtionsvara eller värden att kämpa för* (Lund, 2001).

[32] Hornborg, 'Att återförtrolla'.

[33] Bays, *The Journey*, v.

full expression of your true self',[34] 'there is a huge untapped presence inside',[35] 'as if they are one with everything, or are part of everything – that it is a true realization of Source'.[36]

CoachCompanion is one of the coaching enterprises that in 2009 openly referred to spirituality as their primary instrument and qualification:

> The organisers of the training also recognise the spiritual dimension of the work. We are convinced about our connection to a universal energy and our potential to achieve flow in our lives through this insight.[37]

Despite their references to spirituality as a ground for the coaching practices, CoachCompanion was hired in 2009 by the public Swedish Employment Service to coach the unemployed. Otherwise the science-like concept of 'inner potential' is preferred, and CoachCompanion's idiomatic use of potential and coaching is similar to other companies' descriptions: 'The aims of coaching are: To evoke the best of the client; To set *free the potential* of the client.'[38]

Leadership and Education

Finding one's 'inner potential' is not a solitary mission; rather, the aid of an initiated coach or therapist is greatly needed in this search. This requirement is, of course, the selling argument; otherwise no business could be established. But how do the new self-certified leaders compete with the formal qualifications society has set up for established professions? And how do they manage to gain acceptance of the concept of inner potential from public institutions such as schools, hospitals, or health centres?

---

34 Ibid.

35 Ibid., vi.

36 Ibid., 163.

37 CoachCompanion, http://www.coachcompanion.se/pages/utbildnings_arrangor.html [accessed: 8 August 2011], my translation. The link to this reference could still be found on the internet today (8 August 2011), but it is no longer displayed as a link to the company's main website and as a leading device. One reason could be that one of the highest circulation Swedish newspapers published a high-profile scoop about employment coaching and heavily criticised some of the coaching companies (about 10 per cent) for being too involved in neospirituality and New Age (Claes Pettersson and Camilla Sundell, 'Här avslöjas miljardfiaskot', *Aftonbladet*, 7 November 2009). This withdrawal of a reference to spirituality from the website of CoachCompanion could be seen as a strategic move into the more science-like 'inner potential' discourse and concepts.

38 CoachCompanion, http://www.coachcompanion.se/?p=887 [accessed: 8 August 2011], my translation.

Firstly, the profession of coaching individuals' 'inner potential' has to be combined with leadership and titles that instil confidence and trust. In Sweden the title of 'registered psychotherapist' (*legitimerad psykoterapeut*) is established in medical schools and protected by the state. But new titles, such as accredited, authorised, diplomaed, licensed, or certified therapist/coach, have been designed by the layman therapists/and coaches, all of them without academic qualifications. It is hard for the untrained eye to clearly see the difference between the formal, established and protected title 'registered psychotherapist' and the other look-alike titles. By mirroring the formal qualification title, they attract attention and instil confidence.

The Journey layman therapists market themselves as accredited or authorised Journey therapists, and it is Bays herself who keeps control of this title. The new forms of leadership also become a way of establishing new hierarchies in relation to other alternative therapies. Or as the Swedish Journey therapist emphasises on her website:

> It is thus important to know that, if you are having major problems in your life, you have to go to an authorized accredited Journey therapist, who in order to keep the accreditation has to have it updated every year and do the accreditation week once again every three years.[39]

The new leaders may have simply self-certified themselves, or attended courses at private educational centres that offer certifications to layman therapists or coaches.[40] These courses can vary between attending a weekend workshop or attending more regular meetings. The training programmes for layman therapists could be a mixture of references to one or two scholars, to spokesmen for the New Age like Deepak Chopra, a course manual, or 'canonical' literature (of which selections might vary, from self-help literature and New Age-inspired books to scientific journals, especially scholars who have studied the mind-body connection), personal experiences, and neospiritual rhetoric. The Swedish Journey therapist refers to NLP (neuro linguistic programming, a science-like practice) and 'the Nobel Prize nominee Candace Pert' to strengthen her message about cellular healing.[41] But it is mainly Bays's book *The Journey* which holds the key to the method and theories of healing, so also for the Swedish layman therapist.[42] Brandon Bays's life story of her self-healing is, of course, of great importance for authorising her teachings among the practitioners.

The leaders of CoachCompanion use the title 'diplomaed' coach and offer a course of four meetings and one day in order to earn the diploma to become a

---

39 Resanterapi, http://www.resanterapi.com/resanterapi.htm [accessed: 8 August 2011].

40 Hornborg, 'Rites for Modern Man'; Hornborg, 'Att återförtrolla'.

41 Resanterapi, http://www.resanterapi.com/brandon.htm [accessed: 8 August 2011].

42 Ibid.

coach. As in other coaching practices, they introduce their leaders in a personal manner and add personal descriptions as a qualification and guarantee of good coaching. A description of the coach's personality is included in the list of the staff's qualifications at CoachCompanion:

> Distinctive characteristics which make my coaching successful: responsibility, emphatic, keen, intuitive, creative, positive, energetic … [a]s a coach I would describe myself as interested, pushy, not full of prestige and with an optimistic view of people.[43]

The holistic view of the individual in treatments are also hallmarks of the 'authentic' coach and CoachCompanion stresses: 'We are very meticulous about living the same way as we teach. That's why our core value is a guiding principle for us whatever we are doing.'[44]

The aim is to create a friendly, homely atmosphere as in CoachCompanion's presentation of their enterprise: 'we are known for our cozy and warm atmosphere. Our participants, customers and clients have fun with us.'[45]

When the Swedish government allocated money for employment coaching, the first requirement included a 'qualification system' – but since there are no formal external reviewers of coaching education, it was up to the companies or coaches to proclaim their qualification. The man in charge of procuring the coaches described on a Swedish Radio news programme the qualification for the coaching job as:

> Coaching is not an authorised profession, there are no formal qualifications, you might have worked with individuals and persons in different situations. You must have the competence to meet people in crisis and help them get on in life, and all those who have experience of doing so could certainly work with this too.[46]

Often the coaches give references to the certifications from the coaching trade organisations. But Anne Scoular, who teaches coaching at the London Business School in England, comments on the certifications: 'Part of the problem is the

---

[43] CoachCompanion, http://www.coachcompanion.se/wp-content/uploads/2010/06/Presentation-av-coachcompanions-jobbcoacher7.pdf [accessed: 8 August 2011], my translation.

[44] CoachCompanion, http://www.coachcompanion.se/?p=66 [accessed: 8 August 2011], my translation.

[45] Ibid.

[46] SR – Swedish Radio, http://www.sr.se/cgi-bin/ekot/artikel.asp?Artikel=2548447 [accessed: 8 June 2009], my translation.

number of different certificates: in the UK alone about 50 organizations issue certificates; buyers are understandably confused about which one is credible.'[47]

The second requirement of the coach is to 'meet people in crisis and give them further help in life' and having 'experience of doing so'.[48] This requirement reflects a therapeutic approach in coaching, although coaching for the unemployed was said not to include therapeutic treatment. The diffuse borderline between coaching and therapy is discussed by Coutu and Kauffman with collected data from 140 leading coaches (US 71 per cent, UK 18 per cent), data which the authors invited some experts to comment on. One of the commentators raises the important question 'Coach or couch?' since in nearly all cases (97 per cent) the coaches were *not* employed to discuss personal problems, but in 76 per cent of the commissions the coaches chose to discuss the private life of the clients.[49] Thus it seems as if coaching in most cases also puts a therapeutic approach on the agenda.

Instant Transformation and Intense Emotions

The services of the layman therapists or coaches fit the condition of modernity with its focus on the individual, including facing a life world full of risks and shortcomings. The fear is of being ordinary; not being enchanted. In such a case, the risk is for individuals in modern society to be treated as a boring television programme, the listener switching channel to find another 'conversation partner', or like standing alone at a mingle party, since you have 'nothing of interest' to offer the other participants. The gap for the individuals between the experience of daily life and dreams of what life could be – displayed in talent shows, movies or in the parables telling successful changes in the life of the main character in self-help literature – is to be overcome in the individual-centred performances in which the 'mission' of the coach or layman therapist is to guide their 'clients' to the inner potential. There, it is said, lies the secret of healing and prosperity.

The individual's experiences of efficacy and intense emotions are mostly the characteristics of these modern, individual-centred practices. That is why the new leaders design personally constructed practices, invented for the needs of the participant. Before the coaching session starts, CoachCompanion first offers clients the most suitable coach for the client or company.[50] On the company's website, clients testify to the successful matchmaking: 'In my new work as director of education I knew I needed a coach, but I could not precisely express who or

47 Diane Coutu and Carol Kauffman, 'What Can Coaches Do for You?', *Harvard Business Review*, January (2009): 96.

48 SR – Swedish Radio, http://www.sr.se/cgi-bin/ekot/artikel.asp?Artikel=2548447 [accessed: 8 June 2009], my translation.

49 Coutu and Kauffman, 'What Can Coaches', 92.

50 CoachCompanion, http://www.coachcompanion.se/wp-content/uploads/2009/05/coaching-far-chefer-ledare.pdf [accessed: 8 August 2011].

what I needed. … The coach I was introduced to really showed me how to fit into the special situation I'm in right now.'[51]

The Journey therapy uses individual-centred practices, and the practitioners stress the therapeutic function of the method, saying that it speaks to 'the heart' and promises a more instant effect and healing than clinical therapy can offer. The Swedish Journey therapist claims: 'To find one's inner potential in an easy way, in just a few hours, and clear out all blockages in a much faster, deeper and more effective way than any other existing method, was a fantastic experience.'[52] The websites are designed like commercials, here selling instant relief. On the websites many of the participants talk directly to the imagined reader about how the courses changed their outlook on life.[53] The focus on the individual, and the search for the personal pattern, apparently evokes strong emotions, since the layman therapy or coaching not only concerns the participants' role as professionals, but also becomes a way to better present their 'inner self': 'Besides learning what professional coaching is about, I made my own individual journey in personal development. I got insights concerning myself which led to true changes in my life and have made me feel much better.'[54]

Since the new practices mirror other publicly run practices, such as school medical services, and respond to the 'language of individualistic enterprise culture',[55] they feel like natural ways of acting and being. When the individual's familiarity with the discourse of self-realisation in late modern society is combined with the individual-centred ritualising processes, it triggers feelings and enhances performance, and the intense effects of conversion among the participants are typical of these courses.[56] The emotion of being 'new-born' also motivates the participants to be devoted 'missionaries for the cause', and this is one of the important ways of advertising the healing courses, through being marketed to friends or colleagues at work. This 'mission' is important, since it adds a normative and political dimension to stories of healing. Thus the 'converts', or healed ones, construct their life stories into models in order to encourage others to change their

---

51 CoachCompanion, http://www.coachcompanion.se/?p=181 [accessed: 8 August 2011], my translation.

52 Resanterapi, http://www.resanterapi.com/jag.htm [accessed: 8 August 2011].

53 CoachCompanion, http://www.coachcompanion.se/?p=16 [accessed: 8 August 2011].

54 CoachCompanion, http://www.coachcompanion.se/?p=16 [accessed: 8 August 2011], my translation.

55 Paul Heelas, 'The New Age in Cultural Context: The Premodern, the Modern and the Postmodern', *Religion*, 23/2 (1993): 107; see Salamon, 'Going Global', and Karen Lisa Goldschmidt Salamon, 'Prophets of a Cultural Capitalism: An Ethnography of Romantic Spiritualization in Business Management', *Folk: Journal of the Danish Ethnographic Society*, 44 (2002): 89–115.

56 See also the study of *est* by Peter Finkelstein, Brant Wenegrat and Irvin Yalom, 'Large Group Awareness Training', *Annual Review of Psychology*, 33 (1982): 515–39.

lives, or for society to employ the specific method, which they said had affected their possibility to make the best of their lives.[57]

Many of the new practices take place at conference centres, or at special events. The temporary separation from family or from the workplace creates a short-term new group identification – a *communitas* – and within this group the participants can formulate, compare, and discuss the specific experience of a transforming and enlightening journey, including putting their life story into the Grand Narrative which is commonly constructed by the specific therapy or coaching enterprises and also found on their websites under 'references' or 'clients'.

Individual-centred practices usually generate intense emotions, but the risk is also that they may fail. But the idea is that if failure occurs, it is in the heart of the individual and not the responsibility of the coach or layman therapist. One enterprise, which offers coaching for unemployed, thus writes this about the job coach's responsibility:

> The one you are coaching is fully responsible for everything … his or her project to find a job, his or her life, family, economy and dog … [i]t is not you as a coach who shall deliver or produce anything. … It is the responsibility of the unemployed to reach the goal, whatever their circumstances are. If there are no jobs, the individual needs to take more responsibility. To wait and hope that it will be better is to be a victim of the circumstances.[58]

The coach only models the technique of how to find the 'potential' and then it is up to the individual to fulfil the search for this inner, hidden power. There are, however, two ways of failing. In the cases of employment coaching the declared aim was to get a job, but even if this failed, the participants still said that they were fully content. Discontents of societal problems – unemployment – are overshadowed by having found the inner potential of possibilities. Just partaking in the coaching practices made them experience feelings of change and self-affirmation:

> I got the tools to manage by my own, I know that everything is now possible if I only believe in myself …

> She [the coach] made me realize what my ambition was in life and how by myself I could make this come true …

> By focusing on my inner strength and qualities I got my motivation back and could focus on what I really wanted …

[57] AnnChristin Winroth, 'Vardagligt och livsviktigt berättande om hälsa och bot', in Motzi Eklöf (ed.), *Perspektiv på komplementär medicin* (Malmö, 2004), 140.

[58] Hälsoakademin Europa, http://www.haeu.se/node/132 [accessed: 4 April 2011].

> I have moved from an insecure young woman who didn't believe in herself and her ideas to a strong woman with all trust within, looking bright on the future ...[59]

But the greatest risk of failure is if intense emotions default. This scenario could at worst be turned into a total failure for the individual. Now not only is there no job, but also the 'inner potential' seems to be absent. Kirsten Bovbjerg has examined the correlation between the increasing stress in society and the pressure of the individuals to always mobilise the 'inner potential'.[60] In her study of courses in personal development at work places, Bovbjerg found, that despite all the courses, the level of stress was increased, which also created an increasing market for new courses in how to manage stress or to enhance potential at work. Furthermore, failure for the individual becomes paradoxically a success for the coaches/ therapists: more courses to sell! Bovbjerg's study is also supported by Karin Askeland, who refers to cases in Norway where a new category of patients are looking for help in hospitals – those who have been under too much pressure from their coach. The strategy of these individuals has been to acquire more help from their coaches, until they collapse under the work of steadily working to improve.[61]

Therapy and Coaching as Commodities

Coaching and the layman therapy are clearly products of a market society and as such they have become commodities which are marked as any other therapeutic, self-help service.[62] Mikaelsson, who has studied the New Age literary market, comments on the development of creating a market for the individual in buying books and treatments thus: 'The prosperity gospel can be said to represent a summit in this adaptation to the capitalist, consumerist society' and she compares how the 'Western religious gurus' are 'playing the prophet role'.[63] Since Mikaelsson wrote this in 2001 the construction of contemporary society as a therapy culture,[64] and

---

[59] Hälsoakademin Europa, http://www.coach.haeu.se/coach/hur.html [accessed: 16 February 2011].

[60] Kirsten Marie Bovbjerg, 'De menneskelige potentialer i en "stresstid"', in Joel Haviv (ed.), *Medarbejder eller modarbejder – religion i moderne arbejdsliv* (Århus, 2007), 55–80.

[61] Maj Karin Askeland, 'A Reflexive Inquiry into the Ideologies and Theoretical Assumptions of Coaching', *Coaching: An International Journey of Theory, Research and Practice*, 2/1 (2009): 65–75.

[62] Hornborg, 'Rites for Modern Man'; Hornborg, 'Att förtrolla'; Jenny-Ann Brodin, *Religion till salu?: en sociologisk studie av New Age i Sverige* (Stockholm, 2001).

[63] Lisbeth Mikaelsson, 'Homo accumulans and the Spiritualization of Money', in Mikael Rothstein (ed.), *New Age Religion and Globalisation* (Aarhus, 2001), 94–112.

[64] Frank Furedi, *Therapy Culture: Cultivating Vulnerability in an Uncertain Age* (London, 2004).

of a new selfhood which not only puts responsibility on the individual to find the means for healing and insight, but also a moral duty to find the authentic self and be true to oneself,[65] has created an increasingly profitable sphere for creative and imaginative entrepreneurs to find niches from which to offer solutions for a variety of problems. The philosopher Charles Taylor speaks of an 'expressive' selfhood, in which individuals experience an 'intimate contact with oneself'.[66] But this discovery of an inner self also becomes a discovery of self-authority, or to put it in Taylor's words: 'Being true to myself means being true to my own originality, which is something only I can articulate and discover.'[67] This modern search for the inner self is articulated as an 'I-project' – it is only I who know my inner self – but this project on the market has become a 'we-project' – it is only the coach or the layman therapist who knows the path to guide the individual to the 'inner Source'.

Journey layman therapy originated as a self-help manual, as 'hardcore therapy'. But the basic idea of a guide for self-help practices has been transformed into a range of commodities – individually-centred practices – and sold on the market. One Journey practitioner comments thus on the commodification of the therapy:

> I think it is very interesting how the original book of *The Journey* says you can do it at home with a friend and doesn't mention anything about the need for a trained therapist (as far as I can recall). Then obviously someone realised they could make a lot more money out of it by insisting on the need for a trained therapist.[68]

The Journey has become a huge, commercialised industry, now offering a range of products including the Journey manual, a variety of courses, and items such as books, CDs, and Journey cards.[69] The layman therapy training is built up step by step at weekend workshops, promising deeper and deeper knowledge.[70] The total price for the step-by-step model of education to become an accredited or authorised therapist is hard to estimate, but comes to about 10,000 euros. This includes a basic course containing a message which has to be developed by attending other weekend courses. 'Follow-up' courses are common, offering to update certifications and give feedback to the practitioners.[71] The Journey also offers a variety of practices useful for children, such as *Liberating Kids' Shining Potential*, with the aim to teach Journey layman therapists to help children with

---

65 Charles Taylor, *The Ethics of Authenticity* (Cambridge, MA, 1991), 29.

66 Ibid., 27.

67 Charles Taylor, 'The Politics of Recognition', in Amy Guthman (ed.), *Multiculturalism: Examining the Politics of Recognition* (Princeton, NJ, 1994), 43.

68 Personal communication, 13 October 2008.

69 (The) Journey, http://www.thejourney.com/products/ [accessed: 8 August 2011].

70 Resanterapi, http://www.resanterapi.com/utbildning.htm [accessed: 8 August 2011].

71 Ibid.

situations ranging 'from dealing with emotional upsets and traumas, separation and divorce, school and learning difficulties, to handling behavioural problems, and even coping healthily with death and bereavement'.[72] According to the Swedish Journey layman therapist, the method has been used in schools to prevent bullying and aggressive behaviour, and she is now offering her courses to elementary schools: 'If you are a parent, or you work in schools, and find children not feeling well, and want to try the Journey therapy for children, give me a call, and we can talk.'

In 2009 CoachCompanion was offering 65 hours of training to become a diplomaed coach, or a five-day intensive course at a cost of 3,200 euros (before VAT).[73] Their 'Career View' model is a one-day course at a cost of 1,200 euros. This offer includes a one-year licence, but in order to keep the licence a further yearly payment of 400 euros is required.[74] Many of the coaching courses build their selling concept of showing a continuous requirement for follow-up courses or reconnecting courses.[75]

As previously mentioned, CoachCompanion has reached agreements with the Swedish public employment service, and they also offer coaching to schools in order to instruct teachers to find solutions to conflicts in the classroom, increase the scope for children in the learning processes, and how to use a coaching approach when meeting other colleagues and parents.[76]

Concluding Remarks

Coaching and layman therapy are clearly reflections of the contemporary consumer society both in their efforts to build up both models *of* society, that seem 'natural' to the participant, since the practices reflect societal structures and the marketplace, and models *for* society which will give the participant space to create powerful means to turn dreams into reality and hope for better circumstances in life.[77] These practices also promise (instant) success, both in life and at work. In doing so, they clearly express a prosperity religion. One tendency is clear in the new practices: structural problems are mostly not depicted as a consequence of structural pressure at work, but as the consequence of a lack of connection with the inner self. The message is that 'it is you who are the problem', and it is up to the individual to find the means of coping. In this way neoliberal society has found a

---

72 (The) Journey, http://www.thejourney.com/seminars-and-schedule/seminar-details/7/Liberating-Kids'-Shining-Potential/ [accessed: 8 August 2011].

73 CoachCompanion, http://www.coachcompanion.se/?p=16 [accessed: 24 July 2009].

74 Utbildning, http://www.utbildning.se/Certifieringsutbildning_i_Karriaermodellen_Career_View_48311.htm [accessed: 19 July 2009].

75 Ibid.

76 CoachCompanion, http://www.coachcompanion.se/?p=459 [accessed: 8 August 2011].

77 Clifford Geertz, *The Interpretation of Culture: Selected Essays* (New York, 1973), 93.

way of constraining citizens; no one is to be blamed for failing but individuals are not enlightened and empowered enough by the inner potential.

The second tendency is the new systems of certification, often implying dissolution of the borders between the professional and the private, including leadership. The authenticity of the coach or therapist is a guarantee of creating authentic meetings with the client. When coaches introduce themselves on websites, they usually add personal profiles, and they promote the 'authentic being' – a person who is living fully, according to their teachings. The new 'authentic being' and transformation, which are commonly displayed on the enterprises' websites by 'clients', are also of importance. Their stories of successful (instant) healing processes could be read purely as commercials for selling courses. But the life stories are also elements of the individual-centred performance, and by telling them, they may facilitate the performative effect, that is, experience the transformation of getting in touch with their enchanted selves and potential for self-affirmation and prosperity in life. They are stories of conversions, including the mission to attract other presumptive 'clients', who read the stories and feel inspired to partake in practices that promise instant transformation and healing.

The third tendency is the clear ambition on the part of the new practitioners to collaborate with public institutions. If New Age practices began in the counter-culture movement as alternatives, the 'Next Age' practices are marketed more as scientific practices directed towards the individual in order to get in touch with what is said to be their potential for self-affirmation or prosperity in life. The specific concept of spirituality as a universal, empowering force, dwelling in the inner Self, seems in many cases not to have been an obstacle in the way of coaches collaborating with secular public institutions. Further, the more common use of the science-like 'inner potential' as a discourse within neospirituality has hardly been discussed at all in Swedish contexts, and the public institutions seem not only to have accepted the concept, they promote it, especially when it comes to coaching. It seems as if secularisation in Swedish society has mainly been a question of keeping traditional religion out of the public domain, while the neospiritual rhetoric or practices are instead becoming more commonly accepted. Marketed as 'coaching', or 'therapy', they promise redemption for the hidden individual potential, and have successfully introduced new ways of enchanting the public practices of contemporary Swedish society.

Chapter 12
Valuing Spirituality: Commodification, Consumption and Community in Glastonbury

Marion Bowman

Introduction

To write about 'valuing spirituality' in the context of Glastonbury – the small town in the south west of England that has been variously hailed as Avalon, the cradle of English Christianity, epicentre of New Age in England, the heart chakra of planet earth, a global 'power place', and much more besides[1] – is to be deliberately ambiguous. 'Valuing spirituality' might connote the metaphysical value of spirituality, involving assumptions around humans as spiritual beings with spiritual needs to explore and fulfil. It might conjure up a set of assumptions (positive or negative) around the economic value placed upon and derived from spiritual goods and services; spiritual commodification and consumption as expressions, enablers, or exploiters of contemporary spiritual seeking; or (following the logic that we pay for what we value) a reordering of priorities away from the accumulation of purely 'material' goods. In the sometimes tense interaction between 'incomer' spiritual entrepreneurs and visionaries on the one hand and Glastonians on the other, the rhetoric of valuing spirituality revolves around the desire of the former for a more general recognition of Glastonbury's status as a sacred site, or at least the acknowledgement that Glastonbury's spiritual 'USP' (unique selling point) has value for the town as a whole, even for those who do not share the vision(s). The importance of 'valuing spirituality' (both metaphorically and in monetary terms), as well as the promotion, expression, and negotiation of myriad spiritual values, lie at the heart of many of the town's enterprises.

---

[1] See Marion Bowman, 'Ancient Avalon, New Jerusalem, Heart Chakra of Planet Earth: Localisation and Globalisation in Glastonbury', *Numen*, 52/2 (2005): 157–90; Adrian J. Ivakhiv, 'Power Trips: Making Sacred Space through New Age Pilgrimage', in Darren Kemp and James R. Lewis (eds), *Handbook of New Age* (Leiden and Boston, MA, 2007), 263–86.

As I have remarked elsewhere,[2] commodification is an aspect of contemporary spirituality which attracts considerable critical attention and negative comment. 'Spiritually shopping around' and the business of 'selling spirituality' are often portrayed popularly as proofs of the essential superficiality, gullibility, and narcissism of the clients and the cynically capitalist, exploitative tendencies of the providers of such goods and services. Academic critiques of such phenomena display a range of attitudes and analyses, from a hermeneutic of suspicion to more sympathetic accounts.[3]

Drawing upon fieldwork data from the 1990s to the present, and the results of a small-scale pilot survey of Glastonbury's spiritual economy conducted in 2007, Glastonbury is examined here as an example of a specialised site of religious and spiritual consumption where (in common with other pilgrimage sites) it is assumed that commercial transactions can have sacralised meanings and value. The significance of this for the construction of spiritual identities and communities is explored, alongside the issue of whether countercultural spiritual practices have been co-opted by capitalism, or, conversely, spiritual entrepreneurs in any way challenge or reappraise existing commercial and organisational practices.

Glastonbury

When I say that I work on Glastonbury, people often assume I mean the Glastonbury Festival of Contemporary Performing Arts, actually held in the nearby village of Pilton on Worthy Farm. Glastonbury Festival caters for consumption of diverse kinds, including spiritual goods and services in areas such as the Healing Field, and it has been argued that Glastonbury Festival can be viewed as an 'agoratopia': a utopia which is structured by the market and organised by marketing practices.[4] Nevertheless, I am referring here to the small town of Glastonbury (with a

---

2 Marion Bowman, 'Understanding Glastonbury as a Site of Consumption', in Gordon Lynch, Jolyon Mitchell and Anna Strhan (eds), *Religion, Media and Culture: A Reader* (London, 2011), 11–22.

3 Kimberly J. Lau, *New Age Capitalism: Making Money East of Eden* (Philadelphia, PA, 2000); Douglas Ezzy, 'The Commodification of Witchcraft', *Australian Religious Studies Review*, 14/1 (2001): 31–44; Adam Possamai, 'Cultural Consumption of History and Popular Culture in Alternative Spiritualities', *Journal of Consumer Culture*, 2 (2002): 197–218; Adam Possamai, 'Alternative Spiritualities and the Cultural Logic of Late Capitalism', *Culture and Religion*, 4/1 (2003): 31–45; Michael York, 'New Age Commodification and Appropriation of Spirituality', *Journal of Contemporary Religion*, 16/3 (2001): 361–72; Jeremy Carrette and Richard King, *Selling Spirituality: The Silent Takeover of Religion* (London, 2005); Guy Redden, 'The New Age: Towards a Market Model', *Journal of Contemporary Religion*, 20/2 (2005): 231–46; Andrew Dawson, 'Consuming the Self: New Spirituality as "Mystified Consumption"', *Social Compass*, 58/3 (2011): 309–15.

4 Gretchen Larsen, Michael Macaulay, Daragh O'Reilly and Marion Bowman, 'Producing Agoratopia: Festival Tales from Glastonbury' (unpublished paper, 2012).

population of around 9,000 inhabitants), situated in an area of drained marshland known as the Somerset Levels, in the south west of England. There has been settlement in the area since prehistoric times, and the town contains a variety of striking natural features, including the Tor (a curiously contoured hill which can be seen for miles around), the chalybeate spring at Chalice Well (whose water stains red), and a thorn tree that flowers both in spring and in December. Physically at the centre of the town are the ruins of Glastonbury Abbey.

Glastonbury's economy was negatively affected during the twentieth century by declining agricultural activity and most significantly by the shrinkage of the area's considerable leather-related industries from the 1970s, although there is still building and engineering activity, and some light industry. In addition to the weekly street market, and the Country Market which is held in the Town Hall, the Glastonbury Carnival (part of the network of West Country Carnivals, derived from November 5th celebrations) attracts many visitors, and ventures such as the Frost Fayre in December (with communal singing of Christmas carols, street stalls, and so on) are designed to boost interest in the town. However, very obviously in relation to the High Street, and pervading the town, Glastonbury has developed a unique spiritual service industry on account of its distinctive religious and 'sacred' status.

Glastonbury is one of the most popular and multivalent pilgrimage sites in the UK, exerting an attraction for a variety of spiritual seekers on account of the many myths that surround it and the myriad claims made for it.[5] Some believe that Glastonbury was a significant prehistoric centre of goddess worship, while others regard it primarily as a Druidic site where, it is claimed, there was a great European centre of learning. For numerous Christians, Glastonbury's status rests on it being the first place where Christianity took root in England, allegedly brought there by Joseph of Arimathea. Even more significantly, many believe that Jesus himself came to Glastonbury, and some are convinced that Jesus will return there at the time of the second coming.[6] Glastonbury is regarded by some as an exemplary site

---

[5] See for example Irving Hexham, 'The "Freaks" of Glastonbury: Conversion and Consolidation in an English Country Town', *Update*, 7/1 (1983): 3–12; Marion Bowman, 'Drawn to Glastonbury', in Ian Reader and Tony Walter (eds), *Pilgrimage in Popular Culture* (Basingstoke and London, 1993), 29–62; Bowman, 'Ancient'; Marion Bowman, 'Going with the Flow: Contemporary Pilgrimage in Glastonbury', in Peter Jan Margy (ed.), *Shrines and Pilgrimage in the Modern World: New Itineraries into the Sacred* (Amsterdam, 2008), 241–80; James P. Carley, *Glastonbury Abbey: The Holy House at the Head of the Moors Adventurous* (Glastonbury, 1996); Ruth Prince and David Riches, *The New Age in Glastonbury: The Construction of Religious Movements* (New York and Oxford, 2000); Adrian J. Ivakhiv, *Claiming Sacred Ground: Pilgrims and Politics at Glastonbury and Sedona* (Bloomington and Indianapolis, IN, 2001); Isabel Laack, *Religion und Musik in Glastonbury: Eine Fallstudie zu gegenwärtigen Formen religiöser Identitätsdiskurse* (Göttingen and Oakville, CT, 2011).

[6] Marion Bowman, 'Taking Stories Seriously: Vernacular Religion, Contemporary Spirituality and the Myth of Jesus in Glastonbury', *Temenos*, 39–40 (2003–2004): 125–42.

of Celtic Christianity, and it has been identified with the legendary Isle of Avalon, where King Arthur was taken for healing after his last battle; feminist reworkings of the Arthurian legend[7] have added to Glastonbury's mystique. Now perceived by many as the 'heart chakra' of planet earth, Glastonbury is also regarded as a centre of earth energies, a node where ley lines converge and generate powerful forces for healing and personal transformation. One of many Glastonbury-related websites proclaims:

> It's a sacred place, an energy-field, a crossing of paths and karma-exchange, a place where the veils are thin, where faiths meet, light meets shadow and healings and breakthroughs happen.[8]

Many people on varied 'spiritual paths' narrate how they have felt 'drawn' to Glastonbury.[9]

In response to this hugely varied interest in Glastonbury, a unique spiritual service industry has arisen. Around 40 per cent of the town's retail outlets are what might be broadly termed 'alternative' shops selling goods intended to enhance and expand people's spiritual lifestyles and practices. There is a huge variety of healing on offer; annual events bring in people from Britain, Europe, America, and elsewhere; there are specialist bed and breakfast options; and complex patterns of 'portfolio working' within which people combine, for example, clairvoyance and part-time shop work. All this in turn generates more visitors, for part of Glastonbury's importance and value to a variety of people is as a site of spiritual consumption. However, Glastonbury's 'shopscape' and hinterland of alternative goods and services are predicated upon the spiritual values and ways of valuing and expressing spirituality that is practised and promoted by its spiritual entrepreneurs.

Material Culture, Pilgrimage, and Glastonbury

To contextualise Glastonbury's current status as a specialised site of religious and spiritual consumption, it is helpful to consider briefly the role of material culture and ways in which commercial transactions can acquire sacralised meanings, particularly in relation to pilgrimage sites. David Morgan contends,

> If culture is the full range of thoughts, feelings, objects, words, and practices that human beings use to construct and maintain the life-worlds in which they exist, material culture is any aspect of that world-making activity that happens in

---

7 See for example Marion Zimmer Bradley, *The Mists of Avalon* (London, 1986).

8 'Visiting Glastonbury', http://www.isleofavalon.co.uk/pilgrims/index.html [accessed: 6 January 2012].

9 Bowman, 'Drawn'; Bowman, 'Flow'.

> material form. That means things, but it also includes the feelings, values, fears, and obsessions that inform one's understanding and use of things.[10]

While anthropologists and ethnographers have paid considerable attention to religious material culture, there has been a tendency to underplay its importance in some spheres of religious studies, under the influence of a rather Western, Protestant, intellectual, text-based – and text-biased – approach to the study of religion, which is suspicious or dismissive of visual and material expressions of religion. As McDannell comments, 'Traditionally, scholars have understood the religious impulse as leading away from the material toward the spiritual'.[11] However, observably, pilgrimage centres worldwide traditionally often have been and continue to be places rich in material culture, with distinctive economies which have developed to serve both residents and visitors. Places perceived as special or sacred are frequently sites of commercialism, with 'religious' artefacts, relics, medals, statues, books, leaflets, pictures, souvenirs, and other aspects of material culture on sale, and locations where various forms of quasi-financial transaction with the divine might be enacted, such as the donation of money, ex-votos or services promised in return for answered prayers and healing.

Coleman and Elsner refer to the souvenirs that pilgrims take home as 'containers of the sacred' asserting,

> Pilgrimage is as concerned with taking back some part of the charisma of a holy place as it is about actually going to the place. One of the most characteristic aspects of pilgrimage art in all the world religions is the proliferation of objects made available to pilgrims and brought home by them as reminders and even as tangible channels of connection with the sacred experience. In this way, the influence of the site can be retained in the domestic or mundane context to which a pilgrim has returned.[12]

They point out that the value of objects and gifts purchased at a shrine or religious centre is not so much to do with monetary considerations but with their origin at a pilgrimage centre. Furthermore, the 'memorabilia of pilgrimage' also mark the pilgrim's identity as one who has made the journey. The meanings of and significance invested in such objects and transactions are therefore complex, leading McDannell to caution, 'If we immediately assume that whenever money is exchanged religion is debased, then we will miss the subtle ways people create and maintain spiritual ideals through the exchange of goods and the construction of

---

[10] David Morgan, 'The Materiality of Cultural Construction', *Material Religion*, 4/2 (2008): 228.

[11] Colleen McDannell, 'Interpreting Things: Material Culture Studies and American Religion', *Religion*, 21 (1991): 371.

[12] Simon Coleman and John Elsner, *Pilgrimage Past and Present in the World Religions* (Cambridge, MA, 1995), 100.

spaces'.[13] Notwithstanding the distinctive conditions of contemporary capitalism, secularity/post-secularity, globalisation, the impact of new media, and so on, some of the behavioural traits and rationales in relation to material culture and economic transactions observable in Glastonbury, though perhaps now more varied and 'exotic' than they have been in the past, have long histories and numerous analogues within the vernacular traditions of many religions.

The Development of Glastonbury's 'Spiritual Economy'

While speculations about Glastonbury's prehistoric spiritual and pilgrimage status are plentiful, in terms of contextualising the present spiritual service industry, Glastonbury Abbey is the logical place to start. By the Middle Ages, Glastonbury Abbey was a major Marian shrine, a pilgrimage site rich in relics and associations with numerous saints and royalty, and a centre of learning boasting a magnificent library.[14] The Abbey moulded the physical landscape and by its presence, activities, and significance shaped and influenced the life of the town.

The ground plan of the town exemplifies the extent to which it literally grew up around the Abbey. The monastery played a major part in developing various markets in Glastonbury, with the Abbey as a major landowner, wooltrader, and provider of a range of pilgrim attractions to the town, such as relics, a reputedly miraculous image of Our Lady, and the body of King Arthur allegedly discovered by monks in the Abbey grounds in the twelfth century. (It is worth remembering that some of the claims made for and by Glastonbury Abbey, in terms of its antiquity, which relics it possessed, and so on were contested even in the Middle Ages.) The town in response provided visitor goods and services, in addition to the regular domestic economy. However, the Abbey was brutally suppressed in 1539 at the time of the Reformation, passed into private hands, and fell into ruin. After that, Glastonbury's economy no longer primarily depended on or benefitted from religious associations. There was a brief flurry of activity in the eighteenth century when Glastonbury aspired to become a spa town, with curative claims being made for the waters of what is now known as Chalice Well at an outlet near the Abbey, but this was short-lived. From the 1870s sheepskin processing became increasingly important to Glastonbury's fortunes, an industry that remained significant for a century.

The development of rail travel and the restoration of public access to the Abbey grounds following their purchase by an Anglican-backed Trust in 1908 boosted Christian pilgrimage and tourism to Glastonbury (in relation to which a number of souvenirs were produced, mainly focused on the Glastonbury Thorn). As the twentieth century progressed, however, spiritual seekers, visionaries, and

---

13 Colleen McDannell, *Material Christianity: Religion and Popular Culture in America* (New Haven, CT and London, 1995), 6.

14 Carley, *Glastonbury*.

creative practitioners of various sorts found themselves drawn to Glastonbury, giving rise to a remarkable degree of religious speculation, experimentation, and artistic creativity involving people such as Frederick Bligh Bond, Alice Buckton, Rutland Boughton, Wellesley Tudor Pole, and Dione Fortune.[15] A distinctive spiritual and creative subculture began to flourish. The decline in the local leather industry in the 1970s coincided with Glastonbury increasingly gaining a media reputation as a centre for 'hippies', 'New Age Travellers', and people seeking alternative lifestyles and spiritual experiences.[16] Pilgrimage to Glastonbury once again gained momentum, but the reasons pilgrims, visitors, and incomers gave for feeling called there multiplied in number and complexity in relation to various late twentieth-century religious and spiritual trends.[17]

Since the 1970s in particular, some people in Glastonbury have commonly spoken of 'Glastonians' and 'Avalonians'; the former are primarily local and/or 'mainstream' people who think of themselves as living in a small market town in Somerset, while the latter, generally incomers, perceive that they are in some way in Avalon, a sacred and spiritually significant location. Ivakhiv[18] talks in the Sedona context of 'spiritual immigrants', those starting as pilgrims or tourists but ending up as permanent residents. Many townspeople refer to 'the Alternatives' as a generic description of the people, businesses, events, and visitors connected with the (non-Christian) spiritual service industry. In Glastonbury there have been long-term, ongoing tensions and differences in perceptions relating to the contribution of 'alternative' businesses and Glastonbury's status as a multivalent spiritual centre to the town's economic welfare, with some seeing it as either irrelevant or indeed inimical to the town's prosperity. It has been a frequent complaint among Avalonians that although they have revitalised the high street and brought employment and visitors to Glastonbury, their concerns and visions for the future of the town have been largely discounted by the Glastonians. Conversely, many local people felt threatened and displaced by the economic and social changes of the 1970s, involving what were regarded as not simply countercultural but anti-social groups, individuals, lifestyles, and spiritualities. On the whole there is a high level of tolerance, and inter- and intra-community relations have improved greatly, with many of those involved in 'alternative' activities having now become long-term Glastonbury residents, but some locals still feel puzzled by or resentful of the plethora of 'alternative' shops, religious groups, businesses, and visitors there.

Among the Avalonians, since the 1970s there have been noticeable developments in the types of religiosity practised, the range of 'alternative'

---

15 See Patrick Benham, *The Avalonians* (Glastonbury, 1993); Tracy Cutting, *Beneath the Silent Tor: The Life and Work of Alice Buckton* (Glastonbury, 2004); Tim Hopkinson-Ball, *The Rediscovery of Glastonbury: Frederick Bligh Bond Architect of the New Age* (London, 2007).

16 See Hexham, 'The Freaks'.

17 Bowman, 'Ancient'; Bowman, 'Flow'.

18 Ivakhiv, 'Power', 275.

businesses, and attitudes to commerce. Although the countercultural aspect was particularly pronounced in the 1970s, since the 1990s there has been a more relaxed attitude to money and business among many people in Glastonbury who consider themselves spiritually active. As one shop-owner told me, 'There's no point in being spiritual but bankrupt'. A number of entrepreneurs mentioned during interviews, however, that there is still a problem with 'poverty consciousness' among some people in town, those who retain anti-materialist sentiments resent paying for 'spiritual' goods and services and are somewhat judgemental of successful business people. Conversely, some businesses struggle to keep costs low to the extent that they find profit almost impossible; one catering business owner confided that they only just keep going, but I have witnessed payment being waived or negotiated in cases of hardship in that establishment. The possibility of combining the spiritual and material is occasionally reinforced in courses in Glastonbury, one example being The Prosperity Seminar, a day event held in 2007 by Steve Nobel,[19] a 'core concept' of the course being that 'you can live a spiritually and materially blessed life'.[20]

The Contemporary Spiritual Milieu: Catering for and Creating Community

A variety of religiosity is found in Glastonbury, including different forms of Christianity, Buddhism, Sufism, Indian-derived praxis with diverse foci and forms, Goddess Spirituality, Druidry, Wicca, Celtic spiritualities, assorted Paganisms, and an eclectic range of individually-crafted beliefs and practices. One distinctive feature of contemporary Glastonbury's role as a pilgrimage centre is the diversity of beliefs and praxis found in the town, with clusters of events, shops, goods, services, workshops, and even accommodation specifically associated with them.

Christians of all sorts still visit Glastonbury, attracted by the Anglican or Catholic Pilgrimage; by the Abbey ruins; by the Shrine of Our Lady of Glastonbury in the Roman Catholic church; to visit St John's Church and to attend talks and residential events at Abbey Church House (the Anglican diocesan retreat house). The Abbey's shop and some churches provide the opportunity for the purchase of goods specifically connected with Glastonbury's Christian heritage. Those more interested in Buddhism and Indian-oriented or derived religiosity and praxis might stay at Shekinashram (with its daily morning *arati*, *kirtan*, and meditation); attend workshops relating to various schools of yoga; participate in events run by the Triratna Buddhist Community (previously known as the Friends of the Western Buddhist Order); shop at Enlightenment or Natural Earthling for devotional objects and yoga requisites; sample Tibetan pulsing healing, and so on. Pagans of different sorts might be attracted to Glastonbury for seasonal ceremonies and events; for workshops or longer-term training programmes at the Isle of Avalon Foundation

[19] Author of *The Prosperity Game* (Findhorn, 2006).

[20] Isle of Avalon Foundation leaflet.

and elsewhere; to sample shamanic healing; and to explore the growing number of shops catering for pagan lifestyles such as Magick Box, Cat and Cauldron, and Lillith. Goddess devotees might come for the annual Goddess Conference; to visit the Goddess Temple for seasonal ceremonies, healing sessions, or to purchase candles, music CDs, and other items there; to participate in long-term training as a Priestess or Priest of Avalon and to shop at the Goddess and the Green Man.

While some townspeople and non-religiously motivated tourists may simply be aware of a mass of 'alternative' shops, events, and services, a variety of interconnected markets are being addressed. For pilgrims and visitors coming with specific foci, Glastonbury can provide specialist services, confirmatory or inspirational experiences and goods which might function as 'containers of the sacred' that can act as a link with the place on returning home. On numerous occasions, whether buying a candle from the Goddess Temple, mementos from the stall at the Roman Catholic Pilgrimage or a crystal from StoneAge (clearly sourced far from Glastonbury), people have described their purchases as 'special' because 'they come from Glastonbury'. Purchasers sometimes further enhance the Glastonbury connection by bathing a crystal in Chalice Well water, or touching a candle to a flame at an event then extinguishing it in preparation for travel. Participants of both the Anglican Pilgrimage and the Goddess Conference have described coming to Glastonbury as their 'annual fix', giving them a sense of *communitas* and sustaining them at home in places where they lack like-minded others. While there are clusters of consumption, there is obviously crossover between them. I have accompanied Anglican pilgrimage participants exploring 'alternative' shops such as Yin Yang, while people of many persuasions (dowsers, Sufis, Arthurian enthusiasts, Goddess devotees, British Israelites) visit the Abbey. Meanwhile, restaurants, cafes, the fish and chip shop, the bakery, the pharmacy, the Post Office, bed and breakfast establishments, banks, supermarkets, and charity shops all benefit from the range and quantity of visitors to the town.

While shops and businesses generally strive to be financially viable, there are sometimes other considerations in play, for having a shopfront in Glastonbury can be and has been seen as a way of staking a claim there. When Sheikh Nazim, the leader of the Sufi Naqshbandi-Haqqaniyya, visited Glastonbury in 1999 and declared it 'the spiritual heart of England' he urged his followers to establish a presence there; this has been achieved through the Healing Hearts Charity Shop, which also functions as an informal centre for dispensing booklets by Sheikh Nazim and information about his teachings. The coming and going of shops, the recent growth in the number of pagan-oriented shops, the preponderance of bookshops over crystal shops, or the failure or success of certain shops or ventures might not simply reflect the entrepreneurial skills of the owners but can also be a marker of trends. Movement *within* Glastonbury is also a common phenomenon. When the Goddess and the Green Man moved from the Glastonbury Experience courtyard onto the high street, for example, this was regarded as significant progress in terms of the growing popular acceptance of the beliefs represented.

It should also be noted that not just what is being consumed but methods of consumption have altered with the rise of 'virtual' Glastonbury, whether delivering a petition to the Roman Catholic Shrine of Our Lady of Glastonbury online, experiencing Glastonbury initially or even solely through virtual pilgrimage sites, or receiving goods from Glastonbury through the websites of shops based there. (One fascinating result of my survey of Glastonbury businesses was that 74 per cent of the businesses trading online considered it important to their customers that they are Glastonbury-based.) In addition, the nature of religious consumption has changed and developed in relation to emergent patterns and trends in contemporary religiosity; as Ezzy points out, 'the market is not a neutral influence on contemporary religious practices'.[21] While the spiritual economy and certain sectors of the regular economy may appear to be focused primarily on pilgrims and visitors, Glastonbury residents and entrepreneurs are central to any understanding of Glastonbury's latest incarnation as a pilgrimage centre. The development of non-aligned or de-institutionalised spirituality, the movement away from membership of institutions, and the increasing importance of networks and the formation of new forms of community are all observable and significant there. In the words of the Holism Network, a not-for-profit organisation based in Glastonbury,

> [a] central idea of contemporary spiritual culture is the empowerment of individuals and that it is important for people to maintain their independence and freedom. It does not have a centralised organisation. It does, however, have many small groups and centres, and there is a general sense of a community or network of like-minded people.[22]

It is assumed that people need and want to exercise a degree of choice in relation to ideas, beliefs, practices, and goods and services derived from and influenced by a wide variety of sources in order to produce what are valued by participants as highly personalised forms of religiosity. However, this is not a solitary task; it is done in the context of shared outlooks, networks, and a sense of higher purpose.

The ideas and principles operational among many engaged in Glastonbury's spiritual economy as both consumers and producers can be encapsulated by Possamai's description of 'perennism', a 'syncretic spirituality':

> 1. that interprets the world as monistic (the cosmos is perceived as having deeply inter-related elements; it recognises a single ultimate principle, being, or force underlying all reality, and rejects the notion of dualism; e.g. of mind/body);
>
> 2. whose actors are attempting to develop a human potential ethic (actors work on themselves for personal growth); and

21 Ezzy, 'Commodification'.

22 'Holistic Map UK', http://www.holisticmap.org/about/ [accessed: 22 February 2012].

> 3. whose actors are seeking spiritual knowledge (the way to develop oneself is through the pursuit of knowledge, be it the knowledge of the universe or of the self, the two being inter-related).[23]

While discussion of spiritual consumption frequently centres on what Possamai describes as the 'hermeneutically deficient term'[24] New Age, perennism encompasses a variety of worldviews, including the Aquarian and (neo-)Pagan. Perennists, according to Possamai, 'construct their sense of self, their subjective myth, through consuming religions/ spiritualities, indigenous culture, history and popular culture'.[25] The shared assumption of many visitors to and residents of Glastonbury is that spiritual seeking is an ongoing project, requiring constant exploration and experimentation. As Sutcliffe says of contemporary spiritual seekership, 'multiple seeking proceeds multi-directionally and synchronically: an array of spiritual resources are exploited more or less simultaneously. Ideas, methods and techniques are decontextualised and reconstituted in new settings and adventurous juxtapositions.'[26] Part of the attraction of coming to Glastonbury (whether as a one-off pilgrim, regular visitor, or permanent resident) is that such resources and juxtapositions can be encountered there.

Hanegraaff characterises the 'New Ager' as the 'ideal consumer', claiming,

> the fact that every New Ager continually creates and re-creates his or her own private system of symbolic meaning and values means that spiritual suppliers on the New Age market enjoy maximum opportunities for presenting him or her with ever-new commodities[27]

It is worth noting, however, that suppliers are themselves frequently consumers. Despite some critiques, it is not necessarily the case that they are exploitatively or impassively providing goods to and services for unknown clients. In Glastonbury there is an observable extent to which many spiritual entrepreneurs are sourcing and developing goods, events, and products for themselves and for each other, and doing so with a purpose. As Redden remarks, 'While the instrumental aspect of market relations means that there is no bar to some of those purveying New Age products from seeking profit as an end in itself, a case could be made that much New Age commerce is value-driven'.[28]

---

23 Possamai, 'Alternative', 33.

24 Possamai, 'Cultural', 199.

25 Ibid., 210.

26 Steven J. Sutcliffe, *Children of the New Age* (London, 2003), 204.

27 Wouter J. Hanegraaff, 'The New Age Movement and Western Esotericism', in Darren Kemp and James R. Lewis (eds), *Handbook of New Age* (Leiden and Boston, MA, 2007), 48.

28 Redden, 'The New Age', 244.

Redden's insights on the nature of this commercial activity are particularly relevant to the Glastonbury context, arising from his studies of body, mind, spirit fairs where 'products are presented side-by-side and the activities of many otherwise independent actors are interwoven'.[29] He refers to the fairs as 'intermediary spaces' on account of 'their function of catalysing networked relationships between diverse actors (both providers and participants) through presentation of multiple options for belief and practice',[30] and notes that '[v] alue-relativism, rather than simply being a hallmark of New Age teaching, is an operating principle of New Age markets in knowledge and practice'.[31] Arguably Glastonbury itself is such an 'intermediary space' and while there are undoubtedly strongly held, exclusivist beliefs among some religious groups and individuals who visit and live in Glastonbury, on a day-to-day basis value-relativism is the *modus operandi*.

There are pilgrims and other visitors to Glastonbury who feel drawn to the place (often repeatedly and regularly), but who are nevertheless content to return home from it. As already noted, however, some feel that they must stay. In its booklet *Glastonbury: A Pilgrim's Perspective*,[32] the Glaston Group described itself thus:

> We are an eclectic and evolving group, with a diverse range of beliefs and interests. We too were drawn here, as pilgrims in search of truth and the sacred. Whilst some pilgrims come and go and return again, we put down our roots and stayed.

The Glaston Group was responsible for bringing to fruition the vision of the Pilgrim Reception Centre (PRC), 'open to all people on all paths', providing specialist information and advice for the pilgrim/spiritual tourist. The PRC has become a significant integrative force within Glastonbury, providing a forum for people of very different spiritual persuasions resident in or connected with the town to work together, fostering mutual respect and understanding. A growing number and range of people see Glastonbury's future primarily as a pilgrimage centre, with their role being to draw people to the town and to support them materially, therapeutically, and spiritually while there. While some look with regret to the loss of the prosperity and employment brought by the tanneries and the leather industry, there are those who regard the period from the Reformation to the twentieth century as anomalous, a time when the town became temporarily distracted from its true function as a sacred centre. For people like this, Glastonbury's restoration as a specialised site of religious and spiritual seeking, instruction, healing, experience, and consumption has only just begun. These are often the people who

29 Ibid., 237.

30 Ibid., 237.

31 Ibid., 242.

32 Glaston Group, *Glastonbury: A Pilgrim's Perspective* (Glastonbury, 2005), 13.

see themselves as operating pragmatically on the basis of spiritual values, thereby enhancing the spiritual value of Glastonbury.

Glastonbury's Spiritual Economy

In 2007, with funding from the British Academy and drawing on the survey expertise of Sarah Robinson of Boundaries Unlimited, I conducted a small-scale, questionnaire-based, pilot survey among a range of goods-and-services-related businesses in Glastonbury, complemented by interviews with both 'spiritually inspired' and mainstream business people.[33] I wished to look at different examples of spiritual entrepreneurship and the self-narration of such entrepreneurs, to examine the extent of similarity and contrast with classic pilgrim economies, to assess the degree to which this sector is compatible with, complementary to, or at odds with the 'regular' economy and to sample the awareness and opinions of the mainstream businesses of alternative events and businesses.

Conventional business surveys of Glastonbury tend not to do justice to the diversity and creativity of economic life there, because the ways people make a living, the sorts of goods (spell kits, wands, Tibetan singing bowls) and services on offer (past life regression, spiritual house cleansing), do not easily fit into mainstream categories or SIC (Standard Industry Classification) codes. Nearly 60 per cent of respondents were self-employed, and Glastonbury's reputation as a religious and spiritual centre influenced the decision of 46 per cent of those who responded to the survey to be involved in business there ('I visited Glastonbury to engage with its spirituality, then felt compelled to live here'; 'I prayed to God and was told to come here'; 'to share in the spiritual and other alternative activities taking place in and around Glastonbury'). For 49 per cent of the respondents, Glastonbury's reputation as a religious and spiritual centre had an impact on the type of business they had decided to run in Glastonbury ('Over the years we have gradually changed the emphasis from a basic B&B as it was before we bought it to a more spiritual basis'; 'Many visitors come with a spiritual focus so what I have to offer makes sense here').

Seventy-three per cent of questionnaire respondents believed that religious and spiritual events in Glastonbury have a positive impact on their business, a result not simply relating to those involved in 'alternative' activities. One couple who had run a 'traditional' bed and breakfast for many years, for example, appreciated that 'alternative' events, ceremonies, and so on now provide year-round visitor attractions, whereas in the past they used to close over winter. The expansion in the range of people coming to Glastonbury was commented upon, reflecting the opportunity to cater to a variety of tastes and pockets; for example, more than

33 All organisations who responded to the survey are referred to as businesses even though a number were set up as 'not for profit' organisations and charities; we received 110 responses.

one businessperson mentioned the growing strength of 'the pagan pound' while a shopworker in a (now defunct) menswear shop commented that 'the cloak and crystal brigade must have money trees growing in their gardens'. One proprietor of a pagan lifestyle shop confirmed,

> More middle-class people come to Glastonbury now than ever. At one time it was the real sort of early twenties, hippy-style people or the middle-aged Christian. … That was all there was. … Now you have the massive difference of many more middle-class pagans, because they're more able freely today to express themselves and so they're not afraid to come to town. (Interview, 20 March 2007)

It is important to note that numerous people who have felt called to Glastonbury and operate businesses there donate *gratis* their time, skills, and energy for community and communal initiatives, as Trustees of Chalice Well or the Glastonbury Trust, for example, or organising initiatives in relation to the Glaston Group. The internet has been the vehicle for a form of social bridging in Glastonbury, indicative of other trends towards more cooperative and community-building ventures. Realising that for the most part it was the 'alternatives' who were making best use of the internet to boost business or publicise events, a not-for-profit company Glastonbury Online Ltd was created to assist

> … the development of internet use amongst Glastonbury businesses, community groups & people. Any profits generated are put back into supporting the development of community webpages/websites for local organisations.
>
> Glastonbury Online was formed out of a loose collection of local webworkers and eventually became a company limited by guarantee. We are proud of our good relationships with other webworkers in the town and continue to promote co-operation rather than competition in our community.[34]

The entrepreneurs interviewed so far see no contradiction between spirituality and business, and indeed tend to regard their business as part of their spiritual path, as well as confirmation of their personal skills and qualities. It is quite common for there to be some sort of shrine in shops or business premises, even when the goods or services offered are not overtly spiritual or alternative. One indication of the complex interaction between spirituality and commerce in Glastonbury was the staging of a ritual under the first full moon of 2010 by a number of Glastonbury shopkeepers for the prosperity of the town. In line with the philosophy 'in every life a lesson', even when some business ventures had not turned out well, spiritual

---

[34] 'Glastonbury Online', http://www.glastonbury.co.uk/pages/site.php?pgid=420 [accessed: 22 February 2012].

and personal insights were drawn from the experience, as well as commercial refocusing.

While there are people who undoubtedly make what they describe as a 'comfortable' living from their businesses, there is a notable lack of conspicuous consumption and a certain modesty of lifestyle among them. The importance of 'right livelihood', integrity and balance were stressed repeatedly in the interviews, and the concept of having a business with a purpose came up on a number of occasions. For example, one person involved in the book trade told me,

> I've always wanted to say something but never actually gone as far … but it's books for a better world … we are not just selling books, we are selling books which have some kind of future and that's what ties it into the concept of the New Age. (Interview 15 March 2007)

Very much in the spirit of Ritzer's[35] comparison of 'something' (generally locally or indigenously conceived, made and controlled – rich in substantive content) and 'nothing' (generally centrally conceived, made and controlled – devoid of substantive content), the importance of 'authenticity', fair trade, having a personal relationship with artisans, and having products that are genuinely fit for purpose was stressed. One woman recounted that she had started employing people locally to put together spell kits in preference to her previous supplier, as she needed to be certain that herbs were fresh and candle wax was of a high quality. Another commented on the importance she attached to knowing artisans and sourcing goods herself:

> … people come to us because they know all our stuff is authentic. It's not out of China, it's not a dreamcatcher that just somebody's put together in America, they are all signed by the artist and so our reputation here is for authenticity, and I think that is something that follows through in all aspects of life, being authentic and authentic with yourself – and just find that new product as well! (Interview 27 March 2007)

Other recurring themes included the conviction that there was enough business to go round for everyone and that entrepreneurs could therefore cooperate and interact positively, buy from each other, attend each other's events, and so on. One therapist who is also involved in a herbal products business said,

> I guess it's like a … a flow of business. … It's like an inter connected web, you're tuning into that web of connection and allowing a kind of positive flow of products and services and money and receiving and giving to go round that network and I think … you'll find [it] in a lot of people who have quite a spiritual approach to business. Does that make sense? … I suppose one would hope that

35 George Ritzer, *The Globalization of Nothing* (London, 2004).

> values such as integrity and honesty and compassion, you know some of those values would not be left at the door when you go into the market place, you know, that those were actually integrated into everything that we do. (Interview 13 March 2007)

Related to the concept of being 'called' and the significance of relativism as already discussed, the fact that people were following different paths was generally deemed unimportant as it was assumed that by being in Glastonbury they were part of a larger whole.

Conclusion

In this chapter, the importance of 'valuing spirituality' (both metaphorically and in monetary terms) and the importance of recognising continuity as well as change in religious and spiritual consumption have been stressed, for commercial transactions have had sacralised meanings for centuries in Glastonbury. It has this in common with other pilgrimage centres which frequently generate distinctive economies and are sites of contestation. Glastonbury is now an example *par excellence* of a contemporary pilgrimage centre, with traditional and new forms of religion, traditional and new goods and services, producing a distinctive economy. Pilgrims try to capture some of Glastonbury's charisma through a range of goods purchased there, which they may then further personalise according to their perception of Glastonbury's essence. Notwithstanding the elements of continuity, however, changes in methods of spiritual consumption, the range of goods and services available, and the contemporary impetus for consumption all must be taken into account.

Studying the development of Glastonbury's spiritual economy furthers a more granular understanding of some aspects of contemporary spiritual consumption in relation to both clients and providers. Redden's[36] insights concerning the role of 'intermediary spaces', the importance of value-relativism and the operational significance of commodification and marketisation are particularly relevant. There is diversity not just in the goods, services, and experiences available, but in the meanings and nuances attributed to consumption, as Possamai points out: 'Aquarian perennists (paradoxically) consume in a way that justifies an evolutionary perspective, presentist perennists focus mainly on the present and neo-pagan perennists consume in such a way that it valorizes neo-pagan values and lifestyles.'[37]

---

36 Redden, 'The New Age'.

37 Possamai, 'Cultural', 214.

As Sutcliffe,[38] Hammer,[39] Kubiak,[40] and others have noted, although there is a strong emphasis on the personal quest and individualism within contemporary integrative spirituality, the books on the shelves of individuals following these paths are often remarkably similar. They have frequently attended similar workshops, belong to a variety of overlapping networks, have an interest in and awareness of alternative forms of community, and so on. As a number of parallel clusters of consumption coexist in Glastonbury, the spiritual seeker often feels at home there. This sense of *communitas* is significant, for people on 'personalised' spiritual journeys nevertheless appreciate fellow travellers and confirmation of the validity of their quest.

By seeking to understand how Glastonbury functions as a site of religious experience, spiritual seeking, and consumption, we can usefully pursue a number of questions concerning the construction of religious identities and communities, and the ways in which 'buying and selling spirituality' is perceived and narrated by those involved in such transactions. Dismissing spiritual entrepreneurs as exploitative charlatans, and their clients as deluded fools, is not an acceptable *modus operandi* for getting to grips with a significant economic and business phenomenon which potentially challenges existing organisational and commercial theories and practices. As Watson[41] notes, entrepreneurial identity work involves asking 'who we are' and an individual's biography and life course may be significant in providing the resources through which internal and socially-oriented entrepreneurial identity work is conducted. This is undoubtedly significant in relation to Glastonbury's many and varied spiritual entrepreneurs, who regard their work in the spiritual marketplace as integral to their own spiritual path, as an expression of their spiritual values and as being of service to the spiritual value of Glastonbury.

Since the 1970s the town of Glastonbury has experienced a brutal transition from primarily an industrial and manufacturing economic base to a more varied, service-based (and in one sector, spiritual service-based) economy. With around 40 per cent of its high street outlets now occupied by 'alternative' shops, and a hinterland of spiritually related businesses, healing practitioners of many sorts, specialised bed and breakfasts, diverse devotional communities, and myriad spiritually inspired events and activities, spiritual values and different ways of valuing spirituality have a clear impact on the economy and population as a whole. Researching this relationship between the regular economy and the spiritual

---

38 Sutcliffe, *Children*.

39 Olav Hammer, *Claiming Knowledge: Strategies of Epistemology from Theosophy to the New Age* (Leiden and Boston, MA, 2004).

40 Anna E. Kubiak, 'Old Myths, New Mythicising', in Darren Kemp and James R. Lewis (eds), *Handbook of New Age* (Leiden and Boston, MA, 2007), 255–62.

41 Tony Watson, 'Entrepreneurial Action, Identity, and the Use of Multiple Discursive Resources: The Case of a Rapidly Changing Family Business', *International Small Business Journal*, 27/3 (2009): 251–74.

economy is important, if we wish to understand how new patterns of consumption and production, the structures of late capitalism and the severe financial forecasts for the coming years, affect both the alternative economy and mainstream business models and working patterns.

Bibliography

Abbruzzese, Salvatore, *La vita religiosa. Per una sociologia della vita consacrata* (Rimini: Guaraldi, 1995).

Adams, John H., 'Presbyterian Congregations Use Purpose-Driven Church Model' (8 October 2002), [Online], available at: http://www.faithwebsites.com/sysfiles/site_uploads/pubsartsmeds/pub1756.htm [accessed: 9 December 2011].

Agamben, Giorgio, *Altissima povertà. Regola e forma di vita nel monachesimo* (Milano: Neri Pozza, 2011).

Ahlin, Lars, *New Age: konsumtionsvara eller värden att kämpa för?* (Lund: Teologiska institutionen, 2001).

Altglas, Veronique, 'Indian Gurus and the Quest for Self-perfection Among the Educated Middle Class', in Jörg Stolz (ed.), *Salvation Goods and Religious Markets* (New York: Peter Lang, 2008), pp. 211–34.

Arvidsson, Adam, *Brands: Meaning and Value in Media Culture* (London and New York: Routledge, 2006).

——, 'Entretien avec Adam Arvidsson. "Les marques sont des reliques modernes"', *Les Grands Dossiers des Sciences Humaines*, 22 (2011): 56–8.

Askeland, Maj Karin, 'A Reflexive Inquiry into the Ideologies and Theoretical Assumptions of Coaching', *Coaching: An International Journey of Theory, Research and Practice*, 2/1 (2009): 65–75.

Atkin, Douglas, *The Culting of Brands: When Customers Become True Believers* (New York: Penguin, 2004).

Bäckström, Anders, 'Believing in Belonging: The Swedish Way of Being Religious', in Riikka Ryökäs and Esko Ryökäs (eds), *Urban Faith 2000: Publications of Church Sociology* (Helsinki: Helsinki University, 1993), pp. 31–42.

Bäckström, Anders, Grace Davie, Ninna Edgardh and Per Pettersson (eds), *Welfare and Religion in 21st Century Europe: Volume 1* (Farnham: Ashgate, 2010).

Bäckström, Anders, Grace Davie, Ninna Edgardh and Per Pettersson (eds), *Welfare and Religion in 21st Century Europe: Volume 2* (Farnham: Ashgate, 2011).

Bäckström, Anders, Ninna Edgardh and Per Pettersson, *Religious Change in Northern Europe: The Case of Sweden* (Stockholm: Verbum, 2004).

Bains, David R., 'Contemporary Worship: Trends and Patterns in Christian America', in Charles H. Lippy (ed.), *Faith in America: Changes, Challenges, New Directions, Volume 3* (Westport, CT: Praeger, 2006), pp. 1–23.

Barker, Eileen, 'New Religious Movements', in George Ritzer (ed.), *Blackwell Encyclopedia of Sociology* (Blackwell Publishing, Blackwell Reference Online, 2007).
Bastide, Roger, *Les amériques noires. Les civilisations africaines dans le nouveau monde* (Paris: Payot, 1967).
——, *Le sacré sauvage: et autres essais*, Comp. Henri Desroche (Paris: Payot, 1975), pp. 214–36.
Baudet, Clément, 'Les chaleurs du festival Burning Man', *OWNI* (6 September 2011), [Online], available at: http://www.owni.fr/2011/09/06/dans-la-chaleur-du-festival-burning-man [accessed: 20 July 2012].
Bauhn, Per and Jan Svensson, 'Retoriken ändrade välfärdssamhället', *LUM: Lunds Universitet Meddelar*, 11 (Lund: Lunds universitet, 1996).
Bauman, Zygmunt, 'Postmodern Religion?' in Zygmunt Bauman, *Postmodernity and Its Discontents* (Oxford: Blackwell, 1997), pp. 165–85.
——, *In Search of Politics* (Cambridge: Polity, 1999).
——, *Liquid Modernity* (Cambridge: Polity, 2000).
——, *Liquid Fear* (Cambridge: Polity, 2002).
——, *Liquid Life* (Cambridge: Polity, 2005).
——, *Consuming Life* (Cambridge: Polity Press, 2008).
Bays, Brandon, *The Journey for Kids: Liberating Your Child's Shining Potential* (London: Element, 2003).
——, *The Journey: A Practical Guide to Healing Your Life and Setting Yourself Free* (New York and London: Atria, 2008 [1999]).
Beauchemin, Jacques, *La société des identités* (Montreal: Athena, 2004).
Beck, Ulrich, *Risk Society: Towards a New Modernity*, trans. Mark Ritter (London: Sage, 1992).
——, *What Is Globalization?*, trans. Patrick Camiller (Cambridge: Polity, 2000).
——, 'Interview with Ulrich Beck', *Journal of Consumer Culture*, 1 (2001): 261–77.
——, 'The Terrorist Threat: World Risk Society Revisited', *Theory, Culture and Society*, 19/4 (2002): 39–55.
——, *Cosmopolitan Vision*, trans. Ciaron Cronin (Cambridge: Polity, 2006).
——, *A God of One's Own: Religion's Capacity for Peace and Potential for Violence*, trans. Rodney Livingstone (Cambridge: Polity, 2010).
Beck, Ulrich and Elizabeth Beck-Gernsheim, *Individualization: Institutionalized Individualism and Its Social and Political Consequences*, trans. Patrick Camiller (London: Sage, 2002).
Beck, Ulrich, Anthony Giddens and Scott Lash, *Reflexive Modernization: Politics, Tradition and Aesthetics in the Modern Social Order* (Cambridge: Polity Press, 1994).
Beck, Ulrich and Edgar Grande, 'Varieties of Second Modernity: The Cosmopolitan Turn in Social and Political Theory and Research', *British Journal of Sociology*, 61/3 (2010): 409–43.

Beck, Ulrich and Natan Sznaider, 'Unpacking Cosmopolitanism for the Social Sciences: A Research Agenda', *British Journal of Sociology*, 57/1 (2006): 1–23.

Bell, Catherine, *Ritual: Perspectives and Dimensions* (New York and Oxford: Oxford University Press, 1997).

Bell, Daniel, *The Coming of Post-Industrial Society: A Venture into Social Forecasting* (New York: Heinemann, 1973).

Benham, Patrick, *The Avalonians* (Glastonbury: Gothic Image Publications, 1993).

Berger, Peter L., *The Sacred Canopy: Elements of a Sociological Theory of Religion* (New York: Doubleday, 1967).

——, *The Capitalist Revolution: Fifty Propositions about Prosperity, Equality, and Liberty* (New York: Basic Books, 1988).

——, 'Epistemological Modesty: An Interview with Peter Berger', *Christian Century*, 114 (1997): 972–5, 978.

Berger, Peter, Grace Davie and Effie Fokas, *Religious America, Secular Europe? A Theme and Variations* (Aldershot: Ashgate, 2008).

Berger, Peter and Thomas Luckmann, *The Social Construction of Reality* (New York: Doubleday, 1966).

Betz, Hans-Georg, 'Postmodernism and the New Middle Class', *Theory, Culture and Society*, 9 (1992): 93–114.

Beyer, Peter, *Religion and Globalization* (London: Sage, 1994).

Black, D.S., 'Burning Man as Ephemeropolis and the Refusal of Meaning', paper presented at the North American Interdisciplinary Conference on Environment and Community, University of Nevada, Reno (1998).

Boltanski, Luc and Eve Chiapello, *Le nouvel esprit du capitalisme* (Paris: Gallimard, 1999).

Boréus, Kristina, *Högervåg. Nyliberalismen och kampen om språket i svensk debatt 1969–1989* (Stockholm: Tidens förlag, 1994).

Boteach, Shmuley, *Kosher Sex: A Recipe for Passion and Intimacy* (New York: Doubleday, 1999).

——, *Kosher Adultery: Seduce and Sin with Your Spouse* (Avon, MA: Adams Media, 2002).

——, *The Kosher Sutra: Eight Sacred Secrets for Reigniting Desire and Restoring Passion for Life* (New York: Harper One, 2009).

Boudon, Raymond, 'Limitations of Rational Choice Theory', *The American Journal of Sociology*, 104/3 (1998): 817–28.

——, 'Beyond Rational Choice Theory', *Annual Review of Sociology*, 29 (2003): 1–21.

Bourdieu, Pierre, *Distinction: A Social Critique of the Judgement of Taste* (London: Routledge, 1984).

Bovbjerg, Kirsten Marie, 'De menneskelige potentialer i en "stresstid"', in Joel Haviv (ed.), *Medarbejder eller modarbejder – religion i moderne arbejdsliv* (Århus: Klim, 2007), pp. 55–80.

Bowman, Marion, 'Drawn to Glastonbury', in Ian Reader and Tony Walter (eds), *Pilgrimage in Popular Culture* (Basingstoke and London: Macmillan, 1993), pp. 29–62.
——, 'Taking Stories Seriously: Vernacular Religion, Contemporary Spirituality and the Myth of Jesus in Glastonbury', *Temenos*, 39–40 (2003–2004): 125–42.
——, 'Ancient Avalon, New Jerusalem, Heart Chakra of Planet Earth: Localisation and Globalisation in Glastonbury', *Numen*, 52/2 (2005): 157–90.
——, 'Going with the Flow: Contemporary Pilgrimage in Glastonbury', in Peter Jan Margy (ed.), *Shrines and Pilgrimage in the Modern World: New Itineraries into the Sacred* (Amsterdam: Amsterdam University Press, 2008), pp. 241–80.
——, 'Understanding Glastonbury as a Site of Consumption', in Gordon Lynch, Jolyon Mitchell and Anna Strhan (eds), *Religion, Media and Culture: A Reader* (London: Routledge, 2011), pp. 11–22.
Bradley, Marion Zimmer, *The Mists of Avalon* (London: Sphere Books, 1986).
Brenner, David, *Marketing Identities: The Invention of Jewish Ethnicity in Ost und West* (Detroit, MI: Wayne State University Press, 1998).
Brodin, Jenny-Ann, *Religion till salu?: en sociologisk studie av New Age i Sverige* (Stockholm: Almqvist & Wiksell, 2001).
Bromander, Jonas, *Medlem i Svenska kyrkan* (Stockholm: Verbum, 2005).
——, *Svenska kyrkans medlemmar* (Stockholm: Verbum, 2011).
Bruce, Steve, *Religion in the Modern World: From Cults to Cathedrals* (Oxford: Oxford University Press, 1996).
——, 'Les limites du "marché religieux"', *Social Compass*, 53/1 (2006): 33–48.
Burger, Maya, 'What Price Salvation? The Exchange of Salvation Goods between India and the West', *Social Compass*, 53/1 (2006): 81–95.
Caillé, Alain, *Dé-penser l'économique. Contre le fatalisme* (Paris: La Découverte/MAUSS, 2005).
Campbell, Colin, *The Romantic Ethic and the Spirit of Modern Consumerism* (Oxford: Blackwell, 1987).
Carley, James P., *Glastonbury Abbey: The Holy House at the Head of the Moors Adventurous* (Glastonbury: Gothic Image Publications, 1996).
Carrette, Jeremy and Richard King, *Selling Spirituality: The Silent Takeover of Religion* (London: Routledge, 2005).
Carroll, Jackson W., *As One with Authority: Reflective Leadership in Ministry* (Louisville, KY: Westminster/John Knox Press, 1991).
Casanova, José, *Public Religions in the Modern World* (Chicago, IL: University of Chicago Press, 1994).
——, 'Rethinking Secularization: A Global Comparative Perspective', *The Hedgehog Review*, 8/1–2 (2006): 7–22.
Charmé, Stuart Z., 'Varieties of Authenticity in Contemporary Jewish Identity', *Jewish Social Studies*, 6/2 (2000): 133–55.
Chaves, Mark, 'Secularization as Declining Religious Authority', *Social Forces*, 72/3 (1994): 749–74.
Chomsky, Noam, *Necessary Illusions* (Boston, MA: South End Press, 1989).

——, *Profit over People: Neoliberalism and Global Order* (New York: Seven Story Press, 1999).

Church of Sweden Statistics (2011), [Online], available at: http://www.svenskakyrkan.se.

Cimino, Richard and Don Lattin, *Shopping for Faith: American Religion in the New Millennium* (San Francisco, CA: Jossey-Bass, 1998).

Cohen, Steve, 'Cultural (Con)fusion', *Sh'ma*, 34/607 (January 2004): 8–9, [Online], available at: http://www.shma.com/archives/web-edition/ [accessed: 3 October 2011].

Coleman, James, *The New Buddhism: The Western Transformation of an Ancient Tradition* (Oxford: Oxford University Press, 2001).

Coleman, Simon and John Elsner, *Pilgrimage Past and Present in the World Religions* (Cambridge, MA: Harvard University Press, 1995).

Coutu, Diane and Carol Kauffman, 'What Can Coaches Do for You?', *Harvard Business Review* (January 2009): 91–8.

Cush, Denise, 'British Buddhism and the New Age', *Journal of Contemporary Religion*, 11 (1996): 195–208.

Cutting, Tracy, *Beneath the Silent Tor: The Life and Work of Alice Buckton* (Glastonbury: Appleseed Press, 2004).

D'Agostino, Antonello, Roberta Serafini and Melanie Ward-Warmedinger, 'Sectoral Explanations of Employment in Europe: The Role of Services', *European Central Bank, Working paper series*, 625 (May 2006).

Davie, Grace, *Religion in Britain Since 1945: Believing Without Belonging* (Oxford: Blackwell, 1994).

——, *The Sociology of Religion* (London: Sage, 2007).

Davie, Grace, Linda Woodhead and Paul Heelas, *Predicting Religion: Christian, Secular, and Alternative Futures* (Aldershot: Ashgate, 2003).

Davis, Philip R., 'Judaism and the Hebrew Scriptures', in Jacob Neusner and Alan J. Avery-Peck (eds), *The Blackwell Companion to Judaism* (Malden, MA: Blackwell, 2000), pp. 37–55.

Dawson, Andrew, *New Era – New Religions: Religious Transformation in Contemporary Brazil* (Aldershot: Ashgate, 2007).

——, 'New Era Millenarianism in Brazil', *Journal of Contemporary Religion*, 23/3 (2008): 269–83.

——, 'Consuming the Self: New Spirituality as "Mystified Consumption"', *Social Compass*, 58/3 (2011): 309–15.

——, *Sociology of Religion* (London: SCM Press, 2011).

——, *Santo Daime: A New World Religion* (London: Bloomsbury, 2013).

Dawson, Lorne, *Comprehending Cults: The Sociology of New Religious Movements* (Toronto: Oxford University Press, 1998).

de Geer, Hans, *Arbetsgivarna. SAF i tio decennier* (Stockholm: Svenska Arbetsgivareföreningen, 1992).

DeNora, Tia, *Music in Everyday Life* (Cambridge: Cambridge University Press, 2000).

Dobbelaere, Karel, *Secularization: An Analysis at Three Levels* (Brussels: Peter Lang, 2002).
Doherty, Brian, *This Is Burning Man* (New York: Little, Brown & Company, 2004).
Douglas, Mary and Baron Isherwood, *The World of Goods: Towards an Anthropology of Consumption* (New York and London: Routledge, 1996).
Durkheim, Émile, *Les formes élémentaires de la vie religieuse* (Paris: CNRS, 2007 [1912]).
Edgardh, Ninna and Per Pettersson, 'The Church of Sweden: A Church for All, Especially the Most Vulnerable', in Anders Bäckström, Grace Davie, Ninna Edgardh and Per Pettersson (eds), *Welfare and Religion in 21st Century Europe, Volume 1* (Farnham: Ashgate, 2010), pp. 39–56.
Einstein, Mara, *Brands of Faith: Marketing Religion in a Commercial Age* (New York: Routledge, 2008).
Eiseland, Nancy, *A Particular Place* (New York: Routledge, 1999).
Eisenstadt, Shmuel, 'Multiple Modernities', *Deadalus*, 129/1 (2000): 1–29.
Ellingson, Stephen, *The Megachurch and the Mainline* (Chicago, IL: University of Chicago Press, 2007).
Ezzy, Douglas, 'The Commodification of Witchcraft', *Australian Religious Studies Review*, 14/1 (2001): 31–44.
Fader, Ayala, 'Jewish Spirituality and Late Capitalism', in Celia Rothenberg and Anne Vallely (eds), *New Age Judaism* (London: Vallentine Mitchell, 2008), pp. 34–51.
FAS, *Complementary and Alternative Medicine (CAM): A Systematic Review of Intervention Research in Sweden* (Stockholm: Osher Centrum för integrativ medicin, 2007).
Featherstone, Mike, *Consumer Culture and Postmodernism* (London: Sage, 1992; second edition, 2007).
Fine, Robert, 'Civil Society Theory, Enlightenment and Critique', *Democratization*, 4/1 (1997): 7–28.
Finke, Roger and Lawrence Iannaccone, 'Supply-Side Explanations for Religious Change', *Annals of the American Academy of Political and Social Science*, 527 (May 1993): 27–39.
Finkelstein, Peter, Brant Wenegrat and Irvin Yalom, 'Large Group Awareness Training', *Annual Review of Psychology*, 83 (1982): 515–39.
Fishman, Sylvia Barak and Shlomo Fischer, 'Learning Jewishness, Jewish Education, and Jewish Identity', Report for the Jewish People Policy Institute (JPPI), Jerusalem (2012), [Online], available at: http://jppi.org.il/uploads/Learning_Jewishness,Jewish_education_and_Jewish_Identity.pdf [accessed: 17 February 2013].
Foucault, Michel, *Les mots et les choses* (Paris: Gallimard, 1966).
Frisk, Liselotte, 'Vad är New Age? Centrala begrepp och historiska rötter', *Svensk religionshistorisk årsskrift*, 6 (1997): 87–97.

Furedi, Frank, *Therapy Culture: Cultivating Vulnerability in an Uncertain Age* (London: Routledge, 2004).

Galbraith, John Kenneth, *The World Economy since the Wars* (London: Sinclair-Stevenson, 1994).

Gaonkar, Dilip P., 'On Alternative Modernities', in Dilip P. Gaonkar (ed.), *Alternative Modernities* (London: Duke University Press, 2001), pp. 1–23.

Gaulejac, Vincent de, *La société malade de la gestion. Idéologie gestionnaire, pouvoir managérial et harcèlement social* (Paris: Seuil, 2005).

Gauthier, François, 'Le Temple de l'Honneur. Rituels et deuils dans le désert au Festival Burning Man', *Frontières*, 17/1 (2004): 87–90.

——, 'Sous-cultures jeunesse et religion: métal, gothique, hip-hop et techno', in François Gauthier and Jean-Philippe Perreault (eds), *Jeunes et religion au Québec* (Quebec: Presses de l'Université Laval, 2008), pp. 101–22.

——, 'Religion in Contemporary Consumer Societies: In Search of a Global Comprehensive Analytic', *Revue du MAUSS permanente* (1 September 2009), [Online], available at: http://www.journaldumauss.net/spip.php?article539 [accessed: 2 February 2013].

——, 'Les HeeBeeGeeBee Healers au Festival Burning Man. Trois récits de guérison', *Ethnologies*, 33/1 (2011): 191–215.

——, 'Primat de l'authenticité et besoin de reconnaissance. La société de consommation et la nouvelle régulation du religieux', *Studies in Religion/Sciences religieuses*, 41/1 (2012): 93–111.

Gauthier, Francois, Tuomas Martikainen and Linda Woodhead, 'Introduction: Religion in Consumer Society', *Social Compass*, 58/3 (2011): 291–301.

Gauthier, François and Jean-Philippe Perreault, 'Jeunes et religion dans la société de consommation: État des lieux et prospective', in François Gauthier and Jean-Philippe Perreault (eds), *Jeunes et religion au Québec* (Québec: Presses de l'Université Laval, 2008), pp. 9–28.

Gauthier, François and Jean-Philippe Perreault (eds), *Jeunes et religion au Québec* (Québec: Presses de l'Université Laval, 2008).

Geertz, Clifford, *The Interpretation of Culture: Selected Essays* (New York: Basic Books, 1973).

Gellner, Ernest, *Conditions of Liberty: Civil Society and Its Rivals* (London: Penguin Books, 1996).

Giddens, Anthony, *Modernity and Self-Identity: Self and Society in the Late Modern Age* (Cambridge: Polity Press, 1991).

Gilmore, Lee, 'Fires of the Heart: Ritual, Pilgrimage, and Transformation at Burning Man', in Lee Gilmore and Mark Van Proyen (eds), *Afterburn: Reflections on Burning Man* (Albuquerque, NM, 2005), pp. 43–64.

——, *Theater in a Crowded Fire. Ritual and Spirituality at Burning Man* (Berkeley: University of California Press, 2010).

Gilmore, Lee and Mark Van Proyen (eds), *Afterburn: Reflections on Burning Man* (Albuquerque, NM: University of New Mexico Press, 2005).

Glaston Group, *Glastonbury: A Pilgrim's Perspective* (Glastonbury, 2005).

Glazer, Nathan, *American Jewry or American Judaism?* (Cambridge, MA: Harvard University Press, 1988).

Goh, Robbie B.H., 'Hillsong and "Megachurch" Practice: Semiotics, Spatial Logic and the Embodiment of Contemporary Evangelical Protestantism', *Material Religion*, 4/3 (2008): 285–304.

Goswami, Manu, 'Rethinking the Modular Nation Form: Toward a Sociohistorical Conception of Nationalism', *Comparative Studies in Society and History*, 44/4 (2002): 770–99.

Green, Deirdre, 'Buddhism in Britain: "Skilful Means" or Selling Out?', in Paul Badham (ed.), *Religion, State, and Society in Modern Britain* (New York: Edwin Mellen Press, 1989), pp. 277–91.

Grönroos, Christian, *Service Management and Marketing: Customer Management in Service Competition* (Chichester: Wiley, 2007).

Guenther, Herbert V., *Tibetan Buddhism in Western Perspective* (Berkeley, CA: Dharma Publishing, 1989).

Guerra, Alexandre, Marcio Pochmann, Ricardo Amorim and Ronnie Silva, *Classe Média: Desenvolvimento e Crise. Atlas da Nova Estratificação Social no Brasil* (São Paulo: Cortez Editora, 2006).

Habermas, Jürgen, *An Awareness of What Is Missing: Faith and Reason in a Post-secular Age* (Cambridge: Polity, 2010).

Haenni, Patrick, *L'islam de marché. L'autre révolution conservatrice* (Paris: Seuil, 2005).

Halbwachs, Maurice, *La mémoire collective* (Paris: Albin Michel, 1997).

Hammer, Olav, *På spaning efter helheten: New Age, en ny folktro?* (Stockholm: Wahlström & Widstrand, 1997).

——, *På spaning efter helheten: New Age en ny folktro?* (revised edition, Stockholm: Wahlström & Widstrand, 2004 [1997]).

——, *Claiming Knowledge: Strategies of Epistemology from Theosophy to the New Age* (Leiden and Boston, MA: Brill, 2004).

Hanegraaff, Wouter J., *New Age Religion and Western Culture: Esotericism in the Mirror of Secular Thought* (Leiden: Brill and Albany, NY: State University of New York Press, 1998).

——, 'The New Age Movement and Western Esotericism', in Darren Kemp and James R. Lewis (eds), *Handbook of New Age* (Leiden and Boston, MA: Brill, 2007), pp. 25–50.

Hanson, Sven Ove and Anna-Lena Lodenius, *Operation Högervridning* (Stockholm: Tiden, 1988).

Hansson, Ann-Sophie, 'The Psychosocial Work of Environment in the Church of Sweden: An Explorative Study', *Nonprofit Management and Leadership*, 16/3 (2006): 329–43.

Harrington, Austin, 'Dilthey, Empathy and Verstehen', *European Journal of Social Theory*, 4/3 (2001): 311–29.

Harris, Ian, 'Buddhist Environmental Ethics and Detraditionalization: The Case of EcoBuddhism', *Religion*, 25/3 (1995): 199–211.

Hartford Institute for Religion Research, 'Profile of Total U.S. Megachurches' (September 2010), [Online], available at: http://hirr.hartsem.edu/megachurch/megastoday_profile.html [accessed: 21 July 2011].

Harvey, Peter, *An Introduction to Buddhism: Teachings, History and Practices* (Cambridge: Cambridge University Press, 2005).

Hearn, Alison, '"Meat, Mask, Burden": Probing the Contours of the "Branded Self"', *Journal of Consumer Culture*, 8/2 (2008): 197–217.

Hechter, Michael and Satoshi Kanazawa, 'Sociological Rational Choice Theory', *Annual Review of Sociology*, 23 (1997): 191–214.

Hedström, Peter and Richard Swedberg, 'Rational Choice, Empirical Research and the Sociological Tradition', *European Sociological Review*, 12/2 (1996): 127–46.

Heelas, Paul, 'The New Age in Cultural Context: The Premodern, the Modern and the Postmodern', *Religion*, 23/2 (1993): 103–16.

——, 'The Sacralization of the Self and New Age Capitalism', in Nicholas Abercrombie and Alan Warde (eds), *Social Change in Contemporary Britain* (Cornwall: T.J. Press, 1993), pp. 139–66.

——, *The New Age Movement: The Celebration of the Self and Sacralization of Modernity* (Bodmin: Blackwell Publishers, 1996).

——, 'The Spiritual Revolution: From Religion to Spirituality', in Linda Woodhead (ed.), *Religions in the Modern World* (London and New York: Routledge, 2002), pp. 357–77.

Heelas, Paul and Benjamin Seel, 'An Ageing New Age?', in Grace Davie, Linda Woodhead and Paul Heelas (eds), *Predicting Religion: Christian, Secular, and Alternative Futures* (Aldershot: Ashgate, 2003), pp. 229–47.

Heelas, Paul and Linda Woodhead, 'Homeless Minds Today?', in Paul Heelas, David A. Martin and Linda Woodhead (eds), *Peter Berger and the Study of Religion* (London: Routledge, 2001), pp. 43–72.

——, *The Spiritual Revolution: Why Religion Is Giving Way to Spirituality* (Oxford: Blackwell, 2005).

Heinonen, Kristina, Tore Strandvik, Karl-Jacob Mickelsson, Bo Edvardsson, Erik Sundström and Per Andersson, 'A Customer-dominant Logic of Service', *Journal of Service Management*, 21/4 (2010): 531–48.

Hervieu-Léger, Danièle, *Vers un nouveau christianisme? Introduction à la sociologie du christianisme occidental* (Paris: Cerf, 1986).

——, *La religion pour mémoire* (Paris: Cerf, 1993).

——, 'Quelques paradoxes de la modernité religieuse. Crise de l'universel, planétarisation culturelle et renforcements communautaires', *Futuribles*, 260 (2001): 99–109.

Hervieu-Léger, Danièle and Bertrand Hervieu, *Le retour à la nature: au fond de la foret* (Paris: Editions du Seuil, 1979).

Hexham, Irving, 'The "Freaks" of Glastonbury: Conversion and Consolidation in an English Country Town', *Update*, 7/1 (1983): 3–12.

Hopkinson-Ball, Tim, *The Rediscovery of Glastonbury: Frederick Bligh Bond Architect of the New Age* (London: Sutton Publishing, 2007).

Hornborg, Anne-Christine, 'Rites for Modern Man: New Practices in Sweden', in Lina Midholm, Annika Nordström and Maria T. Agozzino (eds), *The Ritual Year and Ritual Diversity: Proceedings of the Second International Conference of the SIEF Working Group on the Ritual Year, Gothenburg June 7–11, 2006* (Gothenburg: Institute for Language and Folklore, 2007), pp. 83–92.

——, 'Att återförtrolla det sekulariserade samhället: Är Sverige på väg in i Vattumannens tidsålder?', *Svensk religionshistorisk årsskrift*, (2007): 33–59.

——, 'Selling Nature, Selling Health: The Commodification of Ritual Healing in Late Modern Sweden', in Sigurd Bergmann and Yong-Bock Kim (eds), *Religion, Ecology and Gender: Contributions from Korea, Canada and Scandinavia*, Studies in Religion and the Environment 1 (Münster, Hamburg, Berlin, Wien, London and Zürich: LIT Verlag, 2009), pp. 109–29.

——, 'Arbetslösa erbjuds kosmisk energi', *Aftonbladet*, Debatt (19 February 2009).

——, 'I coachningland – på spaning efter den inre potentialen', *Chaos: Skandinavisk tidsskrift for Religionshistoriske studier*, 53/1 (2010): 1–16.

——, *Coaching och lekmannaterapi – en modern väckelse?* (Stockholm: Dialogos 2012).

Hybels, Lynne and Bill Hybels, *Rediscovering Church* (Grand Rapids, MI: Zondervan, 1995).

Iannaccone, Lawrence R., 'Religious Practice: A Human Capital Approach', *Journal for the Scientific Study of Religion*, 29/3 (1990): 297–314.

——, 'The Consequences of Religious Market Structure: Adam Smith and the Economics of Religion', *Rationality and Society*, 3/2 (1991): 156–77.

——, 'Introduction to the Economics of Religion', *Journal of Economic Literature*, 36 (1998): 1465–96.

Inglehart, Ronald, *Culture Shift in Advanced Industrial Society* (Princeton, NJ: Princeton University Press, 1990).

——, *The Silent Revolution: Changing Values and Political Styles among Western Publics* (Princeton, NJ: Princeton University Press, 1977).

Introvigne, Massimo, 'After the New Age: Is There a Next Age?', in Mikael Rothstein (ed.), *New Age Religion and Globalization* (Aarhus: Aarhus University Press, 2001), pp. 58–69.

Ivakhiv, Adrian J., *Claiming Sacred Ground: Pilgrims and Politics at Glastonbury and Sedona* (Bloomington and Indianapolis, IN: Indiana University Press, 2001).

——, 'Power Trips: Making Sacred Space through New Age Pilgrimage', in Darren Kemp and James R. Lewis (eds), *Handbook of New Age* (Leiden and Boston, MA: Brill, 2007), pp. 263–86.

Jones, Steven T., *The Tribes of Burning Man* (San Francisco: Consortium of Collective Consciousness, 2011).

Jonveaux, Isabelle, *Le monastère au travail. Le royaume de Dieu au défi de l'économie* (Paris: Bayard, 2011).

——, 'La cultura rivisitata. I beni culturali monastici tra tradizione e modernità', *Proceedings of the III International Symposium of Pontificio Ateneo di S. Anselmo* (Rome, St. Ottilien: Studia Anselmiana, Eos-Verlag, 2013 – in press), pp. 131–49.

Kagan, Jerome, *What Is Emotion?* (New Haven, CT: Yale University Press, 2007).

Kamenetz, Rodger, *The Jew in the Lotus* (San Francisco, CA: Harper, 1994).

Katz, Maya, 'Trademarks of Faith: Chabad and Chanukah in America', *Modern Judaism*, 29/2 (2009): 239–67.

Kay, David, *Tibetan and Zen Buddhism in Britain: Transplantation, Development and Adaptation* (London: Routledge, 2004).

Khandro, Ani Rinchen, *Kagyu Samye Ling: The Story* (Dumfriesshire: Dzalendara Publishing, 2007).

King, Desmond and Fiona Ross, 'Critics and Beyond', in Francis G. Castles, Stephan Leibfried, Jane Lewis, Herbert Obinger and Christopher Pierson (eds), *The Oxford Handbook of the Welfare State* (Oxford and New York: Oxford University Press, 2010), pp. 45–58.

King, Richard, *Indian Philosophy: An Introduction to Hindu and Buddhist Thought* (Edinburgh: Edinburgh University Press, 1999).

Kiser, Edgar and Michael Hechter, 'The Debate on Historical Sociology: Rational Choice Theory and Its Critics', *The American Journal of Sociology*, 104/3 (1998): 785–816.

Kitiarsa, Pattana, *Religious Commodifications in Asia: Marketing Gods* (London: Routledge, 2008).

Klein, Marc S., 'Relooking a Jewish Newspaper', *Sh'ma*, 34/607 (January 2004): 11–12, [Online], available at: http://www.shma.com/archives/web-edition/ [accessed: 3 October 2011].

Klug, Lisa Alcalay, *Cool Jew: The Ultimate Guide for Every Member of the Tribe* (Kansas City, MO: Andrews McMeel, 2008).

Koven, Mikel, '"Cool Jewz": Contemporary Jewish Identity in Popular Culture', special issue of *Shofar: An Interdisciplinary Journal of Jewish Studies*, 25/4 (2007).

Kozinets, Robert V., 'Can Consumers Escape the Market? Emancipatory Illuminations from Burning Man', *Journal of Consumer Research*, 29/1 (2002): 20–38.

Kubiak, Anna E., 'Old Myths, New Mythicising', in Darren Kemp and James R. Lewis (eds), *Handbook of New Age* (Leiden and Boston, MA: Brill, 2007), pp. 255–62.

Kyle, Richard, *The New Age Movement in American Culture* (Lanham, MD: University Press of America, 1995).

Kyrkoordningen (Stockholm: Verbum, 2007).

Laack, Isabel, *Religion und Musik in Glastonbury: Eine Fallstudie zu gegenwärtigen Formen religiöser Identitätsdiskurse* (Göttingen and Oakville, CT: Vandenhoeck & Ruprecht, 2011).
Lacorne, Denis, *La crise de l'identité américaine: du melting pot au multiculturalisme* (Paris: Gallimard, 2003).
Lampman, Jane, 'Megachurches' Way of Worship on the Rise', *Christian Science Monitor* (6 February 2006), [Online], available at: http://www.csmonitor.com/2006/0206/p13s01-lire.html [accessed: 3 June 2011].
Landron, Olivier, *Les communautés nouvelles. Nouveaux visages du catholicisme français* (Paris: Cerf, 2004).
Larsen, Gretchen, Michael Macaulay, Daragh O'Reilly and Marion Bowman, 'Producing Agoratopia: Festival Tales from Glastonbury' (unpublished article, 2012).
Lash, Scott, 'Reflexivity and Its Doubles: Structure, Aesthetics, Community', in Ulrich Beck, Anthony Giddens and Scott Lash, *Reflexive Modernization: Politics, Tradition and Aesthetics in the Modern Social Order* (Cambridge: Polity Press, 1994), pp. 110–73.
Lash, Scott and John Urry, *The End of Organized Capitalism* (Cambridge: Polity Press, 1987).
Lau, Kimberly J., *New Age Capitalism: Making Money East of Eden* (Philadelphia, PA: University of Pennsylvania Press, 2000).
Laval, Christian, *L'ambition sociologique* (Paris: La Découverte/MAUSS, 2002).
Layman, Emma. M., *Buddhism in America* (Chicago, IL: Nelson Hall, 1978).
Lee, Martyn, *Consumer Culture Reborn: The Cultural Politics of Consumption* (London: Routledge, 1993).
Lemieux, Raymond and Micheline Milot, *Les croyances des Québécois. Esquisses pour une approche empirique* (Québec: Cahiers de recherche en sciences de la religion 11, 1992).
Lemmel, Elie, *Les quatre coupes de lait: le développement personnel selon la tradition juive* (Paris: Lev, 2010).
Lewis, James R. and J. Gordon Melton, *Perspectives on the New Age* (Albany, NY: State University of New York Press, 1992).
Linde, Stig, Församlingen i granskningssamhället (Lund: Lunds universitet/Socialhögskolan, 2010).
Linzer, Judith, *Torah and Dharma* (San Francisco, CA: Jason Aronson, 1996).
Lönnroth, Johan, 'Nyliberalismens genombrott i massmedia', *Socialistisk Debatt*, 1/88 (1988): 14–27.
Lorentz, Todd, 'The Dharma and the West: Can Buddhism Survive Consumerism', *Contemporary Buddhism*, 2/2 (2001): 191–9.
Loveland, Anne C. and Otis B. Wheeler, *From Meeting House to Megachurch* (Columbia, MO and London: University of Missouri Press, 2003).
Luckmann, Thomas, *The Invisible Religion: The Transformation of Symbols in Industrial Society* (London: Macmillan, 1967).

Luhmann, Niklas, *The Differentiation of Society* (New York: Columbia University, 1982).

Luntz, Frank, 'Israel in the Age of Eminem', Report for the Combined Jewish Philanthropies (CJP), Boston (2003), [Online], available at: http://www.bjpa.org/Publications/details.cfm?PublicationID=3157 [accessed: 17 February 2012].

Lury, Celia, *Brands: The Logos of the Global Economy* (New York and London: Routledge, 2004).

——, *Consumer Culture* (New Brunswick, NJ: Rutgers University Press, 2011).

Magnani, José, *O Brasil da Nova Era* (Rio de Janeiro: Jorge Zahar Editor, 2000).

Magnusson, Sven, *Stora tankar i vår tid – perspektiv på New Age* (Hölö: Hvrå förlag, 2000).

Mardin, Serif, *Religion, Society and Modernity in Turkey* (Syracuse, NY: Syracuse University Press, 2006).

Martell, Luke, 'Beck's Cosmopolitan Politics', *Contemporary Politics*, 14/2 (2008): 129–43.

Martikainen, Tuomas and François Gauthier (eds), *Religion in the Neoliberal Age: Modes of Governance and Political Economy* (Farnham: Ashgate, 2013).

Martin, Bernice, 'From Pre- to Postmodernity in Latin America: The Case of Pentecostalism', in Paul Heelas (ed.), *Religion, Modernity and Postmodernity* (Oxford: Blackwell, 1998), pp. 102–46.

Martin, David, *A General Theory of Secularization* (Oxford: Blackwell, 1978).

——, *On Secularization: Towards a Revised General Theory* (Farnham, 2005).

Marx, Karl, 'On the Jewish Question', in *Early Writings*, ed. and intro. Lucio Colletti, trans. Rodney Livingstone and Gregor Benton (Harmondsworth: Penguin Books, 1975), pp. 211–42.

——, *The Poverty of Philosophy* (Moscow: Progress Publishers, 1975).

Matthews, Bruce, 'Buddhism in Canada', in Charles S. Prebish and Martin Baumann (eds), *Westward Dharma: Buddhism Beyond Asia* (Berkeley, CA: University of California Press, 2002), pp. 120–38.

Mauss, Marcel, 'Essai sur le don', in *Sociologie et anthropologie* (Paris: Presses Universitaires de France, 1973), 149–279.

Mayer, François, 'Biens de salut et marché religieux dans le cultic milieu', *Social Compass*, 53/1 (2006): 97–108.

McDannell, Colleen, 'Interpreting Things: Material Culture Studies and American Religion', *Religion*, 21 (1991): 371–87.

——, *Material Christianity: Religion and Popular Culture in America* (New Haven, CT and London: Yale University Press, 1995).

McGuire, Meredith, *Lived Religion* (Oxford: Oxford University Press, 2008).

McKenzie, John S., 'Keeping It Real!: Constructing and Maintaining Traditional Authenticity in a Tibetan Buddhist Organization in Scotland', *Sociological Research Online*, 16/3 (31 August 2011), [Online], available at: http://www.socresonline.org.uk/16/3/7.html [accessed: 15 September 2011].

McMahan, David L., 'Repackaging Zen for the West', in Charles S. Prebish and Martin Baumann (eds), *Westward Dharma: Buddhism Beyond Asia* (Berkeley, CA: University of California Press, 2002), pp. 218–29.

McMullen, Mike and William Kilgore, 'An Analysis of Rick Warren's 40 Days of Purpose Movement', paper presented to the annual meeting of the Society for the Scientific Study of Religion, Portland, OR, 20 October 2006, [Online], available at: http://hirr.hartsem.edu/megachurch/articles/warren40daysofpurpose.pdf [accessed: 13 June 2011].

Mellado, James, 'Willow Creek Community Church (B): Cracks in the Foundation', Harvard Business School Publishing, Case Study #9-899-123 (1999).

Michaelson, Jay, 'Marketing Undermines Judaism', *Sh'ma*, 34/607 (January 2004): 4–5, [Online], available at: http://www.shma.com/archives/web-edition/ [accessed: 3 October 2011].

Mikaelsson, Lisbeth, 'Homo accumulans and the Spiritualization of Money', in Mikael Rothstein (ed.), *New Age Religion and Globalisation* (Aarhus: Aarhus University Press, 2001), pp. 94–112.

Miller, Donald E., *Reinventing American Protestantism* (Berkeley and Los Angeles, CA: University of California Press, 1997).

Miller, Vincent J., *Consuming Religion: Christian Faith and Practice in a Consumer Culture* (New York: Continuum, 2003).

Monroe, Kristen R., 'A Fat Lady in a Corset: Altruism and Social Theory', *American Journal of Political Science*, 38/4 (1994): 861–93.

Montemaggi, Francesca E.S., 'Misunderstanding Faith: When "Capital" Does Not Fit the "Spiritual"', *International Journal of Interdisciplinary Social Sciences*, 5/5 (2010): 179–92.

Moore, R. Laurence, *Selling God: American Religion in the Marketplace of Culture* (New York: Oxford University Press, 1994).

Morgan, David, 'The Materiality of Cultural Construction', *Material Religion*, 4/2 (2008): 228–9.

Morris, Paul, 'Freeing the Spirit of Enterprise: The Genesis and Development of the Concept of Enterprise Culture', in Russell Keat and Nicholas Abercrombie (eds), *Enterprise Culture* (Chatham: Mackays of Chatham, 1991), pp. 21–37.

National Jewish Population Survey 2000–2001: Strength, Challenge and Diversity in the American Jewish Population (New York: United Jewish Communities, 2004), 16, [Online], available at: http://www.jewishdatabank.org/NJPS2000.asp [accessed: 17 February 2013].

Nattier, Jan, 'Who Is a Buddhist?: Charting the Landscape of Buddhist America', in Charles S. Prebish and Kenneth K. Tanaka (eds), *The Faces of Buddhism in America* (Berkeley and Los Angeles, CA: University of California Press, 1998), pp. 183–95.

Nelson, David, 'Advertising Judaism', *Sh'ma*, 34/607 (January 2004): 3–4, [Online], available at: http://www.shma.com/archives/web-edition/ [accessed: 3 October 2011].

Neusner, Jacob, *Transformations in Ancient Judaism: Textual Evidence for Creative Responses to Crisis* (Peabody, MA: Hendrickson, 2004).

Niculescu, Mira, '"Juif-bouddhiste?" Conflictualités internes et intracommunautaires autour des adhésions au bouddhisme par des juifs français', in Anne-Sophie Lamine and Nathalie Luca (eds), *Quand le religieux fait conflit. Désaccords, négociations ou arrangements* (2013, forthcoming).

Niebuhr, Gustav, 'Megachurches – Second Article of a Series: The Gospels of Management; The Minister as a Marketer; Learning from Business' (18 April 1995), [Online], available at: http://www.nytimes.com/1995/04/18/us/megachurches-second-article-series-gospels-management-minister-marketer-learning.html [accessed: 13 June 2011].

Nobel, Steve, *The Prosperity Game* (Findhorn: Findhorn Press, 2006).

Normann, Richard, *Service Management: Strategy and Leadership in Service Business* (Chichester: Wiley, 1991).

Nussbaum, Martha C., *Upheavals of Thought: The Intelligence of Emotions* (Cambridge: Cambridge University Press, 2001).

Oliver, Ian P., *Buddhism in Britain* (London: Rider and Company, 1979).

Öljarstrand, Anneli, *Den mångtydiga församlingen: organisering, roller och relationer i spänningen mellan sekularisering och desekularisering* (Östersund: Mittuniversitetet, 2011).

Orléan, André, *L'empire de la valeur. Refonder l'économie* (Paris, 2011).

Oviedo, Lluis T., 'Approccio alla realtà delle nuove fondazioni', in Roberto Fusco and Giancarlo Rocca (eds), *Nuove forme di vita consacrata* (Roma: Urbaniana University Press, 2010), pp. 163–76.

Pace, Enzo, 'New Paradigms of Popular Religion', *Archives de sciences sociales des religions*, 64/1 (1987): 7–14.

——, 'Salvation Goods, the Gift Economy and Charismatic Concern', in Jörg Stolz (ed.), *Salvation Goods and Religious Markets: Theory and Application* (Bern: Peter Lang, 2008), pp. 149–70.

Paine, Jeremy, *Re-Enchantment: Tibetan Buddhism Comes to the West* (New York: Norton, 2004).

Palmisano, Stefania, 'Moving Forward in Catholicism: New Monastic Organizations, Innovation, Recognition, Legitimation', *International Journal for the Study of New Religions*, 1/2 (2010): 49–63.

——, 'Ambiguous Legitimation: Grassroots Roman Catholic Communities in Italy and Ecclesiastical Hierarchies', *Temenos*, 47/1 (2011): 31–60.

Parsons, Talcott, 'Introduction', in Max Weber, *The Sociology of Religion* (London: Methuen, 1965 [1922]).

Partridge, Christopher, *New Religions: A Guide* (New York: Oxford University Press, 2004).

Pastors.com, 'About Pastors.com: Rick Warren, Founder', Saddleback Church, [Online], available at: http://pastors.com/about/ [accessed: 13 June 2011].

Pettersson, Claes and Camilla Sundell, 'Här avslöjas miljardfiaskot', *Aftonbladet* (7 November 2009), [Online], available at: http://www.aftonbladet.se/nyheter/article12378730.ab [accessed: 8 August 2011].

Pettersson, Per, *Kvalitet i livslånga tjänsterelationer. Svenska kyrkan ur tjänsteteoretiskt och religionssociologiskt perspektiv* (Stockholm: Verbum, 2000).

——, 'The Nordic Paradox: Simultaneously Most Secularised and Most Religious. A Case Study of the Increasing Role of the Church of Sweden in Public Disaster Management', in Hans Georg Ziebertz and Ulrich Riegel (eds), *Europe: Secular or Post-Secular?* (Berlin: LiT Verlag, 2008), pp. 79–92.

——, 'Majority Churches as Agents of European Welfare: A Sociological Approach', in Anders Bäckström, Grace Davie, Ninna Edgardh and Per Pettersson (eds), *Welfare and Religion in 21st Century Europe: Volume 2* (Farnham: Ashgate, 2011), pp. 15–59.

Polanyi, Karl, *The Great Transformation: The Political and Economic Origins of Our Time* (Boston, MA: Beacon Press, 2001).

Portier, Philippe, 'Les mutations du religieux dans la France contemporaine', *Social Compass*, 59/3 (2012): 193–207.

Possamai, Adam, 'Cultural Consumption of History and Popular Culture in Alternative Spiritualities', *Journal of Consumer Culture*, 2 (2002): 197–218.

——, 'Alternative Spiritualities and the Cultural Logic of Late Capitalism', *Culture and Religion*, 4/1 (2003): 31–45.

——, *Sociology of Religion for Generations X and Y* (London: Equinox, 2009).

Powers, John, *Introduction to Tibetan Buddhism* (New York: Snow Lion Publications, 1995).

Prebish, Charles, *Luminous Passage: The Practice and Study of Buddhism in America* (Berkeley, CA: University of California Press, 1999).

Prebish, Charles S. and Martin Baumann (eds), *Westward Dharma: Buddhism Beyond Asia* (Berkeley, CA: University of California, 2002).

Prebish, Charles and Kenneth Tanaka (eds), *The Faces of Buddhism in America* (Berkeley, CA: University of California Press, 1998).

Premfors, Rune, 'Coping with Budget Deficits in Sweden', *Scandinavian Political Studies*, 4 (1984): 261–84.

Prince, Ruth and David Riches, *The New Age in Glastonbury: The Construction of Religious Movements* (New York and Oxford: Berghahn Books, 2000).

Redden, Guy, 'The New Age: Towards a Market Model', *Journal of Contemporary Religion*, 20/2 (2005): 231–46.

Reimers, Eva, *Dopet som kult och kultur* (Stockholm: Verbum, 1995).

Riggs, John W., 'The Megachurch and the Liturgical Renewal Movement' (2002), [Online], available at: http://reformedtheology.org/SiteFiles/PublicLectures/RiggsPL.html [accessed: 13 June 2011].

Riis, Ole and Linda Woodhead, *A Sociology of Religious Emotion* (Oxford: Oxford University Press, 2010).

Ritzer, George, *The Globalization of Nothing* (London: Sage, 2004).

Ritzer, George and Nathan Jurgenson, 'Production, Consumption, Prosumption: The Nature of Capitalism in the Age of the Digital "Prosumer"', *Journal of Consumer Culture*, 10/1 (2010): 13–36.

Rocca, G., *Primo censimento delle nuove comunità* (Roma: Urbaniana University Press, 2011).

Rojas, Mauricio, *Paradoxen SAF och den svenska modellens uppgång och fall* (Stockholm: Timbro, 2001).

Roof, Wade Clark, *A Generation of Seekers* (San Francisco, CA: HarperCollins, 1993).

——, *Spiritual Marketplace: Baby Boomers and the Remaking of American Religion* (Princeton, NJ: Princeton University Press, 1999).

Rosenblatt, Gary, 'Eminem Jews Rap Establishment', *The Jewish Week* (2 May 2003), [Online], available at: http://www.jewishfederations.org/page.aspx?id=42782 [accessed: 17 February 2013].

Roszak, Theodore, *The Making of a Counter Culture* (London: Faber and Faber, 1970).

Rothenberg, Celia, 'New Age Jews: Jewish Shamanism and Jewish Yoga', in Celia Rothenberg and Anne Vallely (eds), *New Age Judaism* (London: Vallentine Mitchell, 2008), pp. 1–18.

Roy, Olivier, *Globalized Islam: The Search for a New Ummah* (New York: Columbia University Press, 2004).

Saddleback Church: Purpose Driven Life, 'About the Author: Rick Warren', [Online], available at: http://www.purposedrivenlife.com/en-US/AboutUs/AboutTheAuthor/AboutTheAuthor.htm [accessed: 9 August 2011].

SAF, 'Varför skall näringslivet informera?', *Fakta och synpunkter från SAF*, 1 (1972): 1–27.

Salamon, Karen Lisa Goldschmidt, 'Going Global from the Inside Out: Spiritual Globalism in the Workplace', in Mikael Rothstein (ed.), *New Age Religion and Globalisation* (Aarhus: Aarhus University Press, 2001), pp. 150–72.

——, 'Prophets of a Cultural Capitalism: An Ethnography of Romantic Spiritualization in Business Management', *Folk: Journal of the Danish Ethnographic Society*, 44 (2002): 89–115.

Salkin, Jeffrey K., 'New Age Judaism', *The Blackwell Companion to Judaism* (Oxford: Blackwell, 2003), pp. 354–69.

Samuel, Geoffrey, *Civilised Shamans: Buddhism in Tibetan Societies* (London: Smithsonian Institution Press, 1993).

Santana, Richard and Gregory Erickson, *Religion and Popular Culture* (Jefferson, NC: McFarland, 2008).

Sargeant, Kimon Howland, *Seeker Churches: Promoting Traditional Religion in a Non-Traditional Way* (New Brunswick, NJ: Rutgers University Press, 2000).

Sassatelli, Roberta, *Consumer Culture: History, Theory and Politics* (London: Sage, 2007).

Satz, Debra and John Ferejohn, 'Rational Choice and Social Theory', *The Journal of Philosophy*, 91/2 (1994): 71–87.

SCB, Statistiska Centralbyrån, *Sjukfrånvaro och ohälsa i Sverige: en belysning utifrån SCB:s statistik*, 3 (Örebro: SCB-tryck, 2004).
——, Swedish employment statistics (2011), [Online], available at: www.scb.se.
Schmidt, Volker, 'Multiple Modernities or Varieties of Modernity?', *Current Sociology*, 54/1 (2006): 77–97.
Séguy, Jean, 'Les sociétés imaginées: monachisme et utopie', *Annales. Économie, Sociétés, Civilisation*, 26/2 (1971): 328–54.
Sennett, Richard, *The Culture of the New Capitalism* (New Haven, CT: Yale University Press, 2006).
Sh'ma, 34/607 (January 2004), [Online], available at: http://www.shma.com/archives/web-edition/ [accessed: 3 October 2011].
Shay, Scott A., *Getting Our Groove Back: How to Energize American Jewry* (Jerusalem: Devora, 2007).
Sheler, Jeffrey L., *Prophet of Purpose: The Life of Rick Warren* (New York: Doubleday, 2009).
Simmel, Georg, *The Philosophy of Money* (3rd enlarged edition, London: Routledge, 2004 [1900]).
Singer, Ellen (ed.), *Paradigm Shift: From the Jewish Renewal Teachings of Reb Zalman Schachter-Shalomi* (New York: Jason Aronson, 1993).
Slater, Don, *Consumer Culture and Modernity* (Cambridge: Polity, 1997).
——, 'The Sociology of Consumption and Lifestyle', in Craig Calhoun, Chris Rojek and Bryan Turner (eds), *The SAGE Handbook of Sociology* (London: Sage, 2005), pp. 174–87.
Snow, David A., James A. Bany, Michelle Peria and James E. Stobaugh, 'A Team Field Study of the Appeal of Megachurches: Identifying, Framing, and Solving Personal Issues', *Ethnography*, 11/1 (2010): 165–88.
Sointu, Eeva and Linda Woodhead, 'Holistic Spirituality, Gender, and Expressive Selfhood', *Journal for the Scientific Study of Religion*, 47/2 (2008): 259–76.
Sökaren, 2 (1981).
Sökaren, 1 (1985).
Sökaren, 6 (1994).
Sonsino, Rifat, *Six Jewish Spiritual Paths: A Rationalist Looks at Spirituality* (Woodstock, VT: Jewish Lights Publishing, 2000).
Sorj, Bernardo, *A Nova Sociedade Brasileira* (third revised edition, Rio de Janeiro: Jorge Zahar Editor, 2006).
Spangler, David, *Emergence: The Rebirth of the Sacred* (New York: Dell Pub., 1984).
Speck, Simon, 'Ulrich Beck's "Reflecting Faith": Individualization, Religion and the Desecularization of Reflexive Modernity', *Sociology*, 47/1 (2013): 157–72.
Spohn, Willfried, 'Multiple Modernity, Nationalism and Religion: A Global Perspective', *Current Sociology*, 51/3–4 (2003): 265–86.
St John, Graham, 'Going Feral: Authentica on the Edge of Australian Culture', *Australian Journal of Anthropology*, 8/2 (1997): 167–89.

——, 'Alternative Cultural Heterotopia and the Liminoid Body: Beyond Turner at Confest', *Australian Journal of Anthropology*, 12/1 (2001): 47–66.

Stark, Rodney, 'Secularization, R.I.P.', *Sociology of Religion*, 60/3 (1999): 249–73.

Stark, Rodney and William S. Bainbridge, 'Towards a Theory of Religion: Religious Commitment', *Journal for the Scientific Study of Religion*, 19/2 (1980): 114–28.

Stark, Rodney, Eva Hamberg and Alan S. Miller, 'Exploring Spirituality and Unchurched Religions in America, Sweden, and Japan', *Journal of Contemporary Religion*, 20/1 (2005): 3–23.

Stearns, Peter, 'L'expansion globale du désir', *Les Grands Dossiers des Sciences Humaines*, 22 (2011): 14–17.

Stehr, Nico, *Moral Markets: How Knowledge and Affluence Change Consumers and Producers* (Boulder, CO: Paradigm Publishers, 2008).

Stehr, Nico and Marian Adolf, 'Consumption Between Market and Morals: A Socio-cultural Consideration of Moralized Markets', *European Journal of Social Theory*, 13/2 (2010): 213–28.

Steiner, Philippe, *L'école durkheimienne et l'*économie: sociologie, religion et connaissance (Geneva: Droz, 2005).

Sterling, Bruce, 'Greetings from Burning Man!', *Wired*, 4/11 (1997): 196–206, 274, [Online], available at: http://www.wired.com/wired/archive/4.11/burningman.html [accessed: 20 July 2011].

Stimilli, Elettra, *Il debito del vivente. Ascesi e capitalismo* (Macerata: Quodlibet, 2011).

Stolz, Jörg, *Salvation Goods and Religious Markets: Theory and Applications* (Bern: Peter Lang, 2008).

Sutcliffe, Steven J., *Children of the New Age* (London: Routledge, 2003).

Svenska Dagbladet (*SvD*), 5 October 1980.

Svenska Dagbladet (*SvD*), 10 November 1980.

Svenska Dagbladet (*SvD*), 7 May 1983.

Svenska Dagbladet (*SvD*), 17 December 1986.

Svenska Dagbladet (*SvD*), 14 June 1991.

Symonds, William C., 'Earthly Empires: How Evangelical Churches Are Borrowing from the Business Playbook' (23 May 2005), [Online], available at: http://www.businessweek.com/magazine/content/05_21/b3934001_mz001.htm [accessed: 13 June 2011].

Sznaider, Natan, 'Consumerism as a Civilizing Process: Israel and Judaism in the Second Age of Modernity', *International Journal of Politics, Culture and Society*, 14/2 (2000): 297–313.

——, 'From Citizen Warrior to Citizen Shopper and Back Again: New Modes of Cosmopolitan Citizenship', in Daniel Levy and Yfaat Weiss (eds), *Challenging Ethnic Citizenship: German and Israeli Perspectives on Immigration* (London: Berghahn Books, 2002), pp. 253–67.

Tarlo, Emma, *Visibly Muslim: Fashion, Politics, Faith* (Oxford: Berg, 2010).

Taylor, Barry, *A Pilgrim in Glastonbury* (Glastonbury: Abbey Press, 2010).

Taylor, Charles, *Sources of the Self: The Making of the Modern Identity* (Cambridge: Cambridge University Press, 1989).

——, *The Ethics of Authenticity* (Cambridge, MA: Harvard University Press, 1991).

——, 'The Politics of Recognition', in Amy Guthman (ed.), *Multiculturalism: Examining the Politics of Recognition* (Princeton, NJ: Princeton University Press, 1994), pp. 25–73.

——, *Varieties of Religion Today: William James Revisited* (Boston, MA: Harvard University Press, 2002).

Thompson, Michael, 'The Dynamics of Cultural Theory and Their Implications for the Enterprise Culture', in Shaun Hargreaves Heap and Angus Ross (eds), *Understanding the Enterprise Culture: Themes in the Work of Mary Douglas* (Edinburgh: Edinburgh University Press, 1992), pp. 182–202.

Thornton, Sarah, *Club Cultures: Music, Media and Subcultural Capital* (Middletown, CT: Wesleyan University Press, 1996).

Thumma, Scott, 'The Shape of Things to Come: Megachurches, Emerging Churches and Other New Religious Structures', in Charles H. Lippy (ed.), *Faith in America, Volume 1: Organized Religion Today* (Westport, CT and London: Praeger, 2006), pp. 185–206.

Thumma, Scott and Jim Petersen, 'Goliaths in Our Midst: Megachurches in the ELCA', in Richard Cimino (ed.), *Lutherans Today: American Lutheran Identity in the 21st Century* (Grand Rapids, MI: Eerdmans, 2003), pp. 102–24.

Thumma, Scott and Dave Travis, *Beyond the Megachurch Myths* (San Francisco, CA: Jossey-Bass, 2007).

Torcivia, Mario, *Guida alle nuove comunità monastiche italiane* (Casale Monferrato: Piemme, 2001).

Turner, Bryan S., *Religion and Modern Society: Citizenship, Secularisation and the State* (Cambridge: Cambridge University Press, 2011).

Turner, Fred, 'Burning Man at Google: A Cultural Infrastructure for New Media Production', *New Media and Society*, 11/1–2 (2009): 73–94.

Twitchell, James B., *Shopping for God: How Christianity Went from In Your Heart to In Your Face* (New York: Simon & Schuster, 2007).

Vallely, Anne, 'Jewish Redemption by Way of the Buddha', in Celia Rothenberg and Anne Vallely (eds), *New Age Judaism* (London: Vallentine Mitchell, 2008), pp. 19–33.

Vandenberghe, Frédéric, 'Simmel and Weber as Ideal-Typical Founders of Sociology', *Philosophy and Social Criticism*, 25/4 (1999): 57–80.

Van Hove, Hildegarde, 'L'emergence d'un marché spirituel', *Social Compass*, 46/2 (1999): 161–72.

Vargo, Stephen L. and Robert F. Lusch, 'Evolving to a New Dominant Logic for Marketing', *Journal of Marketing*, 68 (2004): 1–17.

Veer, Peter van der, 'Market and Money: A Critique of Rational Choice Theory', *Social Compass*, 59/2 (2011): 183–92.

Vidich, Arthur (ed.), *The New Middle Classes: Life-Styles, Status Claims and Political Orientations* (New York: Macmillan: 1995).

Warren, Rick, *The Purpose Driven Church* (Grand Rapids, MI: Zondervan, 1995).

Washburn, Sue, 'Purpose-Driven Presbyterians', [Online], available at: http://www.faithwebsites.com/sysfiles/site_uploads/pubsartsmeds/newsletter2623_2.pdf [accessed: 9 December 2011].

Waskow, Arthur, *Down-to-Earth Judaism: Food, Money, Sex, and the Rest of Life* (New York: W. Morrow, 1995).

Watson, J.B., Jr, and Walt Scalen, Jr, 'Upsizing Jesus: Megachurches, the Church Growth Movement, and Image Management in a Consumer Society', in Jon K. Loessin and Scott Stripling (eds), *The Year 2011 Annual Proceedings of the Association for the Scientific Study of Religion-Southwest* (Dallas, TX: ASSR-SW, 2011), pp. 1–12, [Online], available at: http://envirecon.com/assrproceedings2011.pdf [accessed: 9 December 2011].

Watson, Tony, 'Entrepreneurial Action, Identity, and the Use of Multiple Discursive Resources: The Case of a Rapidly Changing Family Business', *International Small Business Journal*, 27/3 (2009): 251–74.

Weber, Max, *The Protestant Ethic and the Spirit of Capitalism* (London: Routledge, 2001 [1905]).

——, *From Max Weber*, ed. Hans Gerth and Charles Wright Mills (New York: Oxford University Press, 1958 [1918]).

——, 'Science as a Vocation', in *From Max Weber: Essays in Sociology*, ed. Hans Gerth and Charles Wright Mills (New York: Oxford University Press, 1958 [1918]), pp. 129–58.

——, *Economia e società* (Torino: Comunità, 1999). Original edition: *Wirtschaft und Gesellschaft* (Tubingen: Mohr, 1922).

——, *The Sociology of Religion* (London: Methuen, 1965 [1922]).

——, *Economy and Society, vols 1–2* (Berkeley, CA: University of California Press, 1978).

——, *Protestantiska etiken och kapitalismens anda* (Lund: Argos, 1978).

Weintraub, Jeff, 'The Theory and Politics of the Public/Private Distinction', in Jeff Weintraub and Krishan Kumar (eds), *Public and Private in Thought and Practice* (Chicago, IL: University of Chicago Press, 1997), pp. 1–41.

Weissler, Chava, 'The Jewish Marketplace', *Sh'ma*, 34/607 (2004): 1–2, [Online], available at: http://www.shma.com/archives/web-edition/ [accessed: 3 October 2011].

Wiig-Sandberg, Unni, *Den nödvändiga riten?: om upplevelser av kvalitet i begravningsgudstjänsten* (Uppsala: Diakonivetenskapliga institutet, 2006).

Willow Creek Association, 'Our Story: Who We Are', [Online], available at: www.willowcreek.com/about/ [accessed: 8 August 2011].

Winroth, AnnCristin, 'Vardagligt och livsviktigt berättande om hälsa och bot', in Motzi Eklöf (ed.), *Perspektiv på komplementär medicin* (Malmö: Studentlitteratur, 2004), pp. 133–46.

Wittberg, Patricia, 'Real Religious Communities: A Study of Authentication in New Roman Catholic Religious Orders', *Religion and the Social Order*, 6 (1996): 149–74.

——, 'Orders and Schisms on the Sacred Periphery', in James Beckford and N.J. Demerath III (eds), *The Sage Handbook of the Sociology of Religion* (London: Sage, 2007), pp. 323–44.

Wolfe, Alan, *The Transformation of American Religion* (New York: Free Press, 2003).

Woodhead, Linda and Rebecca Catto (eds), *Religion and Change in Modern Britain* (New York and London: Routledge, 2012).

Woodhead, Linda and Paul Heelas, *Religion in Modern Times* (Oxford: Blackwell, 2000).

Wuthnow, Robert, *The Consciousness Reformation* (Berkeley, CA: University of California Press, 1976).

——, *After Heaven* (Berkeley and Los Angeles, CA: University of California Press, 1998).

——, *All in Sync: How Music and Art Are Revitalizing American Religion* (Berkeley and Los Angeles, CA: University of California Press, 2003).

York, Michael, 'New Age Commodification and Appropriation of Spirituality', *Journal of Contemporary Religion*, 16/3 (2001): 361–72.

Zeithaml, Valarie A., Leonard L. Berry and A. Parasuraman, 'The Nature and Determinants of Customer Expectations of Service', *Journal of the Academy of Marketing Science*, 21/1 (1993): 1–12.

Ziebertz, Hans-Georg and Ulrich Riegel (eds), *Europe: Secular or Post-secular?* (Berlin: LiT Verlag, 2008).

Zuckerman, Phil, *Society Without God: What the Least Religious Nations Can Tell Us About Contentment* (New York: New York University Press, 2001).

Zwick, Detlev, Samuel Bonsu and Aron Darmody, 'Putting Consumers to Work: "Co-creation" and New Marketing Govern-mentality', *Journal of Consumer Culture*, 8/2 (2008): 163–96.

Index

For Product Safety Concerns and Information please contact our
EU representative GPSR@taylorandfrancis.com Taylor & Francis
Verlag GmbH, Kaufingerstraße 24, 80331 München, Germany